A Dictionary of African Mythology

A Dictionary of African Mythology

The Mythmaker as Storyteller

Harold Scheub

Oxford University Press

2000

OXFORD

UNIVERSITY PRESS

Oxford   New York
Athens   Auckland   Bangkok   Bogotá   Bombay
Buenos Aires   Calcutta   Cape Town   Dar es Salaam   Delhi
Florence   Hong Kong   Istanbul   Karachi
Kuala Lumpur   Madras   Madrid   Melbourne
Mexico City   Nairobi   Paris   Singapore
Taipei   Tokyo   Toronto

and associated companies in
Berlin   Ibadan

Library of Congress Cataloging-in-Publication Data
Scheub, Harold.
A dictionary of African mythology :
the mythmaker as storyteller / Harold Scheub.
p.   cm. — Includes bibliographical references and index.
ISBN 0-19-512456-1
1. Mythology, African Dictionaries.
I. Title.
299'.62'03—dc21   99-35035

The editor and publisher are grateful for permission to include
copyright material. The bibliography includes several sources from
which texts are reprinted in part in the dictionary. Any errors
or omissions in the list are entirely unintentional. If notified the
publishers will be pleased to make any necessary corrections at the
earliest opportunity.

Designed and typeset by Jeff Hoffman

1 3 5 7 9 8 6 4 2
Printed in the United States of America
on acid-free paper

Photograph by Harold Scheub

A Xhosa Mythmaker

Contents

Mdi Msumu

One day, a girl named Kichalundu went out to cut grass. She found luxuriant grass in a certain place, but when she stepped there, she sank into a quagmire.

Her companions took her hands and tried to pull her out, but they could do nothing. As she vanished from sight, they heard her singing, "The spirits have taken me / Go and tell my mother and father."

The girls ran to tell her parents what had happened.

People from the entire countryside gathered at the place, and a man of God told the father to sacrifice a cow and a sheep.

This was done, and they heard Kichalundu's voice again, but it was growing fainter, fainter, and at last she was silent.

They gave up; she was lost.

But after a time, they saw that a tree was growing upon the spot where she had disappeared. The tree continued to grow, and at last it reached the sky.

During the heat of the day, the herd boys would drive their cattle into the shade of this tree, and the boys climbed into the tree's branches.

One day, two of the herd boys climbed higher than the others, and they called, "Can you still see us?"

The others answered, "No! Come down!"

But the two daring boys refused.

"We are going on, into the sky!" they said. "We are going to Wuhu, the world above!"

Those were their last words. They were never seen again.

And the tree was called Mdi Msumu, the Story-tree.

A Mythology without Tales

A mythology without tales is unthinkable. Nevertheless, the man who, a long time ago, went off on his own and discovered the invisible city he named "mythology" because in his language there existed no name more suitable, did not come back with grand and miraculous tales. On returning to his city which awaited him, he did not tell stories of gods forever young nor of the birth of sky, earth, and sea. Not even a winter's tale, not a single "mythological narrative." But all the old men over sixty began at once to mythologize in such a sublime way that enchanted, fascinated children stayed to listen and, little by little, grew old while the old men imperceptibly became like children. The plague had left the city; Plato's city had been saved from unknown evil, and in hushed tones some people diagnosed that which in other disturbed times perceptive minds were to call "broken tradition."

—Detienne, 1986, 132

Introduction

Myth as story: When Pishiboro died, his body rotted and went everywhere and became water, his blood forming hills and rocks. Mbori enclosed all the creatures of the world in a canoe which he sealed up—except for one hole. Mwari tells the plummeting Musikavanhu to point his finger at a falling stone, and the stone becomes the earth. The evil spirit, Chemosit, is half man and half bird, with one leg, nine buttocks, and a red mouth that shines at night. And Kaidara has seven heads, twelve arms, thirty feet, and sits on a four-footed throne that never stops rotating.

The extraordinary world of myth, the palette from which religion has its origins, is a Brueghel painting, awash in the rich and interwoven colors of fantasy, teeming with figures sublime and grotesque. Like a vast and limitless Thousand and One Nights, African mythology is a brilliant fusion of lavish imagination and austere belief, a flowing and unbroken intermingling of richly detailed, endlessly embroidered images moving majestically across the fertile terrain of this infinitely creative continent, a tapestry of images that poetically reveals deeply held faiths. The myths throng with images that are products of a rich fancy and profound thought.

> C'est des mythes et des légendes que sont sorties la science et la poésie . . .
>
> (Durkheim, iv)

Myth as story: Rali, the giant cow on Mount Kilimanjaro; from its tail hang swollen tufts that contain a fat that has the taste of honey and conceals supernatural powers. Kibuka flies into a cloud hovering over the enemy armies, then shoots arrows down at them. A five-hundred-year-old mother gives her son fifteen monstrous heads on his shoulder; when one head is struck off in battle, fifteen others emerge in that position.

In the stories that make up the African myth traditions, there are beginnings—the creation of the universe; and there are endings—the onset of death. Between is the struggle to reachieve the first and to obviate the second. Initial connections between heaven and earth are severed, a separation between God and man the result. To recover those connections, a conflict erupts on the earth between contending forces, sometimes given form in mythic heroes, other times in the ritual struggles of everyman.

Different versions of the same myths can be found throughout Africa—a man refuses to bring his mother-in-law to life, God resides in heavenly two-storied houses, Obatala is sent to create the earth and is detained, Lisa and Gu fashion the world. Similar heroes take varied names—Kudukese and Lofokefoke, Aiwel and Longar and Wan Dyor. There are variants of stories of millet rationing, of the cosmic egg, of the blood of the wives of gods, of the love stories associated with the planned sacrifice of beautiful women.

For all their brightness, and perhaps because of it, myths have long created problems for observers. Long ago, Andrew Lang discussed "the element in myth which seems to us *irrational*" (1887, 6), referring to "the Zeus who, in the shape of a swan, became the father of Castor and Pollux," and observing, "It is this *irrational* and unnatural element, as Mr. Max Müller says, 'the silly, senseless, and savage element,' that makes mythology the puzzle which men have so long found it" (8). "True myth," wrote Robert Graves, "may be defined as the reduction to narrative shorthand of ritual mime.... Yet genuine mythic elements may be found embedded in the least promising stories, and the fullest or most illuminating version of a given myth is seldom supplied by any one author . . ." (I, 13).

Asclepiades of Myrlea called myths "false tales," but Marcel Detienne has observed, "Since its beginnings the myth has the force of a religion and, in its most rudimentary forms, mythic concepts conceal all the riches that anticipate the highest ideals, those that are slowest to take hold in history" (105). And Isidore Okpewho writes, "Myth is not really a particular type of tale as against another; it is neither the spoken counterpart of an antecedent ritual, nor is it a tale determined exclusively by a binary scheme of abstract ideas or a sequential order of elements. It is simply that quality of fancy which informs the creative or configurative powers of the human mind in varying degrees of intensity. In that sense we are free to call any narrative of the oral tradition a myth, so long as it gives due emphasis to fanciful play. It is this quality of fanciful play that provides one solid structural link between several generations of the concept of myth, first as oral narrative and now as fanciful idea (even a dominating one)" (1983, 69).

This is a collection of such African myths—no more than a brief sampling of stories from across the seemingly unlimited and ever-fertile cornucopia that is the African storytelling tradition. It is not a theological study of African religions, not an anthropological, historical, or philosophical survey—the reader will have to turn to Okot p'Bitek, Joseph B. Danquah, Paulin J. Hountondji, E. Bolaji Idowu, Samuel O. Imbo, Alexis Kagame, John Mbiti, V. Y. Mudimbe, Isidore Okpewho, Kwasi Wiredu for such studies.

Nor is this in any way meant to be an inclusive set of African myths. I have selected myths that cover a broad range of the art form in African societies, including stories of origins, heroic epics, and tales that have mythic touches (the stories of Louliyya, Mekidech, and Nyengebule, for example). I have made an effort to include versions and variants of commonly performed stories. And I have included entries that contain only the glimmer, but nevertheless the rich possibilities, of story. This is a selection of myths that are masks, revealing and concealing, an anthology of images that are suggestive of the exuberance and abundance of African myth. The common denominator here, the criterion for inclusion in this selection, has to do with myth as story.

It is the art of the mythmaker that is celebrated here, the language of the storyteller. "The more solitary I become," said Aristotle, "the more I like stories, *myths*" (*Frag.* 668). Georges Dumézil "admitted that he had never understood the difference between a story and a myth" (Detienne, xi).

Myth, as story—the boys climb into the branches of the tree. "We are going on, into the sky!" The tree was called Mdi Msumu, the Story-tree.

Here is one story-tree. . . .

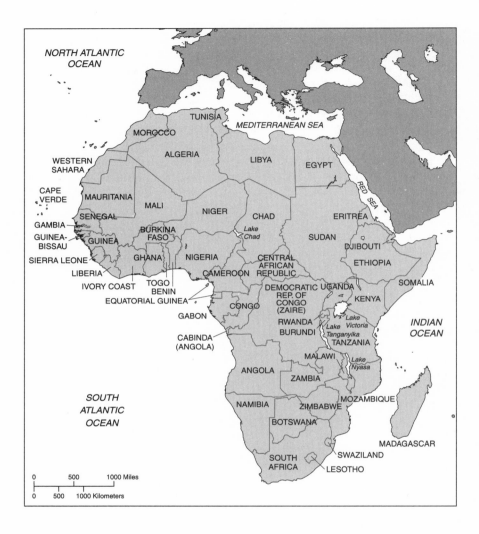

Notes on the Organization of This Dictionary

*T*he many stories in this collection, gleaned from among the literally thousands of stories that compose the mythic traditions of African peoples, are suggestive of the possibilities, hints of the repertories, that exist in the memory and the imagination of mythmakers. Here are four hundred of the thousands of stories in African myth systems. These are arranged in alphabetical order according to the name of the significant figure in the story.

Each entry identifies the culture or language group, along with the country. This is followed by a brief description of the god, hero, or the belief system involved in the title story. Other related stories or variants have sometimes been added to the title story.

Fourteen of these entries have been expanded somewhat to include commentaries on some of the common themes that thread through the myths—themes having to do with the divine trickster and the dualistic god, with the epic heroes and tale characters. These themes are returned to in the third appendix, "The Grand Myth." Because the emphasis is on the mythmaker as storyteller, observations about the art of the storyteller are injected before letter sections, alternating with proverbs having to do with myth.

Sources of the stories and a bibliography can be found at the end of the book. There are three appendices as well, including a country index, a linguistic/cultural index, and "The Grand Myth," an index that breaks the entries into six major themes.

Materials have been largely rewritten for this collection. I have attempted in all cases to remain as faithful to my sources as possible, to stay close to the original source material even when radically abbreviating stories.

Because of the considerable inconsistency in my sources in the use of diacritical marks, I have omitted them here, and refer readers to my sources for the use of such markings. For the sake of clarity, however, I have retained linguistic orthography for such southern African languages as San.

The Mythmaker as Storyteller

All mythmakers depend on story. Who would understand the nature of religion must start with story. It is story that contains within it the deepest-held beliefs, the hopes and fears, dreams and nightmares of a people. If the storyteller is the guardian, the repository, of the past, he is also its interpreter, always in the process of revising history, recasting our notions of origins, and so it is that, within the context created by the story-teller, the past and the present are constantly in a process of becoming, the world of the storyteller a churning cauldron of images that, worked into form, become a momentary means of establishing union between the present living generation and all generations that have preceded it. Nor are the stories that comprise the myths of a people merely fables, explanatory tales, chil-dren's versions of complex adult themes. In a rich and enormously complex way, story is the religious system of a people. It is not a means to understand-ing, not a path to God; rather, it is the means whereby humans, as members of audiences, move to oneness with God. That is the effect of myth, and that is why we humans will not let stories go. They are our means of communing with our deepest beliefs. So myth is not simply the story behind the ritual, myth is the ritual, is the essence of religious faith. The fantasy elements, the "irrational" elements, of myth are at the center of an artistic activity that has the effect of joining the emotions of the audience—for story is always and primarily, if not exclusively, a process of feeling—to the images of the past, those images conjuring up the emotions and then joining them to the past. The enormously complex performance aspects of storytelling, the art of the storyteller, is the key to understanding the meaning of myth.

A Dictionary of African Mythology

Se maintenir en diseuse dressée, figure de proue de la mémoire. L'héritage va chavirer–vague après vague, nuit après nuit, les murmures reprennent avant même que l'enfant comprenne, avant même qu'il trouve ses mots de lumière, avant de parler à son tour et pour ne point parler seul . . .

Assia Djebar

Retaining their role of storyteller, figurehead at the prow of memory. The legacy will otherwise be lost—night after night, wave upon wave, the whispers take up the tale, even before the child can understand, even before she finds her words of light, before she speaks in her turn and so that she will not speak alone . . .

[Tran. Dorothy S. Blair]

A

Abasi's Messenger Is a Vulture (Anang/Nigeria) The supreme god, all knowing, all-seeing, and all-powerful, Abasi moves at times from his place in the sky to the earth, where he struggles with evil supernatural beings and is sometimes challenged by ancestral spirits. Spirits touch people more routinely than Abasi. There are guardian spirits, ancestral spirits, and evil beings. Of significance are the invisible *nnem*, fifty-four spirits who have economic, political, religious, and social functions, and who transport sacrifices to Abasi so that he may make decisions about how to reward the supplicants. ◨ Abasi, when he is in the heavens, continues to have ties to earth by means of the earth spirit, Ikpa Ison, a fertility deity. She keeps Abasi in touch with activities on the earth by means of a vulture. Abasi, having developed a precise moral code, is concerned about those activities, and dispenses rewards and punishments according to whether humans live within the perimeters of that code. Abasi thereby has a shaping influence on the destiny of man.

Abasi's Sexual Prohibition Is Broken (Efik/Nigeria) Abasi Onyong, the god above, the only deity in the universe, dwells in the sky. He created the world, both the good and the evil, and he wars against the evil. A human, before he is born, makes a pact with Abasi as to his intentions when he is born, including his economic state and his longevity. He is expected to fulfill that promise. This arrangement between god and man is called *akana*. Decisions as to where to farm, as to harvests and trading and market days, the appropriate times to go to sea to fish and where to fish—all are influenced by religious beliefs. Abasi Isong, the god below, is the medium through which the supreme god can be reached. ◨ Abasi, the supreme god, created a man and a woman, but because he wanted no one who might contend with him, he decided that they would not be allowed to live on the earth. His wife, Atai, disagreed with Abasi, and so it was that the human couple went to the earth to live. But Abasi did prevail as far as food production was concerned: these humans would not be allowed to cultivate their own foods. Each day, a bell would ring, and the man and woman would have to travel to heaven where they would dine with Abasi. Because Abasi was determined that humans would not forget him, he imposed a further prohibition on them: they could not procreate. But the woman broke God's commands; she plowed the land, growing food for herself. When she shared the food with the man, he concluded that it was even better than the food that they received when they dined with Abasi in heaven. So it is that the man and woman neglected God. Together, they cultivated the land, and they broke Abasi's other command as well: they slept together. When Abasi asked about the whereabouts of the woman, the man lied, saying that she was not well. Because of her pregnancy, he had hidden her from God. And she gave birth to a son. Later, she had a daughter. Abasi was aware of what had happened, and he told Atai that he was right all along, that the humans were neglecting him, had forgotten him. But Atai reassured Abasi. Insisting that humans would never be the equal of Abasi, she brought Death into the world. Death killed the man and his wife, and fomented discord among their children.

Abasi Throws an Ax into a Latrine (Efik/Nigeria) The Efik, who originally lived with other Ibibio groups at Idua, a town near the Oron area, migrated during the first half of the seventeenth century because of a quarrel concerning an ax borrowed from an Ibibio woman by an Efik woman named Abasi. While chopping firewood, Abasi, a legendary woman, broke the ax and, instead of returning it to the owner, left it on the ground. When the Ibibio woman found the broken ax, she told Abasi to repair it. Instead, Abasi deposited the ax into a latrine. The Ibibio woman's husband therefore determined to fight the Efik, but Abasi's husband insisted that the case should be taken to court. During the trial, Abasi cursed the Ibibio people, and they therefore determined to punish her. The Efik began to fight with the Ibibio, and were ousted from the area. Some of the Efik paddled up the Cross River and settled in the Enyong area, where they became known as the Enyong. Other groups paddled down the Cross River and founded Creek Town.

Abasi Ibom Interacts with Man within Two Universes (Ibibio/Nigeria) Abasi, the supreme being, the god of the sky and earth, the creator and governor of all, lives above the earth, in the sky or heavens, perhaps in the sun. Abasi Ibom is concerned with great acts—creation, the ordering of the seasons, control of natural phenomena like rain, thunder, and eclipses—and the lesser deities and spirits have to do with more routine human affairs. Through these spirits, man can appeal to Abasi Ibom, the ultimate arbiter, for intervention. There are two universes, the dominion of God and the domain of man. At the center is man, and his mythic interaction with God occurs at the confluence of those two realms. Man is at the center of a visible, material universe; he is affected by the invisible universe, that of the supreme god and the lesser gods and spirits. There is an interaction of the two universes, man seeking to influence the gods and thereby shape his experience in the visible world, and the spiritual beings motivating man and his affairs.

Aberewa's Pestle Bumps God (Akan, Asante/Ghana) Aberewa, the primordial woman, is a name given to the earth spirit, Asase Yaa. ▣ She pounds her mortar with a pestle as she prepares food for her children, and the pestle routinely bumps against the sky. Annoyed, God, Nyame (the name means both God and Sky), goes away. Now Aberewa attempts to reestablish her relationship with him. To do that, she gets many mortars, piling them one on top of the other. In the process, she moves closer and closer to the sky. Now, to touch Nyame, she needs just one more mortar. She asks a child to get one for her, but he can find none. In desperation, she tells him to take one of the mortars from the bottom of the pile. He does so, and, when the mortar is removed, the entire tower collapses. ▣ In another myth, a love story, Aberewa, the earth spirit, is adored by Twe, a spirit from the water. So profound is his love for her that Twe vows to give fish to her at any time. All she has to do is touch the water. *See also:* Nyame.

Abradi and the Deadly Rabbit (Ama, Nyimang/Sudan) Abradi is the high god, the creator, maker of all things. All-powerful, he is above all spirits: he has given them their power, but is not usually held responsible for their acts. He is in the sky, has never been seen by man, although he is considered to be a presence on the earth. He is treated with reverence, and is invoked in times of drought, epidemic, famine, or family crisis. ▣ In the beginning, the sky was so near the earth that it tended to be suffocating, pressing down on people. When women stirred millet porridge, they had difficulty with the stirring rods because they brushed against the sky. The sky was so low that the women had to bend closely over the pots, and their hands were burned as a result. Finally, one of the women, thoroughly annoyed and exasperated, raised her stirring rod and pierced the sky with the upper end of it. Now the sky, the clouds, the spirits were so enraged that they moved away from the earth. ▣ Long ago, people and animals did not die. But men and rabbits did not get along together. In fact, they despised one another, to the point of attempting to destroy each other. One day, a rabbit took roots from a tree and gave them to a man. The man, unsuspecting, ate the roots, not realizing that they were poisonous. He fell asleep and slept for two days. Then he died. And so it is that death came into the world. ▣ In another myth about death, long ago, when a man died, God said that he was only sleeping, that there was no death. He told the people to place his body to the side for one night, and he would be alive again the following morning. But one time a man died, and a rabbit got to the people before God did. He told them that they should bury the man; if they did not bury him, God in his anger would

A

destroy everyone. The people did as the rabbit advised, and buried him. Later, God asked about the man, and the people told him that they had buried him. God, annoyed that the people had heeded the words of the rabbit, said that this is the way it would be from then on: humans, when they died, would not again come to life.

Abua Moves to Earth on a Rope (Abua/Nigeria) The first man to settle on the earth was Abua. Egule, his wife, is the mother of people. ◧ Abua and Egule, sent by the supreme god, Ake, descended from heaven on a rope. They were the first humans on earth, but animals were already present. Abua's first child was Agana, the first human to emerge from the ground. Because he was the first, he is worshiped as a god. Abua and Egule also bore Otaba, Amogan, and Akpede. Otaba, fond of fish, settled near the water and founded four communities. Amogan, a hunter, lived in the countryside; he established nine communities. Akpede, a doctor, settled near trees that provided the materials for his medicines. His children built the town that bears his name and seven other towns.

Abuk Strikes God on the Toe (Dinka/Sudan) Abuk, the first woman, is the primordial woman later elevated to a god. Abuk, sometimes spoken of as the wife or mother of Deng or of other divinities, presides over women's activities, especially the growing of millet and the brewing of millet beer. ◧ In the beginning, the supreme god allowed Garang, the first man, and Abuk, his wife, to plant one grain of millet a day. That was sufficient; they were able to live from it. But Abuk, hungry, once planted more grains than one, and, as she did this, she struck the supreme god on the toe. He was so irritated that he retreated from humanity, severing the rope that linked heaven and earth. Since that time and because of the activities of Abuk, humans have had to endure sickness and death. *See also:* Deng, Nhialic.

Abu Zayd Struggles with a Jinni (Bani Hilal, Banu Hilal/Tunisia) As a reward for his exploits in battle, Amir Rizq was allowed to marry Amira Khadrs, the daughter of the Sharif of Mecca. Amir Rizq's wife became barren after she bore a daughter. In her despair, she gave a bowl of couscous to the birds, asking the almighty to grant her a son. A black crow landed on the bowl, and Amira Khadrs requested a son with the qualities of this bird, a youth who, when he stabbed with the sword, would cause much blood to flow. God gave her a son as black as night, a boy endowed with the nature of a white or free man—this was Abu Zayd, a mythic hero. But when the birth was reported to Amir Rizq, he banished his wife. ◧ Abu Zayd joined a group of courageous kinsmen. They debated among themselves as to who was the mightiest, Zaydan, who was a great spear thrower; Dhiyab, who was especially impressive in battle; or Abu Zayd, who was compared to a hawk hovering above a bustard, who found adventure in the desert, who trod the wastelands, and destroyed camps with only the owl to tell the tale. The members of this group of three were interchangeable. Dhiyab battled a jinni in a well created by a meteorite, cutting its body in half with his sword. But in some versions of this story, Abu Zayd is the hero. He killed the jinni, the serpent, or the dragon, and inherited a kingdom. In other accounts, the three of them slaughtered the monster. There was then a contest: Who could leap highest against a castle wall in order to touch the monster's severed head? Abu Zayd became the champion, the one who had slain the monster serpent, the jinni. ▣ In another exploit, Dhiyab fought with 'Alan the slave of Zanayti, an enemy of the Hilali. Before the fort of Zanayti, 'Alan tried to overwhelm Dhiyab, but failed. As he retired, Dhiyab's horse leapt over the moat. Dhiyab threw his spear, which pierced 'Alan's eye, went through his head, and was buried in the wall of the fortress. As 'Alan was dying, Dhiyab told him his name; it was the fulfillment of a prophecy having to do with 'Alan's death. *See also*: Antar, Bayajida, Jinn.

Adoudoua and the Wandering Soul (Agni, Baoule/Côte d'Ivoire) The high god, Adoudoua, bred Nyame, god of the skies and symbol of virility, and Assie, the earth goddess and symbol of fertility. He then withdrew. ▣ The human soul, immortal and indestructible, shapes a person's life, determining his behavior. When a man dies, his soul goes to the kingdom of the dead, to reside with the ancestors, with the gods in the heavens. Death is a pleasurable state. If a person does not obey the rules laid down by his soul, there are times when, after death, the soul does not move to the kingdom of the dead but remains on the earth, there to wander, seeking another human body that might enable it to discover the purity that escaped it in its previous life.

Adro Creates Nonhuman Twins (Lugbara/DRCongo, Sudan, Uganda) Adro, the creator, long ago created the world and men. He is the ultimate source of all power and of the moral order. The divinity is conceived of in two aspects: he is Adro (God on earth, immanent), close to mankind, and Adroa or Adronga (God in the sky, transcendent), remote from mankind. Adro made the world; and the hero-ancestors and their descendants, the ancestors, formed Lugbara society, in the shape that it has had until now and that it should continue to have in the future. God's power may be manifested in many ways, in natural phenomena such as lightning and in the form of spirits that are given shrines by humans. He is the fountainhead of all power and authority, of all sanctions for orderly relations between humans. There is a divine spark within every human being, a sign of his divine creation. The soul is weak at birth and increases its strength with age. After death, it becomes an ancestral spirit, an ancestor whose identity is remembered. After death, the spirit of the deceased person returns to live under the ground or on the roof of his home. ▣ In the beginning, the creator Adroa made the first man and woman. They produced another pair of male-female offspring, who did the same in turn. These first couples were essentially nonhuman beings. They acted through magical means and performed marvelous deeds. *See also*: Gborogboro and Meme, Jaki and Dribidu.

7

Agipie Fights with Another God and Thunder Results (Turkana/Tanzania) There are two gods. One is Agipie, a benevolent god who lives in the sky. The other is the opposite, a dangerous god who lives in the world below, in mountains, rivers, and rocks; he has cattle, goats, sheep, and people who are sometimes heard talking. This god causes drowning, creates lightning which strikes people and livestock. ▣ When there is a thunderstorm, it is the two gods fighting, each hurling lightning bolts.

Aido-Hwedo, the Cosmic Serpent (Fon/Benin) Aido-Hwedo dramatizes a creative force that is primal, existing before Mawu-Lisa, the power that enabled that creator god to shape the universe. He remains the servant of Mawu-Lisa, this creative force continuing today, sustaining the shape given to the universe by the creators. ▣ He is mythically viewed as a serpent that carried Mawu-Lisa in its mouth as the creator passed through the universe. When the world had been created, Aido-Hwedo coiled himself around and beneath it; he continues to hold everything in its place, assuring regularity. He revolves around the earth, causing the movement of the heavenly bodies. Aido-Hwedo, found both in the heavens and under the earth, is perceived as the rainbow, as light reflected in water. *See also: Hevioso, Mawu, Mawu-Lisa.*

Aiwel and the Stone that Fell from the Sky (Bor, Dinka/Sudan) The ancestor of the Bor was a youth who came out of a stone. ▣ Long ago, in the time of the mythic hero, Aiwel, the youth took the sheep to pasture, but when they brought them back to be milked their udders were dry. This continued for several days, the boys being thrashed by the elders, who thought they were drinking the milk. At last, one wise old man followed the boys to the grazing ground, and, hiding himself during their noontide rest, he saw a youth milk. Only the old man saw the thief, who ran away and entered a rock. The old man told Aiwel of the incident, who then sent all the cattle and sheep out grazing, keeping the herds separate. Aiwel followed the beasts until he saw a young man come out of the rock and begin to milk the sheep. He stalked and caught him, and, in spite of his turning successively into a hippopotamus, a bird, and a gazelle, held him, though his hand was badly burned. Cattle were sacrificed, and during the ceremony the stone from which the youth had emerged split with a terrifying noise, and, though it was the middle of the dry season, rain fell in torrents. Another sacrifice was made; this time a live cow was pushed into the fissure of the rock, whereupon the rock masses came together. The youth, Fakur, was taken to the village, where he took a little fat from one of the slain bullocks and rubbed it on his captor's palms, which were immediately healed. The stone from which he emerged fell from the firmament, whence came the rain. In the old days, many stones sometimes fell from the sky. *See also: Deng, Longar, Wan Dyor.*

Ajok and the First Rainmaker (Lotuko/Sudan) Ajok, the supreme being, is the creator of everything. The Lotuko also believe in an invisible power called

Naijok, conceived chiefly as bringing death and disease. The spiritual and temporal head of every community of the Lotuko is the rainmaker. Spirits of the dead intercede with Ajok for rain. ◨ The first rainmaker was a mythical person called Ibon, who came to earth in the form of water at Itaraba, near Logurun; he took the shape of a man, married a wife, and left behind him a child and some rain-stones.

Akoma Mba and the Man Who Transformed into a Woman (Fang/Cameroon, Equatorial Guinea, Gabon) The epic hero, Akoma Mba, was carried by his mother for one hundred fifty years, after which he was miraculously born. Because he became a danger to his family, he was given into the care of Mba, a man who married his mother. Mba called his son Wrinkle of Elephant, son of Mba, but his unpredictable behavior did not improve, and so he became known as Akoma Mba, Creator of Mba, the suggestion being that he had created his own father. He became a well-known warrior, evolving into the ruler of the immortal Ekang people. ◨ One Abo Mama, embroiled in an antagonistic relationship with Otungu Mba, a local leader, exiled him to the forest. At the same time, twins were born on the day they were conceived, and they set out to avenge Otungu Mba. One of them, Mengana Mba, first traversed the world on a quest for something to which nothing could be compared. In the process, he was transformed into a woman. When Akoma Mba learned this, he warred against the king of that land, encasing the followers of that king in a rock, which he then took home with him. Those became Akoma Mba's subjects. Then Akoma Mba went to war against Abo Mama, defeating him. *See also:* Zong Midzi.

Akongo Hides in a Forest (Ngombe/DRCongo) Akongo, the supreme being, the everlasting one of the forest, is a spiritual being who has close relations with humans. Though he is a god and is wrapped in mystery, he has the characteristics of humans, and has an intense interest in the activities of men, acting as a guardian of humans. It is not a difficult matter to approach him. Ancestral spirits, with a close association with Akongo, also have an abiding interest in the concerns of men. ◨ The sky is supported by Libanja, who holds it up in the east with a pole, and by Songo, who supports it with a pole in the west. If they become tired and the sky tilts, all humans will become lizards. In the beginning the creator lived among men. But men were quarrelsome. One day they had an intense quarrel and Akongo left them to themselves. He went and hid in the forest, and nobody has seen him since. People today cannot tell what he is like. *See also:* Libaka, Mbokomu.

Alatangana and an Old Man's Revenge (Kono/Guinea) Alatangana is the supreme being. ◨ In the beginning, Sa, an old man, lived with his wife and daughter in murky darkness, a world without other humans, without animals. Alatangana was appalled when he visited the world of Sa, and he therefore created a more inhabitable world, which gratified Sa and his family.

They came to have a high regard for Alatangana, and the god fell in love with Sa's daughter. But when he asked the father if he might marry her, Sa refused. God nevertheless married her, and, because Sa was furious, they moved away, living in harmony, giving birth to seven boys and seven girls, all of different colors, all speaking different languages. Alatangana could not understand the words spoken by his children and, sensing that this was the vengeance of Sa, went to him. Sa said that he was indeed responsible, and so it was that the human races originated. Sa then ordered them to disperse to the far parts of the world. But they continued to live in darkness. They asked Alatangana to do something about their plight, and he sent two birds to ask Sa for advice. Sa sent the birds home, having given them their singing traits: now these birds, when they sang, would summon the light so that humans could emerge from the darkness. This was the beginning of the first day: the sun rose and moved across the sky. Now it was Sa's turn to call upon Alatangana for a favor. Because the supreme god had taken his only child, Sa demanded that Alatangana provide him with one of his own children whenever Sa requested one. They would be selected in Sa's dreams, and would have to come to Sa when he asked. This was the origin of death.

Ale and the Burial of the Dead (Igbo/Nigeria) Everything comes from Ale (Ala), the earth goddess, the spirit of fertility; she is mother and god. She was the daughter of Chi (Chuku), the supreme being, originator of gods and creator of men and beasts. Though he created humans' souls, Chi is a distant god; it is Ale, the mother of Igbo people, who is close to them. Ale is the most cherished and important of the gods; she made the earth, then assured that the peoples of the earth would live under her protection. Also the queen of the underworld, she rules the ancestors who are buried in the earth. She is goddess of the earth, responsible for the place where humans live and plant their crops. She is goddess of fertility, making the seed in the womb grow into a child, and she gives it life, then remains with it during its life, accepting it when life has ended. ⊡ When the earth first emerged out of chaos, Ale decreed that when any man died he should be buried there. From her womb, she bore the earth. When the dead are buried, they turn to earth; the people believe that they are of one body with Ale. The mother of a big bird called Ogbu-ghu, the hornbill, died. In those days, Ale was not present, so Ogbu-ghu could find no place to bury his dead mother. As he flew about, he carried her body on his back, making a grave for her on his head (this is why the hornbill has a mound on his head to this day). Ogbu-ghu flew over the water, seeking a resting place for his mother, but he found none. Then he saw a woman and a man, both very big. They were swimming in the water, creating something: land began to appear. When this land had become expansive, Ale was heard crying out, "When a man dies, let him be buried here." And she stretched her own body over the land. Ogbu-ghu had found a burial place for his mother. *See also:* Chuku.

al-Khidr, the Green One, Tests the Patience of Moses (Arabic areas) al-Khidr, the Green One (Swahili: Hishiri; Fulfulde: Halilu), a mythic hero, was the spokesman for the divine. He was associated with the sea, commanding the obedience of the four quarters; he was the deputy of God on the sea and his representative on the earth. He revealed esoteric doctrines to men of exceptional sanctity. ▣ al-Khidr became immortal when he drank from the Well of Life. He encouraged Alexander, the "two-horned one," so called because, al-Khidr told him, he was the lord of the two horns of the sun. al-Khidr accompanied Alexander in his quest for the Fountain of Life. Alexander did not find the Fountain, but al-Khidr, separated from the two-horned one, accidentally fell into it, and received everlasting life. ▣ Moses, accompanied by his servant Yusha, the son of Nun, journeyed to discover the place where the two seas meet. On their arrival, Yusha found that he had forgotten their fish at a certain rock, and he disclosed that the fish had escaped. They returned to the rock, and it was at that place that they met al-Khidr, the man who had been granted the gift of prophecy. Moses was anxious to follow him, but al-Khidr warned him that to do so demanded great patience and the ability not to be deceived by the outward appearance of events. Moses accompanied him and was tested when al-Khidr scuttled a boat, killed an innocent boy, and repaired a wall for the inhospitable people of a city: Moses lost his patience and demanded an explanation for these apparently iniquitous or irrational acts. al-Khidr explained, indicating that his deeds were in the best interests of all concerned, and that he had acted so under the direction of God. North African traditions associate Rades as the place where al-Khidr built his boat, and Muhammadiya where he repaired the wall. The district of Tilimsan in Algeria is where he encountered Moses and Yusha. The rock where Moses and al-Khidr met is at the Jami' al-Sakhra. *See also:* Irgam Yigfagna.

Alouko Niamie Kadio Descends to Earth (Anyi/Côte d'Ivoire) Alouko Niamie Kadio created the other gods, as well as man, animals, and things. ▣ After creating the world, he descended on a Saturday from his heavenly dwelling, visited the earth, and taught humans all they must know in order to live, as well as all that they must conceal.

Ama, the Potter, Creates the Human Body (Jukun/Nigeria) Ama, the creator, a high god, may be a fusion of two or more gods, being sometimes regarded as a male being, at others as a female, sometimes as the creator, other times as the earth goddess or world mother. Ama, creator of all living things, patron of childbirth, nourisher of crops, identified with the earth, queen of the underworld, sits before Chido, who is always present on earth, creating men and things. ▣ Ama created the world at early dawn. She (or he) made the firmament and holds it up. Ama is the earth: when a man dies he goes to Ama, for every living thing that dies, whether human, beast, or bird, returns to earth. She reigns in Kindo, the underworld, from which humans came, to which they all return, and from which they may return to earth a second time. ☐ She fashions the human body, bone by bone, as a potter builds up her pot strip by strip. When Ama has finished fashioning a man, Chido breathes life into his body, and for this purpose Chido descends to the earth. Similarly, Chido is the giver of grain to men, but it is Ama who fashions it. She is the earth, which is fertilized by Chido in the form of rain. *See also*: Chido, Fi.

Amma and the Egg that Contains the Universe (Dogon/Burkina Faso, Mali) The early story of the universe has to do with a struggle between Amma, the creator, and Ogo, one of her creations. ☐ In the beginning, Amma, alone, was in the shape of an egg: the four collar bones were fused, dividing the egg into air, earth, fire, and water, establishing also the four cardinal directions. Within this cosmic egg was the material and the structure of the universe, and the 266 signs that embraced the essence of all things. The first creation of the world by Amma was, however, a failure. The second creation began when Amma planted a seed within herself, a seed that resulted in the shape of man. But in the process of its gestation, there was a flaw, meaning that the universe would now have within it the possibilities for incompleteness. Now the egg became two placentas, each containing a set of twins, male and female. After sixty years, one of the males, Ogo, broke out of the placenta and attempted to create his own universe, in opposition to that being created by Amma. But he was unable to say the words that would bring such a universe into being. He then descended, as Amma transformed into the earth the fragment of placenta that went with Ogo into the void. Ogo interfered with the creative potential of the earth by having incestuous relations with it. His counterpart, Nommo, a participant in the revolt, was then killed by Amma, the parts of his body cast in all directions, bringing a sense of order to the world. When, five days later, Amma brought the pieces of Nommo's body together, restoring him to life, Nommo became ruler of the universe. He created four spirits, the ancestors of the Dogon people; Amma sent Nommo and the spirits to earth in an ark, and so the earth was restored. Along the way, Nommo uttered the words of Amma, and the sacred words that create were made available to humans. In the meantime, Ogo was transformed by Amma into Yuguru, the Pale Fox, who would always be alone, always be incomplete, eternally in revolt, ever wandering the earth seeking his female soul. *See also*: Doni Dyu, Yo.

Ananse Gets God's Stories (Asante/Ghana) Ananse (Anansi), a divine trickster, mediates between heaven and earth. A master of disguise, deception, and illusion, he tricks gods and humans alike. ☐ Anansi went to Sky God, Onyankopon, and offered to buy his stories from him. Onyankopon told him the price was a python, a hornet, a leopard, and a nature spirit. Anansi agreed on the price, saying that he would add his mother to the price. By tricking the python, the hornet, the leopard, and the nature spirit, Anansi took them, along with his mother, to Onyankopon, who gave him all his stories, stories that thenceforth became known as Spider Stories.

Andriambahomanana Seeks His Sons (Malagasy/Madagascar) The sons of God, Andriambahomanana, with their nurses, Rakoriaho and Ravao, descended to the earth. But these sons of God became lost. Everyone and everything sought them—the stones that were below the ground, the trees that pervaded the earth, the people who lived on the earth, the water and the beasts. But they were found by no one. When a messenger told Andriambahomanana of this state of affairs, God told them to stop the quest. Stones had gone searching below the ground, parts of trees had been buried in the ground while searching—when God said that they should stop, they did so, and this is why there are stones below the ground, why portions of trees are found beneath the surface of the ground. The people who had been searching, who had dispersed in all directions, stopped because of God's command, and for that reason men were scattered abroad in different lands. God commanded that no one mention the names of the two nurses. The reason that the sons of God were lost was connected with the waters, so Andriambahomanana spoke to the waters, ordering them not to rest until Rakoriaho and Ravao, the nurses of his sons, were found. That is why the waters move restlessly night and day, still and always seeing Rakoriaho and Ravao, the nurses of the sons of God.

Andriananahary Sends His Son to Earth (Betsileo, Malagasy, Merina/Madagascar) Andriananahary, the supreme being, is the creator god, maker of earth and sky. But he had little to do with human affairs. Customarily, Zanahary is invoked to initiate ceremonials. The ancestral spirits are much more critical to a ceremonial's success. Andriamanitra is the sweet lord or the fragrant prince. There are four other sovereign lords, and each superintends one quarter of the world. Of these, the Lord of the East dispenses plagues and calamities among mankind, by the command, or permission, at least, of the great god. The others are also subservient to his commands, but are chiefly dispensers of his favors and blessings. The people look upon these four as mediators between men and the supreme being. God is the ruler and dispenser of events. Nothing is unknown to him. Rakelimalaza is venerated as the guardian of the sovereign and the kingdom. Ramahavaly administers to the sick, providing the most effectual remedies for disease. Fantaka and Manjaka-tsi-roa are the guardians of the sovereign and the royal family. Ranakandriana is noted for responding to those who salute him. Rakelimanjaka- lanitra, "little, but ruling the heavens," protects the rice crops from hail by changing it into rain. *Hasina*, a life force possessed by any being, is a supernatural essence that makes something good or efficacious. Along with living people, dead ancestors and ghosts can manipulate *hasina* to work harm or good. ▣ Andriananahary sent down his son Ataokoloinona to see if the earth was suitable for habitation, but Ataokoloinona disappeared into the ground and never emerged again. Andriananahary dispatched his servants, called men, to look for his son. They wandered all over the earth, suffering greatly, because the place was hot and rocky. From time to time, they sent back one of their number to God to ask for new orders, but these messengers, the dead, never returned. To help men in their search for his son, Andriananahary sent rain to cool the burning rocks and to make the soil fruitful.

Anna, Exiled, Becomes a Water Nymph (Carthaginian/Tunisia) Anna, an old woman who was a goddess, was the sister of the Queen Dido. ⬛ After Dido killed herself, the kingdom of Carthage was invaded by Africans led by Iarbas, and Anna was forced to flee. During her flight from an island off the African coast, she was caught in a storm, and landed on the shores of Latium, where Aeneas was ruler. He found her as he walked along the sea, recognized her, mourned Dido's death, and brought Anna to his palace. This displeased Aeneas' wife, Lavinia, and she set traps for Anna. Warned of this in a dream, Anna fled. While she was wandering, she met the god of a stream who carried her off to his bed. Aeneas' servants searched for Anna, following her tracks to the riverbank. There they saw a shape rise from the water: Anna, the exile, had become a water nymph; her new name, Perenna, signified eternity. *See also*: Dido.

Antaeus: The Secret Source of His Strength (Libya, Morocco) Antaeus, in Greek mythology, was a giant, the son of the sea god Poseidon and Gaia, the earth goddess. He lived in Libya or Morocco, and made all travelers fight with him. After he had defeated and killed them, he decorated his father's temple with their corpses. ⬛ Antaeus was invulnerable as long as he kept in touch with his mother (that is, the ground), but Heracles, when he was passing through Libya in his search for the golden apples, discovered the source of his strength, fought with him, and choked him to death by lifting him to his shoulders. When Heracles had murdered Antaeus, he slept with Tinge, Antaeus's wife and the eponym of the city of Tangiers. She gave birth to a son, Sophax, who founded the city of Tingis (modern Tangiers) in honor of his mother. Sophax ruled in Mauritania. This Sophax had a son, Diodorus, who extended his father's empire and founded the dynasty of the Mauritanian kings.

Antar Begins His Quest (North Africa) The story of Antar, a mythic hero, evolved out of a Bedouin tradition. Antar is an Arab hero from Egypt to Morocco. The epic takes place in Nubia, the Zaghawa kingdom of Kanem, and medieval Ghana. ⬛ Shaddad ibn Qurad, a raider of the Bani Abs, captures a slave, Zabiba, and she bears him a son, Antar, who does not know who his father is and grows up as Shaddad's slave. As he grows up, he kills animals with his bare hands and learns the arts of war. He falls in love with his cousin, Abla, and sends her love poetry, which infuriates her father. Shaddad, also angered, plots Antar's death, but when they see him kill a lion with his bare hand, their plans are cooled. Antar later saves the ten sons of King Zuhair; he learns that Shaddad is his father, and when he demands that Shaddad acknowledge this, his father beats him. Antar leaves home, sets out to conquer Algeria and Morocco, and fights with the king of Ethiopia, struggling with mighty forces and with spirits. His quest takes him beyond Arabia and his own time period to Iraq, Iran, Syria, Spain, North Africa, Egypt, Constantinople, Rome, and the Sudan, bringing him into contact with a Byzantine emperor and with Frankish, Roman, and Spanish kings. *See also*: Abu Zayd.

Arebati, the Toad, and Death (Efe/DRCongo) Arebati, the supreme being, created the world, including the first man; he continues to create every person who is born into this world. ▣ In the beginning, death did not threaten people. They did not die: when they became old, God rejuvenated them. When they reached an advanced age, he made them into vigorous young men and women again. One day, an old woman died, and Arebati went out to bring her back to life again. He commanded a frog to move the corpse to one side. But a toad demanded the body for himself. Arebati reluctantly yielded, but said that the toad would have to sit on the edge of a pit with the body. A great misfortune would be caused if the toad fell into the pit. But the toad, refusing to accept this condition, pushed the more nimble frog to one side. But he was so clumsy that he and the corpse fell into the pit. As Arebati had warned, misfortune followed: the old woman did not return to life again, and after her all people were fated to fall into the pit— the grave. Arebati was so affected by this that he wanted to annihilate the toad, but the toad jumped into a deep pool and hid himself in the mud so that God could not see him. So death came into the world. *See also*: Baatsi, Epilipili, Masupa, Tore.

Aruan and the Bell Fastened to His Chest (Kyama/Benin, Côte d'Ivoire) Aruan was a mythic king. ▣ Two sons were born to King Ozolua on the same day by different wives. The one who cried first would become the heir to the throne. Aruan, born in the morning, was a perfect child; the king preferred him, but Aruan was quiet. Esigie, born in the afternoon, was a frail child, but he cried, and therefore became the heir. Aruan became a strong not very intelligent youth; Esigie remained weak, but bright. When they competed, Esigie won and Aruan despaired. Esigie was the rightful heir, but King Ozolua presented Aruan with the royal necklace and a magic sword: the place that he planted the sword would be the new center of the kingdom. Esigie, envious, tricked Aruan so that he planted the sword in undesirable places. Finally, the king told Aruan that when he died he should bury his body at the place where the new capital would be erected. Aruan lived in Udo, Esigie in Benin. When the king died, Esigie infuriated Aruan by stealing the body and burying it in Benin. Ugbeghe, a slave, showing Aruan a great empty pit in a forest, told him that he would prepare an everlasting home for him. When after three days Aruan returned to the spot he found a great lake where the pit had been, a magical lake formed of the slave's tears. Aruan threw a boulder into the middle of the lake. That evening, he heard a thunderous noise as the great stone hit the lake's bottom. Aruan gave orders that he was to be buried in the lake. When Esigie, who was now the king, insisted that Aruan give him the sacred necklace, Aruan refused, and they went to war. Aruan took into battle a large bell fastened to his chest by his hairs; he informed his servants that if he were defeated he would ring the bell, and his wives, slaves, and possessions should thereupon be thrown into the lake. As he marched on Esigie's capital, the bell worked loose and fell with a loud noise. The servants, hearing the sound, carried out their master's wishes. When Aruan discovered this, anguished, he prepared to die. Burying his sword, he cursed the place, forbidding anyone to come near the lake. Then he threw himself into it. When the moon was full, the handle of the sword could be seen above the ground. Aruan wandered about the town of Udo every fifth night, groaning, then returned to the lake. Powerful spirits lived in the lake, and if anyone approached the area, a thunderbolt from heaven would strike him down.

Arum and the Tree that Reached to the Sky (Uduk/Ethiopia) All life comes from Arum, the creator. He created man and everything around him; Arum may destroy man, or allow him to be destroyed. When man dies, he returns to the realm of Arum, which is located primarily below the world that we know, in the earth. ▣ The great Birapinya tree reached up to the sky, which in those days was close to the earth. There were villages in the sky, and people would go and dance up there, using the tree as a route, and the people of the sky would come down to visit the villages on earth. After the tree's destruction by an old woman who considered herself wronged, people were stranded up in the sky, which then retreated very far above the earth. Death, which formerly had been followed by revival, now became a final end for humankind. ▣ In another myth, the moon spat. The lizard was to swallow the spittle, but refused. The moon cursed the lizard: from that time, he would stay on earth in a cold place, and when he died he would not be reborn. And this would also apply to the people on the earth: they would die with the lizard forever. Had the lizard swallowed the spittle of the moon, the lizard and people would have lived forever, would have died and reappeared in the same way as the moon. Arum created humans, and the lizard could have helped them to live forever. ▣ The trickster fox brought fire to the people in the beginning, humanizing them. The fox also taught humans to speak.

Asis and the Girl Who Loved Boys Too Much (Kipsigis/Kenya) Asis, the supreme being, working through the sun, which personified him, created the world's creatures with air, earth, and water. Most living beings came from water. But the creation of man was different, more mysterious: Asis formed earth and water, and from that emerged man. Spirits of the dead mediate between man and God. ◧ The moon, having lesser power, was wrestled by the sun to the ground on the dark side. Because the sun was too hot, the moon melted and drifted away to the dark side to cool off, and since then it has never dared call for a rematch. ◧ In the earliest time, people, living near the great lakes surrounded by the smoking mountains, ignored tradition and so annoyed Asis. They were warned by thunder and lightning that they would be punished by God. But the people continued to ignore the warnings of the elders. Then, for six months, there was no rain. Hundreds of animals died, rivers dried up. The elders wondered how they could placate Asis, god of rain, thunder, and lightning. They informed the people that Asis, the great light, had to be appeased: a girl must be sacrificed. They decided on Cherop, a girl who, it was thought, loved boys too much. When she learned of this plan, she set out with a friend and went to the house of her lover, Sigilai. Along the way, they encountered ogres and lions, and there were struggles. Sigilai's house had been torn apart, and the girls walked on. Finally, they heard the bells attached to the cattle of Sigilai, and heard him singing a love song he had composed for Cherop. They were reunited. Sigilai was understandably not in favor of the intended sacrifice of Cherop. He killed an elephant and a lion to show that he could fight the bird from above who would descend and claim the sacrifice. But he feared that Cherop would have to die. He fought a leopard, and, wounded, was limping. The people came to get Cherop, now known as Nagoro, the sacrificed one, for the ceremony. As she was led to her doom, people wept, clouds gathered, the ground quaked, trees shook, mountains exploded, and a sword was seen glittering and then covered by thick mist. When the mist cleared, a warrior was seen moving around Nagoro. Some thought the man was limping—it must be Sigilai. He struck the big bird with his sword, wounding it. The clouds then opened, and birds and flamingos came from it, and a heavy rain followed. Sigilai married Cherop, and they were happy. *See also:* Wanjiru.

Asis Banishes Men (Nandi/Kenya) Asis is the supreme being. He created the sun and the moon, the sky and the earth first, then fire and water, and thunder with lightning. Then he created the first four living beings on earth: man, people with living souls, and the elephant, the snake, and the cow. He created trees on the hills and grass in the valley. Thunder was a gigantic bird flying through the sky with, in his talons, a spear with a long flashing blade, or a sharp matchet. Asista, the sun, who lives in the sky, is the giver of all good things, and prayers and offerings are made to him; he is a distant being but is the force behind everything. Between him and the living stand the spirits of the dead, Oiik, still members of the nation, who mediate between man and God, and punish the living to prevent them from upsetting the balance of nature by their crimes; they are responsible for sickness and death. They live under the earth, in hills and waterfalls. Two other superhuman beings, the kindly and malevolent thunder gods, Ilet ne-mie and Ilet ne-ya, engage in battles with each other. Chemosit is an evil spirit who lives on the earth and who devours people, especially children. Half man and half bird, he has one leg and nine buttocks; his mouth, which is red, shines at night. He propels himself by means of a stick, which he uses as a crutch. ▣ When the first men lived on the earth, a dog came to them one day and said, "All people will die like the moon, but unlike the moon you will not return to life again unless you give me some milk to drink out of your gourd and beer to drink through your straw. If you do this, I will arrange for you to go to the river when you die and to come to life again on the third day." But the people laughed at the dog, and gave him some milk and beer to drink off a stool. The dog was angry at not being served in the same vessels as a human being, and, though he drank the milk and beer from the stool, he went away angrily, saying, "All people will die, the moon alone will return to life." So it is that, when people die, they remain dead, while the moon goes away for three days and then returns. ▣ When Asista came to the earth to prepare the present order of things, he found three beings there, the thunder, an elephant, and a Dorobo, all living together. One day, the thunder said, "What sort of creature is this man? If he wishes to turn over from one side to the other when he is asleep, he is able to do so. If I wish to turn over, I have first of all to get up." The elephant said, "It is the same with me. Before I can turn over from one side to the other, I have to stand up." The thunder declared that he was afraid of the man and said he would run away to the heavens. The elephant laughed and asked why he was running away, for the man was after all only a small creature. "But he is bad," the thunder replied. "He can turn over when asleep." With that, he fled and went to the heavens, where he has remained ever since. The man, seeing the thunder go away, was pleased. He said, "The person I was afraid of has fled. I do not mind the elephant." He then went to the woods and made some poison into which he dipped an arrow, and, having cut a bow, he returned to the kraal and shot the elephant. The elephant wept and lifted his trunk to the heaven, crying out to the thunder to take him up. The thunder refused, saying, "I shall not take you, for, when I warned you that the man was bad, you laughed and said he was small." The elephant cried out again, and begged to be taken to heaven as he was on the point of death. But the thunder only replied, "Die by yourself." The elephant died, and the man became great in all the countries.

Ataa Naa Nyongmo Causes Earthquakes (Ga/Ghana) Ataa Naa Nyongmo is a supreme being, an eternal, infinite, nocturnal being associated with the sky, the source of life. He created the universe and its creatures, and controls cosmic processes and thereby the lives of mortal creatures. He is nurturing, controlling the falling of the rain and the shining of the sun, determining the growth of plants on which animals and human beings depend for subsistence. Human beings depend on him not only for existence but for the means of perpetuating life. ▣ If humans anger the supreme being by failing to perform certain rites or by violating divine injunctions, Ataa Naa Nyongmo may punish them by withholding the means of perpetuating life or by causing such calamitous events as epidemics or earthquakes. ▣ Gods are immortal, sky-dwelling spirits. They may descend to earth; some are associated with lagoons, mountains, and rivers.

A

Akudlozi iingay' ekhaya.
No spirit fails to go home.

—Zulu proverb

B

Baal Hammon Struggles with the God of Death (Berber, Carthaginian/Tunisia)
Baal Hammon, the supreme being in Carthage, whose name reflects his
fiery, solar aspects, was the creator of the universe; he was king of the
gods, one of the most important gods in the pantheon, universal god of
fertility, god of rain, the storm god. Baal was Shamen, lord of the heavens.
▣ This god of life and fertility struggled with Mot, god of death and
sterility. If Baal were to defeat Mot, there would be a seven-year cycle of
fertility; if he were defeated, there would be seven years of drought and
famine. *See also:* Gurzil, Tanit.

Baatsi Takes the First Man to Heaven (Efe/DRCongo) Baatsi, the creator, made
the first human being out of clay, skin, and blood. ▣ He told man that he
could eat the fruit of any but the tahu tree. After Baatsi became old and went
to heaven, his children continued to obey his rule. Then, when they grew
old, they followed the pattern of Baatsi and went to heaven. But there was a
pregnant woman who very much wanted to eat the fruit of the *tahu* tree.
When she asked her husband to get some of the fruit for her, he refused. But
she insisted, and in the end her husband went to the forest at night and
picked the forbidden fruit. He hid the peelings of the fruit in the forest, but
the moon, seeing all, informed Baatsi. This made God so angry that, as a
punishment, he sent death to mankind. ▣ In another myth, Baatsi remembered the first man, an Efe, whom he had placed on earth, and he dropped a
long creeping plant to the earth, then drew that man to heaven. The hunter
astonished those who lived in heaven, and Baatsi commanded him to go and
hunt. The Efe hunter killed three elephants, and was praised by the people of
heaven. Then Lightning attempted to kill the hunter by striking him, but

each time he did so the hunter was whole again. After a time, Baatsi sent the hunter back to earth, decorated with iron rings and carrying the spears that he had given him. The members of the hunter's family did not recognize him at first, but when they did there was a happy reunion. "Is our father who created all the Efe still alive?" asked his daughter. He assured her that he was indeed alive. *See also:* Arebati, Epilipili, Masupa, Tore.

Bail Delegates Authority (Dilling, Nuba/Sudan) Bail, the one supreme almighty god, exists in a vague realm above. He gives and takes life, but does not directly guide the lives and affairs of mortals, entrusting this work to a number of spirits called Arro. 🔲 These Arro dwell in the next world, but a house is built for each in the community that he represents. The Arro then advise the living chief of the community, controlling the affairs of the community in the next world, looking after the welfare of mortals in this world. They bring prosperity or plagues to reward or punish mortals for their good or evil deeds. Rewards for good deeds are happiness, good crops, fecundity, success in war, and long life; punishments consist of misfortune, bad crops through bad rains or plagues of locusts, sterility, plagues on men and cattle, defeat in war, and death.

Balewa Yola, the Black Horse of Yola, and the Contending Gods (Fulani, Fulfulde/ Nigeria) Because many people in the province of Adamawa retained their traditional religious beliefs, Modibbo Adama launched a jihad against Mandara at the beginning of the nineteenth century. 🔲 While they were attacking them, one of the people of Modibbo, called Bakera, of the Yola royal family, who had a black horse called Balewa Yola, was seeing about his own business, and did not hear what was happening to his countrymen. What engrossed his attention was this: There was a house standing by itself that he discovered close to the side of a moat. In this house, which had a wall around it, he found one of the best-looking women in the city, and he went in to her. He was so preoccupied with this woman that he was not aware that the Mandara had returned and driven out his countrymen. When the woman heard that her people had come back, she tried to detain him. Bakera remained until the husband, without his knowledge, arrived at the entrance. The Mandara woman told him that her husband had returned. She saddled his horse and held the stirrup for him. He mounted as the Mandara man entered and saw someone inside on a horse. He defied Bakera to attempt to escape. Bakera took his spears from the woman, and told the man of Mandara to prepare himself, that he was going out. Then he made his horse plunge forward toward the entrance. As the man awaited him, Bakera went up to him as though they would meet in the entrance, then turned his horse back into the courtyard at a full gallop. The man followed and they went through the courtyard together. When they reached the wall, Bakera pressed his horse forward to jump, and it leapt over both the wall and the moat at one bound. The man of Mandara urged his horse forward, but it jumped over the wall only; it could not clear the wall and the moat. Bakera turned, and struck his horse's quarters. So it was that Bakera escaped from them and departed.

──────── ⧗ **Bata Becomes A Pharaoh** ⧗ ────────

Man Reaches for the Gods. In the complexities of the relationships between humans and gods, mythmakers sometimes move humans toward godliness. Their storytelling efforts take varying forms. In some cases, a person is influenced through his life by the gods, and

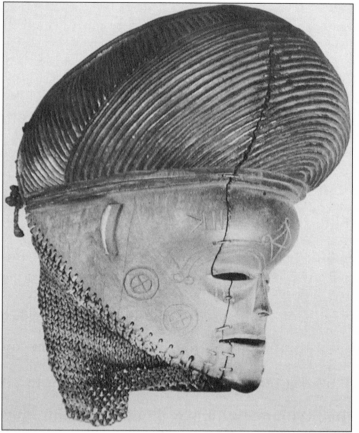

B

Segy Gallery, New York

A Lunda Initiation Ceremony Mask

in certain cases he moves into a state in which he is both human and god, a suggestion that he has successfully navigated the deepening chasm between mortality and immortality. In the language of story-telling, the human in some way touches God, or God becomes a part of him, and so he reaches for that lost unity for which he passionately yearns. ▣ (Egypt) In an ancient Egyptian myth, a man, with the active guidance of the gods, moves to the status of pharaoh, a being who has god in him. When Bata refuses to be seduced by his brother Anpu's wife, she accuses him of wronging her. Bata must flee Anpu's wrath. Ra creates a body of water to separate the brothers, and Bata, protesting his innocence to his brother, severs his penis and throws it into the water. Bata then goes into an acacia forest. The gods, pained because of Bata's loneliness, create a wife for him. But because he has emasculated himself, he cannot consummate the relationship. He informs her that his soul is in a flower at the top of an acacia tree. His wife leaves him, marries a pharaoh, and tells her husband where Bata's soul can be found. The flower is found, destroyed, and Bata dies. Anpu, having killed his wife for her false accusation of Bata, finds his brother's body, and, with the seed from the flower that had contained his soul, gives him life. Bata is now transformed into a great ox, and he reveals himself to his wife at the palace of the pharaoh. The wife has the pharaoh kill the ox. When the ox is slaughtered, drops of blood grow into two great persea trees, and again Bata reveals himself to his wife. She has the pharaoh cut the trees down. When they are felled, a chip from one of the trees enters the mouth of the wife, and she becomes pregnant. A son, Bata, is born to her. When the pharaoh dies, Bata takes his place, becoming pharaoh; he judges his wife, and brings his brother to live with him. The various transformations of Bata, within the context and under the influence of the woman created for him by the gods, lead him from mortality to immortality, lead him to union with God.

Bateta and Hanna Are Created by the Toad and Moon (Soko/DRCongo) Bateta and Hanna were the first humans. ▣ The earth was originally covered with water. Then the water dried up, plants and grass sprang up, trees grew, water flowed in rivers. There was as yet no living being. One day, a toad appeared. In the sky, there was only the moon; on the earth, there was only the toad. One day, the moon told the toad that he planned to create a man and a woman. But the toad wanted to do that: the moon, he argued, belongs in the sky, the toad is a being of the earth. The moon said that the toad's creations had but a brief existence, while the moon's creations were perfect and had everlasting life. But the toad insisted. The moon warned that if he went on with his plan, both the toad and his creations would die, warning that he himself would kill the toad. Nevertheless, the toad insisted, and he created a man and a woman. The moon, angry because the toad dared to be equal to him, moved down from the sky to punish him. The toad's creations, the moon said, were inferior; they would die after just one of the moon's trips around the earth. But the moon decided that he would improve on the toad's creations, giving them longer life and greater intelligence. But while the toad existed, the moon's rage would be dangerous to the humans. The toad therefore had to die. The moon then descended on the toad and consumed him. The moon then tenderly bathed, taught, and molded the humans, much as a potter does. The man he called Bateta, and the woman Hanna. He gave these humans the things of the earth, including an ax, fire, and cooking vessels. Then the moon ascended into the sky.

Bayajida Destroys a Snake and Marries a Queen (Hausa/Niger, Nigeria) Abuya-zidu, a mythic hero, was the son of the king of Baghdad, who was engaged in a war. During that war, the Baghdadi army split into forty groups, of which Abuyazidu led twenty. He marched with his army until they reached Bornu in northern Nigeria; he remained there, helping the sultan of Bornu defend his territory. He became known as Bayajida. ▣ He married Magira, the princess of Bornu, and became famous and powerful. The sultan of Bornu, envying him, conspired to kill him. Bayajida's wife became aware of the plot, and they moved west to Garum Gabas. After a time, Bayajida left his wife, Magira, in Garum Gabas, where she was to deliver a child, and went to Daura, then ruled by a woman whose name was Daurama. There he stayed in the house of an old woman, Ayana, and asked her for water to drink. He was informed that there was a scarcity of water because there was but one well in the town, and it was inhabited by a huge snake called Sarki. Nobody could draw water from it until Friday at a gathering of the entire community. Bayajida went to the well, threw the bucket into it, and drew water with the snake grasping the rope tied to the handle of the bucket. He caught hold of the head of the snake, cut it off, put it in his sack, threw the rest of the body by the well, drank some water out of the bucket, and took the remainder to his hostess, the old woman, who was surprised by his bravery. All these events took place that night. Early in the morning, as people passed the well, they saw the dead body of the snake and notified the Queen of Daura, Daurama, who came to the well and declared that the one who produced the head of the snake would be given half of the town to rule. Many claimed to

B

have killed the snake, but they could not produce the head. The old woman told of her guest who had drawn water from the dreaded well the previous night. Bayajida was summoned to the queen; he produced the head of the snake. When offered half of the town, he refused; instead, he requested the hand of the queen in marriage, and she consented. They were married and lived happily. In time, they had a son, Bawo, who ruled the town after their deaths. Bawo's six sons later became the founders and rulers of six of the seven Hausa states. *See also:* Abu Zayd, Dodo, Korau.

Bumba Vomits Up the Universe (Bushongo/DRCongo) Bumba was the creator.
◧ At the beginning of time, there was only darkness and water, and Bumba, the creator, the first ancestor, was alone. Then he vomited up the sun, and there was light. The water dried up, and the outlines of landforms began to emerge. Bumba vomited up the moon and stars. Then he vomited again, and a leopard emerged, then a crested eagle, a crocodile, a fish, a tortoise, and the lightning, the heron, a beetle, and a goat. Finally, many men came out. Other animals were then created by those creatures: the heron created birds, the crocodile made serpents and iguana, the goat made horned beasts. The fish created the varieties of fish, the beetle created all other insects. The serpents made grasshoppers, and the iguana made creatures without horns. And the three sons of Bumba finished the world. Nyonye Ngana attempted to make white ants, but died in the effort. Chonganda, the second son, created a plant from which all trees and plants have sprung. The third son, Chedi Bumba, created the kite. Lightning became so troublesome that Bumba chased her into the sky, but she continued to strike at the earth. Bumba then showed the people how to draw fire out of trees, telling them that every tree contained fire. He showed them how to bring fire from the tree. When the creation was complete, Bumba gave these creations to the humans.

Bunzi, the Cosmic Serpent, Produces a Rainbow (Woyo/DRCongo) Kuitikuiti's wife, Mboze, the great mother, lived happily with her husband. She became pregnant, and she brought life to and watched over the people. But when she gave birth to a serpent, Kuitikuiti knew that he was not the father. When he learned that the father was his son, Makanga, he killed his wife. The serpent was called Bunzi; she grew up and assumed the rainmaking role of her mother. So it was that when the rains came and the plants grew, the people looked to the sky for Bunzi, and they saw a rainbow.

Voices from the Past, I

I mages from the past form the nucleus of myth, as they do of all story-telling. There is no story without such images, which may range from the violent to the subtle, but which are always, and by definition, emotion-evocative, for there can be no story without emotion. These images, frequently called motifs, contain within themselves the story in microcosm, a cosmic egg from which the myth will be born. The motif may be performed singly or in conjunction with other such images, but it has no life until it is evoked within the context of images from the present. The storyteller, the mythmaker, keeps the past alive, possessing as he does a repertory of such images that are the raw material of the artist, the hues and tones, the motions and spaces, that will provide the context for the organization of contemporary events. Whatever transpires, whatever conspires to form the myth, will always be cradled in these motifs, the music of the past. So it is that the people of the sun are of a different creation from humans: during the sun's night journey, when it has cooled off, they polish it to make it shine brightly, lighting the fires to give it an intense heat. And so it is that !Nariba tosses a stick into the air, where it becomes the sun, cutting the night. Such imagery enables us not only to visualize and otherwise sense ideas and concepts, it becomes in the end the idea itself, the essence of the concept. Most important, images constructed of drama become the means of evoking emotions and, thereby, making members of the audience an integral part of metaphorical imagery.

Chibinda Ilunga Marries the Granddaughter of the Cosmic Serpent (Luba, Lunda/ Angola, DRCongo) Konde, an early leader of the Lunda, had three children, two sons, Chinguli and Chiniama, and a daughter, Lueji. When the sons insulted their father, Konde disinherited them, stating that Lueji would succeed him. And when he died, the brothers submitted to Lueji's authority. She was said to be the granddaughter of Chinawezi, a primordial cosmic serpent. ⊡ One day, an important member of Lueji's kingdom came upon some men cutting up an antelope. They spoke a language he was unfamiliar with. The one who was in charge, a handsome young man, introduced himself as a hunter, Chibinda Ilunga, grandson of Mbidi Kiluwe, the first Luba king. He was invited to the court, where he offered Lueji the antelope he had caught. He had left home because his brother, Ilunga, the reigning king, had insulted him. Lueji and Chibinda Ilunga later married. He initially got along well with Lueji's brothers, but when she transferred the leadership of the people to him, they went into exile. Because Lueji was sterile, she gave her husband a second wife, Kamonga, who bore his successor, Naweji. Then, when Chibinda Ilunga died, Naweji married Lueji. *See also:* Chinawezi, Lueji, Tianza Ngombe.

Chido: When the Sun Fell to the Earth (Jukun/Nigeria) Chido, the supreme being, the sky god, the one who is above, also known as Ama or Ma, is identified with celestial phenomena in general and with the sun in particular. Ama or Ma, the creator god, the earth god, is the fashioner of humans and of everything that lives and grows, and is also the lord of the underworld. Ama endows the corn with its nourishing qualities; Chido sends rain and causes the corn to ripen. When one is about to begin a journey, he appeals for the assistance of Chido and not of Ama, for Chido is above and watches his progress, but Ama is below in the earth. Ama is the female counterpart of Chido—they are a father sky and a mother earth by whose union the crops and other living things are born. ▣ The sun fell to earth one evening among some women who were winnowing corn. One of the women seized it and found that it was nothing but a ram. So she tied up the ram in her house, and the house immediately became filled with light. Next morning, the sun did not rise, and the king promptly gave an order that if anyone was concealing anything strange in his house he was to reveal it. So the woman went to the king and said that she had found a strange ram. She was ordered to release it at once; the ram went up to heaven, and the sun shone once more. *See also:* Ama, Fi.

Chinawezi, the Cosmic Serpent, Makes the Rivers Swell (Lunda/Angola, DRCongo) Chinawezi (Chinaweji) was the governor of the earth. ▣ In the beginning, Chinawezi, the mother of all things, divided up the world with her husband, Nkuba, the lightning. Nkuba moved into the sky, the life-giving rains the result of his urine. Chinawezi, in control of the waters, made the rivers swell when she heard the thunder. *See also:* Lueji, Tianza Ngombe.

Chipimpi and the Head that Thunders (Lamba/Zambia) Chipimpi (Kipimpi), the first chief, was given fire and cultivated plants by his wife, Liulu. ▣ A quarrel broke out between Chipimpi's men, the Goat clan, and his son, Kabunda, and daughter, Lumpuma, both of the Hair clan. Chipimpi decided to separate these two matrilineal clans. ▣ His people, because they insisted on sowing seeds that had been exposed to fire, suffered a serious famine: the rain could make nothing grow in the fields. But Lumpuma and Kabunda were prosperous. Chipimpi's nephew went to visit his cross-cousins, who fed him. He spent the night with Lumpuma, who was pregnant with an infant by her brother, Kabunda. Chipimpi sent the people of his clan to eat with his children. Lumpuma married her cross-cousin. The child she brought forth was called son of an unknown father. ▣ When Lumpuma's husband lost some immortal dogs belonging to his mother-in-law, Liulu, this woman was furious. She insisted that her son-in-law compensate her by killing Chipimpi, who was his father-in-law and his maternal uncle. Kabunda, Chipimpi's son, reinforced this order. The nephew brought the people of his clan together to associate them with his act. The women refused to agree to it, but the men acceded. After spearing Chipimpi twice, they cut off his head. When a new dispute erupted between the Goat clan and the Hair clan, the people of the Goat clan decided to commit collective suicide. Joined together, they threw themselves into a river. One woman only was dragged out in time by her husband, who belonged to the Leopard clan. So it was that the Goat clan survived, from that time dominated by the Hair clan. After the burial of Chipimpi, the villagers were surprised to find the dead man sitting on his front doorstep. They killed him a second time and took the precaution of burning his body. But on returning to the village, they found his head. This still exists. It rolls angrily around whenever one hears thunder. *See also:* Kabunda, Lesa, Luchyele.

Chiti Mukulu's Migration (Bemba/Zambia) Among the Lunda people, there reigned a queen, Mumbi Mukasa. The niece of God, she had fallen from the sky. She had ears that were like those of an elephant. Mumbi Mukasa married Mukulumpe. Among their children was the future Bemba king and mythic founder, Chiti Mukulu. ▣ The sons of Mumbi Mukasa, mobilizing all the workers in the capital, decided to build a tall tower. When the edifice had reached a certain height, it collapsed, killing many people. Mukulumpe, furious, decreed the deaths of his sons, Katongo, Nkole, and Chiti. He put out Katongo's eyes, and Nkole and Chiti, with the help of the blind Katongo, escaped. The father told them that he would pardon them if they returned. But then, to disgrace them, he made his sons sweep the royal village. His anger was assuaged, but when, some months later, the young princes committed other offenses, including adultery with a wife of their father, they were forced to sweep the royal cemetery. Chiti and Nkole, refusing to obey their father, fled with their friends. They were pursued by the followers of their father. Mukulumpe was so annoyed that he sent his wife, Mumbi Mukasa, back to heaven; she died when she got there. The king, made despondent by all that had been happening, called his sons, gave them gifts, then ordered them to live in countries elsewhere. Chiti, Nkole, and their half brother, Kasembe, journeyed toward the east, with a large following. A white stranger called Luchele, a famed diviner, guided them; he left the imprint of his feet on a number of rocks in the country. Chiti led the migration. The hair of Nkole was filled with various kinds of seeds. They crossed the Luapula River and founded a great village. Chiti was sorry that his sister, Chilufya-Mulenga, had not accompanied him to assure the royal succession, according to the dictates of matrilineal descent. But Mukulumpe kept his daughter, who had just reached marriageable age, locked in a house without door or window, a jail surrounded by alarm bells. Chiti's men removed the alarm bells, then, lifting the roof, awakened the princess. On the way back, the prince Kapasa had sexual relations with Chilufya-Mulenga, his sister. Six months later, the pregnant princess revealed what had happened. Enraged, Chiti expelled Kapasa. Before going farther east, Luchele consulted an oracle to ascertain whether the land they were heading for was fertile. The ancestors' response was favorable, and the Bemba people continued their quest under Chiti. In the meantime, Kasembe founded a kingdom along the Luapula River. Months later, the caravan reached the country of the Nsenga chief, Mwase; Chiti made a pact of friendship with him. Chilimbulu, Mwase's wife, seduced the noble stranger by sending him a message: she impressed the splendid tattoos on her breast onto a ball of red powder made from the nkula tree, then had a messenger take this declaration of her love to Chiti. She met him secretly near a stream and, without the husband's knowledge, they lived there together for three days. In the meantime, the husband became suspicious and went to visit his friend's camp. He caught Chiti in the act of adultery, and Mwase wounded him in the arm with a poisoned arrow, killing him. Nkole, succeeding Chiti, had his brother's corpse mummified. Then Nkole organized a military expedition against the regicide's people and killed them all. The corpse of Chilimbulu was cut into pieces. But the skin of her belly, ornamented with tattoos, was dried and preserved as a fertility charm. Since that time, it is said, the king's senior wife covers her loins with this skin when she begins to sow sorghum. The dismembered remains of Chilimbulu and her husband were placed in enormous jars, the jars filled with water and kept at Nkole's village. At that time, Luchele Nganga, the white diviner, reappeared. He built a round house and covered it with iron rods for a roof and glass on top. The mummy of Chiti lay in this sanctuary for several months. Then the remains of Chilimbulu and her husband were burned on a funeral pyre, the smoke from which became thick, suffocating Nkole to the point that he became ill. On the day of Chiti's funeral, he knew that he was dying and had a second grave dug. He ordered that the tomb of Chiti should be at the base of the termite mound and his should be at the top, because he was the elder. The second king was buried beside the first, in an all-white termite mound. *See also:* Mumbi Mukasa

Chiuta and the Chameleon's Message (Tonga/Malawi) Chiuta, the supreme being, a wonder-worker, is the spirit supreme, the self-existent one, the creator, the sustainer of life. He is sometimes called Chandu, the beginner, the first. Man receives his life from him, and death occurs when Chiuta calls. The dead do not go to be with God; the spirits live and move in an underworld, while the abode of Chiuta is above, in heaven. Although Chiuta might be unapproachable by men, he himself is not out of touch with his creatures. He can and does communicate with them; an earthquake, for example, is the voice of God calling to inquire if his people are all there. When the rumble of the earthquake is heard, they all shout in answer, "Yes, yes," and some go to the flour mortars and beat on them with the pestles. The works of Chiuta are often called by his name, especially when they reveal his character as awe-inspiring. Lightning is called Chiuta, as are a heavy thundercloud and other fearful phenomena in nature. ▣ In the beginning, Chiuta told the chameleon and the lizard to take messages to men, the one of life and the other of death. The chameleon was to tell men that they would die, but that they would return again; the lizard was to tell them that when they died they would die for good. The chameleon started, but because he was slow was soon outrun by the swift lizard, which hurried to men with his message that, when they died, they would end their existence. A good while later, the chameleon came along, announcing that though men would die they would return to life again. But he was met by an angry and sorrowful reply: they had already learned that they must die without returning and they had accepted that first message. So death entered the world.

Chuku and the Woman's Long Pestle (Igbo/Nigeria) A pantheon of high gods, headed by Chuku (Chi, Chi-Uku, Chineke, Chukwu, Osebuluwa), the supreme spirit, includes Anyanu, the sun; Igwe, the sky; Amadi-Oha, the lightning; and Ala, the earth deity. Minor deities include water and agricultural gods, spirits that are the personification of destiny, spirits that are the counterparts of living human beings, and the ancestors, who control the fortunes of their living descendants. Chuku is the creator and lord of all created things; he controls all things in heaven and on earth. Three names reveal his different attributes: Chukwu, the great god, the essence of being; Chineke, the spirit who creates; and Osebuluwa, who governs and directs all things. ◪ In the beginning, God lived quite near the earth, and the sky could be touched by man's hand. The blame for the removal of the sky is laid on a woman: One day, a woman was pounding yam in a mortar. At each stroke she lifted the long wooden pestle higher into the air, to bring it down with greater force. Each time she did this she hit the sky. God called out to her to stop, but she paid no heed, and finally God moved away in anger to the distant heights, where the sky has been ever since. ◪ When death first moved into the world, humans sent a dog to Chuku, with the request that the dead be restored to life. The dog loitered along the way, and was overtaken by a toad who had overheard the message and desired to punish humans. He got to God before the dog did, and gave the wrong message, telling Chuku that humans did not wish to be returned to life. Chuku, having agreed to this request, was unable to alter it when the dog finally arrived with the correct request. So it is that death came into the world. *See also:* Ale.

Chwezi Vanish into the Earth (Nyoro/Uganda) The pantheon of Chwezi (Cwezi) spirits constitutes the traditional religion of Bunyoro. The Chwezi, a mystical people who came to Bunyoro many years ago, ruled the country for some generations, then strangely disappeared. They possessed marvelous skills and miraculous powers. The Chwezi constitute a pantheon of contemporary effective spirits, each identified with one of the long-dead if not mythical Chwezi, and each possessing its own individuality and special competence. These spirits are not thought of as the ghosts of real men who died long ago, but rather as unchanging, timeless powers. Before the Chwezi came, there was an earlier dynasty of kings, the last king being Isaza. During his reign, this mysterious people came with cattle from the north and northeast. It is said that they were red and had long straight hair, and by superior magic and ability they obtained supreme power. They set up the empire of Bunyoro-Kitara, and moved with their cattle in search of grazing. The Chwezi built forts and knew the use of bronze. ◪ Ndahura was the son of a Chwezi, Isimbwa, by the daughter of Buchunku, King Isaza's gatekeeper. Ndahura grew up a proud and arrogant young man. When he inherited the kingdom, he extended its boundaries and divided it up among the Chwezi. In the time of his son, Wamara, there was a series of plagues, cattle died, people no longer rendered obedience, and above all there was a plague of smallpox. In disgust, the Chwezi departed. Some say they disappeared in the lakes. When they had gone, people concluded that they were gods who had vanished into the earth, and their spirits were believed to live in large trees and rocks. Ndahura became the god of smallpox. When the Chwezi vanished from the country they left behind them a cult of spirit mediumship of which they themselves were the objects; they thereby bequeathed to the Nyoro people a permanent means of access to the magical wisdom and power that they represented. *See also:* Ndahura, Ruhanga, Wamara.

Tilo ri vangerile rifu eka xipuluku.
Heaven has killed the chameleon.

A ku na munhu la nga lwaka ni tilo.
No man can fight with heaven.

—Tonga proverbs

Da Monzon and the Enemy's Wife (Bambara/Mali) Monzon and his son, Da Monzon, were rulers of Segu (1787–1827). ◘ Insulted because the son of one of his bards decides to remain with Duga, king of Kore, Monzon, a mythic king, sends his son, Tiefolo, to war on Duga. When Tiefolo refuses, he is killed. Monzon's other son, Da, agrees to carry out the king's wishes, and he and his army move to Kore. Duga invites Da to a party. That night, Duga's first wife joins Da when he returns to his army. Da promises to marry her if she will assist him in defeating Duga. She is aware of the secrets of her husband, and she reveals all of this to Da. Duga is defeated. He transforms himself into an eagle and a lion, and, prophesying that Da's father is about to die, he kills himself. Because his father's advisers are opposed to Da's marriage to Duga's wife, they kill her. Then Monzon dies, and Da becomes king. Thiema, the ruler of a province of the kingdom of Segu of which Da is king, revolts, though warned not to do so. He insults Da Monzon, and war is the result. Thiema's army is worsted, until Thiema himself moves into the struggle. Because his body has been washed with magical concoctions, he is invulnerable, and he is successful in his battles with Da Monzon's army, including the great Fulani leader, Hambodedio Pate. Hambodedio is the stronger of the two; Thiema is captured, his province destroyed. Hambodedio becomes Da Monzon's son-in-law. *See also:* Silamaka.

Deng's Tears Are Blood (Dinka/Sudan) Deng, the son of God, is the intermediary between man and the universal spirit. The ultimate spirit who comprises all things is beyond the knowledge of man, but he is revealed to man through his son, Deng. He is sometimes identified with Nhialic, the supreme being. The word, Deng, suggests the firmament, the stars, the rain, the world in general. Deng was married to Aciek ("woman"), who represents the universal mother and existed prior to Deng. Deng fathered sons who became minor spirits. ⊡ The first ancestor of the Adero clan of the Niel Dinka appeared from the sky as a young woman pregnant with her first child. The people reverently formed a circle around her, killed bullocks, and then rubbed her from head to foot with the fat of the animals. Then they built a house for her, but, fearful, they made it unlike other houses so that she could not leave it. After a month, her child was born, but no one came to help her. She called to the people, and they brought her a white cow, a spotted cow, and a bullock. She told them to sacrifice them, then to return to her. They found her nursing a wonderful child whose teeth were adult and whose tears were blood. The mother told them that this was their leader, that they should look after him because she could no longer remain with them. As she spoke, the rain came down in torrents; the boy was therefore called Deng (Rain), or Dengdit (Great Rain). He ruled over them for a long time, and when he was very old he disappeared in a great storm. *See also:* Abuk, Aiwel, Nhialic, Wan Dyor.

Dengbagine and the Parting of the Waters (Zande/Sudan) Dengbagine, a mythic hero, was a priest at the court of King Mabenge. No one knew who his father and mother were. His son was Bakuparanga. ⊡ An army arrived to make war on Mabenge. The opposing armies faced each other across the Uelle River. The river was wide, making it impossible for Mabenge to cross to the other side. Dengbagine was a man who performed wonderful things. He struck the river with his hand bells, and the waters divided, so that there was a path to the other side. When everyone had crossed to the other bank, he struck the waters again, and they closed once more. Mabenge's enemy was then overcome. When they returned, they again came to the banks of the Uelle and were unable to cross over. As before, Dengbagine divided the waters, and the people crossed over with the spoils of the battle, including many captives. But now the elders began to conspire against Dengbagine, telling Mabenge that this man was dangerous because he might use his wonderful abilities to overcome the king. They must therefore destroy him at once. Mabenge, who had been awed by the miracle he had seen Dengbagine perform, agreed with the elders. They seized and bound Dengbagine, intending to kill him. He asked them to tie a stone to his chest, and throw him with it into the water. But they should not stab him with a spear. When they had bound the stone to his chest, he asked them for his hand bells. He held them in his hands as they threw him into the water with the stone tied to his chest. He remained under the water for a time, then rose to the surface with the hand bells in his hands. Everyone saw him as he walked on the water. Beneath the waters, they could hear the beating of drums and gongs along with the chorus of a song from the mouths of many men. Dengbagine began to dance his dance of divination, all the while the drums sounding in the waters, though no one knew who was beating them for him. After he had danced for a long time, he went suddenly into the sky, but his hand bells fell to earth at the feet of Mabenge and entered the earth. He disappeared, and no man saw him.

Dente's Grotto (Ewe/Ghana) Dente is the God of Krachi. 🔲 People come from distant places and ask Dente to advise them concerning their sicknesses and other troubles. He has two priests: a public one, whom everybody knows, and a mysterious, unknown one, an oracle. This god may be approached every seventh day. His dwelling is a cave, and the path by which one reaches it from the town is swept. On the day fixed for visiting the god, the mysterious priest goes into the cave. Gourd-gongs, hand drums, flutes, and other musical instruments begin to sound loudly. The people then go to the edge of the cave, sitting with their backs to the cave's opening; no one may look into it. When they are seated, they hear the god's bells ringing in the cave. Then the crowd is greeted. The entrance to the cave where the god lives is covered. The public priest sits at the entrance; he, too, may not turn and look into the cave. When the oracle speaks, he passes his words on to the crowd. He is the spokesman for Dente, king of all gods; the mysterious priest speaks the words, and the public priest passes them on to the people.

Dido's Fiery Death (Carthaginian/Tunisia) When Mutto, king of Tyre, died, he left his kingdom to his children, Pygmalion and Dido. 🔲 Pygmalion became king, and Dido married Sicharbas, the most important person in the kingdom after Pygmalion. Sicharbas was killed by Pygmalion, who wanted his wealth. Dido, fearful, took her husband's treasure and fled by boat. On the water, she threw what appeared to be containers of gold into the sea, but they were actually filled with sand. She went to Cyprus, where, instructed by the gods, a priest of Zeus slept with her, and then she went to Africa. Dido asked the Africans for land, and was told that she could take as much land as she could envelop in a bull's hide. She had the hide of a bull cut into thin strips, and so obtained much land. She founded a city, shifting the site from a place where they discovered the head of an ox to one where they found the head of a horse. The city grew, became so powerful that a neighboring king, Iarbas, demanded that Dido marry him or he would war with her. Dido did not like the idea, delayed for three months, then threw herself on a funeral pyre and died. *See also:* Anna.

Dikithi Creates a Community by Tearing a Stomach (Mbukushu/Angola, Botswana, Namibia) Dikithi is a creator. 🔲 Old Dikithi, with one leg and one arm, leads people to a new residence. He steals cattle, comes to a river, has the water beaten with a guinea fowl: the water parts and the cattle move to the other side. He slaughters the cattle, and that night eats all the meat in the pots. He steals more cattle, and again eats the meat himself, so that in the morning the people find the pots empty. Kadimba, a trickster hare, puts fireflies on his trousers, and the next night when Dikithi attempts to steal the meat he thinks that Kadimba's eyes are on him. This goes on for some time, Dikithi denied his food because Kadimba is apparently watching. In the end, he decides to return to his original home, killing Kakurukathi, his mother-in-law, before setting out. But the mother-in-law comes to life and gives chase, threatening to cut off Dikithi's testicles. He kills her, or has her killed, a number of times—by fire, locust, a lion, a bird that burns her to death. Dikithi comes down from the tree in which he has sought shelter and makes a whistle of the foreleg of Kakurukathi. His father, the very old Dikithi, demands that his son give him the whistle, but Dikithi kills his insistent father. Then he has a red bird tear open the stomach of the old man, and people and animals emerge to form the nucleus of a community.

Ditaolane, Pursued by Those He Saved, Is Transformed into a Stone (Sotho/Lesotho) Ditaolane is a mythic hero. 🔲 Once, all men perished. A prodigious animal, called Kammapa, devoured them all, great and small. It was a fearful beast—there was such a distance from one end of his body to the other that the sharpest eyes could hardly see it all at once. There remained but one woman on the earth who escaped the ferocity of Kammapa by carefully hiding herself from him. The woman conceived, and brought forth a son in an old stable. She was surprised, on looking closely at the child, to find his neck adorned with a little necklace of divining charms. She therefore decided that his name would be Ditaolane, the Diviner. She was worried about the child being born at a time when Kammapa was ravaging the world. Of what use, she wondered, would his charms be? And she took straw to make a bed for her child. When she went into the stable, she was shocked and terrified: the child had already reached the stature of a fully grown man who was uttering words of wisdom. He went out and expressed surprise at the solitude around him. He asked his mother if they were the only ones on the earth. She told him how, until a short time before, the valleys and mountains were covered with humans, but the beast whose voice makes the rocks tremble had devoured them all. She pointed the beast out to her son. Ditaolane took a knife and went to attack the devourer of the world. Kammapa swallowed him, but he was not dead. Armed with his knife, he went into the stomach of the monster and tore his entrails. Kammapa roared fiercely, then fell dead. When Ditaolane set about opening the beast to get out, the point of his knife made thousands of human beings cry out, beings who were buried alive with him. Finally, he made an opening through which the nations of the earth emerged. Those who had been delivered from death wondered about the identity of the man who had released them. Surely, they reasoned, such a person could not be a man, he was a monster. And they vowed to cause him to disappear from the earth. They dug a deep pit, covered it with turf, put a seat on it, and sent for Ditaolane, telling him that the elders requested his presence. When Ditaolane was near the seat, he pushed one of his adversaries into it, and that person disappeared forever. The people knew that Ditaolane daily rested in the sun near some rushes. They had an armed warrior hide in the rushes, but he was not successful. Ditaolane knew everything, his wisdom always confounding his persecutors. Some of them, attempting to throw him into a great fire, fell into it themselves. One day, they were pursuing him, and he came to the shores of a great river. He changed himself into a stone. One of his enemy, surprised not to find him, seized a stone and threw it to the other side of the river, saying that that is how he would break his head if he caught him. The stone turned into a man again, and Ditaolane smiled at his adversary and went on his way.

Djakomba Sends Men from the Sky (Bachwa/DRCongo) Djakomba (Djakoba, Djabi), the supreme god, reigns in heaven, but no one has seen him. No one knows what he looks like. He speaks through the medium of thunder, and blasts trees and kills men with lightning. Djakomba gives men life and their food; he also sends sickness and death. All people go to Djakomba's place when they die, where they do not have to suffer hardships but are very comfortable and happy, knowing nothing of hunger, thirst, sickness, or death. When a great man dies, one hears distant thunder and the rainbow is seen in the sky. 🔳 Djakomba made everything: the first men came down to earth from the sky from him. The first men were Bachwa, who call themselves "the children of Djakomba"; the other people on the earth sprang from them.

Dodo's Wife and the Boy Who Changed into a Lion (Hausa/Niger, Nigeria) Dodo is an evil spirit, a being who inspires fear, an ancient deity, father of the cardinal directions. He is masculine power, situated spatially between east and south, representing the dry season, dried vegetation, and thunder. Opposite him is his wife, Damina, the bountiful green and moist source of the rainy season when she unites with Dodo's thunder. Dodo is the embodiment of the dead, and principally of the founder of the community. He is social mentor and guardian spirit, and he appears in the pantheon of spirits in the Hausa system of possession trance as well. The concept of the dodo is dramatized in images in myths of origin, in images involved in the Bori cult, in images found in stories of serpents, dangerous water spirits, powerful forces all the more menacing because of their unpredictability. Dodo is not human, but he can speak human languages, and often marries human wives. He is greedy and ruthless, yet these characteristics are sometimes the means of his undoing, as he is often duped by his victims. Dodo is an ogre with creative potential, and is a social symbol. 🔳 The hero, Bayajida, comes to Daura from the east and slays a creature that inhabits a well and refuses to allow water to be drawn except at certain times: this creature is often a serpent, but in some versions of the story Dodo is the spirit of the well. 🔳 There was once a woman who was the wife of Dodo—for Dodo had emerged from the forest and had become a husband. She wanted a human victim, so she came to a town bringing a small basket with a lid on it, and she placed it on the brink of a dye pit, where the people were dyeing, saying that the one who could knock over the basket could marry her. Seeing her great beauty, the men all began to throw—they did not know that she was already married to Dodo. The great men threw first, but they were unable to knock it over and open it.

All threw until at last only a certain small boy was left to throw. He took a small piece of gravel and threw it, and the basket opened. They were married. Three weeks went by, then the woman went to visit her people. The boy's father was a hunter who knew the country; he could transform himself into an elephant, into a lion, anything. He knew that the woman was Dodo's wife, as did the boy. Next day, the boy and his wife went into the forest, and when they had come into the middle of the forest she became a dodo, and rushed up to eat the boy. But he changed himself into a lion. She made as if to spring upon him, but he became a snake, and then she let him alone. The boy became a bird and flew off. *See also:* Bayajida, Jangare.

Doni Dyu, the Seed of All Knowledge (Bambara, Bozo, Dogon, Malinke, Minyanka/Mali) The primary mythic signs, numbering 266, represent the basis of knowledge, Doni Dyu, the seed of knowledge, the basis of creation. The origin of creatures is in the signs. The universe emerged from the spirit and thought of a creator god who first brought forth, out of nothing, these signs that designated in advance all that was to make up the creation. God created matter in the form of a placenta, on the walls of which were engraved the first signs of all that was to be created. The development of beings and things is also prefigured by the 266 primordial signs. This system of signs explains the genesis of a world whose components were all sketched originally in the consciousness of God. *See also:* Amma.

Doondari's Three Descents to Earth (Fulani/Mali, Senegal) Doondari was the creator. ▣ In the beginning, Doondari descended to the earth and created a stone, which created iron, which created fire, which created water, which created air. Doondari, having again descended to the earth, shaped those five elements into man. Because man was proud, Doondari created blindness. When blindness became too proud, Doondari overcame it by creating sleep. When sleep became too proud, Doondari created worry. When worry became too proud, Doondari created death. When death became too proud, Doondari descended a third time, and, as Gueno, the eternal one, he defeated death. *See also:* Gueno.

Dugbo Punishes Men (Kono, Tembe/Sierra Leone) The wife of Yataa and the chief earth god, Dugbo, gives birth to all vegetation and sustains all animals and men. It is her power that produces tropical abundance. The Kono believe that their conduct affects the soil's fertility, and therefore they endeavor each year to maintain Dugbo's favor so that the earth may yield a good harvest. ▣ When one does evil, Dugbo sees it and hands the evildoer over to the sky for punishment. He dies and appears in the sky to receive his justice. *See also:* Meketa, Yataa.

Dzemawon Appears as a Woman (Ga/Ghana) Dzemawon (Numbo) is a powerful and intelligent god, omnipotent and omniscient. He comes and goes like the wind, walking about the world and the towns. ▣ Though invisible, he can for his own purposes take any incarnation he likes. On days dedicated to public worship, one is liable to meet Dzemawon in human form. Presumptuous or inquisitive people invading sacred or forbidden precincts may meet Dzemawon in his own form, which is so terrible that the beholder dies of horror or fear. He is, however, always reasonable and does not harm well-meaning people who meet him by accident. The Asante invaded the country in the days of the Asante king, Ashantosei. The invading army was camped near Nungwa and the Ga were collecting their forces and discussing what to do. Dzemawon rose out of the Sakumo lagoon in the form of a naked and peerless young woman, borrowed a skirt from some women who were washing in the lagoon, and went to the tent of the Asante leader and so fascinated him that he spent the day making love to her in spite of the protests of his impatient captains. This so delayed the attack that the Ga force had time to move around, make a surprise attack on the invaders from the rear, and drive them into the sea.

Dzivaguru and the Rains (Shona/Zimbabwe) Dzivaguru, the god of water, was a simple man who wore his hair long and nothing but a skin about his loins. He wandered about the countryside doing acts of kindness and performing magical wonders. Wherever Dzivaguru went, good rains followed and the people prospered. He controlled the seasons, calling on the rains to fall whenever he considered it necessary. He could walk through the heaviest rainstorm without getting wet. ▣ To thank the god of water for what he did for the people, Chief Gosa, the paramount chief of the Mtawara, gave Dzivaguru a young virgin, Nechiskwa, who was to cook and to care for him. Dzivaguru led a celibate life while on earth, treating the girl with kindness but never once taking her as his wife. He walked into a big pool of water and never came out again. The Mhondoro we Dzivaguru, the Spirit of Dzivaguru, was perpetuated by the people as the supreme spirit.

Dzugudini and the Stolen Rain Charms (Lovedu/South Africa) The sons of the Monomotapa, monarch of the Karanga, quarreled. Each set himself up as an independent mambo, or chief, dividing the empire of their father among themselves. One of these leaders had his capital at Maulwi, in Zimbabwe. He ruled his people not by force, but through his supernatural prerogatives, for he was a sacred king. ▣ He had a daughter, Dzugudini, the mythical founder of the Lovedu people. Though unmarried, she had a son, Makaphimo. Dzugudini refused to reveal the name of the father to her father, the mambo. Her mother stole rain charms and sacred beads, and taught Dzugudini their use. Before Mambo could take action, Dzugudini and her infant son fled to the south, where they settled and founded the Lovedu people. Dzugudini died at Nareni, Makaphimo at Khumeloni. Mahasha, a brother of Makaphimo, sowed seeds, testing agricultural possibilities, and another brother, Mudiga, drove off lions that surrounded his area. Muhale, Makaphimo's son, ruled at Khumeloni, and got Mahasha and Mudiga to rejoin him as leaders. *See also:* Mujaji.

Voices from the Past, II

The mythmaker emphasizes the fact that the stories are ancient. "The art of composing imaginative narratives," says Xhosa mythmaker Nongenile Masithathu Zenani, "is something that was undertaken by the first people—long ago, during the time of the ancestors. When those of us in my generation awakened to earliest consciousness, we were born into a tradition that was already flourishing. Narratives were being performed by adults in a tradition that had been established long before we were born. And when we were born, those narratives were constructed for us by old people, who argued that the stories had initially been created in olden times, long ago. That time was ancient even to our fathers; it was ancient to our grandmothers, who said that tales had been created years before by their grandmothers. We learned the narratives in that way, and every generation that has come into being has been born into the tradition. Members of every generation have grown up under the influence of these narratives. . . ." Regarding the age of stories, Zenani argues that stories have an early provenance: "Their origin is with the ancestors, the ancient grandmothers. In the old days, when we performed these stories, the old people would listen to us. Then they would say, 'This child knows the stories!' Or, 'This one does not know them. He speaks a thing that he does not know. There's no story like this one. This child is just chattering about his own things.' It would be clear that the good storyteller was composing a story that was really ancient—a really genuine narrative."

E

Ebele and the Invisible Hand (Igbo/Nigeria) In ancient times, Ebele, a hunter, was the progenitor to whom all Igbo owed their origin. Where he himself came from is not known. He first lived at a town called Ohanko. There were two towns, Intsina and Eberu, to the south, that were at war with Ohanko, constantly attacking with long spears and poisoned arrows. ▣ Many deaths had resulted when Ebele appeared. Armed with a flintlock, he was present one day when the enemy made one of its periodical attacks on the friends with whom he was staying. Going to their assistance with his weapon, he shot several of the enemy. The others, who had never heard of a gun, seeing their comrades fall as if struck by an invisible hand, came and shook the bodies; finding them lifeless, they fled in terror and never again ventured to attack Ohanko. Ebele, hailed by the people as their savior, settled down among them, and became a man of great influence and substance. Many years passed in peace and quiet. Then a dispute arose between the two leading factions of the town. Because they were unable to settle the matter amicably among themselves, they called him in as mediator. Ebele quickly realized that matters were too far gone for settlement; to avoid an open rupture, he decided to separate the contending factions. It was arranged that one of them would remain at Ohanko and the other would move to Obaku, some three or four miles away. The division, having been agreed to by both parties, was effected without further disagreement or disturbance, and as soon as it was completed Ebele himself took possession of what is now called Ohumbele.

Mythic Commemoration of Man's Godly Activities. The dividing line between myth and tale is as blurred as it is between myth and epic, between tale and epic. In fact, all storytelling involves characteristics of both tale and myth. The narrative movement of each of the genres incorporates the linearity of the tale, and at the core of each is the mythic image, which evokes emotional responses from members of the audience and thereby animates the complex of images that comprise the story. The rich performance of story involves the linear movement, the cyclical organization of images, and the emotional center, all of which comprise myth. This is a story that clearly begins as a tale and ends as a myth, vividly dramatizing the overlapping of the two. ▣ (Ekoi/Nigeria) Sheep and Antelope are farmers, and they share their plantains and coco-yams with the other animals. But when Crocodile requests food, Antelope refuses while Sheep is generous. Crocodile takes the plantains back to his river home, which he shares with Python. They like the food so much that Python takes from his head a shining stone, and Crocodile takes the stone in his jaws and returns to Sheep, the stone lighting the darkness along the way. Sheep is so entranced by the beauty of the stone that he sells his farm to Crocodile in exchange for the shining stone, which he places on the lintel so that it might shine for all the world. But now, without a farm, Sheep becomes hungry. Antelope and the other creatures refuse to share their food with him. Only a fool, says Antelope, would give his all so that a light may shine in the dark. Sheep, weak and faint, seeks food, and comes upon Effion Obassi, God, who is gathering palm kernels. Effion Obassi shares the food with Sheep, and in return Sheep, having returned to his home and once again being refused food by his neighbors, gives God the shining stone. Effion Obassi takes it into the heavens to the sky-people. The lords of the sky place it into a box so that it can shine from only one side. Now the stone is the moon, and it glows for all the world. But sometimes the lid of the box is closed, the moon is dark, reminding the people of the necessity to be generous. In the first part of this story, a tale is told: Sheep and Antelope establish a pattern of generosity, a pattern that is then broken when Sheep sells his farm for a splendid shining stone and all others thereafter refuse to share their food with him. It is at this point that tale becomes myth: Sheep gives the magnificent stone to God, who takes it into heaven and, with it, creates the moon. To bind the myth to the tale, the myth-maker develops the image of the waxing and waning moon: God provides light to remind humans of the generosity of Sheep and Antelope, then withholds light as a warning about selfishness. (See pages 275–79 for the full text of this story.)

Ekineba and the Water People (Kalabari/Nigeria) Ekineba was a mythic being, a mortal who visited the land of the gods. ▣ Ekineba was so beautiful that even the Water People, changing themselves into humans, courted her. The son of the chief priest of Ojoma took a dowry and went to her. Her spirit told her this was the man she would marry. They married, and he took her away in his canoe. Some Water People were upset, and caused a storm to capsize the canoe. Ekineba was taken to the town of the Water People. The mother of the Water People was angry that the canoe had been capsized. When the Water People came home from work, the mother expressed her anger, and they said that they would return her to the land of humans. The chief priest of Ojoma had died, but the son was angry with the gods for not helping him when his wife died. The Water People, before they took Ekineba home, danced for her and told her to beat their drum, the first human to do so. They warned her that at every party she must be the first to beat the drum, to purify the drums. Then they returned her to her home, telling her not to allow her husband to embrace her before he had purified her. He did that, and they embraced. Later, Ekineba told her husband how the Water People had wanted to marry her but she had refused. That is why two of them had taken her away. Then she showed her husband how to make drums, what people should do when she beat them. But some were annoyed that she was always the first to play the drums, and one drummer kept playing before she did. She knew that the Water People were encouraging him, and she did not long to stay in the world of men. She told the people she would be leaving, and she sat and wrapped a cloth around her face. It was evening, and a storm came up: the Water People were coming. She told the people to beat their drums, night fell, a thick cloud descended, and the Water People took Ekineba away.

Elijinen's Torments (Tuareg/Algeria, Libya, Mali, Niger, Nigeria) The world contains both good and evil spirits, jinn or elijinen. Their drumming, singing, and dancing can be heard at times, and food is often left out for them at night. These spirits are not harmful, but they occasionally play practical jokes on people, and they also torture people who displease them. ⧉ Once, the spirits in the mountains of Ihrsan, armed with a spear, struggled against the spirits of the mountains of Adesnu, armed with a sword. During the combat, Adesnu was split asunder and remains so to this day; the crest of Ihrsan was battered with the sword and retains a serrated poll. They do not fight anymore, but they often talk to one another.

Enkai and the Termite Hole (Masai/Kenya) Enkai is the supreme being, the creator. Neiterkob ("that which began the earth," which may also be a reference to Enkai), a minor deity, is the mediator between God and men. Enkai's wife is Olapa, the moon. ⧉ On the volcanic peak of Oldonje Lengai lived Enkai, the god of fertility, the maker of rain, the god of the sun and of love. The first human beings, who came out of a termite hole, settled down in the neighborhood of the mouth of the hole. They had no cattle, but increased and formed a whole village. One day, they heard from heaven Enkai's voice, telling them that seven evenings from then, they must not shut their kraals. The seventh evening came and some did as they had been requested; others were afraid and shut the entrance of their kraals before they went to sleep. They were awakened by a sound from the big opening in the earth, the termite hole: it was cattle coming up and going into the kraals that were open. A little while later, shrill sounds were heard coming from the hole: it was goats and sheep coming up and going into the kraals that were open. When the sun rose, those who had left their kraals open found them full of livestock. Those who kept them shut were sorry that they had ignored the words of God. From the former arose the Masai; from the latter, the Kamba. God then called the Dorobo and told him to come the next day, he had something to tell him. The Masai overheard this, and in the morning he went to God and told him that he had come. God, thinking he was the Dorobo, told him to take an ax and to build a big kraal in three days. When it was ready, he was to go and search for a thin calf, which he would find in the forest. This he was to bring to the kraal and slaughter. The meat was to be tied up in the hide, not eaten. The hide was to be fastened outside the door of the house, firewood was to be fetched, and a big fire lit, into which the meat was to be thrown. He was then to hide himself in the house, and not to be startled when he heard a great noise outside resembling thunder. The Masai did as he was bid. He found the calf, slaughtered it, and tied up the flesh in the hide. He built a big fire, threw in the meat, then went into the house, leaving the fire burning outside. God caused a strip of hide to descend from heaven, which was suspended over the calf skin. Cattle at once commenced to descend one by one on the strip of hide until the whole of the kraal was filled and the animals began to press against one another and to break down the house where the startled Masai was. He went outside and, because he did so, the strip of hide was cut, and no more cattle came down from heaven. God asked him whether the cattle that were there were sufficient: the flow of cattle had ceased, he said, because the Masai had broken God's instruction. The Masai then attended to the animals that he had been given. The Dorobo lost the cattle and has had to shoot game for his food ever since.

Epaphus, the Touch of Zeus (Egypt, Libya) Epaphus was the father of Libya.
🄴 Io, beloved of Zeus, was transformed into a cow; to escape the wrath of jealous Hera, she wandered the earth, finding safety on the banks of the Nile. She resumed her human form and gave birth to a son, Epaphus, or the "Touch of Zeus." Hera transferred her hatred to this son and ordered him hidden away by the Curetes so that Io could not find him. Zeus killed the Curetes, and Io continued her search for her son. She found him in Syria, being reared by the wife of the king of Byblos, and she brought him back with her to Egypt. He became a man, succeeded his adoptive father Telegonus as ruler, married Memphis, daughter of the river god Nile, and fathered a daughter, Libya, who gave her name to Egypt's neighboring country.

Epilipili Is Born of Lightning (Efe/DRCongo) Epilipili was the first; he has always been in existence and will never die. He created all things. The lord of all men, he sees their doings by day and night, even in the darkest forest, and he punishes crime. The rainbow, the terror of all Efe, which has its place in the heavens together with the lightning, is dependent on Epilipili: it may show itself only if he permits. Epilipili dwells above, and the kingdom of the dead is subject to him. He sends all sicknesses. He is also the lord of magic power. He refuses to grant success in hunting to the people until they call upon him for help. 🄴 Lightning and Otu lived together as brother and sister. On one occasion, Moon visited the newly married pair and expressed his astonishment at their attitude toward each other. He scolded Lightning as a dolt who did not know what the woman was there for. Lightning did not learn his lesson until Moon, sensing the desire of the woman, gave her a husband, Mupe. When Otu gave birth to a male child, Lightning sired many children by her, with whom he went to heaven after Otu's death. One, Aporofandza, is the first ancestor and hero of the culture; another, Epilipili, the creator god, has many of the characteristics of Aporofandza. The creator god appears to be a fusion of the two. *See also:* Arebati, Baatsi, Masupa, Tore.

Esu Becomes God's Messenger (Yoruba/Nigeria) Esu is the messenger of the oracle, taking sacrifices to him and bringing his commands to men, acting under his orders and punishing the wicked for him. In a battle with Death he lost his club, but Orunmila recovered it for him and that created a pact between these two divinities. But Esu is also important in his own right, and he is greatly feared for the evil that he can do. He sometimes impels men to evildoing. In this character, he is Elegbara or Shigidi, the avenger. Esu is also

E

47

looked upon as protective and even benevolent: he is called "father." He is said to have two hundred names, which indicates that he is a many-sided, diverse character. Esu is an *orisa* (a god or spirit), so instead of four hundred supernatural powers, the Yoruba often speak of four hundred and one, Esu being the divinity on top of the four hundred. He is regarded as one of the most powerful *orisa*, capable of changing his form at will. Each *odu* (an *odu* is a chapter of Ifa, an immense volume of traditions, consisting of 256 chapters, or *odu*; each *odu* contains from six hundred to eight hundred poems known as Ese Ifa, totaling as many as 204,800 poems) is governed by its own Esu. There are 256 different forms of existence that Esu can assume. But Esu is also a kinsman of the Ajogun, malevolent supernatural powers; the eight Ajogun warlords are his errand boys. Esu is like an impartial judge who mediates between the benevolent and malevolent supernatural powers. He is able to do this by using a sacrifice provided by a would-be victim. When Esu presents the sacrifice to a warring Ajogun, the Ajogun allows his victim to go away unhurt. But if a would-be victim does not perform sacrifice, Esu is not in a position to help him. 🔲 Esu the divine trickster tricked the High God, who then lived on the earth. God became so angry because of Esu's trick that he withdrew from the earth and moved to heaven. Esu was to bring him regular reports from the earth, and so it is that Esu became the messenger between heaven and earth. *See also:* Fa, Ifa, Legba.

E

Ramin mugunta a gina shi gajere.
Dig the hole of evil shallow.

Muni tudu ne, kowa nasa yake hawa, ya fadi na wani.
Evil is a hill. Everyone gets on his own
    and speaks about someone else's.

—Hausa proverbs

F

Fa Is the Will of the Gods (Fon/Benin) Fa, the god of destiny, is the personal fate of each man. Man must be in harmony with his own Fa. ▣ After the world had been created, two men, Koda and Chada, came down from the sky. These two men told the few people on earth that they had been sent by Mawu. They said that all men who are created have their Fa, the sacred word, the writing, with which Mawu creates each person. This writing is given to Legba, Mawu's assistant. The orders given to Legba by means of this writing are called Fa. Legba is sent by Mawu to bring to each individual his Fa. Every man has a god whom he must worship; without Fa, without this writing, he can never know his god. If the people of the earth fail to worship Legba, he will refuse to reveal to them the writing that is their destiny. Each day, Mawu gives the day's writing to Legba, indicating who is to die, be born, dangers to be encountered, fortune to be met. Legba, if he wishes, can change these matters. Though people knew that Fa was the will of the gods, they forgot the importance of Legba. So three other men came to earth at a place called Gisi; they were Adjaka, Oku, and Ogbena. They reported that Mawu said that Legba is very important, that Legba is the son, the brother, and the assistant of Mawu herself. If people on earth are in need of anything, they must first of all address themselves to Legba, who has the power to do as he chooses on earth. Then these prophets showed a man named Alaundje how to make Fa. They had brought with them from the sky the fruit of the palm tree used for divining Fa. Now they showed Alaundje how, when a man wishes to know his destiny, he must enter a forest, take the kernels, throw them, and trace eight lines on the earth. These eight lines reveal the destiny of this man. This same man must then gather the earth on which he has traced the lines of his destiny and put it into a small cloth. This man who now possesses his destiny must give the writing to a scholar to interpret. These same prophets explained each line to Alaundje, along with the meaning of the lines of the hand, lines that correspond to the blueprint of the soul that Mawu gives to all men: by the writing on the hand of man, Mawu makes known her own writing. And as the writing that controls human destiny is in the house of Mawu, it is necessary that Legba be worshiped. *See also:* Esu, Ifa, Legba, Mawu.

Faro and the Albino Twins (Bambara/Mali) Dya and Gla, the forces of creation, arose, and two creators emerged, Faro, who formed the sky, and Pemba, who formed the earth. Faro is a female divinity with a male twin, Koni, who lives in her shadow, owing all that he is to his wife, Faro, considered the ultimate wife and mother. ◧ God made the pond where Faro lived overflow, and a great flood was the result. Faro's people, and also animals, went into an ark, which drifted for seven days. Then the rain washed the sky, and Faro, with the blacksmith, began her reign. They emerged from the ark, built the first village, and the first rains made it possible for the seeds that they planted to grow. Plants and trees grew, and Faro brought into existence animals. Under Faro's guidance and influence, people now experienced night and day, the movement of the seasons, the ordering of life. From her own body, Faro created the life-giving Niger River. *See also:* Mangala, Pemba, Yo.

Fi Helps to Shape Living Beings (Jen/Nigeria) Fi, the supreme being, is associated with the sun. The Jen believe in a second deity, Ma, the servant of Fi. ◧ He fashions all living things as a potter fashions a pot, and if he is careless or in a capricious mood he fashions men in ugly guise. He is the great purveyor, and obtains from Fi all things that are necessary for men, the fruits of the earth and the rain. Among his subordinates are Umwa, the war god, who is attended by Nimbwi, the whirlwind. His immediate officers are the Kue, tutelary spirits, who represent the host of ancestral ghosts. *See also:* Ama, Chido.

F

Experiences of the Present

Storytelling has little relevance, little power, if it is memorized, if it is a static museum piece, if it has become a piece of history. The story, the myth, must always be alive, must contain real and potent linkages to the audience's experience of the present. It is the experience of the present that assures that the mythmaker will people his story with recognizable beings and events. Such contemporary, realistic images are insufficient in themselves, of course; like the motifs, they are the raw material of myth-making. It is not until the storyteller, in performance, unites the two categories of imagery that myth is made. The myth has no previous existence: it exists only in the particular performance, and that performance is nothing if it lacks the vital connections. What happens in a storytelling performance, then, is this: the storyteller takes the venerable images from her memory, unites these with images that are as real as the world that exists outside the storytelling activity, in the process actively enlisting the emotional support of the members of the audience. This combination of activities assures that the past and the present are brought into an artistic relationship one with the other, and it is in this way that story shapes our experience of the present by placing it within the context of the past. Simultaneously, the images from the present influence the way we conceive of the past and provide the materials that enable us to decide what images from the past are relevant. The challenge for the mythmaker is to work the audience's experiences of the present into the perceived historical and cultural experiences as these are documented by and inscribed in the ancient images.

⋈ G ⋈

‖*Gamab's Sharp and Deadly Arrow* (Berg Damara/Namibia) The highest divinity, the supreme being, dwells in heaven and is known as ‖Gamab. He was originally the god of the rising clouds and of thunder and fountains (the word ‖*gami* means "water"). ‖Gamab is not the deity of creation, for the Berg Damara do not believe that the world had a beginning and that it was created. The annual renewal of nature—the regularity of the rainy season, the hunting grounds teeming with game, crops growing fresh and ripening—is the work of ‖Gamab. He provides for the livelihood of all living beings and thus is the maintainer of life. ⊡ He is also the Lord of Death. From his place in heaven, he directs his deadly arrow at the bodies of men who become sick and die. Then the soul leaves the body, departing through the open door of the house. It takes the broad road that leads to ‖Gamab's village, where ‖Gamab gathers around him the souls of the departed. A narrow road, whose destination is not known, branches off from it. At a certain spot on the road is a precipice with a great fire below. If one is careless, he will fall over the precipice. ‖Gamab is the center about whom all deceased Berg Damara, the good as well as the wicked, gather. Whoever approaches the vicinity of the village is met by spirits who lead him into the village. ‖Gamab's village is laid out in the same manner as the Berg Damara villages on earth. In the center is a large fig tree, beneath which burns the holy fire. ‖Gamab, the elder of the village, sits at this fire or rests in his house. The other elders, who once dwelled on earth, also sit at the holy fire. The newcomer takes his place among them. The souls of children who die are delivered to the women in the other world to be educated. *See also:* Holy Fire.

⧧*Gama-*⧧*Gorib and the Hole of the Ancestors* (Khoi/South Africa) ⊡ Heitsi-Eibib was once looking for his people near the place of ⧧Gama-⧧Gorib, an evil being who sent a hare to him to ask him to join in a certain game: if one man quarrels with another, he fills his hand with dust and offers both hands to his opponent. If the adversary is bold, he dashes the dust to the ground, and then the two men fight. This is what happened with Heitsi-Eibib. At first, Heitsi-Eibib was thrown by the hare into a hole, but he said, "Hole of my ancestors, heave up your bottom a little, and give me a lift, that I may jump out." It did so, and Heitsi-Eibib jumped out. This happened twice, after which Heitsi-Eibib threw his adversary into the hole, after hitting him first behind the ear. Then Heitsi-Eibib said, "Hole of my ancestors, heave up your bottom a little, that my children may come out," and it did so, and all his children who had been previously destroyed came out. After this, Heitsi-Eibib cursed the hare and told it that henceforth it should eat only at night. ☐ Heitsi-Eibib then went on to the kraal of |Hau‖Gai╪Gaib, and, when asked what he was doing, said that he was looking for his people. Here also there was a hole, and it was the custom of |Hau‖Gai╪Gaib to place a stone on his own forehead, and ask people who were passing by to take the stone and throw it at his forehead. When they did so the stone bounded back and killed the thrower. Heitsi-Eibib was invited to throw the stone. He promised to do so if |Hau‖Gai╪Gaib would shut his eyes. Then Heitsi-Eibib hit him behind the ear and killed this evil person on the spot, who fell into his own hole. Passing on, he came to a lion. In those days lions could fly, and Heitsi-Eibib saw one of the flying lions in a tree. He burned the tree down, and caused the lion ever after to walk on the earth. He noticed a lion that had been flying in the sky. It pounced down on an ox and devoured it. This made the lion so heavy that when Heitsi-Eibib chased it the lion could not fly, so he cut off its wings. ☐ Heitsi-Eibib was angry with ╪Gama-╪Gorib because he worked so much evil on earth. Heitsi-Eibib managed to distract his attention, and when his rival was not looking he hit his enemy behind the ear. After that the people lived happily. But Heitsi-Eibib was wounded in the knee during the fight, and ever after limped. As people pass his grave they throw on it some pieces of their clothing, or dung from a zebra, or flowers, or branches of a tree, or stones, and if they are hunting they pray to Heitsi-Eibib for good fortune. *See also:* Heitsi-Eibib, Tsui‖Goab.

╪Gao!na and the Tree Whose Name May Not Be Spoken (!Kung/Namibia) After ╪Gao!na, a culture hero with supernatural powers, had created himself, he created the lesser god and then their two wives. The old ╪Gao!na could change himself into other forms, could change people into animals, could bring people back to life. The great god created the earth and gave it its name. In the earth, he created holes for water and he created water. Then ╪Gao!na made the sky, a dome over the earth; he made rain—gentle and violent. He made the sun, the moon and the stars, the wind. He created these things and commands their movements. He created the things that grow from the ground; he created animals, gave them their names. ☐ Then he created human beings, first a woman and then a man, and told

Musée de l'Homme, Paris

Mask Representing the First Ancestor of the Dogon of Mali

them to breathe. When the man asked the woman to give him fire, she did. He married her. ǂGao!na named the first woman, Khwova, for his wife, and he named the first man, ǂGao, for himself. From the beginning, he created men and women to be mortal. He turns the spirits of the dead into ǁgauwasi; they live in the sky with him. He sends them to earth to bring death or good fortune.   □   ǂGao!na has a medicine with which he can renew himself and all those who live in the sky with him. When they get old and he renews them, they do not die. But he has not given human beings that medicine. ǂGao!na gave humans arrows, bows, digging sticks, the knowledge to make things. 🔲 The old ǂGao!na was manlike. ǂGao!na, the great god of the east, is also manlike. He has the power to change himself into the forms of animals or objects and sometimes does so, but in his own form he is a man. The people say he is the tallest of the San, with a big head, black long hair, a long beard, and hair on his chest. He has a horse and rides everywhere across the earth and sky: one can sometimes hear the sound of his horse's hooves passing overhead. ǂGao!na lives in a house at the place where the sun rises in the eastern sky. Near the house is a great tree—one tree. The !Kung fear the tree and the house. The lesser god in the west lives beside two trees, and these two trees have names. The one tree of the great god in the east has no name, or perhaps it has a name that cannot be spoken. The tree is associated with the spirits of the dead. ǂGao!na's house has two stories. It is long, made of stone, with a shining roof of corrugated iron. There are big doors on the ends and small doors on the sides. All the ‖gauwasi (spirits of the dead) live on the lower floor, and ǂGao!na and his wife and children live on the upper floor. No mortal has ever seen ǂGao!na's dwelling place. *See also:* ‖Gauwa, Huwe, |Kaggen, |Kai-|Kini, Pishiboro.

Gassire and the Lute that Sang (Djerma, Soninke/Burkina Faso, Gambia, Mali, Mauritania, Niger, Senegal) In early times, Wagadu faced north and was called Dierra. The last king was Nganamba Fasa, and his strength grew as he fought the Burdama and Boroma. But now he was old and his heroes were old. His son was Gassire, a mythic hero. Nganamba grew so old that Wagadu was lost. But he did not die, and a jackal therefore gnawed at Gassire's heart. He daily watched for his father's death. He fought as a hero against the Burdama and Boroma. He heard his deeds praised, but he was miserable as he listened to the strains of Nganamba's breathing: Gassire wanted his father's sword and shield, and his longing grew. Then a wise man told Gassire that his father would die but Gassire would not get his sword and shield. Others would inherit those; Gassire would get a lute, and that lute would cause the loss of Wagadu. Gassire called the wise man a liar. The next day, he did battle with the Burdama alone, telling the other heroes to remain behind. His sword was like a sickle, and the enemy feared him, and fled. The other heroes gathered the spears of the vanquished Burdama, and sang Gassire's praise; never before had Wagadu won so many spears. Women bathed him, men sang his praise. He went to the fields and heard the partridges. A partridge told of its battle with a snake. All will die, it sang, but the Dausi, the song of its battles, would not die, it would outlive all kings and heroes. Gassire went back to the wise old man: Do men also know the Dausi, and can the Dausi outlive life and death? The old man said, You are hastening to your end. And since you cannot be a king you shall be a bard. Because Gassire cannot be the second of the first rank (i.e., the king), he shall be the first of the second rank. And Wagadu will be lost because of it. Gassire had a smith make him a lute. The smith said he would make the lute but the lute would not sing. Gassire told the smith to do his work and "the rest is my affair." When Gassire struck the lute, it would not sing. The smith said that Gassire had to give the piece of wood a heart, "Carry it into battle, let the wood absorb blood, your pain must be its pain, your fame its fame." The wood must be penetrated by and be a part of Gassire's people. But, he said, Wagadu will be lost because of it. Gassire took his eight sons into battle. His eldest son was killed, and as Gassire carried his body back the blood of the youth dropped on the lute that Gassire also carried on his back. Still, the lute did not sing. He rode into battle again, for seven days, each day carrying back one of his dead sons, and the blood dropped on the lute, blood flowed everywhere, the women wailed, the men were angry, the old wise man said that Wagadu would be lost for the first time. With his last son, Gassire went into the desert. Many heroes rode with him. Deep in the desert, at night, a restive Gassire heard a voice: the lute was singing the Dausi. When it sang the Dausi the first time, King Nganamba died, Gassire's rage melted, and Wagadu for the first time disappeared. See: page 280.

||Gauwa and the Hole of the Forefathers (!Kung/Angola, Namibia) The gods live in the sky, the great god in the east at the place where the sun rises, the lesser god in the west where the sun sets. The great god created himself, then the lesser god, then two wives, one for himself and one for the lesser god. The wives bore six children to the gods, three boys and three girls. The great god created the earth, men and women, and all things. He named himself and then gave names to the lesser god and to their wives and children. He called himself Hishe, the one whom none can command. He caused death among humans, caused the rain to thunder. He has other divine names, including ≠Gaishi ≠gai. The children of the gods were turned into the two stars in the vertical axis of the Southern Cross that now bear their names. 🔲 ||Gauwa first lived in a very big hole which he made by pushing the earth out with his head. There were two entrances: one faced toward the sunrise, one faced toward the sunset. He later made a house, tied together with wire with poles made of iron. It was built up off the ground, on the iron poles which were stuck into the ground and rose up into the air. When a person is sick with a sore throat, the sickness has been caused by those irons that stick into the air. If ||Gauwa does not like a person, he can hurt him with those irons. There are two trees near ||Gauwa's house. They have names. Nothing else on the earth or in the sky bears those names. The remote forefathers came out of a hole in the ground, at the roots of an enormous tree, which covered a wide extent of country. Immediately afterward, all kinds of animals came swarming out after them. There is a great hole in the Marootzee country out of which men first came, and their footmarks are still to be seen there. One man came out of it long ago, but he went back and is there yet. The cattle came from the same hole. See also: ≠Gao!na, Goha, Hishe, Huwe, |Kaggen.

Gborogboro and Meme Create the First Beings (Lugbara/DRCongo, Sudan, Uganda) The creator god created a man, Gborogboro, the person coming from the sky, and a woman, Meme, the person who came alone. The Lugbara are descended from these first creatures put on earth by God at the beginning of the world. ▣ Meme was full of wild animals, who sprang from her womb. The gazelle burst out, followed by the other beasts. After the animals had left Meme's womb, the creator god put children in it. Meme bore a boy and a girl. These siblings produced another male and female pair, who did the same in their turn. There were several generations of siblings, after which the heroes, Jaki and Dribidu, were born. Mankind was thus separated from God in the sky, and this was followed by the separation of peoples. At one point, humans built a tower to the sky, but it was destroyed. *See also*: Adro, Jaki and Dribidu.

Gihanga Gave Men Teeth (Hutu, Nyarwanda, Tutsi/Rwanda) Gihanga was the first man. ▣ Two beings, Kigwa and Nyiramaboko, fell from heaven to earth. They were spotted like leopards, and had tails. They lived together, and had a son called Gihanga (from -*hanga*, to grow teeth). He was the first man, and to him were born three sons, Gatutsi, Gahutu, and Gatwa, the fathers of the three peoples of those names. Other men were created by Imana, but he made them without teeth, and they all flocked to Gihanga to be given teeth, as soon as they discovered that he had the power to do this. He also gave names to all creation. *See also*: Imana.

Gihanga and the Herd that Rose from a Lake (Nyarwanda/Rwanda) Gihanga, the son of Nkuba Lightning, the lord of heaven, was the founder of the Rwanda mystical kingdom, the cultural hero who brought fertility and prosperity, a great hunter. He became the first king of Rwanda. He married a Rwanda princess to become the founder of the dynasty. ▣ Gihanga, inventor of techniques for pottery making and the forge, domesticated a large herd of wild cattle who one day mysteriously rose from the depths of a lake.

Gila and the River-man (Anuak/Sudan) The Anuak trace their origin to the country of Dimo of the Shilluk; they were led northward and eastward by Gila, a mythic hero and brother of Nyikang, whom they call Akango. Gila was regarded as a powerful chief but not really a king; it is his grandchild, Cruvai, whom the Anuak consider their first sovereign. ▣ One day, two Anuak women caught a large fish, which on being seized turned first to a snake, then crocodile, and then man. This river-man was taken to the house of Gila, where he stayed until he had gotten the younger daughter of Gila with child, when he went back to the river. She gave birth to Ucoda, who returned to his father in the river. Later, she brought forth Cruvai, also by the river-man, afterward recognized as the first king of the Anuak. Cruvai married his sister and sired a boy and a girl, whose descendants, for they too married, became the Anuak people. Soon there appeared from the river a mysterious stranger, Ucoda; he brought with him the Ucok and Gurmato necklaces, part of the insignia of royalty, and Cruvai gave him his daughter Kori Nyairu in marriage. *See also:* Nyikang.

Gion's Universe (Jukun, Kororofawa/Nigeria) Gion, the chief divinity and supreme being, with a dog with a head like a lion, controls the tornado. The first fruits are taken to the chief priest, Akondu, to give to Gion. In seasons of drought, Akondu calls the king of the water, to whom offerings are made. ⊡ The sun is called Myino, the moon is called Sun (king). The sun goes to the west and rests. There are seven suns. The moons live in the east. The moon travels day and night, but if it is not seen at night that is because the sun catches it. If there is an eclipse of the moon, the people beat drums to make the sun let the moon go. If a meteor is seen, they put their ears to the ground, and think that it means that some man is dead. Each star represents the soul of a man. The moon is a boy who waxes and wanes. There are twelve of these boy moons. They go away and rest, and return to youth. They live in water. Sacrifice is made to the moon if the moonlight falls into the house.

Goha and the Hole from Which Man Emerged (San/Botswana, Namibia, South Africa) The male god, who is above man, is Goha. The female god, who is beneath man, is Ko; her attendants are called Ganna. One becomes a rain-maker by praying to God and burning different things in the fire. To procure rain, an ox is killed; its fat is chopped and mixed with different kinds of wood and leaves of trees, and all these are then burned. ⊡ There is a great hole in the Marootzee country out of which men first came, and their foot-marks are still to be seen there. One man came out of it long ago, but he went back, and is there yet. The cattle came from the same hole. Matoome was the first man, and had a younger brother of the same name, and a sister whose name was Matoomyane. She was the first who came out from the hole, and had orders respecting the cattle, and was appointed to superintend them. But her brother Matoome came out, and without permission he went and led the cattle around the end of a mountain, which so enraged his sister, who possessed medicine for the preservation of life and death, that she returned to the hole, carrying with her the precious medicine, in consequence of which diseases and death came into the world, and persist to this day. *See also:* ‖Gauwa, Ko.

Goroba-Dike (Fulbe/Mali) Goroba-Dike was a mythic hero. ⊡ Goroba-Dike, a younger son and therefore with no inheritance, wanders about Bamana country in a destructive mood. Finally, under the influence of his griot, he goes to the country of Hamadi Ardo, where he disguises himself as a peasant and works for a blacksmith. Kode Ardo, the daughter of the king, is sought after by many men, but she will marry none but the one whose finger her tiny ring will fit, the finger of a true Fulbe. All men try, but it will fit none. Then the ragged Goroba-Dike tries, and it fits. But this is not what Kode Ardo had hoped for: she despises him because of his poverty and his appearance. In the meantime, Hamadi Ardo is warring on armies of cattle-raiding Tuareg, and all his men go to war, including the disreputable Goroba-Dike. Instead of mounting a hero's steed, he gets on a lowly donkey and rides off in the wrong direction. All jeer at him, especially his wife and the blacksmith for whom he works. But when he arrives in the thick of the battle, he is magnificently transformed: he becomes a splendid fighter on a horse, and no one knows him. During the battle, he helps the king's sons-in-law who are in distress, but only if each will give him an ear in payment. Reluctantly, they agree to do this. Then Goroba-Dike transforms back into the peasant on the donkey; his wife is ashamed, and the smith scorns him. This pattern continues until the enemy is defeated. At one point, Goroba-Dike's wife is being kidnapped, and he is wounded as he rescues her. Not knowing his identity, she bandages his wound with a part of her dress. Later, he produces the ears to disclose the real hero, and produces the dress fragment to reveal to his wife who saved her. The smith is punished, and Goroba-Dike becomes the king.

Gu Makes the World Habitable (Fon/Benin) After Mawu and Lisa, the ranking deity in the sky pantheon is Gu, god of metal and god of war, representing one of the principal forces in the world that is helpful to humans. He is not conceived of in the way that others in the sky pantheon are viewed; he is seen as a person or an instrument in the hands of Mawu-Lisa, a godly force with a body of stone and a head of iron. As a person, he is the heavenly blacksmith, patron of the blacksmiths of the earth and inventor of all crafts, and is identified with iron. ▣ When Lisa came to earth, he brought Gu with him to educate humans in the use of tools, home building, and agriculture. (For the story of Lisa and Gu and the journey to the earth, *see:* Lisa.) Some think that Gu existed even before Lisa, that his trip to the earth with Lisa was not his first, that he was with Mawu when Mawu created the world at the beginning. It was later when the creator, in his character as Lisa, was again accompanied by his helper or instrument, Gu, who traveled over the earth. He gave man tools and taught him the art of the smith. Lisa helped humans to surmount any obstacle they encountered, then re-ascended to the sky and returned the wand to his father. Mawu said that gold and other metals were costly, that iron must serve all mankind. Pleased with what Lisa had accomplished, Mawu gave him the sun from which he could keep watch over the realms of the universe. When Lisa went to the sun, he took Gu with him. Gu is also spoken of as a smith, and, because he is thought of as always at work in his smithy, he is conceived of as living only in the open. At the same time, Hevioso caused the first fall of rain, and Mawu, source of fertility, set down the first seeds that were sown in the fields prepared by Lisa and Gu. *See also:* Hevioso, Lisa, Mawu, Mawu-Lisa, Ogun.

Gueno's Eye Becomes the Sun (Fulani/Senegal) In the pantheon of gods, Gueno is the creator. ⬛ The mountains were initially soft, but Gueno, the god of creation, and eternal, gave the power to the one-eyed king, the sun, to harden the mountains under the intensity of his gaze. At the beginning of time, the sun was Gueno's eye. Then, when the creation was finished, Gueno removed it from its socket to produce the one-eyed monarch, since his single eye was sufficient to see everything that occurs on earth and to heat and light it as well. *See also:* Doondari, Kaidara.

Gurzil Dispels the Darkness (Libya) Gurzil, the sun god, was worshiped among the Huwwara of Tripolitania well into the eleventh century, long after the Arab conquest. This deity was a protector, a guide, and a dispeller of darkness. In his solar aspect, he was identified with the two-horned Carthaginian Baal Hammon. He was not a major deity of cultivation or fertility, but rather a god of prophecy, a seer whose associations were with the departed, and whose—at times—enthroned, faceless mass appeared to represent the image of the deceased in a seated posture, wrapped for burial. He was the oracle of prophecy who advised by his foreknowledge, and who was also a divine guide. ⬛ In ancient times the Libyans were familiar with the priest-king who was at the same time a fighter for his faith. Nabis, who was a Libyan in Hannibal's army, was a chief and priest of Amen. He was well-armed, and under the protection of Amen rode fearlessly into the thick of battle shouting the name of his god. From his helmet hung the sacred bands of Amen, while his dress was that of a priest. More often the symbol of the Libyan sun-god was a bull or a ram known as Gurzil. *See also:* Baal Hammon.

Akukho kufa kunjani.
It matters little what kind of death one dies.

Elokuf' alityeli.
Death gives no notice.

—Xhosa proverbs

H

Hambageu Rises from the Dead (Sonjo, Sonyo/Tanzania) Hambageu was a man worshiped as a god. ▣ In the country of Sonjo lived Hambageu (Khambageu). He came to the world not in a natural way; he had neither mother nor father. He was first seen at Tinaga in a state of poverty. After a time, he built a house and lived there with five goats. One day, the people of Tinaga went to clean a water furrow. Because Hambageu ignored the call, he was fined one of his five goats. But the next day he still had his five goats, despite the fact that one had been slaughtered. A week later, the villagers went to dig the furrow again. Hambageu refused to respond to the call, and four goats were taken from him and slaughtered. The next morning, they learned that the five goats were still alive. They then decided to assassinate Hambageu. When he learned of the plot, he sent for an old blind woman. She refused to go, so Hambageu sent someone who brushed her eyes gently with a fly whisk, and the woman regained her sight. She came to Hambageu, and he told her to throw some bones at a place called Samunge in Sonjo. People arrived at his house carrying clubs, and Hambageu fled to Samunge where the woman had thrown the bones. The people of Samunge supported him. With his fire stick, in a wonderful way he kindled some guinea-fowl feathers and threw them at the Tinaga, who were wounded seriously and fled. From that day, the people of Samunge idolized Hambageu as the creator of the earth, loving him tenderly, making him their God. He made his home and married there. He did not claim to be God, but because of his daily acts and because he had no parents and as he himself could not explain how he came to the world, they considered him to be God. Hambageu had so many children that, except for two of them, he decided to change them into stones. He turned them into stone before the people's eyes. Later, he decided to expel one of the two sons. The remaining son, Aka, was loved by his father. Now Hambageu was old and weak, and Aka carried on his father's activities. One evening, inviting the Samunge to a dance, Aka flew directly into the sky like a bird and was seen no longer. This so distressed Hambageu that he moved to Belwa in the chiefdom of Sonjo. When the Samunge asked him to return, he agreed to do so. He told the people that in years to come they would observe curious changes: red people would come and dominate the country; these people would also pass overhead, flying like birds in wooden canoes. He decided not to return to Samunge, and he made Belwa his home. He told them that when he died he was not to be buried: his corpse was to be placed on top of a huge stone and left there to dry. Then the Samunge could take the corpse for burial at Samunge. He died, but the corpse was buried before the Samunge arrived to take it to their country for burial. A quarrel arose, and they decided to exhume the corpse. The grave was empty, and they learned that the corpse had not been removed by anybody. He must have risen from the dead, as during his long life he displayed countless wonders that none on earth had ever seen. From that day, the Sonjo believe that Hambageu was God and is still God and will remain God. He will return to the Sonjo country at the end of the world. This event will take place one morning when two suns will rise, one in the east and one in the west; at midday both suns will meet, and there will be much fire smoke and noise, all the birds will leave the forest and fly away, and there will be general confusion all around. No living Sonjo has seen Hambageu, but he is regarded as the God of the Sonjo and is worshiped as God.

Hathor, a Mother-figure with a Fearful Side (Egypt) Hathor is one of the oldest deities of Egypt. She was depicted in various forms, the oldest being that of the cow. Het-Hert, the name of the goddess, means the house above, the region of the sky or heaven. She represented the part of the sky in which Horus, the oldest form of the sun god, had been conceived; her domain was in the east of the sky, but in time she came to represent the entirety of the sky. She was the great mother of the world, and the old, cosmic Hathor was the personification of the great power of nature that was perpetually conceiving, creating, bringing forth, rearing, and maintaining all things. Hathor was a fertility figure, protector of women, goddess of song and dance. ▣ Ra sent Hathor to find some potential assassins. She pursued them as a lion, found the assassins, and killed them. But in her fury she continued to destroy humans, and the land was wounded, the Nile disordered. Ra mixed intoxicants, made them look like blood; Hathor as Sekhmet the lion drank it up and became intoxicated. Then the lion was transformed again into Hathor, the land was healed, the Nile rose again. *See also:* Horus.

Hathors Decree a Destiny (Egypt) The Seven Hathors, goddesses of fate, determined the destiny of a child at birth. ▣ A king had no son. He prayed to the gods for a child, and they ruled that his prayers would be answered. His wife bore a son. The Hathors then decreed his destiny: he would die by a crocodile or a serpent or a dog. The king was so upset that he had a house built in the desert, completely furnished and with people—the child would not leave this house. When the child was grown, he saw a dog and wanted one. The king ordered that a little pet dog be brought to him. As the child grew into manhood, he asked his father why he was kept isolated. He knew that he was destined to three fates, but wanted to go his own way. The king agreed, gave him arms and the dog, and the youth journeyed in the desert, living on the game of the desert. And he came to the prince of Naharaina, who had a daughter and no other children. A house had been built for her, with seventy windows seventy cubits from the ground. The chief said to the sons of other princes that the one who reached the window of his daughter would marry her. Now the youth came from the desert, was bathed and per-fumed, and he told them that he was the son of an officer of the land of Egypt, that his mother was dead and his father had remarried. This woman, when she bore her own children, came to hate him, and he became a fugitive. They embraced him. Then he saw the other young men trying to climb the build-ing, day after day. He climbed the building, reached the window of the daugh-ter of the chief of Naharaina, and she kissed and embraced him. When the prince was informed of this, he asked which son of the princes had done it. He was told that it was the son of an officer of the land of Egypt, fleeing from his stepmother. The prince was angry, insisting that he would not give his daughter to an Egyptian fugitive. They told the youth to return to where he had come from. But the young woman refused to allow him to go, insisting that she would neither eat nor drink if he left. Then the father ordered that the youth be killed, and she said that she too would die. The prince then sum-moned the youth and his daughter to his presence, asking who the young man was, and he repeated the story of the stepmother. The prince then allowed the young man to marry his daughter, giving him house, servants, fields, and live-stock. After a time, the youth told his wife of his three fates—crocodile, ser-pent, dog. She insisted that his dog be killed, but he would not do that. She was afraid and would not allow her husband to go out. In another Egyptian town, a crocodile emerged from a river and moved to the town where the youth was. But a strong man in that town kept the creature from escaping for two months. One evening, while the youth slept, a serpent moved to bite him, but his wife saw it and had her servants give it milk; it became drunk and the wife then killed it. She told her husband that the first of his dooms had been eliminated. Days passed, and the youth went to work in the fields, followed by his dog. Later, he followed the dog to a river, entering the river with the dog. Then the crocodile emerged, and it took the youth to the place where the strong man was. And the crocodile said to the youth, "I am your doom, fol-lowing after you . . ." (The papyrus breaks off here.)

Hebieso and Abui, the Flash of Lightning, the Rumble of Thunder (Awuna/Burkina Faso) Hebieso and Abui, gods of destiny, are represented by thunder and lightning. They control the destinies of man, and if rightly propitiated with sacrifices and offerings will confer upon him everything that he desires and protect him from everything that he fears. 🔲 The male god, Hebieso, all-devouring in his wrath, manifests himself in the forked flash and deafening roar of the imminent thundercloud, while the voice of the feminine Abui, of gentler attributes, is heard in the low rumble of distant thunder. Anyone killed by lightning is supposed to have incurred that extreme penalty for some offense against Hebieso, and the body is left unburied and dishonored.

Heitsi-Eibib Parts the Water (Khoi/South Africa) Heitsi-Eibib (Kabip) was a mythical ancestor hero. All the actions ascribed to him were those of a man, but of one endowed with supernatural powers. He died and rose again many times; he was a rich and powerful chief, a seer and thaumaturgist, and a great hunter, but he was also full of tricks and his character was not alto-gether blameless. His graves, heaps of stone piled up high, were found all over the country, and no Khoi would pass one without adding to it a stone or branch or some similar object, sometimes also muttering a prayer for good luck and success in hunting. But he never commanded the same respect and reverence in the eyes of the Khoi as did Tsui-‖Goab. Heitsi Eibib could take many forms: sometimes he was handsome, or his hair grew down to his shoulders; at other times, it was short. 🔲 Once, when he was travel-ing with many people, an enemy pursued them. When they came to a body of water, he said, "My grandfather's father, open so that I may pass through. Then close yourself afterward." The water parted, and he and his people went safely through. Then their enemies tried to pass through the opening, but when they were in the middle of it, it closed on them and they perished. 🔲 A man made a large hole in the ground and sat by it. He told those who passed by to throw a stone at his forehead. But when a person did this, the stone rebounded and killed the person who had thrown it, and he fell into the hole. At last, Heitsi-Eibib was told that many people were thus dying. So he went to that man who challenged Heitsi-Eibib to throw a stone at him. He declined to do that, but he drew the man's attention to someone on one side, and when the man turned around to look, Heitsi-Eibib hit him behind the ear. The man died and fell into his own hole, and there was peace and the people lived peacefully. *See also:* ‡Gama-‡Gorib, Hishe, Tsui‖Goab.

Hevioso and Atmospheric Phenomena (Fon/Benin) The group of deities known as the thunder pantheon constitutes a duality of which the thunder gods are one term. The general term for this group of gods is So, and the head of it is called Sogbo, an androgynous being living in the sky who produced a num-ber of children. The two eldest were twins, Agbe, a male, and Naete, a female. 🔲 Sogbo sent them to rule over the world below, with the sea as their home. Naete and Agbe produced children, one of whom was exiled by his father from the sea because of his penchant for sinking boats. A number of the children reside in lagoons. Other sons are responsible for the rising and falling of the tides, and one of them sometimes causes boats to sink and fishermen to die. Avrekete, a daughter, a messenger between gods and humans, is the repository of the secrets of her parents and therefore guardian of the sea's treasure. Other children of Sogbo live in the heavens and have various functions. One of them controls the nurturing rain; another has control of the temperature and has the capacity to create hail-storms. The voice of yet another can be heard in the thunder. Another draws the moisture from the waters of the sea to create rain. Gbade is the youngest of the children, and he has no particular function. A divine trickster, he does as he pleases and he can be heard in the booming sounds of thunder. More than any of his siblings, he is a killer. Sogbo presented him with Aido-Hwedo, the rainbow serpent, who accompanies Gbade to the earth when someone is to be killed. All of these gods have power to strike humans with lightning. ⊡ There is a clear distinction between the sky and the earth. It is the water, the rain that is showered on the earth from the sky, and the return of water to the heavens from the seas, that establishes a linkage between the two realms, providing a tie between humans and the gods. The water is necessary to the prosperity of the people on the earth, but the water is both creative and destructive. That destructiveness is seen in the flooding of the seas and also in the destructive powers of the gods as manifest in their control over the lightning. While Sogbo's children have enormous powers, including the power to destroy, they do not have the facility to give life. Only Sogbo possesses that power. And, even though it appears that she has little to do with the day-to-day activities of humans, she is generous and it is she who is in the end the life-giver. These life-giving qualities of Sogbo are matched by the death-dealing activities of her children, and so a balance is achieved between them. Humans live in a world in which life and death, the sky and the earth, are richly joined by the waters and the rains. *See also:* Aido-Hwedo, Gu, Mawu, Mawu-Lisa, Sagbata, Sogbo.

Hishe, the Moon, and Death (Aikwe, Auen, Naron/Namibia) Hishe (Hise), God—heaven, the sky—lived in the east. Some say he is the same as Heitsi-Eibib, the Khoi divinity. Some Naron identify Hishe with !Khuba or !Xuba, who lives in the sky or is the sky—they pray to him for health and long life. ‖Gauwa is a spirit whom some believe to live with Hishe in the east, and who appears as the wind storm. Some identify Hishe and ‖Gauwa as the same being. The name ‖Gauwa is also given to disembodied human spirits. The !Kung of southern Angola also know Huwe and ‖Gauwa, but do not speak of the dead as ‖Gauwa: he appears in thunder and lightning; the stars are his fire. Some Naron believe in ‖Gauwa as the supreme being. ⊡ In olden times, the trees were people, and the animals were people. One day, Hishe commanded them to be animals and trees. Then he called the first captains of the white men and of the black men, and told them to take the cattle and goats, and live by them. He told the first captain of the San to take the bucks and live by them, to take rope and make traps, to hunt and live in the countryside. Hishe produced wild beasts and plants originally, and human beings, and gave them their present form. 🔲 The moon is connected with life and death: Moon said, "People shall die and come back again as I die and come back again." But Hare contradicted Moon and said, "They shall die and stay dead and not come back again." Then Moon became very angry, and took his ax and hit Hare on the mouth, cleaving it. The hare singed her kaross in the fire and threw it at the moon's face, and burned his face. The moon's face is black from the kaross. The moon cried and caught the kaross and threw it away. The hare said, "Of men, the one who marries many women shall be killed." The moon contradicted him: "The man shall not die. The man has leave, and he to each woman shall give children, so that they may bear many people, many men may bring forth, many women bring forth, many San." *See also:* ǂGao!na, ‖Gauwa, Heitsi-Eibib, Huwe, |Kaggen.

Holy Fire and the Circle of Religious Ideas (Berg Damara/Namibia) The first circle of religious ideas is grouped around the personality of ‖Gamab, the second around the harmful forces, of whose nature only vague conceptions exist. There is a third circle of religious ideas, whose center is the holy fire. It is at the same time the incorporation and the visible form of the thoughts that compose the first and second circles. 🔲 The holy fire is the center of the village. It burns near the village tree. Wherever possible the village is laid out where there is a shady tree. When such a tree has been selected, a cut is made in its bark and the heart blood of some game is poured into the cut. In this manner, the tree is consecrated as the village tree. On its eastern side, the holy tree will burn in the future. There, the elders will sit in council. When the field crop area is exhausted and the hunt has become unprofitable, the people must settle elsewhere where the prospects of livelihood are more favorable. In doing so, they never forget to take a burning or glowing piece of wood from the holy fire. It is the office of the great wife to carry this brand at the head of the procession. On the way, the campfire is lighted with it. From the campfire, a suitable brand is again removed, and the procession continues until a new site has been selected, when the village fire is lighted with it. *See also:* ‖Gamab, Kamangundu.

Horus's Struggle with Set (Egypt) Horus, the falcon-headed god, son of Isis and Osiris, was a sky god whose left eye was the moon and whose right eye was the sun. Heru-Behutet is the greatest of the forms of Horus, representing as he does that form of Heru-Behutet that prevailed in the southern heavens at midday, typifying the greatest power of the heat of the sun. It was under this form that Horus waged war against Set (Typhon). Heru-Behutet is the power that dispels darkness and night, drives away clouds, rain, and storms, and fills heaven and the world with his brilliance and light. He created himself, renews his birth daily, year by year performs his course in the heavens, bringing in his train the seasons and their proper produce. He is identified with Osiris, and the goddesses Isis and Nephthys are said to help him to emerge from the abyss of Nu. ▣ He made the heavens to be the dwelling place for his soul, and he created the deep that it might serve as a place in which to hide his body. As god of light, he fought against Set, the god of darkness, and as the god of good against the god of evil. From the height of heaven, he was able to see his father's enemies, and he chased them in the form of a great winged disk, attacking them with such wrath that they lost their senses and could not see with their eyes, hear with their ears. See also: Hathor, Isis, Osiris, Ra.

Huveane and the Fleeing Bundle of Grass (Pedi, Venda/South Africa)

Huveane and the Fleeing Bundle of Grass (Pedi, Venda/South Africa) Huveane (Hobyana, Khudjana) is a mysterious being, sometimes called the creator of heaven and earth, the first ancestor. Sometimes he is referred to as the son of the creator. He is a divine trickster. ▣ He once modeled a baby in clay and breathed life into it. He kept his child in the hollow of a tree so that his parents would not know about it, and he stole out every morning to feed it. Because of his extraordinary activities, the people decided to destroy him, fearing that he would bring them to harm. They put poison into his milk, but he poured it on the ground. They dug a pit by the fireplace, but instead of sitting next to it, he sat with his brothers, and one of them fell into the pit. They dug another secret pit, and he leapt over it. A man with a spear was wrapped in a bundle of grass, and Huveane was told by his father to go and get the bundle. But when he came near to the bundle, he threw his own spear at it and the man inside fled. He told his father that he tried to do what his father told him to do, but the grass ran away.

Huveane Moves Away from Humans (Sotho/Lesotho) The high god is Huveane, the creator who made heaven and earth. ▣ Huveane made the sky and earth, and when he had finished he climbed into the sky by driving in pegs that he put his feet on, taking out each peg as he stepped onto the next, so that people would not be able to follow him. He has lived in the sky ever since.

Huwe's Hairy Home (!Kung/Botswana) Huwe (Xu) wards off disease, gives plenty, and protects the San from danger. The supreme being is a good being to whom the people attribute the creation and maintenance of all things. Huwe, anthropomorphic, looks like a San and speaks !Kung. This god is often prayed to, especially for rain and success in hunting, as well as in cases of illness, because he made all things, can do everything, knows everything, and he is given the first offering of the chase. The rain comes at his command as a mist out of the earth, and then falls down, thereby making thunder and lightning. ▣ He lives in the sky in a house with two stories, the lower of which is occupied by himself, his wife, and many children, while the upper is occupied by the souls of the dead, Xa. This house is similar to the ordinary San house, but its exterior is hairy like a caterpillar. Honey, locusts, fat flies, and butterflies are found here in superabundance, and the great captain feeds on these. The souls of the dead merely sit around and eat

H

nothing. Huwe summons musicians and gives them supernatural powers; he is the lord over rain and lightning, as well as over the spirits, ‖gaunab, and through their leader he sends good fortune in hunting or in the collection of veldkos. If anybody thinks or speaks evil of him, he punishes the evildoer with lightning; otherwise, he takes little interest in the doings of the San. *See also:* ‡Gao!na, ‖Gauwa, Hishe, |Kaggen, Xu.

Hyel and the Corpse in the Tree (Bura, Pabir/Nigeria) Hyel, the supreme deity, was originally a moon deity. The chief of the people belongs to the order of divine kings. When he dies, it is said that God has fallen. He does not actually die, but he goes away for a time. With his person is bound up the well-being of the people and the productiveness of the crops. At his death, there are rituals that resemble a process of rebirth by which the chief is converted into a god. The central religious festival of the year is the Mambila, a feast of all souls, especially the souls of the chief's forefathers. When a man dies, his soul goes to join his grandfather's, but returns to the town each year at the Mambila feast. The festival is held at harvest, and the chief takes the principal part. There are rain rites, prayers to the royal ancestors for the increase of the people, their crops, and their cattle. Each year at the maize harvest, every man who has lost a father or mother selects three heads of corn, dresses them carefully, burning off the sheath, and places them on a tray that he sets by his head at night. The spirits of the dead father and mother come and eat the soul of the corn. ▣ Long ago, there was no such thing as death. All were therefore surprised when a man died. They sent a worm to ask the sky what they should do. The sky said they should hang the corpse in a tree and throw mush at it until it came back to life. Then no one else would ever die. On the way back, a lizard named Agadzagadza, having overheard the words of the sky, ran ahead of the worm to deceive the people on the earth. Agadzagadza therefore ran very hard. When he reached the earth, he told the people that the sky said they should bury the corpse. The people did this. Later, when the worm arrived and gave them the true message, they were too lazy to take the corpse from the grave. They refused to do what the sky asked them to do, and people still die. *See also:* Iju.

Mythmaker and Audience

A story never occurs in a vacuum. There is always an audience, large or small: the creation of myth is always a social event, necessarily involving an audience whose emotions are evoked and a storyteller who works those emotions into form. That formal result is the combination of imagery and emotion, a sacred place where a human being comes into contact with his god. There is a conjunction of the storyteller who possesses the images from the past, the audience that is enveloped in the imagery of the present, the emotions evoked and the emotions worked into form. This is the sanctity of mythmaking, the place where all comes to a focus, and this is what must be comprehended if one is to understand the force of story in religious belief. The audience, by means of its emotional contributions, expands and therefore redefines the term "audience," because it is not merely a group of spectators. It is that, a critical and eager company of peers of the performer, but it is also an integral and crucial part of the performance. In fact, there can be no performance without the active participation, which means the emotional involvement, of the members of the audience. Those emotions are a part of the canvas of performance, the tones of performance, the story itself, the means whereby the audience is itself worked into the very context of story. What the mythmaker does is unite the members of the contemporary audience and the images of former times, images that contrive to form the essential foundations of the society from which that audience emerges. During the performance, the audience, then, more than passive onlookers, are imbued with images, themselves an integral part of those images.

1

Man's Heroic Activities Result in Permanent Good. The epic is the mythic inventory of a society. It contains elements of a culture—the way it was, the way it is, the way it shall be. It traces the roots of the hero and renders the vision, focusing on the struggle to bring these into a viable relationship. The hero bridges past and present to pose a new world. The activity of the epic, as of all storytelling, has to do with chaos and order. The mythmaker moves hero and god into union, with the result that the godly activities become the template for human activities. Every hero follows a similar journey that takes him from the familiar to the unfamiliar, on a dangerous passage, to a struggle with the forces of the underworld, to a wresting of some life-giving elixir from a death-dealing force. Then there is a return to the familiar world, but all has changed; the world can never be the same. ▣ (Malagasy/Madagascar)—Father Sky welcomes his five sons—the Prince of the East, the Prince of the North, the Prince of the South, the Prince of the West, and the Prince of the Middle. But Father Sky is disappointed with the Prince of the Middle because he has not sired a child. Cannons are fired for all the sons, but that for the Prince of the Middle is fired into the ground. His wife,

Rasoabemanana, humiliated, goes to Ranakombe, a seer, to get help for her barrenness. He warns her that the birth of a son will mean her death, but she persists. She soars into the heavens and gets a grasshopper, then the grasshopper helps her to secure a child-bearing talisman. All of nature reacts. Ranakombe, again warning about the child's destiny, has cannons fired. The grasshopper leaps into the fire, then moves into the mother's womb through her head, and remains in her womb for ten years. Now this child, Iboniamasiboniamanoro, causes his mother to wander the earth, seeking a place where he might be born. He finally decides that it should be a farm. He asks his mother to swallow a razor, and he cuts himself out of her womb. His mother dies, and nature reacts. The child leaps into a fire, is not harmed, but will not be quiet until the cannons are fired into the four cardinal directions. Ranakombe gives names to him, and, after rejecting a number of names, he accepts his name, Iboniamasiboniamanoro. He remains in the fire. Nature responds. At a distant place, the villainous Raivato strangely thinks about his future enemy. Iboniamasiboniamanoro grows up. As he does so, he proves his abilities by fighting other children. He routinely defeats them. Now he wants to marry. He praises himself, and Ranakombe tells him what he must do to get his wife. He must get a bull, move through trees that are impostors, get talismans, stop a whirlwind, roast a bull, dive into water with the talismans, stay under water until daybreak, and he will have his wife. Iboniamasiboniamanoro does this. He becomes an irritable trickster, causing people's goods to fall into a ditch. His mother challenges him four times, and each time he rises to her challenge, defeating a crocodile, two ogres, and a swallowing monster. He opens the swallowing monster and releases the people who are inside. Iboniamasiboniamanoro, although his mother suggests alternative brides, insists that he go to seek Iampelasoamananoro, who has been kidnapped by Raivato. To gain access to Raivato's homestead, Iboniamasiboniamanoro, after learning the old man's habits, kills Ikonantitra, Raivato's old retainer, and puts on his skin. As Ikonantitra, he enters Raivato's homestead—and a plate and spoon break, a mat flies apart, Raivato's charms rattle. And Iboniamasiboniamanoro as Ikonantitra defeats Raivato at chess and wooden crosses, and in the fields with oxen. Finally, he gets Raivato's charms, then hammers Raivato into the ground and destroys him. He takes Iampelasoamananoro as his wife. Iboniamasiboniamanoro and Iampelasoamananoro are married for ten years. Then, three years before his death, he makes his testament: let no one tamper with the sacred bonds of marriage. And he dies. This is a story of Ibonia's transformation to manhood, but because of his mythic origins and godly nature, his transformation becomes that of human society generally. And, in this case, the elixir that he extracts from the death-dealing forces of the underworld is the covenant of marriage, which is a symbol of life.

Idris, Rejecting His Wardrobe, Defecates (Arab, Berber/Morocco) The sky, which is female, is a spark from hell, which escapes in the morning and returns there at night to lie down and sleep. When there is an eclipse, which is a warning from God, the sun has been swallowed by an ifrit—a jinni, huge and winged, who lives underground. When the ifrit vomits it up, it begins to shine again. The moon is also supposed to be a woman. She is said to be a virgin who has strayed from paradise. She is born at the beginning of every month, and dies at its end. ▣ Idris, a mythic giant who was visiting Fez, asked the inhabitants to make him some clothes. But Idris was a giant, and the Fazi offered him garments that did not fit. Idris was so furious that he defecated before the gate of the city, and Mount Zalagh was the result.

Ifa's Departure Upsets the Gods (Yoruba/Nigeria) Ifa (Orunmila), god of divination, fate, and wisdom, informs mortals of the wishes of Olorun, the sky god, the god of destiny; he was appointed by the supreme god to protect and rule the people. He is consulted before any action is taken—from choosing the time of marriage, building a house, or entering an agreement, to going to war or making peace. Coming after Sango in order of eminence, he has the title of Gbangba, explanation, demonstration, proof. Ifa's secondary attribute is to cause fecundity; he presides at births, and women pray to him to be made fruitful. Obatala causes the woman to become pregnant, while Ifa forms the child in the womb. ▣ Ifa first appeared on the earth at Ife, but his parentage and origin are unexplained. He tried to teach the inhabitants of Ife how to foretell future events, but they would not listen to him, so he left the town and wandered about the world teaching mankind. After roaming for a long time, Ifa fixed his residence at Ado, where he planted on a rock a palm nut from which sixteen palm trees at once grew up. Ifa has an attendant, Odu, and a messenger, Opele. Ifa, the oracle of divination, is named after the deity who controls it. No serious decision is taken without consulting it: a whitened board is employed, about two feet long and eight or nine inches broad, on which are marked sixteen figures. These figures are called "mothers." The sixteen palm nuts are held loosely in the right hand, and thrown through the half-closed fingers into the left hand. If one nut remains in the right hand, two marks are made, and if two remain, one mark. In this way is formed the sixteen "mothers," and from the order in which they are produced certain results are deduced. The interpretation is in accordance with established rule, but that rule is known only to the initiated. The basis of divination is a series of 256 figures (odu) or permutations, each with a name; one of these is arrived at either by casting a chain of eight seeds or by "beating" palm kernels. Each permutation has a number of verses associated specifically with it, each verse being related to a problem which may be similar to that with which the client is confronted. The client does not confide the problem or question that has brought him to the diviner. When, therefore, a throw has been made, the diviner recites the verses of the figure at random while the client listens for a verse dealing with a problem similar to his own and interprets it as he will. Each verse contains specific instructions for solving a problem, the commonest suggestion being that the client should offer a sacrifice. ◘ Some time after settling at Ado, Ifa became tired of living in the world, and accordingly went to dwell in the firmament, with Obatala. After his departure, mankind, deprived of his assistance, was unable to properly interpret the desires of the gods, most of whom became in consequence annoyed. Olokun was the angriest, and in a fit of rage he destroyed nearly all the inhabitants of the world in a great flood, only a few being saved by Obatala, who drew them up into the sky by means of a long iron chain. After this outburst of anger, Olokun retired once more to his own domains, but the world was nothing but mud, and unfit to live in, until Ifa came down from the sky, and, in conjunction with Oduduwa, once more made it habitable. *See also:* Esu, Fa, Legba, Obatala, Oduduwa, Sango.

Iju Makes a Pact with Death (Margi/Nigeria) At Baza, Womdiu, and Wuba, the title of Hyel is used to refer to the supreme being; among the Margi of Bornu the supreme being is known as Tambi. Among the other Margi groups the common term for the supreme being is Iju. He is the firmament, the sun, the moon, the stars, the sender of rain. He is male, fertilizing the earth, Ii. The earth, Ii, female, brings forth. There is thus a form of dualism. But the earth is not definitely personified, nor are prayers addressed to Ii as they are to Iju. ◘ In the beginning, Iju was so close to the earth that men could touch the place of his abode, the sky. In those days, men did not have to farm; they had merely to place clean calabashes on platforms outside their houses and Iju sent his children to fill the calabashes with food. Men were

C.K. Cooke, *Rock Art of Southern Africa* (Cape Town: Books of Africa, 1969), p.30

Rock Art: Masked Figures, Dancing

like the gods: they lived forever. But this state of bliss was ended: a woman set out a dirty calabash and caused a swelling to rise on the forefinger of one of the children of heaven. In his anger at this, Iju withdrew to a distance from men, who, left without food, began to make inroads on the farms of Death, Mptu. (According to another account, it was Iju who led men to the fields of Death so that they might break off heads of corn and eat them. But if they approached too closely to the abode of Death, Iju pulled them back by the chain necklaces which the first men wore.) When Death complained to Iju of the ways of men, Iju made a compact with him that if he would allow men to take seed-corn from his farm Iju would permit him to take the lives of a few men each year, one man here and one man there. Iju did this because he knew that he could restore men to life. So it is that men obtained corn, and death entered their midst. When Death took his first victim, the brother of the victim saw Death and followed him. But when he overtook him, he found him bathing in a field of fire, and fled in terror. A younger brother resolved that he would face Death and slay him. When he found Death bathing in fire, he attacked him with a sword and cut off one leg. So it is that Death is lame. He has two long teeth reddened with the blood of his victims. When Iju saw that men were taking the law into their own hands, he became angry and put dark coloring into their eyes so that they could no longer see Death, which is why the eyes of men are dark. Men did not know what they were doing, but Iju knew what he was doing. When men began to die, they sent a messenger to Iju to ascertain the cause. The messenger was a chameleon, and Iju told the chameleon to say to men that if they threw baked porridge on the corpse the corpse would come to life. But as the chameleon, being a slow traveler, had been absent a long time, men resolved to send another messenger, for death was rampant in their midst. So they sent a lizard, which arrived in the presence of Iju soon after the chameleon had departed. Angered at this second message, Iju told the lizard to dig a hole in the ground and bury the corpse. (According to another account, men sent the lizard to ascertain how to treat a man who was sick, and Iju in his anger ordered that hot gruel be poured over him. This was done, and the man immediately died.) The lizard arrived home before the chameleon and delivered his message, and the corpse was buried. But when the chameleon arrived with his message, men opened the grave in order to throw baked porridge on the corpse, but the corpse was not there. And so it is that men can no longer be restored to life. (According to another account, Iju gave the same message to the lizard he had given to the chameleon, but the lizard falsified the message.) *See also:* Hyel.

Imana and the Childless Couple (Hutu, Nyarwanda, Tutsi/Rwanda)—Imana is the supreme being, the creator. He is good. Ryangombe is his opposite, feared and deadly. 🄴 This is a myth about the fall of man. Imana was alone in the beginning, and he created the heavens and the earth. But the earth was not a mirror of the heavens, it was not the same: it was in fact the opposite, and was characterized by human suffering. But when Imana had initially created all living beings, including humans, animals, and plants, they remained in the heavens with him, and at the beginning humans lived with Imana, ate Imana's plants. And if it happened that a person died, Imana brought him back to life in three days. And so in those early times humans mated and life prospered, and people did not die. The story of the fall begins with a woman whose name was Nyinakigwa: she was sad, because she and her husband were without children. Having thought long about her situation, she went to Imana and asked him to make it possible for her to have a child. He heard her entreaties, and then agreed to provide her with a child. But there was a stipulation: he would provide her with a child with the provision that she must not tell where that child came from. So it was that Imana gave her three children—two of them were sons, Kigwa and Lututsi; one was a daughter, Nyinabatutsi. Nyinakigwa was happy now, and she and her family lived in harmony. But she had a sister who was in a similar state: she was also unable to bear children. When she saw that her sister had children, she became jealous. She beseeched her sister to tell where those children had come from, how she herself might also get children, and she finally got Nyinakigwa to tell her of the origins of those three children. Then she herself went to Imana to ask him to provide children for her as well. And now Imana was angry because he had been disobeyed. Nyinakigwa, knowing that she had broken her word to Imana, turned on her children and killed them. When she had done so, when she had destroyed her children, the sky dramatically opened, and when it had done so the children plummeted to the earth below, where they lived lives of great difficulty and anguish. Now Nyinakigwa was in sorrow, knowing that because of her action her children were living in a land of great suffering. In the end, the two women went to Imana and asked for his forgiveness. And Imana considered their request and agreed that one day the children would have suffered enough and he promised that they would come back to him in the heavens. ◘ In another myth, God and a man, one of his creations, regularly conversed with each other. Then, one day, God told the man that on a certain night he was not to go to sleep, that during that night God would bring him long life. The man did not know that a snake had overheard the words of Imana. And during that fateful night the man did in fact fall asleep, against God's admonition. When Imana came with his good word, his promise of renewed life, the snake answered in the man's stead and God, thinking the snake was the man, gave him the news: he would die but would return to life; he would become old but would shed his skin. And so it would be for all of his descendants. The man awakened, and he continued to await God's message, but it was not forthcoming. He then went to God and asked him about this. It was then that Imana knew that the snake had taken the man's place. He said he could not undo what had been done, but noted that men would henceforth kill snakes. But the man would nevertheless die, as would his children. The snake, on the other hand, would shed its skin, and be reborn. *See also:* Ryangombe.

Imana and the Quest for Death (Hutu, Rundi, Tutsi/Burundi) When Imana, the supreme being, reached the hills above Lake Tanganyika and in the north of Burundi, he was tired. This is because all the center of Burundi is beautiful rolling downland, while to the north and in the Rift Valley, the hills are very steep and high. He was fresh while he was creating the central country, but got tired toward the end, and finished in a hurry. ◘ Death came into the world during the period of Imana's sojourn on earth in visible form. Once Death did not live among people, and whenever he appeared Imana gave him chase — according to some versions, with the aid of his hunting dogs. On one occasion, he was being hunted very violently, and was chased into a narrow place, where he collided with a woman coming from the opposite direction. He asked her to hide him, saying, "Hide me, and I will hide yours." She opened her mouth, and he jumped inside and she swallowed him. Imana then came up and said, "What has happened to Death? Did you see which way he took?" The woman denied having seen him. Then Imana, who knew what had happened, said, "Seeing you have hidden Death, Death will destroy both you and yours." And he departed from her in anger. From that moment, Death spread throughout the land. In Rwanda, the same tale exists, but it is a king, not Imana, who is hunting Death. ◘ At first, Imana lived among men, and he went about among them and talked with them, creating children, causing their development in the womb, until one day he created a crippled child. The parents were very angry, and one of them took a knife and began to watch for an opportunity to kill Imana. Imana, being Indavyi, the seeing one, knew all about it, and said, "If they are going to behave like that, I will depart to my own place, and not show myself anymore. Then I can create as I please, and if they are not satisfied, they can just grumble." Accordingly, he never shows himself anymore, though a few people can see him if they are lucky enough to catch him in an unguarded moment. *See also:* Gihanga.

Inusa and the Gun That Turned to Water (Bachama, Bwaare, Bwaatiye/ Cameroon, Nigeria) While the Bachama were living in Gobirland, there was no Fulani there. The Fulani came from the direction of Egypt, they passed through and went as far as Wukari, and asked for a place to live there. The people of Wukari drove them back. Then they came and met Bawa Jan-Gwarzo, and he allowed them to remain. ⬛ They were there for two years when a certain Fulani, a learned man, was urged by his servant to destroy Bawa Jan-Gwarzo and take over his chieftaincy. The teacher said to wait. They waited five years, and then the teacher told the chief that a message had come from Mecca, that a white crow was needed. The chief raised his hands and many white crows came down. He again raised his hands to the sky, and many black crows descended. He did that again, and numerous crows with white necks came down. The teacher went home and asked his servant if he had ever seen a white crow or a purely black crow. The servant said no. The teacher said he did not know who was greater, he or the chief. They continued to live there. They began their intrigue. The Fulani teacher asked the chief to give him his son so that he could school him. So it was that the chief's son, Inusa, went and lived with the teacher. Meantime, the chief's eldest daughter married and went to live in her husband's town. The chief then became ill and he died. A cock crowed, and she knew that he was dead, and she packed to go to him. Her husband did not believe her, but as they traveled a messenger told them of the chief's death. Inusa was told to come to take the chieftaincy. As he left, the teacher said that if he looked back, they would conquer him. Inusa turned and glanced back. The Fulani then gathered together, and Inusa learned that his teacher was plotting against him. He invited the teacher to come to him, and when he took a gun to shoot him, the gun turned to water. The war began. A woman among the chief's people had supernatural powers. She sent a young man around the wall of the town with a cock, but as he went into the gate, the Fulani cut the wall and entered the town. The Fulani were driven back. They brought more Fulani together, and the battle went against the chief. The Bata people battled, then moved to the countryside. The other people returned to the town. And that was the basis for their separation from the people of Gobir (Gobirland was an area including much of what is now Niger and the northwestern part of Nigeria). The one remaining there said, "My brother is lost."

Ipupi and the Magical Gourd-bow (Kimbu/Tanzania) Ipupi, terror of those who wake, was a great mythic chief of the Nyisamba. He lived on a hill that had a very high rock. ⬛ Ipupi played a magical instrument, a gourd-bow called Isimeli. With this gourd-bow, he could summon people from far distances. Chiefs from many areas would respond, and, when they had gathered, Ipupi gave them their orders. They called him Mwijuxa, the one who knows all things. Then they returned home. Ipupi would punish any chief who refused to come to Nyalanga when called, causing a drought in his chiefdom, sending rats to eat his harvest. Only when such a leader begged for mercy would Ipupi relent, affirming his power to eliminate the chief's lineage. By an act of will, he caused the rain to fall again, or destroyed the marauding rats. If a chief warred on Ipupi, he would stop the army by sending lions. People feared Ipupi because he needed no messengers, he simply used Isimeli. Toward the end of his life, Ipupi climbed the high rock for the last time at sunset and played the gourd-bow. He sang, "Isimeli, you are sweet and fair," and told his people to build a round house. They did that, and he then asked for water; he summoned his great wife. Then, having bathed and anointed themselves, they sat down on stools beside each other. Ipupi played Isimeli for the last time, and, as he did so, he and his wife descended, living, into the earth. The stools went down also, as did Isimeli, the gourd-bow. Ipupi was not buried by the hand of man. No grave had to be dug for him. The place of his descent is where the offerings are made today, but the great rock has split, and the summit has tumbled down.

Irgam Yigfagna (al-Jabal al-Lamma), the Gleaming Mountain (Berber/Algeria, Libya, Morocco, Tunisia) In ancient times, it was thought that the ocean surrounded the earth as if it were a collar. The image was sometimes that of a serpent associated with the depths of the sea and the collar that clasped the earth. The serpent and the ocean were closely linked, the serpent often representative of the ocean. The sea was a supernatural power, and had both destructive and creative possibilities, sometimes hostile to man, sometimes the origin of a god with life-giving powers that could be valuable to those who believed. 🔲 Ibn Fatima was once on a voyage on the Atlantic Ocean to Nul Lamta, when his ship was blown off course and he found himself in a strange place that was shrouded in fog. Not knowing where they were, aware only that he and his sailors were lost, he and his crew abandoned the ship. In a small boat, they moved across the mysterious waters. After a time, they reached the middle of these waters, where they saw many white birds. But they reached land only after their provisions were almost exhausted. They had landed at the foot of al-Jabal al-Lamma, the Gleaming Mountain, but they were told by the Berber inhabitants of the area that they should not approach it. They did not know why this was, but obediently turned to the north of it, avoiding the place. As they moved along the shore, they met someone who asked them how it is that they got lost, and, now inquisitive about the mountain, they asked about the warning that they had received about al-Jabal al-Lamma. The people told them that it contained a mass of venomous serpents that always seemed to strangers to be gleaming objects made of beautifully colored stone. Such strangers were thereby deceived into drawing near, and when they did the snakes would kill them. This is what they learned about the Gleaming Mountain: Irgam Yigfagna is a name that was identified with this gleaming mountain. Jabal Qaf, the mother of mountains, encircled most of the inhabited world. Within this range, the Gleaming Mountain, shaped like half of a scepter, was a major source for rivers that flowed into the Atlantic Ocean. A gleaming pillarlike mountain not far from the sea, it was held in religious awe by the nomadic peoples. Within it seemed to be treasure, what seemed to be beautiful stones. Yet it was the abode of death, inhabited as it was by serpents that protected it from intruders who, deceived by its outward appearance, were drawn to it almost against their will. There was also a sea of darkness here, full of terrors—the dangers of mists, storms, and shipwreck. The sea was mysteriously linked to the desert mountain; both were the gate of death, yet at the same time the source of precious stones, sea creatures, bottles containing jinn (who haunted the mountain), and demigods. There was also a holy man—now Moses, now al-Khadr, now some other saint or prophet—who was always present. The crew presented the Berber with gifts in gratitude for their safety, bought mounts from them, and departed for Naghira, the capital of the Gudala. They stayed for some time with the Gudala, drinking camel's milk and dried camel's flesh until they journeyed with them to Nul. Five rivers descended from al-Jabal al-Lamma. The middle river was called Nahr al-Hayyat, the river of snakes. There were many snakes around al-Jabal al-Lamma and nearby mountains, sent by God as a punishment to the people of those regions, but more a blessing than a punishment because the people found them delicious to eat. The sea, the serpent, the holy man, and the Gleaming Mountain are unified. See also: al-Khidr.

Isis and the Secret Name of Ra (Egypt) Isis (Aset, Aust, Eset, Hest, Mert, Selkit, Unt), the goddess of protection, was the daughter of Get, the earth, and Nut, the sky. Her brothers were Osiris and Set; her sister, Nephthys. ⊡ Isis mourned for her husband, Osiris, when he was assassinated by his jealous brother, Set. She sought his body, recovered it, but it was stolen by Set, who then cut it in pieces. Isis recovered the parts of Osiris's body and restored him to life. ⊡ She kept her son, Horus, hidden until he was old enough to avenge the death of his father. She introduced marriage. She was a goddess of protection, was prayed to by the sick, and, with other gods, she protected the dead. She was involved in rites having to do with the dead. The goddess Isis wished to know the secret name whereby Ra lived, and as the god refused to impart it to her she determined to destroy him. She made a serpent in the form of a dart, and having worked magic on it, she threw it on the path over which Ra would pass. When the god came to the serpent, it bit him, and but for the incantations of Isis after he had, when about to expire, revealed his secret name to her, he would have perished. ⊡ In another myth, Isis was hiding from Set in the marshes. As she moved to a town, she asked a rich woman for shelter, but the woman refused to open her house to her. But a poor girl, the daughter of fishermen, invited Isis into her humble home. The seven scorpions that accompanied Isis, disgusted by the rich woman's treatment of the goddess, crept under the door and stung the rich woman's child. When that woman expressed sorrow for her acts, Isis laid her hands on the child, comforting him, and she gave the child life. See also: Osiris, Ra.

Asiyeweza kutuumba, kutuumbua hawezi.
He who cannot create us cannot uncreate us.

Kuna uzima na kifo.
There is life and there is death.

—Swahili proverbs

J

Jaki and Dribidu and the Leper Woman (Lugbara/DRCongo, Sudan, Uganda)
The creation and subsequent happenings occurred at a place called Loloi. The last pair of siblings produced the two hero-ancestors, Jaki and Dribidu, who came to the present country of the Lugbara and there sired many sons, the founders of the present clans. They were not human as men are now: Dribidu, the hairy one, was covered with long hair over most of his body. He was also known as Banyale, eater of men, since he ate his children until he was discovered and driven out of his earlier home on the east bank of the Nile. Dribidu died on Mount Eti, and Jaki on Mount Liru. They accomplished supernatural deeds, were involved in fantastic adventures. Each one of them met a woman with leprosy and was given fire by her to cook his food. Each cured the woman, then had sexual relations with her. This led to a dispute with her kin, and each had to pay a fine along with a dowry. This was, it is said, the origin of war and dowry. Each acquired a knowledge of fire from indigenous people, and each was a rainmaker, the first among their people. *See also:* Adro, Gborogboro and Meme.

Jangare: Haj Ali Glimpses the Mythical City of Spirits (Hausa/Niger, Nigeria)
There is a world of spirits that are more or less inimical to human beings unless propitiated. They are called Bori, and are a mixture of ancestors, jinn, local deities, and marabouts. Each person has a familiar Bori of the same sex and generally one also of the opposite sex, in constant attendance. The spirit world of Jangare, the mythical city in which Bori spirits are said to live, is the place from which they move like the wind when they wish to intervene in the lives of mortals. Jangare is governed by a king, and he is surrounded by a royal court. There are twelve houses in Jangare, each headed by a super-

natural spirit, *iskoki*: Sarkin Sulemanu, Sarkin Aljan Biddarene, Malam Alhaji, Kuturu, Sarkin Filani, Sarkin Aljan Zurkalene, Sarkin Aljan Shekaratafe, Mai Dawa, Sarkin Arna, Sarkin Gwari, Barkono, Batoyi. Jangare is said to be in the Red Country, between Aghat and Asben. No living person has ever seen this city close, but all travelers know of its whereabouts and, should anyone enter it, he will never be heard of again. ▣ One day, Haj Ali, while going across the desert to Hausaland, halted for a few minutes, and, on proceeding again, he saw four caravans going in different directions. He did not know which was his, for all appeared to be alike, but he chose that which he thought was taking his own route, and started to follow. All at once, he heard the lowing of cattle, the beating of drums, and the sounds of a great city, and looking up he saw Jangare far ahead of him. As he knew it immediately, he hurriedly retraced his steps, and soon saw some of his own people who had been sent back to find him. The Bori come at night, it is said, and call people from a caravan by name, and if they answer and go, they will be lost, just as will be stragglers in the daytime. Often in the early morning, travelers will hear cocks crowing nearby, and sounds of a city awakening, but when they arise they will see nothing, and they will know that they have been sleeping near the city of Jangare. *See also*: Dodo, Jinn.

Jeki la Njambe, the Son of God, Has a Hostile Relationship with His Father (Batanga, Duala, Malimba, Pongo/Cameroon) Njambe, the future father of Jeki and a famous man, has nine wives (he has been married for 146 years), nine fields under cultivation, many canoes, slaves, and cattle. His senior wife is initially barren, and Njambe therefore remains distant from her. She finally gives birth to a daughter who is abducted by a spirit. The second time she is pregnant, she remains so for an inordinately long time. Jeki, her son, speaks in her womb, departs from her body at times, and identifies the place where he wishes to be born. Before he is born, many wonderful weapons emerge. Njambe, his father, attempts to kill his son, sending him to events where this is certain to occur. But Jeki always triumphs, his brothers are killed instead, and he brings them back to life. He goes into the underworld, the land of the spirits, and brings home the sister who had been abducted before he was born. He engages in adventures involving crocodiles and whales and water spirits, struggles with fantasy characters, and remains protected by his mother by means of a supernatural amulet. He sometimes destroys his enemies in flames, then eats the ashes. He is killed a number of times and resurrected by his mother, his sister, or another being called Jeki. He encounters an old woman with long breasts, and heals her. He is married in the end, and takes over Njambe's position.

Jinn: A Serpent Helps Abu Zayd (Arab/Western Sahara) Jinn are spirits. Nature is full of living beings that are superhuman, the jinn or demons. These jinn are not pure spirits but corporeal beings, more like beasts than men, for they are ordinary represented as hairy, or have some other animal shape, as that of an ostrich or a snake. Their bodies are not phantasms, for if a jinni is killed a solid carcass remains. But they have mysterious powers of appearing and disappearing, or even of changing their aspect and temporarily assuming human form, and when they are offended they can avenge themselves in a supernatural way, by sending disease or madness. They have, for the most part, no friendly or stated relations with men, but are outside the pale of man's society, and frequent deserted places far from the wonted tread of men. In the Sahara and adjoining African regions, serpents and jinn are the common denizens of water points, caves, tree roots, low-lying thickets, and groves, and both beings are often confused as common protectors of hidden treasures. 🔲 As the poet Abu Zayd Muhammad (Abu) 'l-Khattab al-Qurashi accompanied a party of riders on a journey, they saw a great snake (shuja') dying because of the heat. They told Abu to kill it, but he allowed it to live. He cooled the snake with water from his water skin, and it slid away to its lair. The party continued its journey and accomplished its aims. When they returned, they passed that same river valley where the serpent lived. Abu was delayed, because his camel was tired. Alone in the strange place, he was afraid, but he heard the voice of a friendly jinni. It gave him a fresh camel so that he could continue his journey. When he got home, he gratefully released the second camel. Then he heard the jinni's voice, telling him that it was the serpent that he had befriended in its agony, and that the camel which had brought him to safety had been his reward. Within the haunted deserts and thickets of the Sahara and Arabia, the serpent was both a friend and a foe to man; in its form was the supernatural, always prepared to help or to hurt mankind, depending on the nature of the jinni, or the intentions of its human confronter. Hausa call them aljannu, iskoki, ibilisai. See also: Abu Zayd, Jangare, Juntel Jabali.

Jok and the Tree of Life (Acholi/Uganda)

Jok (Lubanga) is the supreme being. But he is not wholly accessible to humans. There are other spirits, also called jok, who carry out God's wishes, involved in the daily world of humans, touching humans positively and negatively. Spirits of the dead continue to influence humans. Jok is present everywhere, in all things: he created the world—the heavenly bodies, the landforms of the earth, the beasts and humans. He taught humans to cultivate, and gave them fire. 🔲 Jok created the world, then placed into the skies the heavenly bodies, the sun, the moon, and the stars. And he planned to give to man the fruits of the tree of life, so that he would never die. Man was therefore called to the heavens; Jok awaited him. But the man was in no hurry to move to the skies, and God became angry. In his anger, he took the fruits of the tree of life and gave them to the sun, to the moon, to the stars, so that they lived forever. Then, when man finally arrived in the skies, it was too late: the fruits of the tree of life were gone, and so man would not live forever. 🔲 In another myth, man died but, after a brief time, returned to life. He was told by Jok to take one grain of millet, grind it, and that would provide him with sufficient food. When humans broke Jok's instructions and ground a large amount of millet, they no longer returned to life once they had died.

Jok and the Man Who Fell from the Sky (Lango/Uganda) Jok, the supreme being, is like moving air; he is omnipresent, like the wind, but is never seen, though his presence may be felt in whirlwinds or eddies of air, in rocks and hills, in springs and pools of water, and he is especially connected with rain-making. He is an indivisible entity permeating the whole universe. Any inexplicable or mystifying occurrences are attributed to the presence of Jok. The failure of the rains, destruction caused by hail, lightning, and locusts, are believed to be manifestations of his power. Jok is the creator of the world and of man, the dispenser of death, and the decisive force in determining the period of a man's existence. He is responsible for all births. Rich harvests are sent by him, as are the rains that ensure a good harvest and the dry season favorable to hunting. Jok, accessible to the prayers of the people, punishes neglect and those who doubt him. The spirits of the departed become eventually merged in Jok, all the long departed merging into one preexisting deity called Jok, a plurality of spirits unified in the person of a single godhead, a spiritual force composed of innumerable spirits, any one of which may be temporarily detached without diminishing the oneness of the force. Jok created the two worlds contained in the Lango cosmology together with their inhabitants. He set the stars between the upper and the nether worlds and so ordained the Milky Way as to arrange for the two diverse seasons necessary for man's life and happiness. ▣ In April and May, 1918 there was a terrible drought. That same year, a man had fallen from the sky, descending near the river Moroto, bringing with him a bag of money, a leg of a cow, and four soldiers. He spoke Lango without any accent. He said that, although he had come from a place where there are many cattle and great wealth, he would consent to live here on earth. Orweny of Bata, a powerful man of god, asked him about the drought; having come from the realm of Jok, he would surely have information. The stranger told him that the drought had resulted because a certain spirit had committed adultery with another, then refused to pay compensation. For that reason, the wronged spirit had stopped the rain. Toward the end of May, Orweny, using his enchantments, was able to achieve the punishment of the erring spirit along with the payment of compensation. Rain fell in June. *See also:* Polo.

Juntel Jabali Wrests the Secret of Weaving from Jinn (Tukulor/Senegal) The Mabube are masters of weaving, experts in its techniques and magic. ▣ In a myth having to do with the origin of weaving, jinn play a central role in the craft, along with activities of a semidivine ancestor, Juntel Jabali. From Juntel Jabali, the Mabube have inherited their lore and magic, and they are descended from him. Jabali Nango was the son of 'Nango, son of Feynar. Jabali married a jinni, and they had a son, Juntel, the one who brought weaving to man. Juntel was sent by his father to learn fishing, and while he was collecting firewood for the grilling of fish, he encountered a jinni weaving in the forest. Juntel secretly watched as the jinni wove, the jinni speaking loudly, pronouncing incantations with each thing he did. Juntel returned again and again to watch the jinni weaving in the forest, and he learned much. Then he decided to take the loom for himself. When he saw the jinni, he recited an incantation to make himself invisible. He crept quietly, but stepped on a piece of wood. The jinni lifted the cloth-beam from his lap and ran out of the loom. Juntel collected the loom parts, removed the threads, rolled them together, and returned with them to the canoe. When Juntel's mother saw the equipment, she knew from whom he had taken the loom: it was from her people. There were still many things he did not know about weaving, how to set up the warp, thread up the loom, start weaving a new warp. His mother taught him what he did not know, how to grow cotton, make threads, and wind bobbins. When people asked Juntel for a particular number of cloths, he spoke his mother's name and created the number of cloths required. *See also:* Jinn.

Juok and the Dog That Preserved Mankind (Anuak/Sudan) Juok (Jwok), the creator, the supreme being, was an androgynous god, an all-powerful and omniscient spirit. ▣ He had sons—first an elephant; then a buffalo, a lion, a crocodile; after that, a little dog; and, finally, man and woman. When he saw the humans, beings without hair, Juok told the dog to throw them away. The dog took the humans to a tree, and put the children into a hole in that tree. Then, without his knowledge, the dog milked a cow from among God's herds and fed the children. The children grew up, got too big for the tree, so the dog took them to the country, where they built a house. They became a man and a woman. When the dog brought them to God, Juok wanted to kill them, but the dog asked him to let them live as his brother and sister. As the land was getting crowded, God decided to allocate land to his people. He would deal with the elephant, buffalo, and lion first, with the man and woman last. But the dog knew that if they went in last they would get nothing. They must go in first, pretending to be the larger animals. When God asked who he was, the man said he was the elephant, the buffalo, and the lion, and God gave him all the spears. When the larger animals arrived, God realized what had happened, so he gave the crocodile teeth, tusks to the elephant, horns to the buffalo, claws to the lion. The man, when he met those creatures, killed them with his spear, so they went onto the plains. And man took the best place. The name of the first man was Otino. The name of the first woman was Akongo. ▣ Juok decided to cast a rock into a river so that when a man died he should die forever. When Dog heard that the beasts had been summoned to council by God, he told man to look after the cattle, he would go and listen to God. But man said he would listen to God himself. Dog knew that man would misunderstand Juok's words, but he gave way. Up to that time, man had died for a few days only and had then come to life again. God had summoned all the beasts to come and throw the rock into the river and so terminate man's life. When God spoke to the beasts, man did not clearly understand what he said, as Dog had foreseen, so that the beasts cast the rock into the river. Dog, while herding, heard a great splash and ran to see what had happened. When he saw that the rock had been cast by God into the river, he showed man where the rock had fallen and told him to collect all his people to pull it out of the river. But man said that he was tired, he might hurt himself. Why should he pull it out? Dog tried to pull it out by himself, but it was too heavy; it kept rolling back again, and the people did not help him but only stood on the bank and laughed. So he bit as large a piece out of the rock as he could manage and carried it home with him. In consequence of Dog's action, man takes a long time to die. If Dog had not saved a portion of the rock, man's life would be very short. ⚄ Once men had no knowledge of fire. People placed their porridge in the sun and after warming it a little in this way they ate it. One day it rained all day long, and the dog was wet and miserable. He went from house to house seeking shelter, but everyone turned him from their door. He reached the house of a woman with a small daughter. The daughter started to drive the dog away, but the mother rebuked her, saying that the dog was like a human being and ought to be allowed to enter houses to dry himself if he wanted to do so. The dog entered the house and lay there until his coat was dry. He then asked the woman where her fire was. She said that she had no such thing, so the dog told her to place a heap of dry grass before him and when she did so he urinated on it and made fire. He told the woman to blow on to the fire and heap sticks on it to keep it alive. He said, "When everybody else drove me away from their houses, you alone allowed me to enter, so I have given you fire. When the other people ask you to give them fire, make them pay a necklace of dimui beads for it." So when people asked the woman to give them fire, she replied, "No, I cannot give it to you for nothing. Its owner said that I was to take a dimui necklace for it." Many people came to the woman and paid her for a portion of her fire, and so spread it to all mankind.

Juok and the Struggle Between Sun and Moon (Jo Luo/Sudan) Juok was the creator. ⚄ He once asked the sun and the moon if there were now more or fewer people on the earth. The moon answered that there were many people. But the sun said that this was not true because people were always dying. Juok said that he wanted the people to die as the moon dies, then be returned to life again after a month. The sun was envious of the moon, because the moon knew more about people than he did. The people always hid themselves when the sun came, because he was so hot. He therefore fought with the moon, throwing him—the scars (the lunar seas) are still to be seen on the moon. Juok felt sorry for the sun because she was alone, and decided to give her a brother or sister. Spider intervened, saying that if there were two suns the people would die. The sun condemned the spider for rejecting Juok's proposal, saying that from that time spiders would have to hide during the time that the sun was out. They could come out only at night. ⬚ The first fire was brought by a dog. This dog went into the Juok village and found Juok in a blacksmith's shop. The fire was burning there. The dog said that it was very cold, and he kept moving nearer and nearer to the fire. When he got too near, his tail caught fire and he ran away. While he was running, he wagged his tail and in this way set fire to the *abolo* tree and other trees and grasses. The people asked the dog where he had found the fire. He said that he had brought it from the house of Juok, but it was kept in the *abolo* tree. Therefore, if people want to make fire, they take sticks from the *abolo* tree and use them for kindling. *See also:* Nyikang, Wac.

Juok and the Creation of the Races (Shilluk/Sudan) Juok (Jwok), the supreme being, created the world, its plants, animals, and people. There are three levels of belief: the recognition and worship of Juok, the cult of Nyikang and the kings in whom he has been reincarnated, and the cult of the ancestral spirits. Juok is spirit that is universal, formless, and invisible like the air. He is above Nyikang and men, though he is approached principally through Nyikang. Sacrifices are made to Nyikang to cause him to move Juok to send rain, to prevent misfortune, remove sickness. ⬚ Using different types of earth, God created people in three types, black, white and brown. The white man was made from white loam; the brown man was made from the desert sand; and the black man was formed from the fertile riverside clay. *See also:* Nyikang, Ukwa.

Juon Lets Men Hear the Sound of the Dance (Burun, Meban/Sudan) The creator and supreme god, Juon (Juong), molded all men out of earth. ⬚ While engaged in the work of creation, he wandered about the world. In one land, he found a pure white earth or sand, and out of it he shaped white men. He came to Egypt, and out of the mud of the Nile he made red or brown men. Then he came to the land of the Shilluk, and finding black earth he created black men. ⬚ In the process of modeling humans, he took a lump of earth, thinking that he would make a man who could talk and run, who would have two legs, like the flamingo. He did that, then considered that the man must be able to cultivate his millet, so he gave him two arms, one to hold the hoe, the other to do the weeding. But he knew that the man must be able to see the millet, so he gave him two eyes. And he also knew that the man must be able to eat his millet, so he gave him a mouth. Juon thought, further, that the man must be able to dance, to speak, to sing, so he gave him a tongue. And God knew that the man must be able to hear the sound of the dance, the speeches of great men, so he gave him two ears. And God sent into the world a perfect man.

J

The Unifying Rhythm

Patterning is the crucial artistic aspect of mythmaking, and it is the mark of an accomplished storyteller who can rigorously take the emotions that he has evoked and work them into the artistic form of the experience. Repetition seems straightforward enough, and indeed when children perform stories it is readily discerned. But in complex story, it becomes an exceedingly subtle and potent tool. This is the craft of the accomplished artist—the patterning of imagery, and the interworking, interweaving of a variety of patterns, giving the mythic performance its texture, and binding the members of the audience, for the moment of performance, into a unified group. There is no story without patterning. It provides the form of the story, which is to say the meaning. It is pattern that links the two repertories of imagery, by so doing weaving the emotions engendered by the one into the images that compose the other. It is pattern that brings the storyteller, who possesses a part of the raw material of performance (images from the past and affiliated emotions), and the audience, which is another part of the necessary raw material of performance (images from the present and associated emotions), into union, and it is in that union that meaning, message, idea is to be discovered. Patterning is provided not only by verbal repetition but also by nonverbal elements of performance. Rhythm is the essence of storytelling no less than it is of all art. Observers sometimes become snarled in the obvious surface morality of stories, and thereby neglect their more complex meanings. The language of storyteller is intricate, composed of much more than obvious superficial homilies.

K

Kabunda, Whose Mother Brought Fire (Lamba/Zambia) Kabunda was a mythic ancestor. ▣ When humans cultivated only millet and were still ignorant of fire, the men of the Goat clan found a woman who had become lost—her name was Kinelungu or Konde, and she belonged to the Hair clan. Lwabasununu, chief of the Goat clan, married her. She brought with her the seeds of various cereals and agreed to reveal the secret of fire to her husband on condition that his people abandon patrilineal filiation. She also demanded that on Lwabasununu's death his power be split between two principles: authority, *bufumu*, would continue to be exercised by men, but sacred power, *bulopwe*, would be transmitted through women. When the son who sprang from their union, Kabunda, killed the elder son of Lwabasununu, his half brother, all the members of the Goat clan drowned themselves in the Zambezi River

Kaggen Imagines the Earth

Everyman's Two Sides Are Represented by the Divine Trickster. The creator god, when he is cast in the role of divine trickster, suggests the order-chaos duality of the creator, this character mirroring the duality of the universe as the supreme being moves to bring order to disorder. The divine trickster embodies godly elements, incongruous though it may seem. There is a strange affiliation of the sublime and the grotesque in this wonderful character, an intensely focused summary of the forces at large and in struggle during the age of creation. The idea that the creation of the universe is intimately bound up with belief in an almighty being is revealed in a myth having to do with a San divine trickster, in which the creator god imagines the new world; from the rich and productive possibilities of his own inner struggle and creativity emerges a world that is never wholly severed from an initial oneness with God. ◧ (San/Botswana, Namibia, South Africa) |Kaggen (Cagn, Dxui, ǂGao!na, ‖Gauwa, Hishe, Huwe, |Kaang, Kho, Thora), the San supreme being, is a creator god. A mantis, he is also a divine trickster. He creates, but he also has a destructive urge. He has godly knowledge, yet he is capable of acts of mortal stupidity; he is sublime, he is also obscene. |Kaggen was the first being; he gave orders and caused all things to appear. He used to dwell with men on the earth, but how he came into the world no one knows. He used to be a kindly god, but he could not cope with the stubbornness and opposition of mankind, could not establish his ways in peace, so he went away. He could change himself into any animal form, a mantis, an eland bull. He loved the elands: today, no man knows where |Kaggen is; only the elands know. ◧ |Kaggen, revealing his trickster nature, takes away the sheep of some ticks. His dispute with the ticks establishes a necessary disjuncture in the mythical world that will lead to its dismantling and reconstruction in earthly terms. The ticks, who possess shelter, domestic animals, and clothing, bloody and defeat |Kaggen, but must now experience God's revenge. What was the environment of the ticks in the world of myth is now recast because of the divine wrath of the trickster-god in human terms: it is the origin of San civilization. God dreams, and his dream, an awesome fancy, is fulfilled; it is a vision of genesis, of the first creation, fraught with the prophecy that orders all things. |Kaggen dreams that all the ticks' homes, their domesticated animals, their weapons, and their fire arise and come to the place of the San. The San world is coming into existence, with domesticated animals, clothing, utensils, fire, symbols of civilization. But |Kaggen goes further; he now orders living beings as well. The ticks will henceforth have to drink blood; they

will no longer have fire. They will drink the blood of other creatures. God's curse becomes an origin. When his family awakens, it
finds that what he had dreamed is now reality. The sheep and
houses, the pots that the San would cook in, all things of San civi-
lization are now present. |Kaggen then continues the process of first
ordering. Ichneumon, God's grandson, will become an insect; the
mother of Ichenumon will become a porcupine, his grandmother a
hare. |Kaggen himself will become a mantis. The creation is com-
plete. But it is then destroyed, engulfed by a swallowing monster,
All-devourer, a fabulous mythical villain, fearful father of the porcu-
pine. |Kaggen inexplicably and against the advice of the porcupine
invites the fire-breathing All-devourer to his home, and an awful pattern of destruction begins, as the monster scorches then swallows
everything—plants, the things of the home, the domesticated animals, finally the people—including God—themselves. God has cre-
ated fire. Everything that |Kaggen has created goes into the monster's
belly. This second part of the story, a fantasy restatement of the
things envisioned by |Kaggen in part one, ends with a second cre-
ation, wherein |Kaggen's offspring and his grandchild are taught to
withstand the deadly heat of the fiery All-devourer. This crucial pattern counters that of the destructiveness of the monster. When they
are prepared to contain the great forces that |Kaggen has given
them—the fire, symbol of civilization, but also, unchecked, symbol
of returning chaos—re-creation can take place. Everything returns
from the stomach of the swallowing monster, and the dream of god,
culture hero, and divine trickster, is now fulfilled. As ambiguous god
and man, |Kaggen bestrides the two worlds, leading early humans
from the one to the other. ▣ |Kaggen, smarting because his chil-
dren have killed the eland he created, moves to action. In his venge-
ful anger, he pierces the eland's gall, which blinds him, and he has
created night. In his benevolence, he wipes his eyes with an ostrich
feather, throws the feather into the sky, and creates the moon.
▣ Once |Kaggen, going along in the darkness, threw his shoe into
the sky and it became the moon. Now the moon walks in the night,
feeling that it is a shoe; shining in the night, it makes enough light

for travelers. ⊡ The sun, once a man who lived on earth, was left-handed because from his right armpit shone forth a great light. If he put down his arm, darkness fell everywhere; when he lifted it up, it was like day. The greatest of his light and warmth fell around his own house. When he lay down to sleep, all others in that village were cold in the dark. So the women got together and told the children, when they found him asleep, to throw him into the sky. "As you throw him," they said, "tell him that he must become the sun, that he must pass along the sky and be hot so that the rice may dry." When he fell asleep, the children saw that the light from his armpit made a little spread of light upon the ground. They grasped him firmly and threw him into the sky, saying, "Grandfather, become the sun, which is hot, so that the rice may dry. Make the whole earth warm and light. Shine, take away the darkness." It was done, and the children then went home. Now the sun comes, the darkness goes away; the sun sets, darkness comes, the moon comes at night. The moon, |Kaggen's shoe, goes along in the night, taking away the darkness. ⊡ The sun, when he moved into the sky, drove the moon away. He went after it with a knife and cut it. "Sun, leave the backbone for the children!" the moon cried. The sun consented and left the moon his backbone. Sometimes that is the way people see him, just his thin backbone in the sky, curved like |Kaggen's shoe. Then the moon is a new moon, but he knows that he will be whole again. He puts on a new stomach, he grows large again; he is whole, and goes by night, feeling that he is |Kaggen's shoe which walks in the sky by night. ⊡ Another origin myth of the San tells of remote forefathers emerging from a hole in the ground at the roots of an enormous tree that covered a wide extent of the country. Immediately afterward, all kinds of animals came swarming out after them in great numbers. *See also:* ǂGao!na, ‖Gauwa, Hishe, Huwe, Kho.

with the exception of one woman, Kabilo, from whom all existing members of the clan are descended. Kabunda, now leader of the Lamba, had relations with his sister, who gave him a son. This son combined in his person the two principles of power, *bulopwe* and *bufumu*. By the matrilineal rule that prevailed thenceforth, the son was considered the uterine nephew of his father. *See also:* Chipimpi.

Kahina: They Say the Jinn Spoke to Her (Lamtuna/Morocco) Kahina was a mythic epic Berber hero, a half-historical, half-legendary queen and prophet who fought against an Arab conqueror in A.D. 699 and was victorious. Two Lamtuna men, Abu Bakr b. Umar and his cousin Yusuf b. Tashfin, army leaders in Morocco and the southern Sahara, struggled for power, dividing the Almoravid Empire between them. In 1067, affairs were firmly in the hands of the Amir Abu Bakr b. Umar, and the country obeyed him. ▣ The influence behind both men was a woman endowed with magic, skill, and shrewd judgment. She was a beautiful woman known as Zaynab al-Nafzawiya. Her renown and her life became known to the peoples of the Masmuda. Their shaykhs and princes used to seek her hand in marriage, but she insisted that she would marry only the man who ruled the entirety of the Maghrib. They therefore despised her. Strange stories were told about her; some said that the jinn spoke to her, were her servants, others that she was a witch. She became known as Kahina. ▣ The Amir Abu Bakr b. Umar, informed of her beauty, married her. She promised to give him much wealth. She made him enter, blindfolded, a subterranean dwelling. When she removed the blindfold and he opened his eyes, he saw rooms filled with gold, silver, gems, rubies. Abu Bakr b. Umar was amazed at what he saw, the gold and silver. Kahina told him that all this was his wealth, that God had given it to him, that she had delivered it to him. Then she again blindfolded him and brought him out; he did not know how he had entered or how he had departed. Zaynab—Kahina—was a remarkable woman.

K

Kaidara, with Seven Heads, Twelve Arms, and Thirty Feet (Fulani/Senegal) Kaidara, god of gold and of wisdom, is a beam that comes from Gueno. When he makes himself visible, he does so in the guise of deformed old men or beggars, to confuse opportunists. As god of gold, Kaidara resides, with gold, in the ground. To get to the supernatural spirit and, thereby, the gold, travelers must cross eleven strata and trials. Gold and knowledge are united in Kaidara, an extraordinary being with seven heads, twelve arms, thirty feet, perched on a four-footed throne that rotates constantly, the structure of the world and of time. ▣ The journey to the underground, the move to Kaidara, is a movement into an esoteric realm. The first phase ends with the encounter with Kaidara, an effort rewarded by the gift of nine oxen laden with gold. Kaidara gives gold at this initial phase, not knowledge. The second phase describes the return of the voyagers to the earth's surface; during this phase of trials, their conduct will determine their outcome, for gold is ambiguous: it may help in the acquisition of wealth, power, or wisdom. Gold is the foundation of knowledge; it must be used to acquire wisdom. *See also: Gueno.*

|Kai |Kini *and the Fire Sticks* (!Kung/Namibia) |Kai |Kini was the fire-bringer. ▣ There was a time when no one had fire except one man, |Kai |Kini. He had fire, the name of which was Doro, made with fire sticks. While other people ate raw food, |Kai |Kini cooked his food with this fire. ǂGao!na,

walking in the veld, came upon the place where |Kai |Kini was living. He was not there, but his children were, eating cooked |karu. ǂGao!na asked for some, found it very good, and asked how it had been cooked. The children told him that their father cooked the food. ǂGao!na, returning the next day for more, saw |Kai |Kini and his children digging for food in the ground. He hid and watched. They went back to their home and |Kai |Kini got his fire sticks from the place where he had hidden them. He twirled the male stick against the female stick, saying, "Fire will come, fire will come." When the fire was made and the food was cooking, |Kai |Kini hid his fire sticks again, ǂGao!na watching all the time. When the food was dished up, he came out from his hiding place, sat down by the fire, and they ate together. ǂGao!na suggested that they play a game. He made a jani toy, placing on it a guinea-fowl feather, weighting it with a nut. He tossed the toy into the air with his stick, and when it floated down, he ran, caught it, tossed it up again and again without it ever falling to the ground. |Kai |Kini wanted to play. ǂGao!na gave him the jani, but |Kai |Kini could not throw it very high. ǂGao!na said the guinea-fowl feather was no good, they must put a big paouw feather on it. This they did, and this time the jani flew high. ǂGao!na then released the wind and, blowing from the eastern side, it swept the jani toward the west. |Kai |Kini followed it, fascinated, tossing it higher each time he caught it. ǂGao!na followed |Kai |Kini and, when they came to the place where the fire sticks were hidden, ǂGao!na seized them and ran with them into the veld. As he ran, he broke them into little pieces, throwing them over the entire world. "All the world is going to get fire now," he said. "Fire, fire, go over the world." Since then, there has been fire in every piece of wood; all men can get it out and cook their food. |Kai |Kini stopped playing and looked at ǂGao!na. ǂGao!na told him, "It is not right that you alone should have fire. From now on, you will not be a person." And he changed |Kai |Kini into a bird named ǂOre. *See also:* ǂGao!na, ||Gauwa, |Kaggen.

Kalala, Who Devoted Himself to War (Holoholo/DRCongo, Tanzania) In ancient times, people did not know war, sickness, death. Then Mwamba, a woman, arrived from the southwest with her fifteen children. Kalala, the eldest, had spears, and when he saw a column of black ants he announced that he would devote himself to war. His mother laughed and Kalala, grown evil, buried her alive. He came to five men who sat at the foot of a gigantic tree that joined heaven and earth. Kalala killed three of them; the other two fled. When he caught them, they offered to renounce war. They organized a dance, bringing together many people in the village of Chief Ilunga Nsungu, who lived on the other side of the Lualaba River. While Kalala was asleep, the followers of Ilunga Nsungu dug a great ditch, covering it with a mat. Kalala woke up, and the dancing resumed. His hosts invited him to rest on the mat, but Kalala stretched out beside the concealed trap. Then one of the two men he had spared climbed up the great tree to the sky. Five months later, as that man had not returned, his companion decided to join him. The second man met the first coming back to earth. He told his companion that, in the sky, he had met a great black goat with a fiery tail (Nkuba Lightning); it had ordered him to make war. The two companions seized Kalala and threw him into the ditch, which they filled in. Kalala's fourteen brothers searched for him. They discovered the grave of their mother. Arriving in the country of Ilunga Nsungu, they killed women working in the fields. Ilunga Nsungu, defending himself, hurled at his enemies three pots, which contained smallpox and some bees. Many slaves were killed, but the fourteen brothers continued the war. In the end, Ilunga Nsungu asked for peace. Then he asked them to cut his hair, as friends do. But his great head of hair was very tough and only the youngest brother succeeded, by licking it. Furious at the youth's cleverness, the others killed him and cut up his body. Ilunga Nsungu collected the pieces and put the body together again by magic: the youth came back to life. Ilunga Nsungu kept him hidden in a house, so that his brothers would not find him. After drinking heavily, Kalala's brothers began the war again. The youngest brother, saved by Ilunga Nsungu, gave his benefactor a great magical calabash. Ilunga poured out the water it contained from the top of a high mountain and the sons of Mwamba were drowned. The youngest brother remained with his protector who sent him to collect bird traps along the river. The captured birds asked him to spare their lives; in return, they gave him supernatural aid in case of sickness. The youth let them go, returning empty-handed. Ilunga Nsungu, spying on him, discovered that he talked to the birds and set them free. He attacked the boy and cut him into pieces. But the birds came in great numbers and put him together again, carrying him through the air, depositing him before the house of his maternal aunt. The people of Mwamba took up arms and a terrible war ensued with Ilunga Nsungu. He blew in vain on the magic calabash: no water appeared. He finally sued for peace and paid tribute to the people of Mwamba.

Kalitangi, Who Vies with God (Ovimbundu/Angola) Kalitangi was a mythical hero. ▣ Leopard, instead of eating Goat, befriends her. They agree that when they give birth they will eat the children. Leopard gives birth, and they eat the child. But Goat takes a long time to give birth, and Leopard keeps threatening to eat her. Finally, she starts to give birth: she bears a spear, arrows and a bow, gun and ammunition, and at last Kalitangi, who says, "I am Kalitangi. I talk back to Suku [God]." Whenever Leopard attempts to kill Kalitangi to eat him, Kalitangi threatens him with one of the weapons. Eventually, he kills Leopard. Suku in heaven learns of Kalitangi, and he sends for Goat; she does not return to earth. Kalitangi, with other animals, goes to Suku to get his mother. They must bore through a mountain to reach Suku's large village. Now Suku and Kalitangi begin to vie with each other, tricking one another by transforming and defying the other to discover the trick. To get his mother back, Kalitangi must defeat Suku in this risky contest. In the end, Suku has Kalitangi climb a tree. Before he does, Kalitangi asks God to wear his belt. Suku then sends the tree into the sky, but Kalitangi commands his belt to squeeze Suku, who must therefore bring Kalitangi back to earth. With the assistance of a fly, Kalitangi identifies the box in which Suku has hidden his mother, and they go off together.

Kalumba Forges the Sun (Luba/DRCongo) Kalumba (Sendwe Mwlaba) is the creator god. ▣ In the beginning, Kalumba came from the east and was the one who forged the sun. He is black and resembles man. He sits far away from the earth; the sky is near in comparison. Kalumba was alone. He took a stick and held it in his arms. He said, "My child." He carved a stick in human form. He stood it up. Kalumba (also the word for wind) blew on the stick. The carved form walked. This carved form had no name. After walking, it bore twins. Kalumba showed them things for food. ▣ Sendwe Mwlaba sent two people, a man called Kinbaka-Baka and a woman called Kinbumba-Bumba, the parents of all mankind, to spy out the land to the west. They found it all dark, all night, and returned to report this. The moon was in the sky, but it became necessary for Kalumba to forge the sun. They slept, and saw only the moon. They said that where they had come from there was light, that they would return home and bring the sun. They went back to report. They said, "Give us a sun, we will go and wash the land." They washed the land, and could see one another. They brought a dog, named Kalala Kabwa; they brought birds that make a noise before sunrise. They brought a fire-making stone and iron. They brought with them the power of reproduction, *ngoya* (God had earlier created Ngoya, the queen ant), for animals, plants, and people. There were many small rivers. Kalumba, the creator, sent the names for them. ▣ These first people in the land had two children, twins, a boy and a girl. Kalumba knew that both Life and Death, wrapped up in grass cloth and tied to a pole as if for burial, would pass along the path to try to reach the people. So he appointed Dog and Goat to guard the path in order to allow Life to pass, but not Death. Kalumba, the creator, sent both Dog and Goat to guard the path. He said, "Go, lie on the path." Dog said, "I shall not go to sleep while I am guarding!" Dog and Goat talked crossly to each other. Goat said, "If you undertake to guard the path, you will surely fall asleep!" Dog said, "No, I shall not sleep." Goat said, "See how I jump around. I am lively, I could not possibly fall asleep." Finally, Goat's feelings were hurt, and he went home, leaving Dog to guard by himself. Dog stayed there to guard the path. He made a fire—and went to sleep. Then Death slipped past him. When Goat returned, they swore at each other because of what had happened. Next day, Goat watched. He did not sleep on the path as he was guarding. Life came along, and Goat caught him. People said, "If Goat had watched, Death would have been intercepted." Dog cursed Goat, saying, "You have ears far apart, and horns between." Goat cursed Dog, saying, "You have shiny eyes that are always looking for something to steal." ▣ The sun and the moon each claimed to be greater than the other. They brought their dispute to Kalumba, who decided in favor of the moon, because it gave life to men: on one of its thirteen annual journeys, the moon brought back the rain, causing the plants to grow. Incensed at this verdict, the sun threw mud in the moon's face. Since that time the moon has produced less light than the sun. ▣ At the beginning of time, men lived in the same village as Kalumba. Tired of the noise of their quarrels, the creator dispatched humankind to earth. There they suffered from hunger and cold, and came to know sickness and death. A diviner advised them to return to the sky to find immortality. So they began to build an enormous tower of wood, with its foundations in a *lusanga* tree. After many months of labor the builders arrived at the sky. They entered the celestial domain, beating a drum and playing a flute to make the news known to those who remained on earth. But these were too far away to hear. When he heard the noise God became angry and destroyed the tower, killing the musicians. *See also:* Nkongolo.

Kamangundu Emerges from Omumborombonga, the Tree of Life (Damara, Herero/Namibia)

Ndjambi Karunga (Mukuru) is the heavenly God. He lives in heaven, yet is omnipresent. His most striking characteristic is kindness. Human life is created by and dependent on him, and all blessings ultimately come from him. He who dies a natural death is carried away by Ndjambi. As his essence is kindness, people do not fear but venerate him. As his blessings are the gifts of his kindness without any moral claims, the belief in Ndjambi has no moral strength. "He stays in the clouds because, when the clouds rise, his voice is clearly heard." ▣ The first people originated from a mythic tree, an Omumborombonga tree, growing between the Kaokoveld and Ovamboland. Makuru, the old one, with his wife, Kamungarunga, and his cattle are descended from this tree, but everything else in the world has a different origin. The Ovambo migrated southward from the upper reaches of the Zambezi at the same time as the Herero. On reaching the present Ovamboland, the Herero continued in a westerly direction, moving toward and through the Kaokoveld southward in search of suitable pastures for their large herds of cattle, while the Ovambo, being an agricultural people, decided to remain. They, in common with the Herero, are descended from the Nangombe ya Mangundu. Nangombe came from the east with his brother, Kathu. At the great Omumborombonga tree in the Ondonga area, the two brothers separated, Kathu leading the Herero onward in search of pastures for their herds, while Nangombe with his followers settled on the fertile plains of the present Ovambo territory. Nangombe and Kathu are the sons of Mangundu; it is not known whether Mangundu was their father or mother. The center for religious worship was a place where a weak fire glimmered and was blown up into a blaze only on festive occasions. This fireplace was separated from its surroundings by means of stones or a thorn hedge. In close proximity, a branch of the Omumborombonga tree lies as a permanent representative of the ancestors. The holy fire is a gift from Mukuru. ▣ Out of the Omumborombonga tree came forth in the beginning a man and a woman. The woman was called Kamangundu, and

K

from her sprang the Herero, Ovambo, Tswana, and Nama. ▣ The Berg Damara originated in the following manner: A discontented Herero girl ran away into the field, and there fell on a flat rock, upon which the Berg Damara and the baboons who live in the mountains on edible bulbs were born. The oxen also came out of the Omumborombonga tree, while the sheep and goats sprang from the flat rock in the Kaoko. When the children of Kamangundu came out of the tree, the people killed an ox. A woman came and took the liver for her children; from these came the black people. Another woman took the lungs and the blood for herself and her children; from these came the red people. By the slaughtered ox, the people began to quarrel as to who should have the skin, which the Herero, considering themselves to be the first among the nations, seized upon. Now began the enmity and separation of the people. First, the Herero beat and drove away the Ovambo, who went to the north; afterward, they returned and made peace with them. The Tswana went to the east, where they remained for a long time. Subsequently, they returned and robbed the Herero, but were finally repulsed by them. *See also:* Holy Fire, Karunga.

Kambili, Who Does Not Want to Stay in the Womb (Mandinka/Mali) Kanji, a general of Imam Samory Toure, leader of the Mandinka, tells Samory that he has nine wives but none of them has yet given birth. Samory calls experts to discover if Kanji will have a child and who the mother will be, but they are unable to help. But one holy man states that Kanji's first child will be born of Dugo, a despised wife who has been forced by the chief wife to live in a goat pen. The name of the wife who will bear the child is kept secret so that co-wives do not kill her out of jealousy. The holy man convinces the wives that they must not spend the night with Kanji for a month, and during this time, he sneaks Dugo into Kanji's bed after nightfall and sneaks her out before daybreak. Dugo becomes pregnant. The first wife discovers this and accuses her of having relations with the goats. She swears to Samory that this is the case and declares that she will sweep his compound with her buttocks if it is not so. After some difficulty with Kambili, who does not want to stay in the womb, the nine months eventually pass and Kambili, resembling his father perfectly, is born in the goat pen. The first wife is made to keep her promise, and Dugo is brought back to Kanji's compound to live. The first wife, jealous, attempts to kill Kambili but is caught by Kanji, who kills her. Dugo becomes the favored wife. Kambili spends his youth hunting; he kills every possible animal. He marries Kumba, who was promised to one Cekura, who becomes angry at this betrayal. Cekura, having the power to transform himself into a lion, sets out to ravage the village. Samory calls on the hunters to stop the lion-man. Kumba knows who the lion-man is, and, to develop an antidote, she requires hair from Cekura's head, underarm, and crotch. She goes to Cekura and, pretending that she loves him, tricks him into giving her the needed hairs. She returns with them, and a sacrifice is made. Kambili, having consulted a spirit to determine where best to set the trap for the lion-

K

man, ties a boy under a tree and climbs up into the tree with his weapon. Kumba gives the boy a talisman to protect him from the lion-man, then, transforming herself into a lion, lures Cekura to the trap. She brings Cekura to the tree, but he has a powerful medicine that causes Kambili to fall asleep. The boy sings a song to awaken Kambili, who fires his rifle, killing the lion-man with one shot. At a celebration, Samory gives gifts to Kambili and a song of praise is sung for Kumba.

Kana, the Name of Three Boys (Ganda/Uganda) Human history begins with a first family, the head of which is Kintu. There are three children in this family, all boys. Initially, all are called Kana, "little child." Because this is confusing, Kintu asks God if they may be given separate names. God agrees, and the boys are given two tests. First, six objects are placed on a path by which the boys will pass—an ox's head, a cowhide thong, a bundle of cooked millet and potatoes, a grass head-ring for carrying loads on the head, an ax, and a knife. When the boys come upon these things, the eldest takes the bundle of food and starts to eat. What he cannot eat he carries away, using the head-ring for this purpose. He also takes the ax and the knife. The second son takes the leather thong, and the youngest takes the ox's head, which is all that is left. In the next test, the boys must sit on the ground in the evening with their legs stretched out, each holding on his lap a wooden milk-pot full of milk. They are told that they must hold their pots safely until morning. During the night, the youngest boy, dozing off, spills a little of his milk, and he asks his brothers for some of theirs. Each gives him a little, and his pot is full again. Just before dawn, the eldest brother suddenly spills all his milk, but his brothers refuse to help him because it would take too much of their milk to fill his empty pot. In the morning, their father finds the youngest son's pot full, the second son's nearly full, and that of the eldest empty. He gives his decision, and names the three boys. Because he chose the millet and potatoes, peasants' food, and because he lost all the milk entrusted to him, showing himself unfit to have anything to do with cattle, the eldest, and his descendants after him, is always to be a servant and a cultivator, carrying loads for his younger brothers and their descendants. He is named Kairu, peasant. The second son, because he chose the leather thong for tying cattle and had spilled none of his milk, providing some only for his younger brother, will, with his descendants, have the respected status of cattleman. He is called Kahuma, little cowherd; the cattle-herding people of this part of the interlacustrine region have since been called Huma or Hima. The third and youngest son, because he had taken the ox's head, a sign that he would be at the head of all men, will be his father's heir; he alone had a full bowl of milk when morning came, because of the help given him by his brothers. He is named Kakama, little Mukama or ruler. He and his descendants become the kings of Kitara, later to be called Bunyoro. The father tells the two elder sons that they should stay with their younger brother and serve him always. And he tells Kakama to rule wisely and well. *See also:* Kintu, Ruhanga.

Musée de l'Homme, Paris

A Bakota Head, Eyelids Sewn Together as a Sign of Death

Kanu, Annoyed, Moves from Earth (Limba/Sierra Leone) There is a single high god, Kanu, called Kanu among the Safroko Limba, also called Masala (Sela Limba) and Masaranka (Tonko Limba). But little is known about him. Kanu is the supreme being, originator of all things. ▣ He lives in the distant sky. In the beginning, humans dwelled with Kanu; all were together here below. A deer and python were seeking food, and the python chased the deer, wishing to eat it. Kanu called the deer and python to him, but the python seized and ate the deer. The python, moving on, came to ants that wished to eat the python. Kanu called the ants and the python to him, warning them that their actions would cause him to disappear. But the ants seized the python and ate it. The ants were pursued by fire; again Kanu confronted them, and the fire consumed the ants. The fire was met by water; again there was the meeting with Kanu, and the fire was eaten up by the water. So it was that Kanu left the earth and went to the sky. It was because of the obstinacy of the python.

🄻 Kanu made medicine that would assure humans of eternal life. He instructed the snake to carry the medicine to the Limba. But the toad took it instead, and when he jumped he spilled it. Kanu said that because of what the toad had done he would give no more of the medicine. That is why the Limba die.

Kapepe and the Magical Feather (Lenje/Zambia) Kapepe is a mythic hero. 🄻 He moves to heaven to marry the daughter of the supreme god, Lesa. Along the way, an old woman gives him a magical feather that assists him when he is in difficulty. He struggles with various creatures and moves across a forbidding landscape, and finally arrives in the city of God, where he is able to overcome tricks and pass through ordeals. He marries God's daughter, then moves back to the earth, again confronted by discouraging obstacles. His wife becomes bored with life on earth, and she returns to the heavens. Kapepe follows her, and remains in the heavens.

Kar and the Rope between Sky and Earth (Nuer/Sudan) Kar (Jakar), a Gaarwar ancestor, descended from heaven by a rope that connected the sky with a tamarind tree, probably the tree in Hang country beneath which mankind is said to have been created. He then cut the rope (sometimes it is a tree) between sky and earth so that another ancestor, War, could not return after being enticed down with the smell of roasted meat.

Karkur, the Heap of Stones (Hausa/Niger, Nigeria) In parts of North Africa, there are heaps of stones to which each passerby adds a similar article, the piles being usually by the tomb of a marabout. 🄻 In Nigeria, where such a sacred place exists, it is pointed out by a learned marabout. The reason for adding to the pile is to make certain that the journey on which one is going shall be successful, for by depositing something, the holy man will remember and help one in whatever one is going to do, while by passing by without paying any attention, he will become angry and thwart one.

Karunga, Emerging from the Earth, Has a Race (Herero/Namibia) Karunga, the supreme being, the creator, the molder, sometimes characterized as Eyuru, heaven, is situated so high and is so superior to men that he takes little special notice of them. Karunga is a good being, the preserver of life. It is not he who kills people or brings trouble to them. The ancestors have the power to punish people for their offenses. He influences the powers of nature. The rain comes from him; he is in the rolling thunder, he hurls the lightning.

🄻 Karunga and his wife, Musisi, had two children: a girl, Tyinondyambi (Shinondyambi), and a boy, Tyarura (Shalula). Karunga, coming out of the earth, created three couples: from the first man and woman came the Ovambo; from the second couple, the San; and from the third, the Herero. He called the wife of the third couple Kamangundu. ▣ In the beginning, Karunga instituted a race, the prizes offered being a field pickax, a pointed digging stick, and a bullock. The Ovambo seized the pickax, the San the digging stick, and the Herero the bullock. *See also*: Kamangundu.

Kashindika Wants a Sun and a Moon (Lala/Zambia) Lesa and Mushili had two sons, Kashindika, the elder, and Luchyele, the younger. ▣ These sons of God were sent by their father from heaven to earth to build villages. They came to earth, which was the property of their mother, and found complete darkness, a place with neither sun nor moon. They decided that Kashindika should go to Lesa to get a sun and moon. He arrived, and they killed an ox. In the evening, meat-relish was cooked and porridge was served, and they took it to the house where the chief's son was to sleep. Lesa kept a great fat dog, and it went to where Kashindika was. When he saw it, he picked up the tongs and gave the fat dog a blow on the backbone, and it went away cringing. When it got light, Lesa told him to choose the packages of the sun and moon, because there were very many packages in the storehouse. He went home empty-handed because he did not see the sun or the moon. Then Luchyele set off to get a sun and moon. They killed an ox. But he, when the fat dog came, took some relish and put it in a pot with a large lump of porridge, and gave it to the dog. When it had finished eating, the dog told him that it would identify the packages containing the sun and moon. Luchyele did as the dog told him. Then, when he got to the village, he put the package of the sun in the east, and that of the moon in the west; he put the package containing the hornbills with the sun, and that containing the cocks in the verandah of the house. They heard the hornbills, and all was bright as the sun came up. They were happy. So the sun stayed on the earth. ▣ The elder, Kashindika, was jealous, and he concluded that Lesa favored Luchyele. At dawn, he went to Lesa's to get the world-destroyer, poison, to kill people. He called Lesa "enemy," because he refused to give him the sun, giving it to Luchyele instead. "Now I want the world-destroyer." Lesa refused. Kashindika said he would just take it then. He took the poison and went home. When he got to the edge of the village, Luchyele's wife, who was making porridge in her house, died with the porridge-paddle in her hands. The people wondered if Kashindika had poisoned her. They buried her. Then they found Kashindika's wife dead too, and they went and buried her as well. Luchyele decided to live somewhere else, and he went off to the east. Kashindika went in other direction, to the west. It is believed that all who die go to the west, to Kashindika's, while all good things come from the east. *See also*: Lesa, Luchyele.

Kaumpuli, the Child without Arms and Legs (Ganda/Uganda) Kaumpuli was the god of plague. ▣ Kaumpuli's father, Prince Kayemba, brother of King Juko, fell in love with a woman named Naku, and wished to marry her. But the gods objected, warning the king not to allow his brother to marry this woman. Kayemba, disregarding the warning, married Naku; she became the mother of Kaumpuli, a child without arms and legs. Because Kayemba was afraid of this child, he sent the mother and child away by canoe to Busoga. The priests of Busoga warned the chiefs not to receive Naku, and she was sent back to Uganda. Driven away from each place to which she went because of the child, she was at last allowed to settle at Bugoya. The child had a nurse, Nabuzana, who was fond of him and who tended him to the time of his death. After his death, he was declared by the gods to be the god of plague; a temple was built in Bulemezi in his honor, and the remains of Kaumpuli were placed there. The god resided in a deep hole in the temple, securely covered to prevent him from escaping and harming the country. The hole could only be covered efficiently by wildcat skins, and hundreds of these little animals were needed each year to cover it. Plantain stems were first laid over the hole, then the skins were placed on them and weighted by stones around the edges. It was believed that, but for this covering, the god would come out in a puff of smoke, and if he escaped he would destroy the country. King Juko was forbidden to look toward Bulemezi, because it was believed that he would die if he did so. For years, it was the duty of one of his wives to hold a bark cloth before him to prevent his eyes from wandering toward Bulemezi when he went out. One day, this wife was ill, and the king looked toward the hill on which Kaumpuli's temple stood, and a few days later he died.

Kaura Duna: A Struggle between Gods (Hausa/Nigeria) Kaura Duna is a mythic figure. ⬛ The Battle of Badar was the Prophet's first battle, that of Tabuka the last. The great-grandfather of the Tabuka was Kal'ana, who challenged God. He raised a large army and had them shoot into the skies. God ordered an angel to drop to the earth limbs of a giant human body to deceive Kal'ana. In the end, a gigantic human head plummeted down, and King Kal'ana declared victory. Many in heaven asked God for permission to go to earth to punish Kal'ana; God allowed two mosquitos to descend. They entered his ears and for seven years caused him intense pain. Satan went to the palace to heal the king's head, but he did so as a joke, and the king of Tabuka, the large city, died. Years later, a Muslim merchant in Medina told of the mighty city of Tabuka, ruled by heathens. The Prophet was urged to go to battle against the king of Tabuka. A spy informed the king of Tabuka, Kaura Duna, of the pending invasion. In the meantime, the Prophet was choosing a husband for his daughter, Nana Fadima. Ali wanted to marry her, but a wealthy man employed an old woman to sow deceit, and Ali was given the impression that Fadima preferred that man. He was intensely disappointed. He met an orphan who had accidentally spilled his milk on the ground, and Ali squeezed the earth to recover the milk, with the result that the earth swore that when Ali died it would make his grave uncomfortable. Ali was so angry about his situation that he lost his sight, so that when the battle with Tabuka approached he had to stay home. The Prophet's army went to battle, and, because of the arrogance of Kaura Duna, won the first battle. But the Prophet's armies were concerned about the absence of Ali, the Sword of God. Ali recovered his sight, a divine horse was prepared for him, and he roared into battle with such exuberance that the Prophet had to keep him under control. Ali destroyed the enemy, then faced the notorious giant of a man, Kaura Dunhu Duna, who, defeated, informed the king. Now the king himself had to face Ali. His five-hundred-year-old mother gave him magical potions that she had inherited, giving him fifteen monstrous heads on his shoulder. When Ali struck one head, fifteen others emerged in that position, and so the king developed, in the battle with Ali, scores of heads. But Ali, in the heat of the struggle, purposefully paused briefly, and the king turned around with his real human head to see what was the matter. Ali at once cut off that head with his famous sword, and all the other heads fell off as well, and the king of Tabuka was dead. Tabuka was vanquished.

Kejok, Born Mysteriously, Restores Life (Dinka/Sudan) Kejok was a mythic hero. ⬛ About the year 1700, a woman called Quay, the wife of Cheng, an Iyat Agar of the Akorbil clan, visited a pool at Korather close to Shambe which is believed to have been the home of Desheik, the ancestor of the Dinka. Quay mysteriously became pregnant without any human agency, and after a few days' pregnancy gave birth to a boy called Kejok who grew to manhood in a few months, and performed miracles. He had a brother called Menyang whose son, Lual, lost the sight of one eye; Kejok extracted the eye of a hartebeest and restored his sight. Later, a cow called Iyar, the property of Menyang, died and the carcass was cut up and divided among the people, but Kejok reassembled the skin and flesh, and brought the cow to life again. He had the power of producing water from the ground by tapping it with his hand. Menyang, filled with jealousy at the powers possessed by his younger brother, accused him of witchcraft, a quarrel ensued, and Kejok left his people, declaring that he would return to God his father, but that he would again appear at some future time. He was never seen again, but his memory is held sacred among the people. ⬛ In March 1921, a pool appeared near Khor Lait in the country of the Itay Agar Dinka in the eastern district of Bahr El Ghazal Province. It was believed to be inhabited by Kejok, and the messianic expectation arose that he was about to manifest himself again to his people and to bring them untold wealth and happiness. The incident was invested with religious significance and caused great excitement, which rapidly spread to other Dinka communities. Pilgrims flocked to the spot, sacrifices were offered, and there was much talk of signs and wonders and a general feeling that the miracle boded well for the Dinka and ill for the foreigners.

Kemangurura and the Monster (Kikuyu/Kenya) Kemangurura was a mythic hero. ⬛ A very strong youth, Kemangurura could kill two thousand men at a single stroke. He went to the home of a rich man, Njoroge wa Mbogwa, who had in an enclosure a monster called Hitimondo. The monster abused Kemangurura as he went by, and the young man asked Njoroge if he could strike Hitimondo. But Njoroge said he would take care of the matter. Then the Masai descended on the Kikuyu, with destructive results. The elders concluded that only Kemangurura could help them, and they asked him to do so. But he said he would not help them unless he was allowed to hit Hitimondo. The elders asked Hitimondo to consent to be struck by Kemangurura, but the monster refused because the elders would not give him the calf of their black cow. The elders then asked the black cow to deliver a calf, but the cow declined because the people had refused to give it good grass when it was hungry. The elders went to the rainmaker and pleaded for rain so that the cow could have good grass. The rainmaker refused, because they prevented him from eating a striped mouse. They went to the mouse, but he said they chased him when he was eating millet. They asked a woman who was harvesting millet for grain for the mouse, but she said they had refused to give her a knife. Fatigued, the elders went to the blacksmith and asked him to make a knife, but he said no, they had given him no charcoal. Dejected, the elders went to the forest to make charcoal. They gave it to the smith, got the knife, the millet, the mouse, the rainmaker, the grass, the calf, and Hitimondo ate the calf. And now Kemangurura clenched his fist and hit Hitimondo on the head. The monster fell to pieces like a calabash, his bones crushed. Now Kemangurura, enjoying himself, took clubs the size of hills and enormous spears and shield, and went to Masai country, where the people were feasting and dancing. He threw a club, and two thousand Masai fell dead. With the single survivor, Kemangurura rounded up the cattle and took them to his Kikuyu country, and he was made leader of the people.

Kho and the Origin of Death (San/Botswana, Namibia, South Africa) 🖥 Kho, the supreme being, the moon, sent an insect to earth to tell humans, "As I die, and dying live, so you shall also die, and dying live." Along the way, the insect was overtaken by a hare. The insect told the hare of his mission. The hare said that he, a faster runner, would take the message. He ran off, and when he got to earth, he told humans that he had been sent by the moon to tell them, "As I die, and dying perish, in the same manner you shall also die and come wholly to an end." When the hare told the moon what he had said, the moon struck him on the nose, which is why the hare's nose is slit. *See also:* |Kaggen.

Khuzwane Left His Footprints in the Rocks (Lovedu/South Africa) Khuzwane (Mwari), the supreme being, is the creator of the world and humanity. But he is remote from humans. The gods of the Lovedu are their ancestors, deceased fathers and mothers who guard one in death as they did in life. Ancestors are protectors; no harm can befall one unless the ancestors are neglectful. They are responsible for the fertility of the crops. 🖥 Khuzwane left his footprints on rocks in the north when these rocks were new and soft. But no one knows what has happened to him. *See also:* Mujaji, Mwari.

Kibo and Mawenzi, Atop Mount Kilimanjaro (Chaga/Tanzania) Kibo and Mawenzi are mythic beings. ▣ The majestic symbols of the land are the two giant glaciers, Kibo and Mawenzi, that make up Mount Kilimanjaro. Kibo, the spotted one, is so called because the dark naked stone appears in big, steep patches above the snow and ice fields. Mawenzi (or Mawenge) means the crumpled, the jagged, broken one. One day, the fire in Mawenzi's hearth had gone out. He went to Kibo to get some fire. Kibo was in the middle of pounding dried bananas. Mawenzi greeted him. Kibo returned the greeting, gave him fire, and made him a gift of a few bananas. Mawenzi went away and put out the fire, then went back to Kibo. He said that his fire had gone out on the way. Kibo muttered, but once again gave him a few bananas. When Mawenzi had gone a little way, he once again put the fire out, and returned for the third time to Kibo. But when he was greeted, this time Kibo did not answer. Instead, he raised his pestle and beat him with it. This is how Mawenzi became so jagged. ▣ In a broad pit on Kibo is supposed to live a giant cow, called Rali. From its tail hang big tufts that contain a fat that tastes like honey and conceals supernatural powers. For this reason, people have climbed up to cut off some of these precious tufts. The cow stands with its tail toward the opening of the pit. The people creep up very carefully, cut a few tufts very quickly with their swords, and move away rapidly. Because of her size, the cow can only turn around slowly since its body fills nearly the whole pit. But if she has managed to turn around, she lets out a mighty sound and the break from her mouth is like a hurricane that blows down onto the plains. It carries the offender through the air and smashes him on the plain. Twenty men once went up to get these tufts for the chief, and only two came back. This cow has only one calf, which takes her place when she dies. This cow sustains the sun so that it always renews its strength to overcome the clouds, which in the rainy season often keep its rays from the earth for months at a time. If the cow were found and killed, endless rain would start to fall that would kill everybody.

Kibuka Shoots Arrows from Clouds (Ganda/Uganda) Kibuka (Kyobe), the god of war, was the brother of Mukasa, the highest of the Ganda gods, and the son of Wanema, a god. ▣ During the reign of Nakibinge, the Nyoro were at war with the Ganda. King Nakibinge, after several indecisive battles, sought the aid of the god, Mukasa. They were pleased when Mukasa sent his brother, Kibuka, to assist the king. Mukasa warned him never to let his enemies know where he took up his position in the battle, and he further cautioned him to have no dealings with Nyoro women. Now the king felt confident of victory, and he personally went to the war, taking up a position as general of the army. Kibuka flew up into a cloud and hovered over the enemy; during the battle, he shot down arrows and spears on them, while the Ganda army pressed them in front. The battle ended in favor of the Ganda, and the Nyoro withdrew to a safe distance to consider what they should do. The Ganda had taken some women prisoners, and Kibuka was attracted to one of them. He had her sent to his house. At night she escaped, after having discovered his secrets, who he was and where he posted himself during the battle. She carried the information to her people, who decided to attack the Ganda again the next day, keeping a sharp lookout for Kibuka and his cloud. When the battle was at its height, Kibuka came sailing over the enemy in his cloud and began to hurl down his weapons upon the Nyoro. Some of their archers, however, sent a volley of arrows into the cloud, and Kibuka was mortally wounded. He fled away in his cloud to Mbale in Mawokota, and alighted upon a large tree, where he died. When Kibuka was wounded, he dropped his shield; the Nyoro took it, but many of them fell ill because they kept the shield. *See also:* Mukasa.

Kintu Seeking Life, Finds Death

A Dualistic God Suggests the Dualism of Man. In the movement to the contemporary age, humans frequently express their free will and thereby separate themselves from God. This is a part of the differentiation process that characterizes the age of creation. As humans separate themselves from God, they lose an essential godly quality, everlasting life. For a variety of reasons, as they distance themselves from God, they become mortal: death comes into the world. Death is sometimes the result of an act of free will on the part of the human, but it can also result from an accident, the growing distance between heaven and earth, the anger of the gods. To dramatize and symbolize the forces active during the early creative period, God is frequently depicted as a complex, ambiguous figure, both creative and destructive, the two contending forces combined within a single being. That being becomes a means of revealing the transformational processes at work during this time. In some cases, that dualism is suggested by the offspring of the creator god, a creative daughter and a destructive son, for example. 🔲 In a story from eastern Africa (Ganda/Uganda; Masai/Kenya), god and human come together in the marriage of Kintu and the daughter of God, and they move to earth to begin the new world. But along the way, they break God's command, and Death comes into the world. The children of God, Nambi and Walumbe, represent his duality, his life-giving and death sides, the two forces at large during the period of creation: When Kintu first came to Uganda, he found that there was no food at all in the country; he brought with him one cow and had only the food that the animal supplied him with. In the course of time, a woman named Nambi came with her brother to the earth and saw Kintu. The woman fell in love with him, and wishing to be married to him pointedly told him so. She, however, had to return with her brother to her people and father, Gulu (Mugulu), who was king of heaven. Nambi's relations objected to the marriage because they said that the man did not know of any food except that which the cow yielded, and they despised him. Gulu, their father, said that they should test Kintu before he consented to the marriage, and he accordingly set tasks for him. Kintu, sometimes with the help of nature, cleverly completed the tasks, and Gulu gave him his daughter in marriage, sending the couple to earth. But he warned them not to return to heaven. If they did so, Gulu's Son, Walumbe (Death), would follow them. When they discovered that they had forgotten to bring grain for the fowl, one of them returned to heaven, and Walumbe followed them to earth. Death kept asking them for their children, and they refused to give them up. Then the children began to die. Kintu complained to Gulu, who sent another son, Kaikuzi, to help them. The brothers contended with each other, but in the end Walumbe escaped and fled into the earth. From that time, Death has lived upon the earth and killed people whenever he can. *See also:* Kana, Walumbe.

Kisra, Pursued, Widens a River (Bargu/Benin) Kisra was a mythic hero. ⊡ He arose in Mecca, preaching a new religion, and was driven from there with his followers by the Muslims. In other accounts, Kisra, the head of a tiny clan, caused a great stir by refusing to accept the reforms of the Prophet or to be converted to Islam. There was a struggle, and he was defeated. With his followers he was forced to cross to Africa and eventually to traverse the continent until he came to the Niger River. Tradition connects the Yoruba emigration to that of Kisra. The Yoruba may have been a part of the clan of which Kisra was the head; they unsuccessfully attempted to persuade Kisra to lead them, and eventually went without him. Kisra's followers at last crossed the Niger at Illo, and the river was immediately afterward widened to its present size by a miracle. It is not certain who caused the miracle. It may have been Kisra, who, being pursued by Muslims, thus brought pursuit to an end, or it may have been the Muslims, who thereby prevented the unbelievers from ever returning to Mecca. When the river was crossed, Kisra expressed his intention of finally settling down. The people, who had so long held together, now broke up. Minor chiefs, perhaps the younger brothers of Kisra, founded the towns of Nikki and Illo. They still looked, however, to Kisra as their leader, both spiritual and temporal. He himself set up the kingdom of Busa, and his semi-priestly status has been handed down to every succeeding king of Busa and is largely responsible for the sphere of their influence.

Kiumbi, Angered, Retreats into the Sky (Asu, Pare/Tanzania) Kiumbi, the creator, created the ancestors and all things that they required. These ancestors became mediators between God the creator and the living members of society. Kiumbi had his dwelling place in the sky. ▣ Formerly Kiumbi had regular commerce with people. But the people disobeyed him, eating eggs that he had ordered them not to eat. They did this because they were cheated by a person whose name was Kiriamagi. As a result, God withdrew himself to a distant abode. Now the people were alone, without fellowship with God. But he sometimes visited them. ▣ People attempted to build a tower to reach God's place and thereby attain the former fellowship with him. But the higher they built, the farther God's place receded. ▣ Eventually, God punished the people with a severe famine, during which all the people died except two youths, a boy and a girl. All the people on earth descend from this pair. Since then, man's fellowship with God has been remote, and communication with him has to be sought with the ancestors who are closer to him than the living members of the society.

Ko, a God, Dances with Mortals (San/Botswana, Namibia, South Africa) Ko is the god who is below. The San had a name that they gave to God who is above them, and another to God who is under them. The former is a male, the latter a female. The male god they call Goha, the female Ko, and her attendants are called Ganna. When the San dance, Ko sometimes comes and informs them where game is to be procured, and, when any animals are killed, certain parts of them must be eaten only by particular persons. She is a large, white figure, and sheds such a brightness around that they can hardly see the fire for it; all see and hear her as she dances with them. Should a man be permitted to touch her, which seldom happens, she breathes on his arm, and this makes him shoot better. She eats nothing but bulbous roots. After Ko comes up from the ground and dances a short time with them, she disappears, and is succeeded by her nymphs, who likewise dance awhile with them. ▣ One man said that when he died, he knew that he would be eaten up by a wolf, and that would be the end of him. When a San died, they made a grave and buried him in it with his face toward the rising sun. Were they to put his face toward the west, the sun would be longer in rising the next day. Another said that when one dies, they put the assegai, or spear, by his side, so that when he arises he will have something to defend himself with and procure a living. If the living despise the dead person, they provide no such assegai, so that when he arises he may be either murdered or starved. They suppose that sometime after they arise they shall go to a land where there will be abundance of excellent food. *See also:* Goha.

Korau Discovers the Hidden Strength of His Rival (Hausa/Niger, Nigeria) Korau was a mythic hero. ▣ The first Katsina dynasty was founded by Kumayo, a grandson of the legendary Bayajida of Daura fame; he ruled at Durbi ta Kusheyi near Mani. The last chief of Kumayo's dynasty was Sanau. About the middle of the thirteenth century, a malam of western extraction, Korau, came from Yandoto, an ancient capital near modern Chafe, and killed Sanau, establishing a new dynasty. ▣ Korau was a professional wrestler and a former playmate of Sanau. He knew that Sanau was unequaled at wrestling owing to a certain charm that he wore around his waist. Though not of royal blood, Korau was a titleholder. He was invited by Sanau to a feast. Having persuaded Sanau's wife to steal this charm, Korau challenged him to a wrestling bout. The contest occurred at the traditional place, in the vicinity of the tamarind tree known as Bawada, which stood on the site of the residence of the reigning king. According to custom, the king was honor bound to accept such a challenge. Robbed of his hidden strength, Sanau was quickly thrown and, while he was on the ground, Korau stabbed him to death. The short sword with which Korau murdered Sanau is preserved among the insignia of Katsina, where it is known as Gajere. Some historians say that Korau lived about 1260. *See also:* Bayajida.

Koulotiolo Voids the Superhuman Condition (Senufo/Côte d'Ivoire, Mali) Koulotiolo was the creator god. Genesis was in two stages, the first devoted to basic infrastructure, the second marked by the presence of men. ▣ On the first day, Koulotiolo was born out of nothing, and with his divine words erected his celestial home. He lighted the sun in order to illuminate the day and created the moon and the stars to illuminate the night. On the second day, Koulotiolo let a part of the firmament fall, creating the earth and raising the mountains. On the third day, he sent rain to the earth and made the rivers run. He created the first man on the fifth day. A kind of superman who was called Wouloto, he was tall, white, naked, and mortal, but he possessed a soul called Pil. He drank only water, symbol of life. From the sixth day, the earth was populated with animals and the running rivers were filled with fish. These creatures did not yet know material want and, not knowing murder either, lived in peace. The seventh day there were many changes: trees began to bear fruit and animals to reproduce. Wouloto, for the first time feeling the pangs of hunger, tasted the fruit, became a vegetarian, and from then on was subjected to physiological laws, at the same time losing his superhuman condition. Beginning on the following day, in order to satisfy his instincts, Wouloto, tired of looking far for his food, discovered the usefulness of agriculture, invented the hoe, and became a farmer. His tools, which were first made of wood, were later made of stone and finally of iron. A great tree called *seritegue* provided Wouloto with fibers for making his clothing. In certain myths, the idea of a couple composed of two partners of distinct sex is replaced by the notion of an androgynal single person or double. The ninth day marked the awakening of the sexual instinct. Feeling lonely, Wouloto asked the creator to give him a female companion. She was called Woulono; she was as white as her husband, whom she aided in the fields and with whom she went to drink at the river when the sun went down. In order to understand each other, the two partners of this first couple for the first time used a language. Finally, on the tenth day, the married couple built themselves a house with lumps of earth and thatch, to shield themselves around their hearth from inclement weather. The woman invented the first pot to transport water from the drinking trough. Thus, the first household was founded and the first stage of creation was completed. But a good deal of work remained to be done. In this phase, events were influenced by a female being, Katieleo, a direct emanation of the original male force, Koulotiolo. On the eleventh day, a historical period opened that evolved and continues up to our time. Having mastered the principal handicrafts—hunting, stock breeding, fishing, pottery making, basket weaving— the primordial couple gave birth in the course of time to numerous children. Among these children of different colors and languages was a boy from whom later descended all the African people. Unfortunately, these children did not understand each other. As soon as they became adults, they dispersed to all corners of the world.

Kudu and the Tree of Life (Benga/Equatorial Guinea, Gabon)   ⊡   The beasts all lived in one place. Only the python lived alone, thirty miles from the others. There was a tree called Bojabi, but the animals did not know its name. Therefore, when there was a famine, they did not know if the fruit of the tree could be eaten. They sent the rat to the python to learn about the tree. The python told him the name of the tree, that the fruit was Njabi. But on the way home, the rat forgot the name. The other animals beat him, then sent the porcupine to the python. He also forgot the name of the tree, and was beaten. Then the antelope forgot, and all the animals sent forgot, even the ox and the elephant. Finally, Kudu the tortoise remained, and everyone laughed when he said he would go. His mother told him to drink no water while at sea, to eat no food on the way but only in the town. Nor should he obey the call of nature at sea, only on shore. The others did these things, she said, and that is why they forgot. Kudu went to the python, and obeyed his mother's injunctions, and on the way home he sang a song that incorporated the names of the tree and its fruit. Even when the canoe was upset, he kept repeating the name Bojabi. When he finally got home, he told the animals the name of the tree, and it is then that the animals were able to gather the life-giving fruits from the tree. The animals now declared that they had two kings, Kudu and the python, the one with wisdom and the other with skill.

Kudukese Dies Three Times (Hamba/DRCongo) Kudukese was a mythic epic hero. 🔲 Hunters move through a fantasy forest and come upon a tree containing many women. They attempt to get to the women but cannot. Then Kudukese appears. He uses magic to get to the women, and takes one of the women for himself, then distributes the others among the animals. He struggles against enemies who attempt to take his wife. He dies and is revived twice. When he dies a third time, killed by a sorcerer, he does not revive, and his wife, pregnant, is taken by his killer, who is also destroyed. Kudukese's wife gives birth to rivers, a great spider, and to Okangate, destined to become a hero: he speaks before birth, is born fully grown. His mother dies when he is born, and Okangate, smarting when he is teased because he has no mother, brings her to life. He embarks on a quest to determine the fate of his father, bringing home to his mother after each expedition animals, blacksmiths, the sun, and the moon. He has assistance from the spider. In the end, all—Okangate, his mother, the spider—die of hunger. *See also:* Lofokefoke.

Kwege's Identity Is Stolen (Zaramo/Tanzania) 🔲 A man dies and leaves his son, Kwege, and a slave, Bahati, in the care of his wife. The woman belongs to the sky clan, and rain must never be allowed to fall on her or she will die. One day when rain threatens, the mother sends Kwege to get vegetables for dinner, but he refuses. She goes, telling him that if she dies it will be his fault. When she is in the garden, a cloud gathers, it rains, and she dies. Kwege mourns the death of his mother, and he and Bahati go to his uncle's place. Kwege is handsome; Bahati, ugly. If Kwege steps over a log in the path, he will die; he must be carried over. Bahati agrees to do this, but only if Kwege gives him an article of clothing. By the time they get to the village, Bahati has all of Kwege's clothing, and he introduces himself to the uncle as Kwege, treating Kwege as his slave. Kwege is therefore made to keep the birds from the corn, and as he does so he sings a song lamenting what has happened to him: "Bahati is turned into Kwege,/I weep in the speech of the birds." His dead parents, having both been transformed into birds, see what has happened, and Kwege tells them the story. The father flaps a wing, and a bundle of cloth falls out; he flaps the other wing, and beads and a gourd filled with oil fall out. His mother flaps her wing, and food is provided. Then they bathe him and anoint him. Kwege hides all these things and returns, but he shines brightly because he has been anointed, raising suspicions. This goes on, and the uncle's son follows one day and sees what is happening. He tells his father that Bahati is Kwege, that Kwege is Bahati. They kill Bahati, and Kwege's identity is restored.

Kwoth and the Cutting of the Link between Heaven and Earth (Nuer/Sudan) God, the supreme being, is Kwoth, Spirit; God is Kwoth Nhial, Spirit of the Sky. There are other and lesser spirits, Kuth Nhial, spirits of the sky or of the above, and Kuth Piny, spirits of the earth or of the below. The name Kwoth suggests both the intangible quality of air and the breathing or blowing out of air. Nhial is the sky, and is also associated with rain and thunder. Though the sky is not God, and although God is everywhere, he is thought of as being in the sky. Anything connected with the firmament has associations with him. Nuer sometimes speak of him as falling in the rain and as being in lightning and thunder. The rainbow is called the necklace of God. The sun belongs to God, and the moon and the stars also. God is spirit, which, like wind and air, is invisible and ubiquitous. But though God is not these things, he is in them in the sense that he reveals himself through them. He is in the sky, falls in the rain, shines in the sun and moon, blows in the wind. ▣ There was once a rope between heaven and earth. When a human became old, he would climb the rope to God in heaven; there he would be rejuvenated, then returned to earth. One day, a hyena and a weaver-bird entered heaven by this means. God gave instructions that they should be watched, that they should not be allowed to return to earth, where they would surely cause trouble. But they escaped one night and climbed down the rope. When they were near the earth, the hyena cut the rope and the upper part was drawn into heaven. So it was that the connection between heaven and earth was cut, and those humans who grow old must now die. Above all else, God is thought of as the giver and sustainer of life. He also brings death.

K

Ngai ni nene.
God is great.

Ngai ni nguru.
God is old.

—Kikuyu proverbs

L

Trickster Symbolizes Contending Forces in a Transformation. God may be a divine trickster, both noble and outrageously debased, a spirit of order and a spirit of disorder, by turns creative and destructive. The divine trickster is a symbol of the transformation period that characterizes the age of creation. As he moves from the one stage of creation to the next, he embodies the changes. The move is from the perfection of God (the creative side of the divine trickster) to the flawed human (the destructive side of the trickster). The trickster can take on heroic dimensions, both hero and trickster being on the boundaries. But the trickster is forever liminal, the hero only for a time. As the creative characteristics of the trickster move to the ascendancy, that character journeys into the aura of the hero, but even as the hero takes center stage, accepting the applause of all, the trickster remains dancing grotesquely in the background, ever present, ever prepared to unleash new forms of mischief and destruction. ▣ (Fon/Benin) Legba, the seventh and youngest offspring of Mawu, the creator god, is a major figure in the Fon pantheon of gods. He is the linguist, the Fon divine trickster. He is a guardian of entrances, and has much to do with a human's personal destiny, or

Fa, who had sixteen eyes, the nuts of divination. He lives on a palm tree in the sky. From this height, Fa can see all that goes on in the world. Every morning, Legba climbs the palm tree to open Fa's eyes. Like most tricksters, Legba is mischievous, a boundary character who ignores social restrictions. His trickery knows no limits, and even God can become the target of his antics. He is amoral, his behavior lacking restraint: his activities are usually meant to fulfill his own desires and satisfy his gargantuan appetites. But when it comes to a choice, he favors humans against the gods. Often, when he has indulged in trickery, he seeks to find solutions to reestablish equilibrium. Because of this trickster's antic nature, Mawu informs him that he cannot give him a kingdom to govern, nor can he be made subject to the great energies of the universe. He is given the task of visiting the kingdoms ruled by his brothers, then to give his account of the gods: he thus becomes Mawu's linguist, his spokesman, intermediary between men and gods, between gods and the creator. But there are always questions about his moral judgment, about his sense of responsibility. He is forever unpredictable, untamed. 🄴 When God and Legba lived near the earth, Legba was always being reprimanded for his mischief. He did not like this and persuaded an old woman to throw her dirty water into the sky after washing. God was annoyed at the water being constantly thrown into his face, and he gradually moved away to his present distance. But Legba was left behind, and that is why he has a shrine in every house and village, to report on human doings to God. 🄴 In another myth, Legba, with Minona and Aovi, his siblings, makes up a funeral band, to earn cowries. They fight over the division of a single cowrie, asking three passing women to adjudicate their dispute. When they disagree with the judgments of the women, they kill them, and Legba has sex with the corpses. By means of trickery, Legba ends the pattern of dispute. In the process of their work, they encounter the King of Adja, whose son is impotent. The son asks Fa for a powder to make him virile; Legba switches the medicines, rendering all men of the kingdom impotent. Legba flees, and has sex with his mother-in-law. Three cases are therefore brought against

Legba in court: in the case having to do with the murder of and sex with the three women, Legba argues that by breaking the pattern he arrested further deaths; in the case of his mother-in-law, he insists that he thought that she was his wife. And in the third case, he himself takes the powder that he gave to the men, but he has again tricked them and switched the medicine. Then, flamboyantly, he has sexual relations with the king's daughter. Legba has crossed normal social boundaries. He has removed the potential for sexual relations from the human community; then, by restoring it, he re-creates it, ritualizing it, rendering sexual activities not an animal but a human activity, a social activity. He links sexual relations to ritual. When he restores sexual potency to the men, it is no longer the unchecked sexual activities that he has engaged in throughout the story, but a domesticated, acceptable form of sexual activity, an activity given sanction through ritual. The danger of chaos is checked, extra-social activities reined in, social institutions given their form. Legba is thus the material that is pre-order and post-order. He is the raw data that represents all of humanity, and humans experience him in the process of becoming ordered and socially acceptable. *See also:* Esu, Fa, Ifa, Mawu, Sagbata.

L

Lesa's Wife's Death Means Death for All (Lala/Zambia) Lesa (Cuuta, Lucele, Mulenga) created the world. He lives in the sky, and is spoken of in connection with rain and the phenomena that accompany rain. ▣ There was a woman with only one breast to suckle two children. This woman caused the human race to fill this world. From her were born two children, Mushili, a woman, and her brother, Lesa. The brother and sister were married, and from their incestuous union sprang good and evil. They had two children, Luchyele and Kashindika. Luchyele went to the home of his father to be given two packages containing the sun and the moon. The one who sent Lesa to marry his sister was the one who had one breast, their mother. Mushili, Lesa's wife, died when Lesa, who had gone to get wisdom, was away. When he came back, he found that his wife was dead, and that they had buried her; he told them they had done wrong to bury his wife in his absence. Because they buried his wife, he said, all people will die and be buried. Lesa went to Mushili-mfumu's, because there lived there Chaalula (Changer), Chaabala (Starter), and Chintu-mukanyo-kufwa (Thing-which-prevents-death). But things could not be changed. Lesa asked Chintu for something to prevent death, but he refused. 🔲 Dog was discontented with his lot: although he helped man to hunt game, he was just thrown food on the ground and was not allowed to share his master's food from the eating basket. He went off with his complaint to Lesa, and on the way he met other discontented animals. Elephant was discontented because she had only one child at a birth, Lion because he had to eat his meat raw. They all arrived at Lesa's village, and were listened to with sympathy, until Wagtail came and gave the game away. He pointed out that Dog ate human excrement and so was not fit to eat with man, while if Elephant increased rapidly, no one else would be able to live on the earth, because everything would be trampled. As for Lion, if he could use fire, he would set light to men's houses and kill them all. Because of Wagtail's service to man in speaking up before Lesa, he is never killed, but is allowed to hop about the village of man unmolested. *See also*: Kashindika, Luchyele.

Lesa and the Bundle of Death (Lamba/Zambia) Lesa (Lyulu, Mulungu, Nyambi, Shyakapanga), the creator of all things, is the high god, the supreme being. 🔲 The earth is flat, and the dome of the sky comes down and meets the earth at its confines. At the ends of the earth, the clouds come downward to touch the earth, and the dwarf dwellers at land's end cut off slices of the clouds, take them to their homes, and eat them as their staple food. The sun, a huge globe, travels across the dome of heaven until it reaches land's end, then it secretly travels back at night, very high up, behind a bank of clouds. On the sun are people of a different creation from humans, who have daily duties. During its night journey, when it has cooled off, they polish it to make it shine brightly, and then they light the fires, so that great heat is given out. It begins to cool down as it gets to the west. There is another army of workers who drag and push the sun on its daily journey, and yet another who take it back at night. The moon does its work by night. It too has workers, who wash it clean. Every day they cleanse it, rubbing it vigorously. The stars are the favorite attendants of the moon, who is their chief. All are round, and the twinkling of some is because of the making of fires on them. Above the dome of the sky is a great lake of water, kept back by a bank or weir. There are guardians of this lake, and it is their duty to guard the bank. The lightning is believed to be caused by the people guarding the weir. Thunder is said to be a noise made by the guardians of the weir; they shake huge metal drums. 🔲 Lesa is conceived of as living in his great village, seated on a metal throne. The village is so great that the ends of it cannot be seen. Lesa sits alone on his throne—he has no wife. All the people in the village of Lesa eat food from the great eating table of the chief, and the food is so good that if any drops onto the ground they pick it up and eat it. There is no river in Lesa's country, nor is there grass in the courtyard, which is smooth and made of metal. There is no water, only honey. Only at night does Lesa leave his throne to enter his house. There is no sleep there; sleep will end when Lesa takes the people from the earth. He sits on this throne judging the affairs of people in his country. He has councillors who assist him in these cases and watchmen who carry messages to his headmen. 🄷 Long ago, the chief on earth used to travel from place to place, but eventually he desired to settle down. He therefore sent some of his people to Lesa to fetch seeds, that he might sow them and have his own gardens. When his messengers reached Lesa, they were given some little bundles tied up, and instructed not to undo a certain one of the bundles, but to deliver them to their chief. The messengers had to sleep on the road, but their curiosity overcame them. They began to undo them. When they opened the forbidden package—the package of death—death spread abroad. Fearfully, they went to their chief, and confessed to him that one of their number had opened the little package and let death escape. And death entered the world. 🄷 In another myth about death, God sent the chameleon to the people with this message: "Tell the people that when they die they will return again." The chameleon set off on his journey, stepping slowly and deliberately, rolling his eyes around at every step. After some days, God sent the lizard with another message: "Tell the people that when they die they will die forever!" It was not long before the lizard overtook and passed the chameleon, reached the people, and delivered his message. Sadly late, the first messenger arrived with his message of life, but the people would not believe him. They hated him for his delay, and killed him.

──── ⬐ *Lesa: Man Takes the Place of God* ◪ ────

Humans, Moving into New Identities, Touch God. Humans living in the contemporary age struggle to recover a fabled oneness with God and the universe. Cultural rituals and institutions are meant to help in this regard. As people attempt to recover the primal union, they undergo ritual changes in their lives. During these reshaping periods, they are adapting new identities, casting off their old identities. While involved in this transitional period, they are marginalized, shifted to the periphery. The movement to new identity is characterized by chaos and order. 🄷 (Lamba/Zambia) A lion and a cow give birth to children, Lion-child and Cow-child. As the two children grow to manhood, they set things right in three environments—in the animal world, they overcome a lion who has killed a cow; in the human world, they defeat three old men who hold a community hostage; and in the world of God, they insist that God respond to the petitions of humans. In this movement from the animal to the human to the celestial realms, the two are gaining insights into their world, in the process rejecting the might is right dictum, and so purging themselves of any such antisocial ideals. They steadily move through the worlds, leaving the animalistic concept of the strong overwhelming the weak behind, and so they slowly move along a trajectory that leads them to godliness. To make this point even more dramatically, the storyteller has Cow-child, now having achieved his majority, take over the role of God in the end. At one point, a part of Cow-child's recollection of his mother is destroyed, suggesting that he has left that part of his world behind. Similarly, Lion-child, eschewing the idea that might is right, gives life to Cow-child rather than destroy him as his mother destroyed the cow. Order and humaneness are thus established by Lion-child and Cow-child. In the process, the links with the past must necessarily be cut, so that the initiate can move into his new state of full humanity. Change has occurred, as the creatures, Lion-child and Cow-child, move from the animal world into the human world and to the world of God. Even as these two central characters move through each of these worlds, taming the villains and making the three worlds more humane, they are at the same time purifying themselves, eliminating, through their humane acts, the animal parts of themselves, shedding their pasts, sloughing off their primal forms, moving from animal to human, from one state into a new state, and simultaneously moving the world from a world in which beings destroy one another like animals, or where humans exploit one another, or where God is a being with destructive attitudes towards humans, into a more enlightened dispensation.

Leve and the Water of Life (Mende/Sierra Leone) Leve, a name for the supreme deity of the Mende, was female, later to be supplanted by a masculine god, Ngewo, now the more commonly used term. Leve initiated the moral codes that determine good social behavior. He brings society into being, and when men cannot fulfill their proper functions in society, or when they desire to take on new functions, they are born again. Leve and Ngewo have blended into a single god. ⊡ In ancient times, people forgot god, neglecting to pray to Ngewo, not bringing a certain herb for the ancestral spirits. Then life changed for them, and they were plagued by disease and death. One night, the voice of Leve could be heard, directing the people to bring the herb, along with palm-oil rice and water for the dead, informing the living that they must pray to Ngewo. The people went out that night, seeking the origin of the voice that they heard, and they came upon a man whom they had thought dead. He was sitting under a tree covered with the leaves of the herb, and he carried palm-oil rice and a shell containing water. The people watched, as the man poured water on the ground, announcing that it was for the ancestors, at the same time asking the ancestors to care for their living children. Then he sprinkled water on the people, and ate the herbs. The villagers also ate the herbs, and from that period things improved for them. *See also:* Ngewo.

Leza and the Eternal Serpent (Fipa/Tanzania) [◨] Leza came to earth and asked who did not wish to die. Man and all the animals were asleep. Only the serpent was awake, and he promptly responded. That is why humans and all other animals die, and the serpent does not die unless it is killed. Every year the serpent changes its skin and so is renewed.

Leza and the Tower to Heaven (Ila, Kaonde/Zambia) Leza, the supreme being, is closely identified with nature; as Lubumba, the creator, he is above nature, and as Chilenga he is regarded as the grand institutor of customs. So close is the connection between God and nature that rain is given the same name, Leza. People pray to him on occasion; prayers are also addressed to the mizhimo, the ancestral spirits; the mizhimo mediate between God and man. [◨] In the beginning, a man descended from above accompanied by his mother, his wife, his mother-in-law, cattle, goats, and dogs. The women herded the cattle but used to quarrel about it. Consequently, the cattle frequently got lost. One evening, the cattle had not returned and it was too late to find them. The next morning they went into the forest to look for them, and found that they had turned into buffalo. That was the first misfortune. After a time, another misfortune arrived: the mother of the man's wife died. The woman told her husband that they must bring back her mother. The man refused, insisting she would turn up of her own accord. When the man's mother died and he wanted to go to get her, his wife refused because of his earlier attitude about her mother. That is why people die and do not return. [◨] A very old woman, in ancient times, was perplexed by the riddle of this painful earth; she set out to seek Leza and to demand from him an explanation. She was an old woman of a family with a long genealogy. Leza, being Shikakunamo, the besetting one, killed her mother and father while she was a child, and over time everyone connected with her died, even the children of her children. She became withered with age, and it seemed to her that she herself was at last to be taken. But a change came over her: she grew younger. Then came into her heart a desperate resolution to find God and to ask the meaning of it all. Somewhere up in the sky must be his dwelling. She

L

cut down tall trees, joining them together and planting a structure that would reach to heaven. As it was getting to be as she wanted it, the lowest timbers rotted and it fell. She fell with it, but without being killed or breaking a bone. She again erected the structure, but once again the foundations rotted and it fell. Somewhere on earth there must be another way to heaven. She traveled through many countries, seeking the place where earth and sky touch, to find the road to God and to ask what she had done to him to deserve these afflictions. She never found where the earth ends, but though disappointed she did not give up her search. People asked her what she sought, and she said, "I am seeking Leza." Why did she seek Leza? How had she suffered? Because, she said, she was alone, a solitary woman. How are you different from others? they asked. "Shikakunamo sits on the back of every one of us, and we cannot shake him off." She never obtained her desire: she died of a broken heart. From her time to this, nobody has ever solved her problem.

Lianja, Sprung from His Mother's Tibia, Avenges His Father's Death (Mongo/ DRCongo) 🔲 Bokele, a boy, is born miraculously: the wives of Wai were all pregnant, the pregnancy of one of them was so prolonged that she was scorned. An old woman took an egg out of the womb of this wife, and a handsome boy, Bokele, hatched. Because the world was in darkness, Bokele, with the assistance of a hawk, a turtle, and wasps, stole the sun from those who controlled it and brought it back to his community. From that same land of the sun, he brought back Bolumbu, his wife. Lonkundo, their son, died twice and was restored to life. He was taught how to build traps by his father, and he dreamed that he caught the sun. But it was Ilankaka whom he had snared, a beautiful shining woman. He married her, and her unborn child, Itonde, fully grown, left her womb at night to get food. A hunter, he caught a bird. When Itonde set the bird free, it gave him a bell called "the world," a bell that would grant his wishes. His father renamed him Ilele, and the youth became his father's successor. Ilele met Mbombe, wrestled with her, the first of her suitors to defeat her, and he married her. An ogre killed him, and Mbombe gave him life. He was killed in another fight. Mbombe gave birth to insects, birds, communities of human beings. And within her womb was Lianja, already talking—he emerged a man, armed, from Mbombe's tibia. He had a twin sister, Nsongo, shining like the sun. They leapt onto the roof, soared into the sky, and returned. Now Lianja set out to avenge the death of his father. He killed Indombe, a python, that transformed into a spirit. The twins went to a river, separating themselves from the animals. Indombe had cursed plants so that they did not grow: Lianja lifted the curse. He settled the people in their several communities, then he climbed a tree and, with his sister on his hips and his mother on his shoulders, he vanished into the sky. *See also:* Mbomba Ianda.

Libaka, Tree of Covenants (Ngombe/DRCongo) 🔲 Libaka, the sacred tree (the word means union), is a symbol of the unity of the seen and the unseen, of the living community and the ancestors who have died. When a village is built on a new site, it cannot be really recognized as a village until the chief has planted Libaka, this silk-cotton tree, in front of his house. Libaka is consecrated by hunting. At the end of the final hunt, each hunter cuts a special stick that he plants in the ground close to Libaka. They are all tied together and to Libaka with a special cane, tied with seven knots. Libaka is treated with respect. Two important covenants are those of peace and of friendship. It is essential that these covenants be made at Libaka, for then the ancestors are witnesses to and sharers in them. *See also:* Akongo, Mbokomu.

Libanza and Nsongo Move to the Heavens (Boloki/CAR) Libanza was the first man. ◙ He lived on the earth and was the first to go to heaven. His mother first gave birth to elephants, to animals of the countryside, to flies and insects, to the amphibia. Then she told Libanza to come out, but before he would do so he ordered his mother to scrape her fingernails. When she had done this, he threw out spears, shield, a chair covered with brass nails, and finally came out himself. Libanza's father was trapped and killed while stealing some fruit for his wife. He acquainted his wife with his death by causing a horn he had left her to overflow with blood. As soon as Libanza was born, he inquired about his father and the manner of his death, and set himself to punish the one who had killed him; after a series of efforts to do this, he was successful. As Libanza and his sister, Nsongo, journeyed, Libanza changed himself into a boy covered with yaws. A hunter met them and made them his slaves. Their new master was not very successful as a hunter, so Libanza told him to give him the snares—he would try to catch some monkeys. He appeared to be a weak boy covered with yaws, and his master therefore laughed at him. But he gave the boy the snares, and Libanza quickly caught thirty monkeys. While the hunters were dividing the monkeys, Libanza and his sister fled. At a large town, he again turned himself into a boy covered with yaws. The people of the town were pounding sugarcane to make sugarcane wine. A man claimed them as his slaves. Libanza told them to give him a pestle—he would crush the cane. The people laughed that so small a boy should make such a request. However, Libanza used the pestle with such vigor that it snapped in two. He broke all the pestles they had in the town except the last one, and with that he ran away. Nsongo saw a man whom she wanted to marry. Libanza changed himself into a shell, then into a saucepan, and followed the man. But the man ran away filled with fear. Libanza then turned himself into the handle of an ax, and, when the man came to pick up the handle, Libanza caught him and led him to his sister. This person had only one leg and stumps for fingers, and Nsongo, when she saw this, refused to have him for a husband. They resumed their wanderings. Nsongo saw a bunch of ripe palm nuts, and she asked her brother to ascend the tree and cut down the nuts. Libanza climbed the palm tree, and as he ascended it the palm tree grew higher and higher, until the top was hidden in the heavens. There Libanza alighted, leaving his sister down below on the earth. Nsongo, alone on the earth, heard a rum-

L

bling noise. She thought it was her brother, Libanza, scolding up above. She called a wizard and asked him how she could rejoin her brother. The wizard told her to call a hawk and send a packet with it to her brother. She should put herself into the packet. The hawk reached the place where Libanza was; when he opened the parcel, his sister emerged. Libanza became a blacksmith. There was in that country a person whose name was Ngombe; he swallowed people every day. Libanza, with molten metal, killed the swallower of people. *See also:* Motu, Njambe.

Libanza Punishes the Slothful (Upoto/DRCongo) Libanza is the supreme being. 🔲 Libanza sent for the people of the earth and the moon. The people of the moon hurried to the presence of God, and were rewarded for unhesitantly responding to God's command. Because they came to Libanza at once when he called them, they would never die. They would be dead two days each month, for rest, then would return in splendor. When the people of earth finally came before Libanza, he angrily told them that because they did not come to him at once, they would die one day and not revive, except to come to God.

Libya,Whose Son Carries theWorld (Libya) Libya was a daughter of Epaphus, son of Io and Zeus. Epaphus and Io were identified with Egyptian mythic figures, Apis and Isis. Among the children of Libya was Atlas, who bore on his shoulders the world. She also bore Agenor and Belus, mythical figures in Phoenicia and Egypt. 🔲 A queen of the land of Libya was Lamia, one of Zeus's lovers. Hera, jealous, killed the children of this union, and Lamia, in her fury, killed children and devoured men whom she seduced.

Likuube's Jealous Wife Originates Death (Nyamwezi, Sukuma, Sumbwa/Tanzania) Likuube, the supreme being, a very remote spirit, created the world. He is also called Limi (Sun) and Kilya Matunda (Creator). 🔲 He created a man and a woman who lived in Mwirunde, in heaven above the earth. They descended from there in the form of rain. They multiplied, dispersed, and populated the earth. 🔲 A powerful creator, Kilya Matunda, made all things, including stones, plants, animals—and finally two women, Nabashindi and Nashingo, whom he married. Nabashindi was clever at basket making, Nashindo made pottery. One day the two women, wanting to display their skill, produced perfect examples of their art. They called their husband to judge. Kilya Matunda, impressed with both the basket and the pot, and uncertain as to which of the two he should give the prize, decided to test the durability of the two pieces. He threw the basket and then the pot to the floor. Nabashindi, having won the contest, became the favorite wife of Kilya Matunda. She died first, and he buried her in her house, remaining there day and night, pouring water over the grave. When Nashingo brought him food, she put it in front of the door because she was not allowed to enter the house. A plant grew on the grave of Nabashindi, and when Kilya

L

saw it, he was pleased, knowing now that she had not died, that life is immortal. He left the house one day to collect fuel, and when Nashingo saw this, she entered the house to satisfy her curiosity. She was surprised when she saw the plant on the grave. She realized that it was Nabashindi, and took a hoe and destroyed it. Blood came out of the stem and filled the room.

Liongo's Fatal Weakness Is Discovered (Pokomo, Swahili/Kenya) Liongo was an epic hero. 🔲 In the city of Shanga lived a great and strong man, Liongo. He was an oppressive man, so the people decided to make him a captive. They imprisoned him, but he escaped and continued to harass the people. They again seized him, and bound him in chains. His mother sent him food each day. Months passed, and Liongo sang beautiful songs, entrancing all who heard them. People came to the prison to hear him sing. He composed songs with encoded meanings that only his mother and her slave could decipher. He sent a message thereby to his mother, telling her to put a file in a cake. The mother did this, and Liongo then asked for a horn, cymbals, and a gong: he was going to take leave of the people. He sang while others played the musical instruments, all the time filing the fetters. When the people looked up, they saw that he had broken the door down and had come outside to them. They fled, but Liongo caught them. And he continued to harass and kill people. They tried to seize him again, but he saw through their plot. They finally discovered his one weakness: his nephew discovered that Liongo could be killed if he was stabbed in the navel with a copper needle. The people gave the nephew a needle, and he stabbed his uncle in the navel. Liongo awoke because of the pain, and, taking his bow and arrows, went to a place near the water wells. He knelt down there, readying himself with his bow. And there he died. In the morning, the people who came to the wells to draw water saw Liongo, and they thought he was alive. They told his mother to speak to him, and she found that he was dead. They buried him. His grave is to be seen at Ozi to this day. Then they seized that young man, Liongo's nephew, and killed him.

Lisa, God's Son, Goes to Earth (Fon/Benin) Lisa is a creator. Mawu is one of twin creator deities; the other is Lisa. 🔲 Mawu created the earth, and after the creation retired to live in the sky from which he (Mawu is sometimes considered female) never desired to descend and return to earth. From his place on high, he saw that nothing went well on earth, and that men showed no interest or intelligence in putting to use the things on earth. They had no way of cultivating the earth, or of making cloth, or of building a shelter; they seemed to be unable to cope with the simplest problems. One day, Mawu sent his only child, Lisa, to earth. In his hand Mawu had put a certain metal that could cut. Mawu had held it like a wand when he had created the universe. He told Lisa to go to earth and clear the forests, and show human beings the use of the metal so that they might fashion tools which would enable them to obtain food, to cover their bodies, and to make shelters. Lisa came to earth with Gu, the god of metal and of war, and he cut down the trees, taught men how to make shelters, and instructed them how to dig the ground. He gave them his father's message, saying that without metal man could not survive. Lisa reestablished the world, then re-ascended to the sky and returned the wand to his father. For a reward, Mawu gave Lisa the sun as his dominion, since from that place he could watch over the universe. *See also:* Gu, Mawu, Mawu-Lisa, Nana-Buluku, Sagbata, Segbo.

Lofokefoke: The Waters Part for Him (Mbole/DRCongo) Lofokefoke is a mythic hero who appears in both animal and human form. 🄴 A hunter comes to a tree filled with women. He cannot get to them, so he sends for Bakese Bonyonga, who lives in the land of the spirits of the dead. Bakese succeeds, and also, with the help of his wife, overcomes animal foes. Bakese fights the people of Bosunga and is killed. Bosunga takes Bakese's wife. She becomes pregnant, and will eat only certain foods that Bosunga must gather. In the process, Bosunga is killed by the spirits of the dead. The wife laments the death of her first husband, and soon all who were killed by Bakese come to life. She gives birth to seven children, including Lofokefoke, the last born, miraculously born. He asks about the place where his father has died. He performs deeds that reveal his invulnerability. He kills an elephant, but it comes to life and escapes him. Lofokefoke and his brothers pursue it, until it is found dead in his village. Lofokefoke plays a game with elephants, using a tree as a bat, throwing the ball as high as the sun. When he returns home, he destroys many people. When he comes to the Lomami River, the waters part for him. He arrives in the villages of his brothers, fighting with them. He fights his senior brother, Basele, kills his sister Mangana, resumes his battle against Basele, engages in many other fights, hunts, killings, and extraordinary feats. When he attempts to destroy all hippopotamuses in the Lomami River, Lofokefoke and all of his children are killed. *See also:* Kudukese.

Loma and the Two Grains of Millet (Bongo/Sudan) Loma is the supreme being. The world and men were created by Loma and his feminine aspect, Ma Loma; he remains intrinsic to all creation. He is present in every object and creature, and manifests himself through them. Of the varied expressions of this god, Loma of the forest is the most important. 🄴 In ancient times, people lived in close proximity to Loma. This union came to an end when one of his orders was disobeyed. Loma had instructed people to take just one grain of millet for preparing food—this one grain would multiply, so that everyone would be satisfied. Then a man married a woman from another village. She brought with her a gourd full of millet. She took two grains to prepare food, but it did not multiply as usual. Loma became angry. "I told you to take just one grain of millet, but you did not obey me. From now on, food will not multiply any longer." So it is that Loma retired from the people into his village in the east, and since then people do not approach him directly. *See also:* Loma Gubu.

L

J. Stuart, *uKulumetule* (London: Longmans, Green, 1925), p. 105, and Allen F. Gardiner, *Narrative of a Journey to the Zoolu Country in South Africa* (London: William Crofts, 1836), p. 58.

Zulu Mythmakers

Loma Gubu Protects Nature (Bongo/Sudan) Loma Gubu is lord of the forest. The creator, Loma, created the world, men, and in addition to the Loma spirits, he created other Loma that are his reflections—one of them, Loma Gubu, the Lord of the Forest, plays the most important role in the everyday life of the Bongo. He created the mountains, the rivers, the trees, and the animals of the forest. ▣ Because of the way men destroy the things of nature, Loma Gubu has become hostile to them. It is Loma Gubu who decides if a hunting expedition is successful, and his anger has to be appeased if hunting accidents are to be avoided. The animals that are hunted are this god's property, and his judgment is severe if they are maltreated. Those who deal with animals in a negative way are apt to die prematurely. When a sick person becomes unconscious, it is thought that his soul has been taken to the court of Loma Gubu, where a decision is made as to that person's fate. Animals are witnesses in this court, revealing the actions of the person being tried. If the lord of the forest finds him guilty, the soul does not return to the body but appears at the court of Loma, the creator. If it is determined that the sick person's attitude to animals was humane, the soul returns to the body, and the illness ends. *See also:* Loma.

Longar Defends the Fabulous Pastures (Dinka/Sudan) Longar was a mythic hero. ▣ A man called Jiel attended a lions' dance. When a lion asked him for his ring, he refused, and the lion cut off his thumb and pulled off the ring. Jiel died, leaving an old wife with a daughter. She wept by the bank of the river, where she told Malengdit, a power of the river, to whom smallpox was attributed, that her husband was dead and she had no son. Malengdit told her to come to him in the river, to lift her skirt, drawing the waves toward her with her hand so that they might enter her. Then he gave her a spear and a fish to sustain her, and told her to go swiftly home, for she had conceived a son. She went home and bore a male child whom she called Aiwel, a child born with its teeth complete, an augury of religious power. One day, while Aiwel was still a tiny baby, his mother went out, leaving him sleeping in the house. When she returned, she found that a gourd of milk that she had left in the house had been drunk; she punished her daughter for taking it, though the girl denied that she had done so. When this happened again, the mother pretended to leave Aiwel alone in the house with a gourd of milk, but hid herself where she could watch him. She saw him get up and drink the milk. She told him that she had seen him, and he warned her that if she told anyone she would die. She did tell someone else, and she died. He left his mother's people and went to live with his father, the power in the river. When he was a grown man, he came back from the river with an ox that had in it every known color, including the color of rain clouds. This was the ox by the name of which he was to become known: Longar. Aiwel Longar lived in the village tending the cattle that had belonged to Jiel. There was a drought in the land and all the people had to take their cattle long distances to find water and grass for them. The cattle of the village were thin and dying, but those of Aiwel Longar were fat and sleek. Some of the young men of the village, spying on him to see where he watered and pastured them, found that he took his cattle outside the village; there he would pull up tufts of the grass from beneath which springs of water flowed for his herd to drink. Longar knew that they had spied on him, and when they returned to the village and told the people they died. He then called together the elders of the village and said that they should all leave their land, for cattle and men were dying, and they too would die there. He offered to take them to fabulous pastures where there was endless grass and water and no death. The elders, refusing to be led there by Longar, set off alone. Aiwel Longar left the people, and God placed mountains and rivers between him and them. Across one river that the people had to cross, God made a dike like a fence. As the people tried to pass this fence of reeds to cross to the other side, Longar stood above them on the opposite bank of the river, and as soon as he saw the reeds move as men touched them, he threw his fishing spear at them, killing them as they crossed. Then a man named Agothyathik made a plan to save them from the fishing spear of Longar. He had a friend take the sacrum of an ox that he had fastened to a long pole and move through the water, holding out the bone so that it would move the reeds. Longar darted his fishing spear at the bone, which he mistook for a human head, and was held fast there. Agothyathik seized Longar, and they were locked together until Longar was tired. He told Agothyathik that he should call his people to cross the river in safety. Some feared to do so, but to those who came, Aiwel Longar gave fishing spears. When he had given out his powers with the spears, he told Agothyathik and the other masters of the fishing spear to look after the country. He would leave it to them to do so and would not intervene except when they encountered difficulties too serious for them to deal with alone, and he would then help them. *See also*: Aiwel, Wan Dyor.

A Human Struggles with the Worse Side of Her Nature. The language of storytelling is, as this tale clearly demonstrates, universal. Wherever the tale is told, at its heart is myth. In this case, a fantasy ogre contains the emotional message of a transformation of two youths into new identities. It is not that fantasy is myth, or that the ogre is mythic; the combination of youths undergoing transition in the real world within a fantasy context creates myth. ▣ (Egypt) A king and his wife were childless. The wife pledged to God that if she had a child she would make three wells and fill them—with honey, butter, and rose water. They had a child, a boy, Yousif, and in their joy forgot the pledge. The boy grew up, and while the king slept he heard a voice telling him to fulfill his pledge. But the king forgot. And the boy became ill and no one could cure him. Then the king remembered, and the wells were built, and filled with honey, butter, and rose water. Then the king invited his people to come and empty the wells, which they did. An old woman came and, finding the wells empty, sponged drops off the walls, filling the three cans that she carried. Yousif was playing with a ball; he hit the woman with the ball and everything that she was carrying was spilled. She wondered what she could do to such a young boy, and she cursed him with Louliyya, daughter of Morgan. When he asked about Louliyya, he was told that he was too young to know. Finally, a servant told him that she was a beautiful young woman whom he would have to find. He upset his parents when he told them that he was going to quest for her. He went from country to country, seeking her. Finally, an ogre caught up with him, and when Yousif told him he was seeking Louliyya, the ogre sent him to his brother, who sent him to his brother, and on to the next brother, and finally to a sister of the ogre. If that sister had red chickens around her and was well-groomed, he should not speak to her; if she had green chickens, her breasts thrown over her shoulder, and her hair a mess, then he could speak to her. When he arrived, she had red chickens. Later, when she had green chickens, he addressed her. He told her that he sought Louliyya, and she asked why, he was too young to die. She told him to hit a ball with a racket, then follow the ball. Yousif followed it a long way and came to a great palace in the middle of the desert, a

⧫

L

⧫

tall palace with no windows or doors. He saw a small window at the top. Then a great ogre came along, singing to Louliyya, asking her to let her hair down. She did that, and the ogre climbed her hair to her window. Later, when Yousif called to her, she warned him about her father. He went up and told her that she was predestined for him. The ogre was her father, she said, and there was no escape. When the ogre came, she transformed Yousif into a pin. The next day, retransformed, Yousif and Louliyya escaped, allowing the furniture to answer when the ogre called for her. Now he pursued them, and Louliyya with a needle created a field of thorns, then a comb became a hedge of bamboo, her mirror a lake. The ogre and his dog drank the water from the lake until the ogre exploded. As he died, he threw pins at them, and Louliyya became a dog, Yousif a lark. Louliyya, as a dog, arrived at his parents' place. Yousif kept flying over the house. Yousif's mother petted the dog, found three pins in its head, pulled them out, and the dog became the beautiful Louliyya. Louliyya got sugar and attracted the lark, pulled the pins out of its head, and the bird transformed into Yousif. They married.

L

Luchyele: Footprints in the Stones (Lamba/Zambia) ⬛ Lesa, the deity, visited the earth in the beginning under the name of Luchyele. Luchyele came from the east, arranging the whole country, rivers, hills, anthills, trees, and grass. He came with numbers of people, planting the nations and communities in their respective places, and passed on to the westward. Markings on sandstone in the Itabwa plain, not far from Chiwala's village and Ndola township, are pointed out as being the footprints of Luchyele and his people as they passed. It is said that the stones then were soft like mud, but that as soon as Luchyele had passed the mud hardened, and the marks have thus been preserved ever since. Luchyele went back to his heaven, high in the sky, but promised his children he would return. When there is thunder and lightning, the Lamba say, "God is scolding us!" ⬛ Lesa sent a chameleon from heaven with a message to the earth: "When people die, they will live again." But the chameleon walked very slowly, and Lesa then sent another messenger, the lizard, saying, "When you die, you die forever." The quicker lizard reached the people first and cast them into despair with his grim tidings. *See also:* Chipimpi, Kabunda, Kashindika, Lesa.

Lueji Inherits Her Father's Kingship (Lunda/DRCongo) Lueji (Luweji, Lweshi), mythic queen of the Lunda, was a descendant of the primordial serpent,

Chinawezi, and wife of the hero, Chibinda Ilunga. 🔲 Hunters from the great lakes in the north crossed the Congo River. Kalundo, chief of that group, a man who had abandoned his own people because his claim there to the succession had been postponed, together with his followers founded a new state called Luba. Others joined them; other states came into being, including the Bungo. The Bungo were divided into distinct peoples, each governed independently by its own chief, who possessed as a mark of distinction the *lukanu* bracelet, a special insignia that distinguished lord from slave. The chiefs of these peoples were relatives; all respected the most senior, Iala Macu (Iyala Maku, "mother or source of stones"), a name given him because he had been an accomplished hurler of stones. The main residence of Iala was Nkalanyi between the Kalanhi and Kadishi Rivers. Iala, by his first wife Nkondi yaMateti, had two sons, Chinguli (or Kinguri) and Iala, and a daughter, Lueji (Luweji Ankonde), to whom her mother's name was given as a surname. The sons were idle and drunken, and the father, as he grew older, concluded that he should not confer the leadership on either of them. At one point, the drunken sons beat their father bloodily. His daughter, Lueji, cleansed and healed him. The dying Iala asked friends and relatives to recognize his daughter as his sole heir. Iala Macu then surrendered the *lukanu* bracelet to Lueji that it might be placed on the arm of the man whom her heart might choose to be the father of her sons, who would be of her blood and would succeed her. Because Lueji was young, Iala provided for councillors to assist and advise her, and to defend her from her cruel brothers. He died, and Lueji took over, became an effective ruler, and gained the affection of the people. Eventually, she was advised to marry so that the question of succession could be settled. But she could not find a man she loved. Meanwhile, the great hunter Ilunga, son of the late Mutombo, king of the Luba, was hunting, carrying with him the ornamental ax that was his symbol of authority. He and his group came upon the young women of Lueji as they were bathing, and asked them for salt. The women reported the matter to Lueji, who invited the hunters to cross the river and come to her. She had the handsome hunter sit on the stone used by her father as a throne, and she heard his story, how he intended to leave his land. He showed her the ax, and she showed him the *lukano* bracelet that she had inherited from her father. She asked him to remain there, to teach the Bungo how to use the weapons. He now had access to the bed of the queen, and he now sent his ax back to his home, to Cassongo, his elder brother, informing him that he would not return to assume the leadership. He and Lueji became more intimate, conversing daily. Ceremonial trees were planted around the stone. Convinced that the spirit of her father had sent this hunter to her, Lueji conferred with her councillors, telling them that she wished to marry him: though a stranger, he was a man of high birth, the brother of Kanioka and Cassongo, her neighbors. The councillors and her people agreed to this, fearing that Kinguri would attempt to recover the *lukano* bracelet. Cassongo received the news favorably. Because Lueji was pregnant and because she feared her brother, she wanted to transfer control of the *lukano* to Ilunga quickly. The ceremony was completed, and the senior councillor slid the bracelet on the arm of Ilunga. He was given powers in the name of the people to join all the small states into a single state under the authority of his future son who would have within him the blood of Iala Macu. He was told to teach the sons of Lueji to be brave. Lueji's son was born: he was Noeji. Ilunga ruled in Noeji's name, and the people, including Lueji, humbled themselves before him. Some of Lueji's people, including Kinguri, found it difficult to perform these humiliating ceremonies. Kinguri now set about to organize a following, and he killed those who opposed his will. In the end, he decided to leave the country, to go to a distant place and organize a powerful state that would one day destroy the state of Ilunga. He and his followers traveled a great distance. Lueji bore six sons. *See also:* Chibinda Ilunga, Chinawezi, Tianza Ngombe.

Lurubot Receives Rain-stones from God (Lokoiya, Oxoriuk/Sudan) The oldest remembered ancestor of the Lokoiya or Oxoriuk is Lurubot, who at least ten generations ago purchased Pirisak Hill from Okali of the Luluba by giving him his daughter Aito in marriage, from which time the two peoples have lived in amity. 🔲 Lurubot talked with God, who sent him down two rain-stones from heaven. The rain chief is a person of paramount importance; the rain power is transmitted in the male line, to son, brother, or nephew. The chief of the land, Oxobumiji, performs two annual ceremonies, at the time when the rain breaks and at harvesttime. God is the author of thunder and lightning; he made men, and when he pleases kills them.

Lwanda Magere's Secret Strength Is Discovered (Luo/Uganda) Lwanda Magere was a mythic hero. 🔲 Long ago, there were many battles in Kano between the Nandi/Lango and the Luo. Nandi warriors terrorized the Luo, and with each defeat the Luo were further shamed. Dignity was restored only by the emergence of the hero, Lwanda Magere. In one battle after another, this skilled warrior led the Luo to victory against their enemies. Because of his courage and prowess in war, many women were attracted to him, and he captured some of his wives from vanquished enemies. In all, he had twenty-five wives, including Lango and Luo wives. For years, he successfully led the Luo against the Nandi and Lango, and the Lango sought ways to overcome him. Lango elders deliberated long, and finally had a solution: as a gesture of peace and friendship, they offered Lwanda Magere a wife, a beautiful Lango princess. But her true mission was to discover the strength of Lwanda Magere's strength and to report this to her people. Luo elders pleaded with Magere not to accept the wife, but he refused to listen. And soon, she began to ask him the source of his strength. After much seduction, he could keep his secret no more. He told his wife that his strength in battle was in his shadow; no arrow or spear aimed at his body could harm him, even if it penetrated his shield. To protect his shadow, he always chose to fight his battles in the evening or at night. The Lango wife and spy immediately reported this secret to her people. She told them to lure Lwanda Magere to a daylight battle and to aim their spears directly at his shadow. On the day of battle, the Luo elders cautioned him about going to war. But his pride would not allow him to listen to them. Taking his shield, he led the Luo warriors to war. And the strategy of the Lango worked. The Luo were defeated, and Lwanda Magere was hit where he was weakest—his shadow was assaulted. He died on the battlefield that day. His body turned into a rock.

L

Voices that Are Nonverbal

The emphasis in mythmaking is on performance, and this means that the words, while important, are only a part of the total work. The body of the performer, the tone of the voice, movements that are both subtle and broad, not only enhance and cradle the words of the story, they play decisive roles in establishing the message of the myth. In an art form that places paramount stress on the emotions, nonverbal aspects of performance are of enormous significance. Their effect on meaning is difficult to gauge, but until the language of storytelling is fully understood, what observers conclude is message may be only a vague intimation of the true meaning. What a storyteller does is provide a conduit to the past. The reason for that is not merely to provide an experience of ancient times. The story is never isolated from the immediate world of the audience. If the performer is to be successful, she has to unify these two worlds. One way of doing that is through the rhythm of performance. Closely allied to and a part of that rhythm is the nonverbal character of performance—the body of the artist, movement that is a muted form of dance, the music of the voice, the exploiting of the tonal qualities of the language, the drama of the face, and the shaping force of the hands. All of these assist in working the audience into that channel to the past, so that what seems on the surface to be a vicarious experience becomes in fact a realistic event. There is a joining of ancient and contemporary images largely because of the silent movements, a confined ballet unifying artist and audience, and making possible the communication of a message that is, in essence, a renewed sense of order, a union between God and man.

Makeda Breaks an Oath (Amhara, Ge'ez, Tigre/Ethiopia) The kings of Ethiopia trace the origin of their line to King Solomon. ▣ Tamrin, the merchant of Makeda, Queen of Ethiopia, bringing red gold, sapphires, and black wood to Solomon, was stunned by the splendor of Solomon's kingdom and the wisdom of Solomon. Makeda decided to visit him, and she was entertained lavishly and impressed by his erudition. When she prepared to return to Ethiopia, Solomon was determined to have a child by her. He invited her to sleep in his palace, and she agreed but only if he would swear not to take her by force. He agreed, in return for an oath from her that she would take nothing by force that was in his palace. In the night, she was thirsty, saw a jar of water that Solomon had placed in the center of the room, and crept out of bed to get a drink. Solomon caught her, said she had broken her oath, and so worked his will on her: they slept together. He gave her a ring when she left, telling her that if she had a son to give the ring to him and send him to Solomon. A son was born, Solomon's firstborn son; his name was Menelik, and when he was a man the queen sent him to Solomon. But Solomon did not need the ring: the youth resembled the king in every way. Solomon tried to persuade Menelik to remain and reign in Israel, but Menelik would not. So the king anointed Menelik with the holy oil of kingship so that none but the male issue of Menelik would rule in Ethiopia. The queen had asked for a piece of the fringe of the covering of the Ark of the Covenant, and Solomon agreed. But when Menelik returned with an entourage including Azariah, the son of the high priest, that person smuggled the Ark of the Covenant out of Jerusalem. When Menelik discovered this, he was joyful. When Solomon learned of the loss of the Ark, he set forth with an army, but was comforted when he learned that his firstborn son had it. He kept the loss of the Ark a secret from the people of Israel. So the kings of Ethiopia are the descendants of the firstborn son of Solomon, the heirs of the promise that the kings of the seed of David and Solomon should rule over all the world.

Malikophu Is a Persistent Pursuer (Xhosa/South Africa) Gxam, a young man seeking work, is blinded by two of his friends when they steal his food from him. Crows, wonderful birds of God, magically restore his sight. He then continues his quest, and arrives at the home of Death, Malikophu, a supernatural fiend, who immediately sets about to destroy the youth. With the help of Malikophu's daughter, Gxam is able to fend off Malikophu's assaults. Caught between these twin forces of good and evil, Gxam moves to a new identity, as Malikophu is destroyed and Gxam becomes wed to the daughter.

Mangala Sends Man to Earth in an Ark (Mande/Mali) Mangala is the creator god. ▣ From God's egg came a pair of twins, including a rebel, Pemba, who left the egg before he should have. He moved through space, carrying with him a part of his placenta, which would become the earth. Pemba then had incestuous relations with the earth, and the earth was thereby impure. His twin, Faro, was destroyed because of Pemba's acts, his body cut into pieces, the pieces then becoming trees on the earth. Mangala, God, then brought Faro back to life, made a human of him, and sent him to earth with the original ancestors and the first animals and plants in an ark fashioned of the placenta. The ark landed on a mountain. One of the passengers on the ark was a blacksmith; he brought his hammer down on a rock, and rain came. Faro then created the world out of the seeds of the original egg, and the first people planted the earth in turn with their seeds. Faro continued the primal struggle with Pemba, his brother. *See also: Faro, Pemba.*

Maori Allows the First Man to Go to Earth (Makoni/Zimbabwe) Maori is the creator god. ▣ In the beginning, Maori created the first man, Mwuetsi, the moon. Initially, he installed Mwuetsi in the depths of the sea, giving him a horn filled with oil. When Mwuetsi told God that he wished to live on earth, Maori allowed him to do so, but warned him that death would be the result. When he moved to the earth, Mwuetsi found nothing, and he complained. Maori sent him a woman, Massassi, the morning star. God gave her fire, and told Mwuetsi that she would remain with him for two years. They went into a cave, and Massassi made fire with implements given to her by Maori. Mwuetsi, uncertain as to why God had sent him the woman, touched the oil with his finger, then touched Massassi with that finger. The next morning, Massassi was pregnant, and gave birth to plants and trees that covered the earth. The two were happy, building their home, trapping, and growing food. When two years had passed, Maori took Massassi away. For eight years, Mwuetsi mourned, as Maori reminded him of how he had warned him about moving to the earth. Now God sent another woman, Morongo, the evening star, and said she could stay two years. Mwuetsi touched Morongo with his oiled finger, but she said that he must have inter-course with her. This Mwuetsi did, and Morongo gave birth to the animals of creation. Later, she gave birth to human boys and girls, who grew quickly. Maori sent a storm, warning Mwuetsi that death would be the result of all of this activity. Morongo had Mwuetsi build a door so Maori could not see what they were doing, and they continued to sleep together against God's command. Then Morongo gave birth to dangerous animals—lions, leop-ards, scorpions, snakes. Under Morongo's guidance, Mwuetsi had relations with his daughters, and they bore children, becoming the mothers of the people. Mwuetsi became the mambo, the leader, of his people. One night Morongo coupled with a snake, and when Mwuetsi later wished to sleep with her she was reluctant. Mwuetsi insisted, and in the night his wife's snake-lover bit him and he became ill: rivers and the fruits of the earth dried up, animals and people died. The people learned that only if Mwuetsi was sent back to the depths of the sea would things improve, so his children killed and buried him, along with Morongo. Death had come, as Maori had said it would. But Mwuetsi, the moon, rises from the sea each day, pursuing Massassi, the morning star, across the sky.

Masupa's Command Is Broken (Efe/DRCongo) In the beginning there was only Masupa, a creator. He was alone. He created three children, two sons and one daughter. One of the sons was the ancestor of the Efe, the other the ancestor of the neighboring peoples. 🔲 God communicated with his peo-ple but never showed himself to them. He gave them one commandment— they must never seek him. Masupa lived in a large house in which could be heard the sound of hammering and forging. He was good to his children, and they lived happily. Everything came to them; they did not have to labor. The daughter's task was to gather firewood and water, then place them in front of the door of Masupa's home. One evening, when she was placing the water pot in front of the door, her curiosity overwhelmed her. Secretly, she tried to get a glimpse of her father. She hid behind a post so that she would at least see the arm of her father when he took in the water pot, and she did. God stretched his arm, which was covered with brass rings, to take in the pot. She had seen it—the richly adorned arm of God. But her sin was immediately followed by punishment. In his rage, God called his children and announced to them the fearful punishment they must bear for their dis-obedience: henceforth they must live without him, he was withdrawing himself from them. God gave them weapons and tools, taught them the use of the forge and other things that would be necessary for them as they went through life alone. But he cursed their sister. Henceforward, she was to be the wife of her brothers. In pain, she would bring forth children and be kept to all kinds of hard toil. God left his children in a clandestine fashion, disap-pearing downstream along the banks of the river. Since then no one has seen him. With God went happiness and peace, and everything that he formerly offered them freely went from the people: water, fish, game, and fruit. They must work hard in order to eat their daily bread away from God. Still worse, as punishment for their sins, death was brought about with the first child born of woman. As the woman was filled with anxious forebodings, she herself named the child Kukua kendi, meaning, "Death is coming." The child died two days after its birth. Since then no one escapes the avenger, Death. So it is that death came into the world. *See also:* Arebati, Baatsi, Epilipili, Tore.

Matsieng, Emerging from a Hole, Leaves a Permanent Footprint (Hurutshe/South Africa) Matsieng is the creator god. 🔲 The first human beings and animals came out of Lowe, near Mochudi, in Botswana, emerging from a hole nine to twelve feet deep in a rock in a dry riverbed. On the rock, surrounding the hole, can be found engravings of footprints of men and wild animals. These are the footprints of the first creatures; one of them, pointing toward the hole, is the footprint of Matsieng, the one-legged creator, who retired into the hole when he was disappointed with his creatures. 🔲 In some versions of the creation myth, Lowe was the creator God and Matsieng his servant; Matsieng was ordered to open the hole and make the first creatures. Later, Lowe imprisoned Matsieng in the hole and became the first Tswana chief. 🔲 In another version of the myth, Matsieng was God, and Thobega was the servant and one-legged creator. Matsieng left another footprint in another place, on a rock near the hill, Powe. The first human being to come out of the hole was a girl, Matoomyane, who had two brothers, both named Matoome and who were also created there. This girl had orders regarding the cattle. She was appointed to herd them, but her brother, Matoome, came out, and without permission he led the cattle around the end of a mountain. This so enraged his sister, who possessed medicine for the preservation of life and health, that she returned to the hole, carrying with her the precious medicine; because of this, diseases and death came into the world and prevail in it to this day.

Mawu and the Man Who Tried to Enter Eternal Life without Dying (Anlo/Ghana) Mawu (Adanuwoto, Se) is the supreme being. He is like the wind, revealing himself by what he does. His home is distant, in the sky. After death, the soul returns to its source, the supreme being. As Adanuwoto, he is a creator, a molder, giving form to a formless matter as a potter does. He first made the spiritual counterpart of the universe, and from this the material realm later evolved. 🔲 Death is the gateway to life beyond. Tsali, the deified ancestor of the Tsiame clan, was supernaturally powerful when he lived on the earth, so powerful that he sought to enter the life beyond without first dying. But he was turned back when he got to the bank of the river that separates the material world from the land of the dead. He came back and died before he was admitted into the society of those in the afterlife.

Mawu: People Wipe Dirty Fingers on Him (Ewe/Benin, Ghana, Togo) Mawu, whose name has the meanings of sky and rain, is the spirit of the firmament, the deified canopy of the heavens. He is the all-wise creator and giver of all good things. He is thought of as having human form, but he lives far away, in the invisible sky, and seems remote from mankind, though he is responsible for sending rain and for the food supply. There is a group of pantheons that, among the great gods, are divided into the sky, the earth, and the thunder pantheons; these in turn are succeeded by series of pantheons of lower orders down through the ancestral spirits, personal spirits, and powers. 🔲 Mawu originally lived very close to the humans he had created. Because he was so close, he was, as far as they were concerned, a convenient towel, and the people would wipe their dirty fingers on him. This so annoyed him that he moved out of reach of humanity. And the golden age disappeared. 🔲 In Togo, it is said that children wiped their greasy fingers on the sky when they had finished their meals. 🔲 In Benin, a woman is said to have thrown a pot of dirty water out of her house door into the face of the sky. For these reasons, the sky moved away in anger and lived in the distant place where it is today. 🔲 Men grew tired of dying, and sent messengers to God to ask that they might live forever. They sent a sheep first, but he delayed on the way. A dog was later sent to confirm the message, and he outran the sheep. But the dog gave the wrong message, asking that men might remain dead and not return to earth. The sheep tried to correct this when he arrived, but God had given his decision in accepting the dog's request, and he would not change it. 🔲 Dada-Segbo tried to obtain fire to give it to men. The fire was guarded by a giant, and Dada-Segbo sent the animals one by one to fetch it. The lion tried first, and stole the fire from the sleeping giant, but a bird gave the alarm and the giant snatched back the fire before it reached heaven. The same happened to the monkey, the elephant, and all the other animals. When the effort was given up in despair, the tortoise offered to go. Even though the other animals mocked him, he set out. The tortoise stole the fire and was pursued by the giant. But the tortoise hid the fire in his shell and the giant could not find it. The tortoise kept putting his head in his shell to warm the coal, as he does today. Finally he produced it, and God was able to give fire to men.

Mawu and the Earth That Became Unwieldy (Fon/Benin) Each of the three main pantheons, sky (Mawu-Lisa), earth-smallpox (Shapata), and water-thunder (Sogbo), has certain common characteristics. Each one is headed by deities who are androgynous or a pair of male and female twins; in each there is a youngest god who is mischievous and unpredictable. The three pantheons are alternative ways of viewing the gods and the heaven. The sky pantheon is generally considered the most significant of the three, the gods in the other pantheons being the offspring of Mawu and Lisa. Earth gods and thunder gods are the forces that deal justice to men, smallpox and thunder being their weapons. Mawu, the creator god, is the moon, mother of the gods, of the world, and of mankind, giver of souls to the newborn. Another god, Nana Buluku, had power great enough to create Mawu. 🔲 Mawu (moon, female) and Lisa (sun, male) are supreme. When there is an eclipse of the moon, it is said the celestial couple are engaged in lovemaking. When there is an eclipse of the sun, Mawu is believed to be having intercourse with Lisa. ⊡ Mawu created the universe. And as she went around creating the universe, she rode on the back of Aido-Hwedo, the great rainbow serpent who was so big he could encircle the sky. Every morning, wherever Mawu and Aido-Hwedo had spent the night, mountains stood; in whatever place the great serpent had lain coiled, the mountains rose and towered. When the world was finished, they soon saw that too many things were too big. The earth itself was too big; it was heavy. Mawu saw that it would surely topple. So she told Aido-Hwedo to coil around the earth and steady it. Aido-Hwedo coiled around the earth. Mawu told him to bear its weight, and Aido-Hwedo tightened up a little. Aido-Hwedo encircles the earth today. And to keep himself from slipping, he holds the tip of his tail in his mouth. He cannot bear the heat of the sun, so Mawu caused the sea to rise around him for his dwelling place. He arches across the sky from edge to edge and around the whole curve of the earth below. And his body lies in the sea. Once in a while, he gets tired and uncomfortable and shifts a little to ease himself, and then there is an earthquake in the world. One day he will get hungry and begin to swallow his tail. On that day, the world will fall into the sea. *See also:* Aido-Hwedo, Fa, Gu, Hevioso, Legba, Lisa, Nana-Buluku, Sagbata.

Mawu-Lisa and the Shape of the Universe (Fon/Benin) In the sky pantheon, Mawu, the female, is the moon; Lisa, the male, is the sun. Mawu is a dualistic figure, one side of its body being female, with eyes forming the moon, and bearing the name of Mawu, "body divided." The other portion is male: the eyes are the sun, the name is Lisa. The part of the androgynous figure that is Mawu directs the night, the portion named Lisa has charge of the day. ⊡ The universe is a sphere divided in two, one half fitting on top of the other. They join at the horizon. The earth is on the plane that separates the two halves, the top half of which is the sky. This sphere is encased in a larger sphere, with water between them, the smaller sphere floating in the larger one. The rains and the sea come from these waters. *See also:* Gu, Heviosio, Lisa, Nana-Buluku, Sagbata, Sogbo.

Mbegha's Transformation (Shambaa/Tanzania) ⊡ Mbegha is a mythic hero. ⊡ Mbegha was made king by the people of Shambaai. Because he was considered a supernaturally dangerous being, he was denied his inheritance. He cut his upper teeth first, and was therefore considered responsible for the deaths of his relatives. He became a hunter, and went hunting pigs with the son of a chief whom he had befriended. The chief's son was killed, and Mbegha fled, living in the open, hunting. He lived in a cave in mountains near a place called Ziai. When the women of Ziai went to gather firewood, they saw the smoke of Mbegha's fire. Mbegha told their husbands that he meant no harm, and he gave them gifts of meat, and was given gifts by the people of Ziai. He was welcomed by the Shambaa and taken to Bumbuli, where he killed many wild pigs and was given a wife in gratitude. Then he went to Vugha and killed all the wild pigs there. Mbegha arbitrated disputes, and people were impressed with his reasoning powers. When a lion attacked cows at Kihitu, near Vugha, Mbegha killed it. The Shambaa made him chief of Vugha. From his life in the wild, Mbegha was transformed, in Shambaai, into a protective prince. *See also:* Sheuta.

Mbokomu, a Nuisance, Is Lowered to the Earth (Ngombe/DRCongo) Akongo, the supreme being, is above men and above all spirits. He is associated in a special way with the ancestors, who are powerful and have an interest in the life of the people; they still form an integral part of the community. Akongo is associated with each individual in a particular way, almost in the sense of a guardian angel. He is a spirit with the qualities and characteristics of a human. The approach to him is easy and natural; no intermediary is needed. ◧ People lived in the sky with Akongo and they were happy. But a woman, Mbokomu, became a nuisance. Akongo put her in a basket with her son and her daughter, some cassava, maize, and sugarcane, and lowered them to earth where the family planted a garden. ◧ The mother told her son that when they died there would be no one to tend the garden. He must therefore have children by his sister. The son balked at the idea, but she insisted, and he finally went to his sister, who became pregnant. She met a creature who looked like a man except that he was completely covered by hair. She was afraid, but the creature spoke kindly to her and they became friends. She took her husband's razor and shaved him so that he looked like a man. His name was Ebangala, the beginner. But Ebangala was the evil power of the earth world; he bewitched the woman, so that when her child was born, it grew up under the tutelage of Ebangala, and brought evil and sorrow to men. Over time, the brother and sister had other children. So the earth was peopled. But evil persisted. *See also:* Akongo, Libaka.

Mbomba Ianda Creates the First Humans (Mongo/DRCongo) Mbomba Ianda, the supreme being, the creator, made the earth. He also made the fire, and, because he was lonely, he caused another being to grow out of the fire. They had children, two children born as one. Mbomba Ianda parted them, and they went in opposite directions. When two other children were born, they went in the other two directions. Because these spirits were lonely, they returned to their father and asked for other beings. He created others; they grew, flew, asking for places to live. God, Mbomba Ianda, was the good spirit, on the right; the spirit on the other side was evil. ◧ Mbombe, the first female created by Mbomba Ianda, and her husband, Ilele, went into the forest to hunt porcupines. She became pregnant, and ate only a certain kind of fruit, nsabu fruit. Ilele followed birds to Nsabusabu to get the fruit, struggling with those who guarded the tree, having to escape from the nets that snared him. He was caught and presumed dead by Mbombe. Then Nsongo, a girl, was born. An earlier child, a male, was Jibanza (Lianja). She then had another son, Boilenge; he quested after his father, battling with the Nsabusabu people. When he captured the king of the Nsabusabu, Nsongo married him. The brothers, Nsongo and her husband, and the soldiers journeyed, and met a man who was playing a stringed instrument. He challenged Jibanza, who, when he arrived, transformed himself into a child, telling the man that he wanted to play his instrument. When Jibanza claimed it as his own, the man recognized him. Jibanza, calling himself a king, became a man again, and led his soldiers. They traveled on, seeking enemies, conquering them. Then another Jibanza, Jibanza Jolombongo, who also had a sister named Nsongo, came along, and he defeated the first Jibanza, Jibanza Bolekunge. He lunged at Jibanza Bolekunge with a knife, and that Jibanza Bolekunge disappeared in a flash of fire. Jibanza Jolombongo pronounced him dead, but there was no grave. It rained, and they sent the first Nsongo into the rain to get water. When she went into the rain and filled a gourd, Jibanza Bolekunge appeared, telling her to break the gourd. She feared they would beat her, so Bolekunge took it and broke it. When she returned and told them the gourd was broken, Nsongo, the sister of Jolombongo, was angry, but when she raised her hand to strike Nsongo, her arm was paralyzed in the air. She asked for help, but the same thing happened to all who raised their arms. When they called Jolombongo, he raised his arm with a whip, and Bolekunge grabbed his arm and held it there. They wrestled, and Bolekunge threw Jolombongo to the earth. His sister brought him a knife, and he cut off the head of Jolombongo. Then Bolekunge and the two Nsongos and the soldiers moved on, singing. They came to Mbomba Ianda. Jibanza asked for the sun, and Mbomba Ianda sent a fly to get the sun for Jibanza. The fly failed, so a wasp was sent. It failed, and a hawk was sent. Mbomba Ianda gave the hawk a gift to present to Elima, the god of heaven. The hawk asked for the sun, Elima gave it a clock. The hawk returned to earth, gave the clock to Jibanza, and Jibanza shared it with his sister. Jibanza announced that he was now king. As they moved on t̲ ir journey, Jibanza left people behind at various places to start communities of their own, telling each the name of his nation. He then crossed the ocean, leaving people on every continent, and when he died another king was chosen in his place. That was the beginning of the people of the world. *See also:* Lianja.

Mboom Flings a Mat through the Void (Kuba/DRCongo) Mboom (Mboomaash, Mboomyeec) is a creator god. 🔲 A primeval marsh produced Mboom. The creator created through the power of his word. He began by taking a mat and hurling it through the void: it unrolled and floated, producing the earth. 🔲 Mboom and Ngaan were creators. They each ruled one half of the world. But because of a quarrel over a woman, they moved away from the world that they had created, Mboom going to heaven and Ngaan under the water. To avenge himself on Mboom, Ngaan invented evil and pestilential animals. 🔲 An androgynous gourd broke open and produced mankind. The first man and woman were let down from the skies by a rope. 🞐 Mboom had nine children, all called Woot; they created the world—the ocean, mountains, rivers, forests, stones, fish. One Woot gave an edge to pointed things and one Woot sculpted people out of wooden balls. Death came to the world when a quarrel between two of the Woots led to the death of one of them by the use of a sharpened point. 🞐 Mboom appeared in a dream to a man, Kerikeri, and taught him to make fire by friction. When all fires were accidentally extinguished, Kerikeri sold flames at a very high price. He fell in love with a princess, Katenge. She went to him, cold, and asked him to make a fire. Rubbing sticks, he did so. Then she told everyone his secret. *See also:* Woot.

Mbori Encloses the World's Creatures in a Canoe (Zande/Sudan) Mbori (Mboli, Bapaizegino), the supreme being, is all-powerful and takes an active interest in human affairs. He created the earth, air, fire, water, and animals. Mbori is involved in the creation of individuals; conception cannot take place without his tacit approval, and barrenness occurs because of him. 🞐 Bapaizegino, who is the same person as Mbori, enclosed all the world's creatures in a round canoe that he sealed up except for one hole, which he plugged with wax and marked with *mbiango* juice. Then he sent for his sons, Sun, Moon, Night, Cold, and Stars, to visit him as he was dying. When they arrived at court, they were set the problem of undoing the canoe and discovering its contents. Only Sun was able to do this, because Bapaizegino's messenger had revealed the secret to him. When Sun broke the wax, out poured men, animals, trees, rivers, hills, and grass. 🞐 The reason the moon does not die is as follows: A human corpse and the corpse of the moon lay at the side of a grave. It was said, "Let the frog and the toad jump with them over the grave. Let them jump over the grave with a corpse, and he will never die again." The frog jumped over the grave with the corpse of the moon. The toad intended to jump over the grave with the human corpse, but he fell with it into the grave. Therefore, they said that the moon would not die again, but that man would die permanently. It is for this reason that the moon continues; it comes to daylight, grows old, and changes into a little moon and rises again in the west. When the toad fell with the human corpse, it meant that man would continue to die always and forever.

Mbumba Struggles with Lightning (Yombe/DRCongo) Mbumba, the rainbow, is a water snake who works his way to the sky by climbing through trees. When he reaches the heavens, he causes the rain to stop. The skies are ruled by Nzazi, Lightning, and the earth is ruled by Mbumba. A struggle sometimes ensues between these divinities: it is a cosmic struggle between heaven and earth. 🞐 A myth recounts this epic contest between earth and the sky, between Mbumba and Nzazi; it is a struggle that has to do with the waters, waters that are both life-giving and death-dealing. Mbumba emerged from his watery residence on the earth, and went into the heavens where he visited

Nzazi. They constructed a community, but they quarreled when Nzazi insisted that Mbumba remain in the skies to become the guardian of that community. The result of the dispute was that Mbumba returned to earth to the water. Then, some women came to fish in that water where Mbumba dwelled, but the water dried up and they found him. They moved to kill him, thinking that he was a fish. He thereupon bit one of the women, and the water turned red and, like a snake, he moved out of the water and frightened the women. When they had fled, he again went into the sky, and the struggle between earth and sky continued when Mbumba and Nzazi contended over the lives of humans: now Nzazi went to the earth to take the lives of humans, and Mbumba threatened Nzazi with rain if he did so. The struggle shook the universe, as the two divinities sought to demonstrate their independence of each other. On the earth, Mbumba was assisted by Phulu Bunzi, lord of the waters. When Nzazi moved to the earth, it was Phulu Bunzi who caused him to be overwhelmed by water. It was because of this that a pact was reached between heaven and earth, between Nzazi and Mbumba, a pact devised by Phulu Bunzi. And Nzazi then returned to the heavens. So it was that a harmonious balance was achieved between the heavens and the earth, a balance developed within terms of water, with the ruler of the heavens brought under control by the being who ordered the earth. But that balance would forever be a delicate one, and it would have to be regularly nurtured. The relationship between heaven and earth would remain forever contentious, a contentiousness that was also experienced on the earth: later, when Phulu Bunzi was visiting Mbumba, his son died. Phulu Bunzi blamed Mbumba for the death, and consequently killed him and cut his head off.

Mbungi and the Head of His Wife (Boloki/CAR) ▣ Mbungi told his wife to dig and prepare cassava and cut plantains as preparation for a hunting and fishing trip. They put their goods into a canoe and set out. Mbungi dug a hole and set his traps. The next morning, he found an antelope and a bushpig in the hole. He took these to the camp, cut them up, and gave them to his wife to cook. As she was about to take her portion, her husband pretended to go and ask the forest-people if it was proper for her to eat that meat. He brought back a message that if she ate the meat the traps would lose their efficacy and ensnare no more animals. The husband had all the meat for himself and his wife went hungry. Mbungi found many animals in his traps; the woman, because of the prohibition, did not have any. One day, she made some fish traps and set them, and on her return to the camp the husband wanted to know where she had been. She refused to tell him. She went and found many fish in her traps, which she brought to the camp and cooked. Mbungi returned unsuccessful from his traps. He told his wife to bring her fish to him. But she said that she must first ask the forest-people if he could eat the fish. She brought back a reply that he was not to eat the fish; if he did so the fish traps would lose their effectiveness. Mbungi was hungry. Days passed; he caught no more animals, while his wife always caught many fish.

He became very thin and angry, and he cut off his wife's head, buried it and the trunk in the ground, and went to his town. As he traveled, he heard a voice, telling him to wait, they would go together. He saw the head of his wife coming along the road, calling after him. He cut the head into small pieces and buried it again. But again he heard it shouting. He cut it and buried it again, and again, but it was no use; it continued to follow and call after him. When he reached the town and his wife's family asked him about her, he said that she was coming. He denied their accusations that he had killed her. But while he was denying it, the head of his wife came into the town. When the members of her family saw it, they immediately tied up Mbungi, and they killed him. That is how murder was introduced into the world.

Mdali and the Chameleon's Message (Xhosa/South Africa) Mdali is the supreme being of the Xhosa people, the creator, the molder. Some said that God emerged from a cave in the east, a cave called Daliwe, meaning "creator," from whence originated his name. Mdali was the original name of the creator god, governor of all; as time went on, he became known by other names, Qamatha and Thixo, and the name Mdali has consequently been used less frequently. It is said that Untu was the first man from whom all others are descended. He is thought to be the father of Xhosa and Zulu, and he carried with him the laws of the people. ⊡ God created the first human being by splitting a reed, from which came a man and two women, who were the progenitors of the human race. ⊡ The great being, after creating man, sent Nwabi, the chameleon, to him, to tell him he would live forever. After Nwabi's departure, however, God repented and sent after him Ntulo, the quick-running salamander, to tell man he must die. Ntulo, being swifter, outran Nwabi, and, coming to man, delivered his message. Nwabi then came up and delivered his message, but man answered him, "Go, we have already accepted the message which Ntulo has brought us." And so it is that men die. *See also:* Qamatha, Thixo.

Mebege Creates an Egg (Fang, Pahouin/CAR, Congo, Gabon) Mebege is God. ⊡ He was very lonely, with only Dibobia, a spider, hanging below him above the water. Neither Mebege nor any of his ancestors had more than one offspring. Dibobia, on his web situated between sky and sea, told Mebege that they were alone, they must create the earth. Agreeing, Mebege pulled hair from under his right arm, took substance from his brain, dipped into the sea, and took out a smooth pebble. He blew on them, and an egg was formed. He gave the egg to the spider, who lowered it to the sea. Mebege said that, when the egg became hot, the spider should tell him. When that occurred, Dibobia went to Mebege, who descended and put sperm on the egg. When the egg cracked, people were discovered: Zame ye Mebege (God) on the right and Nyingwan Mebege (the sister of God) on the left and in the center Nlona Mebege (the brother of God, a creator of evil). These were the three children of Mebege. Mebege and Dibobia withdrew, leaving the world in the control of Zame, who saw only sky and water—and a bit of raffia floating on the water. He fashioned a strand of raffia into a cross, then Mebege enabled him to understand that the cross stood for the four directions. He took hair from under his arms, took the lining of his brain, and rolled them into a ball. He blew on them, creating termites and worms. He dispersed them in all directions. With their droppings, they built up the earth. The earth grew in the sea, soft at first, then it hardened, and Zame, his brother, and his sister stepped off the eggshell. Zame planted the cross, which grew into a raffia tree. Then he created man.

Meketa and the First Blacksmith's Bellows (Kono/Sierra Leone) Meketa (Yataa), the supreme being, is omnipotent. The Kono believe that once death comes all trouble is at an end. They believe in a resurrection but in no judgment after death. ▣ After Meketa made all the earth and the animals in it, there were no men and women. God came down to earth and built two houses, the doors facing each other. He made four balls of mud, two large and two small, put a small ball in each house, and fastened the doors. Next morning, there came out of these houses a man and a woman. God came to them and told them they belonged to him; he took the two large balls of mud and rubbed them, telling them never to forget that they would one day become earth again. God told them what to do and left them. Many children were born to these two. The first was a son who became a great farmer and is the father of all farmers. The second was a son who became a hunter and is the father of all hunters. The third was a daughter who learned to weave cloth and is the mother of all weavers. The fourth was a daughter who learned to fish and is the mother of all fisher-people. There were many more who learned different trades and became the mothers and fathers of all these trades. The last child was a son; there was no trade for him to follow, so he thought out one for himself, and began to make implements for his brothers: hoes for the farm, knives for the hunter. The fisher-girl went out one day to fish, and, as she came to the waterside she met a great snake, so large that it was thicker than she was. She at once killed the snake and cut it open, and a wonderful deer leapt out from the inside of the snake; it thanked her and ran off. The hunter had his nets spread in the forest, and this deer got caught in the net. When the hunter came and saw the deer and was going to kill it, the deer told him that if he killed it, he should give its skin to a blacksmith. The hunter killed the deer, skinned it, tied the skin at the neck and at the back, and went home. When he got home, the youngest brother was making knives at the fire and the hunter threw the skin down by the fireside and told his brother about the wonderful deer. The hunter was tired and he sat down on the skin, which was full of air. When he sat on it the air came out and blew up the fire. The youngest cried out at once, "Then I will be a blacksmith." This is how the first bellows was made, and the blacksmith got his trade. *See also:* Dugbo, Yataa.

Mekidech Marries the Daughter of Death (Kabyle/Algeria) Mekidech is a mythic hero. ▣ Mekidech, a dwarf and one of seven brothers, goes hunting. A young woman warns him of her ogre-mother, a death-dealing person. The trickster-hero Mekidech deceives the blind ogre, taking parts of her property from her each night. His brothers, envious, attempt to do the same, but they must be rescued by Mekidech. Finally, he takes the ogre's daughter. He is caught by the ogre and put into a pot. He convinces the daughter that she should release him, and he moves higher in the house. To catch him, the ogre piles wood, and when she is halfway up the woodpile, Mekidech sets it on fire, killing her. He brings the daughter home, and his parents are delighted, but they fear that the daughter will avenge the dead mother. Mekidech makes the daughter promise that she will change into a woman, no longer an ogre. She swears that she will do that, becomes a woman, and is united with Mekidech.

Melqart Dies and Is Resurrected (Carthaginian/Tunisia) Melqart (Melkart), a Phoenician god, chief deity of Tyre and of two of its colonies, Carthage and Gadir (Cadiz), was also called the Tyrian Baal. Protector of the mother city, Tyre, Melkart had to die annually before being resurrected.

Miseke Marries the God of Thunder (Nyarwanda/Rwanda) A woman whose husband is fighting in a war is alone and ill, and she cries out that she will die of cold if no one builds a fire for her. She prays to the thunder of heaven to help her. A cloud appears in the sky, grows, until the sky is overcast. She hears thunder in the distance, sees a flash of lightning, then Thunder stands before her in the likeness of a man with an ax in his hand. He splits the wood and lights the fire with the touch of his fingers. Then he asks her what she will give him. He asks if, when her baby is born, she will give her to Thunder for a wife. She agrees, and Thunder vanishes. A baby girl is born, called Miseke. When her husband returns, she tells him about Thunder and the promise, and the father tells the daughter not to leave the house or Thunder will carry her off. When she grows older, she is kept in the house. Now, every time Miseke laughs, beads drop from her mouth, along with brass and copper jewelry. Miseke's father concludes that Thunder must have sent the beads as gifts to his betrothed. And Miseke continues to remain inside. She is fifteen, her parents are in the garden, and her peers are going to get white ocher. She slips out of the house and goes with them to the stream where the ocher is found. As they dig, it grows dark, and suddenly a man appears, asking for Miseke. He makes each girl laugh to see if beads come from her mouth, and finally Miseke laughs and a shower of beads falls to the ground. Thunder takes her into the sky and marries her. He is a kind husband and they are happy, becoming parents of three children, two boys and a girl. Miseke wants to take her baby girl home to show her to her parents. He provides her with food and companions, and sends her down to earth, telling her to keep to the high road. But they stray from the main road, and are confronted by an ogre. They give the ogre the beer that they carry, then he eats the companions, then the livestock, and finally only Miseke and her children remain. The ogre demands a child, Miseke gives him one of the boys. She sends the other boy for help. The ogre is killed, but before he dies he tells Miseke to cut off his big toe and everything that was taken would be returned to her. The companions and cattle emerge from the toe of the beast, and Miseke arrives at her home. After a time clouds gather, and suddenly Miseke and her children and entourage move into the air and disappear.

Mkhulumnchanti Sends His Messenger to Earth (Swati/Swaziland) The Swati believe in the unbroken continuity of kinship after death and vaguely assume that eventually the wishes of men reach Mkhulumnchanti (Mvelinqangi), the first being, the great ancestor. He is never specifically mentioned in prayer or sacrifice, nor does he intervene in enforcing the ethics of the culture. Having "broken off" from a reed all things on earth, the trees, mountains, and people, and having sent death to man, there gradually intervened between him and mankind the immediate dead, who are bound more closely with the living. ▣ He had a messenger, Mlenzengamunye (Mlentengamunye), the one-legged one, who occasionally descended from the skies in a thick mist and was visible only to women and children. His appearance sometimes heralded fever, but generally he was a messenger of good news. He appeared on top of any mountain or in the form of a cloud, and people were able to see his one leg while the rest of the body was concealed in the cloud. ▣ The sun and moon are personified and mystically associated with human destiny. The sun is spoken of as a male, the moon as his wife; she follows him, is hidden from him, and then reappears. The dominant national ceremony is Incwala, a first-fruit ceremony, a pageant in which the early life of the Swati is reenacted in dramatized form, a ritualization of kingship. The king is identified with the sun at the Incwala, and his close paternal kin are honored as the Mlangeni, People of the Sun. The rainbow is called the Princess of the Sky, and lightning is believed to be caused by the Bird of the Sky, which lives in certain pools.

Modimo's Homes in the Sky and Earth (Sotho/Lesotho, South Africa) Modimo, the creator god, the supreme being, is also called Ralabepa. Of the various gods, perhaps twelve of them, Ralabepa, the father of all might and power, stands as their head. He is feared for his vengefulness and power of fire. He lives behind the land of Sewase, where he is called Ralawimpa. The god of water is Ramochasoa. He lives on the bottom, whence the fountains rise. Ramaepa watches the field, that the enemy may not cross the boundary. Other gods are Makofatsiloe, Maseletsoane, Manakisoe, Ngoalenkalo. A god who is generally known and feared is Sedatyane. Toona is the god of revenge. The god of dance is Lotiloe. Of the celestial bodies, a large comet called Modudutsa is honored. Modimo, invisible, intangible, is remote, inscrutable. Modimo is mother, is light, is in the sky. But he is also associated with the earth. The thunderbolt, appearing to enter the earth, is interpreted as Modimo returning to himself. 🔲 To an evil being known as Moremo, many misfortunes were attributed. At death, men and animals did not cease to exist; they merely left their earthly homes and went to Mosima, the home from which they all came. Mosima was another world, with pleasant green valleys, where they would live an existence similar to that followed on earth. They would cultivate the same crops and herd the same cattle. 🔲 Modimo lives in a hole, but it is not inferior to a place in the sky. Both derive their importance from Modimo's presence. This hole is the abode of the dead, where they find again the company of their kin. The earth is the place where, in Modimo, men have their beginning and meet their end. 🔲 Some say that the creator, with one leg, left his footprints on certain rocks when they were soft.

Modimo and the Origin of Death (Tswana/Botswana, South Africa) The high god is Modimo, the one who goes into the heart of the things he has created, originated, or brought into being. The Badimo are not gods equal in being and power with the one God, but manifestations of him. Like God, they are classified as impersonal, though they have personal attributes. Two of these Badimo (singular, Medimo), Cosa and Nape, are emanations of the most high God: Cosa, the god of destinies, allots to man his life; he stood at the beginning of human history and mapped out the course, together with the events, that would befall men. From this god, Cosa, the Tswana begin their course of time. He existed before the days of Bilo (Bilwe), the firstborn son of man. Nape is the manifestation of the mind of God. There are also earthbound gods, deifications of heroes of a long-gone age: these include Tintibane, child of God and child of earth, and Thobege a phachwa, who is said to have only one leg. The Badimo are not gods or demigods; they are the spirits of the dead, sometimes beneficent but generally malignant. Their leader is Dimodimo, or Dinwe. The Badimo are personal spirits, so closely connected with human life as to share in it. They live in the spirit world nearer to the gods than man. Not only are they hostile to humans, they are the undoers of the things of God, the perverters of his purposes in creation. They incite man to turn away from God, with the result that man becomes an innovator, an originator of customs that were never intended by God. 🔲 There was a cave from which the original man emerged. This cave is called Looe or Lowe, and the dweller within it was called by the same name. Lowe was also called Tauetona, Big Lion. Lowe's footprints can be found at a place called Kopong. He lived in the cave with his dogs, and around him were the beasts of the field. When he came out of the cave, he saw the animals and other created things, and many of the created things were brought into being while he was there. Authority to name them was given to him; he gave a name to all, with the exception of the snake. 🔲 A myth tells of the creation of men and women, both youths in the prime of young manhood, and women, ripe for motherhood—the males living by themselves at a place called Thaea-banna, the originating of men, and the women by themselves in Motlhaba-basetsana, the plain of the women. After the people had been created, they were asked what they wished with regard to death. Should they return after death, or should there be a going away for good? The people were very slow in giving an answer; again and again the messengers came, presumably from God. At last, an answer was sent that the dead should return. This answer was sent by the chameleon, the slow-moving one, but he spent a very long time on the road. After his departure, the people changed their minds, and sent a message to the gods by Kgatwane, the two-legged lizard. He was to ask the gods to let women live and only men die, or, if that could not be, that all should die, saying, "Let death be a resting, and let there be no return of those who die." Kgatwane hurried with his message and arrived long before the chameleon. As this was the unanimous desire of mankind, God agreed; hence, when man dies he does not return. After many days, the chameleon arrived at the abode of the gods and gave the message he had been given by man. God said, "I have already received the message from man, brought to me by the lizard, and I have agreed that man shall die and not return." So it is that death seems to end all, and man does not return to the abode of men.

Monje Ngumyu: To Meet Her Is Fatal (Tangale/Nigeria) Shoro are guardian spirits, nonhuman spirits. Wa mo mamom min gan wabi (Our town's thing which we worship) is a benevolent Shoro, one who looks after people in their habitation and influences for good the hearts of humans.   ▣   Monje Ngumyu, the Beautiful One, is the wife of Wa mo mamom min gan wabi: she is symmetrically formed, with one leg and one centrally placed breast. Her hair is done up on the crown and greased. Occasionally, she goes to the town. Her dwelling is the stony structure of Wa mo mamom min gan wabi. If anyone ever passes by her house and she meets him doing so, that person will die. She kills men.

Mosuor and Those Who Sprang from the Earth (Talensi/Ghana) The ancestor who founded Tongo was Mosuor, the paramount chief of Mampurugu.   ▣   He had to flee the country after being vanquished in a fight for the chiefship. When he reached Tongo, the Gbizug Tendaana, ritual office of the Custodian of the Earth, Genet, was living there. Mosuor came to the house but found nobody there; Tendaan Genet, having seen him coming, had fled to nearby hills. Near a stream not far away, he found a pit. Beside the pit was a tree that was shedding its leaves. Mosuor could see that someone had been carrying water that had spilled onto a path that led to the hills, so he scattered the leaves on the path and hid. After a time, Tendaan Genet came along to get water, the leaves crunching and betraying his presence. The ancestor Mosuor asked him what he was afraid of. Genet said that his gown and the red thing on his head frightened him. When Mosuor found that the Tendaan owned the house, he said that he would stay there with him. Genet would be his Tendaana to carry out the sacrifices on his behalf. Tendaan Genet told

Mosuor of his kinsmen, the Ba'at-Sakpar Tendaana, the Wakii Tendaana, the Degal Tendaana, and the Ka'ar Tendaana, the original inhabitants of the country. They sprang from the earth itself, say their descendants.

Motu, the Cloud-people, and the Origin of Fire (Boloki/CAR) Motu made a large garden, and planted it with many bananas and plantains. The fruit ripened quickly, but when he arrived one day at his garden, he found that the ripe bunches of bananas and plantain had been cut off and carried away. This theft continued, and at last he lay in ambush for the thief. Motu had not been in hiding very long before he saw a number of Cloud-people descending. They cut down his bananas, and what they could not eat they tied into bundles to carry away. Motu rushed out and, chasing them, caught one woman whom he took to his house, and after a short time he married her. She was very intelligent, and went about her housework and farming just like an ordinary woman of the earth. Up to that time, neither Motu nor the people of his village had ever seen a fire. They had always eaten their meat raw, and on cold, windy, rainy days had sat shivering in their houses because they did not know anything about fire and warmth. Motu's wife, however, told some of the Cloud-people to bring some fire with them next time they came to visit her. She taught the people how to cook food and how to sit around a fire on cold days. Motu was very happy with his wife, and the villagers were very glad to have her among them. She persuaded many of the Cloud-people to settle in her husband's village. One day she received a covered basket, and, putting it on a shelf in the house, she told her husband never to open it; if he did the Cloud-people would all leave him. Motu agreed; he was very happy, for he had plenty of people, a clever wife, and the villagers treated him as a great man. But he wondered about the basket. Foolishly, he decided to open it. When his wife had gone as usual to the farm, he opened the basket, and—there was nothing in it. He laughingly shut it up and put it in its place. When his wife returned, she asked him why he had opened the basket. Then, while Motu was away hunting, she gathered her people and ascended with them to Cloud-land, never again to return to earth. That is how the earth-people received their fire and a knowledge of cooking. *See also:* Libanza, Njambe.

Mpaca's Very Long Fingernail (Nyanga/DRCongo) Mpaca is a spirit of the forest. ⬚ Mpaca is male but often appears to be feminine, with abundant hair and long nails, and he is very thin because he does not eat. And he has the ability to change himself into a beautiful young girl. He is always evil, envious, and powerful, possessing an extraordinary sense of smell: he has the snout of an animal. He attacks women when they are alone in the forest, attaching himself firmly on their backs, forcing them to do things for him. But he always ends by being defeated. ⬚ After her marriage, a woman called Nturo quarreled often with her husband. Because she was frequently beaten by him, Nturo decided to hang herself. She came to a small village of which the forest spirit, Mpaca, was the lord. He called her name, Nturo. Then, inside his house, Mpaca leapt on her back. He had a very long fingernail, which he stretched and buried in her neck. Now she did all the work in the house, with Mpaca attached to her back. She complained about this, and Mpaca finally withdrew his fingernail from her neck. The next morning, he went to gather some wood for Nturo. While he was gone, she entered a snail shell. Mpaca returned and, finding that she was gone, stretched out his fingernail, seeking her. But he could not find her. The nail searched everywhere, and finally it came upon the snail shell and plucked out the woman. Once again, Mpaca stretched out his nail, and buried it in Nturo's neck, and she again protested. Her aunt, appearing to her in a dream, told her to prepare some beer. Nturo tempted the spirit with it. He took his nail from her neck so that he could drink. The beer bewitched Mpaca; he became drunk and fell asleep. Nturo cut his throat and returned to her family in the village.

Mregho, the Sacrifice to God (Chaga/Tanzania) Mregho, a gentle, beautiful girl, was very popular, especially with men. Girls would go together to cut grass, but, because of their jealousy, they stopped taking Mregho with them so that they could plot against her. They were also annoyed because she always carried home the biggest and best bundle of grass. One day, they asked Mregho to go with them so that they could show her a new game. Unsuspecting, she watched each girl jump in and out of a big hole they had dug. Her turn came and she jumped into the hole; while she was in it, the girls moved a big stone across it, and Mregho was trapped. Her parents were told by the girls that she had come back with them from grass-cutting and had been seen taking her usual path to her parents' house. Whenever the girls went to cut grass, they passed by the hole where they had trapped her, and they would call her name. Each time they thought she must be dead, but to their astonishment she would answer with a song. Her younger sister, Mlyakicha, started going with the girls to cut grass. They persuaded her to cut on her own while they went to see if Mregho was still alive. She always was, singing her song. Mlyakicha became suspicious. One day, keeping out of sight, she followed them. She heard them call her sister, and heard the song in answer. Later, she went to Mregho and heard the whole story from her. She could not move the blocking stone, so she told her parents. At first, they would not believe her; she persuaded them to go to the pit where they heard their daughter's voice. The three of them rolled away the big stone and helped Mregho out of her prison. She looked healthy. Ruwa, God, had sent small bees to her, and she had lived on honey. Mregho had been engaged to marry a young man called Kiwaro; he was overjoyed to find her still alive. But they could not marry until she had undergone the circumcision ceremony, which fate had delayed. While she was undergoing it, the rains failed. There was no food, and the usual sacrifices were of no help. A doctor said that Ruwa wanted Mregho to be the sacrifice, with small bells tied to her legs, to make the country fertile again. Her parents, adoring her

Bronze Head of a Spirit, Benin

yet unwilling to believe that she had not brought the drought, felt they must obey the doctor, who was the voice of Ruwa. Mregho found herself with bells tied to her legs, and she sang a song of farewell to her parents, proclaiming that she was going to the creator, to the protector. As she sang, a great storm came up, with thunder and lightning, but, although it began to rain very heavily, nobody would open a door to let her out. It went on raining, until the countryside was green again. The people offered their thanks to Ruwa. The chief explained that it had been necessary to offer Mregho as a sacrifice, and it had worked, the rain had come. In fact, Mregho's grandmother had taken pity on her that dark and stormy night, and had hidden her granddaughter in the house, taking the bells off her legs and tying them onto a sheep, which was let loose in the storm. For a time, she had to keep Mregho hidden. But soon it became known that Mregho had been too beautiful to die, and that Ruwa had accepted the sheep in her place. Mregho's troubles finally came to an end—accepted as so beautiful that Ruwa himself wanted her kept alive, she was released from hiding, and was married to Kiwaro.

A Human Finds Godly Links and Stark Reality. The reality of life on earth does not achieve the perfection of God's realm. That domain is the ideal; humans seek to recover that state. Cultural rituals are meant to enhance this process, but such rituals are not a guarantee of perfection. Tales are frequently brutally realistic, recasting traditional motifs—in this case that of a mother, symbol of life, who is, incongruously, also responsible for death. It is this paradox of the human condition, humans caught between the perfection of heaven and the flawed earth, that storytellers frequently depict.

▣ (Chaga/Tanzania) Mrile creates a child from a seed bulb, but his mother, fearing that he is feeding the child his own food, kills the child. Mrile, dispirited and against the pleadings of his relatives, leaves home, sitting on his father's chair, which wafts him into the heavens. As he moves to the realm of God, the king of the moon, he encounters various groups doing the agricultural work of the Chaga people—wood gatherers, grass cutters, livestock herders, cultivators, harvesters, water carriers. Each group shows him the way to God, but only after he has assisted them in their work. Finally, Mrile arrives at the place of God, and he gives God fire in exchange for which God and his people present him with livestock and grain. When Mrile wishes to return to earth, he asks various birds to carry to his family the message of his return. Only one bird is able to take the message, and Mrile returns to earth on the back of a bull, one of the animals given to him by God. The bull tells Mrile that he must never eat of its flesh. Mrile promises, but when his mother slaughters the bull and feeds him the meat, Mrile, not knowing that it is the flesh of the bull, eats it. He then slowly descends into the earth until he sinks out of sight. The reality of life on the earth is the mother, a dualistic person, at once life-giving, in the sense that she wants to nourish her child, and death-dealing, in the sense that her efforts result, both at the beginning of the myth and the end, in death. This dualism, the idea that the obverse of life is death, is the reality of the human condition. Rituals and traditions may move us closer to original godly perfection, but there is no assurance that such perfection will be achieved.

Mubila's Death and Resurrection (Lega/DRCongo) Mubila is a mythic hero. ▣
Yombi's many wives give birth. His most beloved wife is the most junior
wife, and she gives birth to Mubila, destined to become heroic. He speaks
before birth, chooses his own name, is born holding a spear, a knife, a
shield, a belt, and a necklace. He also has a whistle. Mubila puts his followers into a pack that he carries. In him is a mystical guide that helps him
when he needs it. He is strong and a prophet. And he can fly. He can die, but
he also can be revived. After he is born, he builds a village and, with one of
his brothers, moves away from his home and settles there. When his father
dies, Mubila accuses one of his brothers of the death and pursues him, in the
process encountering various obstacles and overcoming them. He marries
Kabungulu, who assists him in his endeavors. His struggles continue. He
marries a second wife and pursues men who have eloped with his sister. He
has encounters with various fantasy characters, faces new problems, and in
the end is attacked and killed. His son goes to get his father's body, and
Mubila is brought back to life. He then goes in search of his murderer and
his murderer's allies. The battles and conflicts both with heroic men and
with animals continue, and Mubila has the assistance of his wife and brothers. He marries a third wife. He undergoes an initiation that requires a second circumcision. He dies once again, and is, once again, resuscitated. He
regularly returns to his village of birth and confronts new problems. He
purifies his home village, and the people rejoice.

Mujaji and the Rain Medicine (Lovedu/South Africa) Mujaji (Modjadji or
Modhadje), ruler of the day, is an honorary title bestowed on the ruler or
queen of the Lovedu. She is also referred to as the rain goddess and transformer of the clouds (Khifidola-maru-a-Daja) because of her ability to produce rain. Four rulers bearing the title "Mujaji" have ruled over the Lovedu
as rain goddesses. The Mujaji line has descended from a mambo, son of the
once mighty Monomotapa of the Karanga empire in Zimbabwe. She possesses a mysterious power and medicine for making rain, and is considered
to be immortal and inaccessible. At the center of the agricultural cycle, rain
is the focus of many human interests: as the elixir of life, it is one of the ultimate bases of man's sense of security, and as a manifestation of celestial
grace, it is the supreme justification of the divine right of the queen to rule.
The chief actor in the rain cult is the queen. During life, she is not merely
the transformer of the clouds, she is regarded as the changer of the seasons
and guarantor of their cyclic regularity; when she dies, the seasons are out
of joint and drought is inevitable. Her very emotions affect the rain; if she is
dissatisfied, angry, or sad, she cannot work well. Her rainmaking is not confined to dramatic ceremonies in time of severe drought; it is conceived of as
continuous care throughout the summer. ▣ Dzugudini, a daughter of the
mambo, had to flee southward because of an illegitimate son, Makaphimo; it
was said that his father was Dzugudini's own brother. Their descendants
about the year 1600 became the rulers of the Lovedu in the mountainous

northeastern Transvaal. Dzugudini's mother stole the rain medicine and the sacred beads, and taught her daughter their value before the daughter fled with them. Initially, the Lovedu were ruled by males, among them Makaphimo, Muhale, Pheduli, Khiali, and Mugede. Mugede committed incest with his daughter, Mujaji I (about 1800), who became the first rain goddess. Her fame spread far and wide, and great leaders such as Soshangana in Gazaland, Shaka of the Zulu, and Moshweshwe of the Sotho appealed to her for rain. In the wars between the Africans during the first half of the nineteenth century, it was Mujaji's reputation that saved her people. About 1850, Mujaji I was succeeded by her daughter, Mujaji II (fathered by Mugede). *See also:* Dzugudini, Khuzwane.

Mukasa and His Place on a Rock (Ganda/Uganda) Mukasa, a god of the Ganda, sought to heal the bodies and minds of men. A god of plenty, he gave the people food, cattle, and children. He was a human being who, because of his benevolence, came to be regarded as a god. Mukasa was the son of Wanema (Mairwa), a god; his mother's name was Nambubi. His younger brother was Kibuka (Kyobe), a war god. 🕀 Before his birth, Mukasa's mother, Nambubi, refused to touch any food except a kind of ripe plantain; she would not eat cooked food. When the boy was born, she named him Selwanga. He declined to eat ordinary food, but ate the heart and liver of animals and drank their blood. While still a child, he disappeared from home, leaving no trace. He was subsequently found on the island Bubembe, sitting under a large tree near the lake. Some people saw him as they passed the place, and told the elders of the village, who went to see him and to find out who he was. They concluded that he had come from Bukasa, and called him a Mukasa (that is, a person from the island of Bukasa); this name attached itself to him from that time. One of the men who went to see him, Semagumba, told his companions that he could not leave the boy on the shore all night, so he carried him up to a garden and placed him on a rock, until they could decide where he was to go. The people were afraid to take him into their homes, saying that he must be superhuman to have come to their island. So it was decided that a house should be built for him near the rock on which he was seated, and that Semagumba should take care of him. They were at a loss as to what to give him to eat, because he refused all things that they brought to him. Finally, they happened to kill an ox, and he asked for the blood, the liver, and the heart, though he refused any of the meat they offered him. This confirmed the people in their opinion that he was a god, and they consulted him about any illness, and sought his advice when they were in trouble. Semagumba became chief priest. For many years, Mukasa lived in the house that they had built for him, and the priests cared for him. He married three wives, Nalwanga, Najembe, and Naku. Some say that Mukasa died and was buried on the island, in the forest near the temple, and others affirm that he disappeared as suddenly as he had come. *See also:* Kibuka.

Mukunga M'bura: The Killing of the Rainbow (Kikuyu/Kenya) Mukunga M'bura, the mythic rainbow, is a predatory monster who lives in water. The rainbow in the water and the sky is not the animal himself but his reflection. When he comes out at night, his tail remains in the water. When the rain comes, the rainbow puts his head out of the water and lies on his back and turns red and is reflected in the sky; at other times, he is green. He eats goats and cattle. ◘ The rainbow that lived in the Lake of Naivasha came out of the water at night and stole the cattle of the Masai, who lived in a village not far from its borders. When he had done this, not only once but twice, the young warriors prepared a reception for him—they made their spears hot in the fire and awaited his coming. The only vulnerable part of a rainbow is the back of his neck. When therefore the monster once more made a descent on the cattle, the young men carefully judged their aim and plunged their spears into his neck behind his head, and the rainbow, wounded, fell dead. ◘ In a myth, a boy herds cattle on the grazing grounds of Mukunga M'bura, who, in retaliation, swallows the boy's father and all the people, the livestock, and the homes, all except the boy. As the boy grows to manhood, he takes a sword and goes to fight Mukunga M'bura, who, fearing the youth, implores him to make a hole in his finger rather than his heart, so that he will survive. The youth does so, and everything Mukunga M'bura has swallowed emerges. The youth initially spares Mukunga M'bura, but later, fearing his evil, he goes back and kills him. But one leg of Mukunga M'bura throws itself into a pool. When, the following day, the youth goes to destroy the leg, he finds no water, only the livestock that had remained in Mukunga M'bura.

Muluku and the Obedient Monkeys (Makua/Malawi, Mozambique) Muluku, the creator, made the earth. ◘ He dug two holes; from one came a man and from the other a woman. He gave them land to cultivate along with tools, seed, and crockery. He told them to plant the seeds, to build a house, and to cook food. Instead, the man and woman chewed the raw seeds, spoiled and broke the crockery, discarded the tools, then went to the forest to hide. Muluku was annoyed. He summoned a male and female monkey, and gave them the same things he had given to the man and woman, and he gave them the same instructions. The two monkeys dug the earth, built a house, harvested the grain, and cooked it in the pots. They ate the food off the plates Muluku had provided. The god was pleased. He cut off the monkeys' tails and stuck them onto the two disobedient humans, saying that they would be monkeys from now on, and the monkeys would be humans.

Mulungu: Man and Hyena, and the Origin of Death (Gogo/Tanzania) Mulungu is the supreme being. He governs man's destiny, heals people, and controls rain. ◘ Man and Hyena had a conversation. Man said, "We want to live always." Hyena said, "You had better not, as we want to eat your dead bodies." Therefore we die, as decreed or desired by Hyena.

Mulungu and the Emergence of Life from a Termite Hole (Kamba/Kenya) The creator of all things, Mulungu gives good things to all humankind. He is invisible: it is not known what he looks like or where he lives. ▣ Of the first men, one pair, a man and a woman, came out of a termite hole. Another pair, a man and his wife, were thrown down by Mulungu from the clouds, bringing with them a cow, a goat, and a sheep. They fell down on the rock Nsaue, southeast of Kilungu, and there built a village. Both pairs had children, who married among themselves and formed new families. From some of their descendants came Kamba clans; others gave origin to the Masai, the Kikuyu. On Nsaue are seen some marks in the rock, which are said to be the footprints of the first men and their cattle; there are also said to be marks of the stool of the head of the family. The first human beings who came up out of the termite hole had various kinds of seeds in their left hands. The first seed was put into the ground in small open places. They did not understand how to work at or loosen the ground. One year, when they wished to sow again, a huge tree had fallen and was found lying over one of the small fields. With great effort, they succeeded in getting the tree away, then they sowed the field. When the crop was ripe, it was found that the plants at the place where the big tree had fallen were much more vigorous than at other places, because the soil there was looser. There were also less weeds. From this arose the idea of loosening the soil with a stick, and in this way came the digging stick. ▣ Man was originally to live forever, but the chameleon, which Mulungu sent to announce the news, lingered on the way and stammered when delivering the message. Meanwhile, Mulungu sent a weaver bird, which flew swiftly and told people that they would henceforth die and disappear like the roots of the aloe tree. Then humans began to die. But the dead continue to live in another world, a world that is similar to that of the living. *See also:* Ngai.

Mulungu and the Origin of Fire (Yao/Malawi, Mozambique) Mulungu is the supreme being, the creator. He is the great spirit of all men, a spirit formed by adding all the departed spirits together. ▣ Ntembe came to the people, and they were eager to see him. They found him sitting on a stone, and he spoke to them. They said they wanted to come and see the great Ntembe, the owner of this land. Ntembe told them they were welcome: "I have come to teach the mysteries." A serpent came along, and Ntembe twisted it around his head. Then, when people passed, they were bitten and died. Mulungu told Ntembe that he had a bad heart, he was killing God's children. Ntembe told Mulungu to take the people away and dwell with them, that Ntembe would remain where he was. Mulungu took the children then and went on high with them. They were happy with God, and Ntembe became a mountain. ▣ In the beginning there was no man, only Mulungu and the beasts. When men were created, Mulungu lived on earth, but went up into the sky because men had taken to setting the bush on fire and killing "his people," the beasts. ▣ Some say that Mulungu was not responsible for the creation of mankind. He and his people, the beasts, lived on the earth. A chameleon found a pair of humans in his fish trap—it was the first man and woman, who had blundered into the trap during the night. The chameleon reported this to Mulungu, who said to wait and see what these humans would do. The man started making fires by twirling a hard stick on a piece of soft wood, setting the grass alight. The beasts fled to the forest, and the chameleon climbed a tree. Mulungu was forced to leave the earth, but he was unable to climb a tree to get there. He therefore asked a spider for help. The spider spun a thread that reached to the sky. Mulungu then ascended to the sky on the thread of the spider to escape the wickedness of humans. Mulungu then said that when men died, they would come up to the sky. So it is that men, when they die, go to heaven to be slaves of God.

Mumbi Mukasa, the Queen with Ears Like an Elephant (Bemba/Zambia) In the land of the Luba was a king, Mukulumpe, the son of Kapopo Lapwa, Mukali wapwa bantu. He ruled his people well, and built a capital called Kalilunga. ⊡ A man brought a message to the king, about a woman with ears like an elephant. When she was asked where she came from, she pointed to heaven. The king ordered that she be brought to him. When the strange woman was brought before King Mukulumpe, he asked where she came from. When she pointed up, the people thought she meant that she had come from heaven. But that is not what she meant. She said that her name was Liulu, Heaven, that she had many brothers and sisters, all of whom despised her because they considered her ugly. Once when her family was journeying, she became lost and went to a village the inhabitants of which brought her here. She said she was Mumbi Mukasa, and she was a queen. Though she had large ears like an elephant, she was a beautiful woman, so the king decided to marry her. From that time until now, all Bemba people have believed that Mumbi Mukasa, daughter of Liulu, came from heaven and had ears like an elephant.

Mungu Casts Man Out of the Sky (Nandi/Kenya) Mungu is the creator god. ⊡ The earth and the sky were once one, until Mungu put the sky above and the earth below. God also made a small human child, and he told him to remain there. The boy grew up. Then God began to search, saying that he wanted to find someone to live with the man. He killed that man, and took out one of his ribs, from which he made a girl who grew up and bore children. God asked them why they bore children. The man said that he did not know that God had forbade them to have children. God said, "I have given you death and health." And he said, "Go."

Mungu: The Moon Is Swallowed by a Snake (Swahili/Kenya, Tanzania) The creator god, Mungu, created the heavens and the earth, and when he fashioned that earth, all was silent: the land was without life, animals and humans were absent from the scene. Water had been created: the oceans were present, and God had created the rain. Fire was produced, and the sun and moon were in the heavens. Mungu had created light, and it was from light that he created human beings; they were placed on the earth, their lives harmoniously linked to the movement of the heavenly bodies—the sun, the moon, the stars. But it is said that such harmony is sometimes interfered with when a snake approaches the moon and swallows it. It is left to Mungu's people on the earth to intervene with the serpent on the moon's behalf until it vomits her up, thereby reestablishing these harmonious relations with the cosmos.

Murungu and the Fruit of the Forbidden Tree (Meru/Kenya) Murungu (Ngai, Mwene inya) is the supreme being, the almighty, all-seer, all-giver, master of life and death, creator of all things and of man. ▣ Humans originally lived at Mbwa. At that time they did not cultivate, they did not need to eat or to wear clothes. God had created a boy first. The boy was not happy, because he had no one to play with. Then a girl emerged, and they played together. They loved each other, and bore a child. God gave them food but forbade them to taste the fruit of a certain tree. A snake, a wise creature, told them that if they ate the fruits of that forbidden tree they would have the intelligence of God. The woman ate a fruit, then offered one to her husband, who refused. The woman insisted, so he took the fruit and ate it. When he did so, his throat-apple came out; this was the origin of the throat-apple. God punished the snake by crushing its head. And he sent the mole to tell the man that all men would die and then arise. While the mole was on the way, he met the hyena. The hyena asked him where he was going. The mole said that God had sent him to tell men that they would die, then rise again. The hyena said that if that happened, what would the hyena eat? When the mole was about to go on its way, the hyena threatened to swallow it. The mole, fearful, went to the humans and told them that they would die and not come back to life. Then the mole returned to God and told him what happened, how he had been intimidated by the hyena. God told the mole that from that time he would live under the earth, far from God in heaven. And to this day, the mole lives in a hole in the earth, coming out only at night when no man sees him.

Mvelinqangi and the Sick Woman (Zulu/South Africa) Mvelinqangi, the creator, came out of the reed. He brought out men, women, animals, corn, and all the fruits of the earth. Men did not have to eat or drink, they did not die. Crops grew, but humans did not know their use. Animals roamed at will, and all were happy. But then a baby emerged, something they had not seen before. Then the mother became ill, something that had not happened before. The people, not knowing what to do, fed her corn and pumpkins that they saw growing, assuming that these would kill her. But she grew healthy and fat. The people tasted the food, and liked it. And they killed livestock and liked the meat. So they brought the more pliant beasts, the cattle and sheep and goats, into enclosures. ▣ When Mvelinqangi had finished his work, he sent two messages, one by a little stone lizard and one by a chameleon. The first message was to be delivered by the chameleon: the people would not die, they would live forever, would die but rise again. Later, he sent the lizard to tell them that they would die and never rise again. Because the chameleon loitered, the lizard passed him and delivered his message. When the chameleon arrived, the people, not knowing what death was, refused to listen to him, saying they had accepted the word brought by the lizard.

Mwari Drops Man from the Sky (Shona/Zimbabwe) Mwari is the supreme being, the giver of rain (he is also known as Dzivaguru, the Great Pool) and therefore the controller of fertility. He is both male and female, god of darkness and of light, god of the skies and of the earth. ☐ He is the creator, and is always present in what he has created. It was in the heavens that he created Musikavanhu. He caused him to sleep, then allowed him to fall from the sky. As he was falling, Musikavanhu awakened, and, looking about him, saw a stone that was also dropping from the sky. Both were moving rapidly. Mwari then spoke to Musikavanhu, instructing him to point at the stone with his finger. This Musikavanhu did, and as he did so the stone, moving at great speed, stopped. Then Musikavanhu moved to the stone, and as he did so, the stone became larger and larger, immense. Musikavanhu plummeted towards the stone, and then his speed lessened, and he moved quietly to the surface of the stone. When his feet touched it, the part that he touched became soft and water emerged. This place became known as the stone of the pool, called Matopos today, and held in sacred awe. Musikavanhu moved about on the surface of the stone, and at night he sat down near the place where Mwari had spoken to him, and he fell asleep. He had a dream: birds soared through the air, animals leapt about. When Musikavanhu awakened, what he had dreamed was reality: birds in the air, animals on the surface. Mwari then instructed Musikavanhu about what he could and could not eat: he could eat fruits and vegetables, but he must not touch the animals. And animals, too, did not eat each other. Again, Musikavanhu slept, and as he did so a snake moved over his body: he awakened, felt strange, had difficulty breathing, and his penis was to him like a snake. A voice came to him and told him to go to the pool. As he went, he encountered a beautiful woman: she was sitting near the pool, on a stone. They looked alike, but she was unable to move. The voice again came to Musikavanhu, telling him to touch her. When he did so, she came to life; then the snake moved across her body, and she felt what Musikavanhu had felt. The voice told him how he must behave, and how he must honor Mwari. And when he had completed the work set for him by God, he would return to heaven. Before he went to heaven, he in his turn instructed his children to obey the laws of God. ☐ Humans now lived in peace on this earth that Mwari had created. But it happened that Musikavanhu's children, drunk, were overcome by pride, insisting that God was dead, that one of them would become God. The voice of Mwari warned them, but they were proud. God's anger deepened, he cursed the earth: sea water became salty, the land dried up, thorns appeared. Rivers overwhelmed people during the rainy season, and crocodiles emerged. The sun became hot, animals ate one another and assaulted humans. And men started to kill each other. ▣ In another myth, Mudzanapabwe, coming from another country, stood on a rock; when he stamped his foot a cloud of dust moved into the sky, transforming into massive mountains. He shot an arrow into the sky; when it hit a rock there was a clamorous noise, the rocks became black. He shot an arrow trailing a string; it bound the rocks and created a land. Rain came, flooding the land. Mudzanapabwe shot another arrow: earth and heaven were separated. The rain ceased, plants grew; when the land dried Mudzanapabwe shot his arrow into the sky, and the rains came. *See also*: Khuzwane.

────── ⧗ Mwindo Moves to the Heavens ◪ ──────

The Heroic Side of Man Soars to the Heavens. The epic hero, mythic, belonging to the realms of earth and heaven and moving between the two, embodies the essential qualities of the relationship between God and man. The heroic epic is a majestic blending of tale and myth, heroic poetry and history, dwelling on major turning points in history, always with a towering historical or nonhistorical figure who encapsulates the turning point, linking pivotal events to tradition. The effect of the epic is to mythologize history, to bring history to the heart of the culture, to endow history with the resonant roots of the society as these are expressed in myth, tale, motif, and metaphor. The significant genre involved in epic is not history but tale and myth. As the tales take routine, everyday experiences of reality and, placing them into the fanciful context of conflict and resolution, with emotion-evocative motifs of the past, give them a meaning and a completeness that they do not actually have, so in epic is history given a form and a meaning that it does not possess unless history is seen as myth. The imaginative environment of epic revises history, takes historical experiences and places them into the context of the culture, giving them thereby cultural meaning. The epic hero, linking heaven and earth, god and human, fancy and reality, gives historical disjunction a cultural continuity. ▣ (Nyanga/ DRCongo) Mwindo, who is to become a mythical king, is the miraculously born son of Chief Shemwindo and his preferred wife. Rejected by his father, who did not want any of his wives to bear sons, the newly born Mwindo successfully escapes his father's attempts to kill him. He is locked in a drum by his father's councillors, and travels in a river in search of his father's sister, who is married to a water serpent. He is liberated from the drum by his paternal aunt, Iyangura, then returns with her to his village in search of his father. Mwindo can walk and talk from birth. He has the gift of premonition and is born with a magical scepter. On the journey home, he performs extraordinary deeds until he reaches his village from which his father has escaped. He destroys the village and sets out, in subterranean travels, in quest of his father. In the realm of subterranean beings and divinities he successfully performs many tasks, until his father is turned over to him. He carries his father home, revivifying on his way the many enemies whom he had overcome. A great council is convened in which all parties express opinions. The kingdom is divided into two parts, one ruled by the hero, one by his father. But the troubles are not finished. Followers of Mwindo, on a hunting party, are swallowed by a dragon, Kirimu. Mwindo defeats the dragon and liberates his followers. But the destruction of the dragon disturbs Lightning, a friend and ally of both Mwindo and the dragon. Lightning takes Mwindo into the celestial realms of Moon, Sun, Star, and others, where for one year the hero undergoes his final purification. He is returned to earth with warnings and prescriptions. Mwindo now rules as a glorious chief, prescribing for his people a set of rules for harmonious inter-relationships. He moves to completeness, to the state of heroism, represented by a movement from what his father represents to what his aunt represents. The symbolism of his aunt is reinforced by Mwindo's journeying in the celestial realm, after which he returns home with a command that all beings are sacred in the eyes of the gods and no human may make decisions as to his fate.

Ngalu geke lo a bie, bii bi yele woma goo.
You are like the new moon: you don't know what is coming after.

—Mende proverb

N

Naka, a Jealous God, Drives His Sister Away (Sonjo/Tanzania) Naka, a god, and his sister, Nebele, were the first beings to appear in the world. They were both creators, Nebele creating everything except man. ▣ Naka, jealous of Nebele's accomplishments, told her that she was but a woman and therefore his property. He prepared to brand her like an animal. Nebele, angry, fled to another world, and has not been seen since. Naka then created a man and a woman, whose children became the founders of all the peoples of the world. Naka gave each group one gift, whatever they asked for. The Sonjo asked for and received the digging stick.

Nambalisita, Born of an Egg (Ambo/Angola) Nambalisita was the first man. ▣ He was not born of any person, although he had a mother and father: he was born from an egg that cracked after having been in the storage basket for several days. His mother had laid other eggs, but had destroyed them. One day, when she chopped into a stump, the stump began to speak and told the woman that when she had another egg, she should not destroy it but should keep it in the granary. It was then that Nambalisita was born. When he emerged from the egg, he said that he was born of no person, that he gave birth to himself. His mother told him that she had been living with his maternal uncle but that he had been killed. Nambalisita engaged in various wonderful activities that revealed his heroic traits, and then he and his mother left his paternal home, pursued by the king of the land. Nambalisita overcame the army of the king, killing his own father when he refused to withdraw. He continued his journeying with his mother, and had various experiences as, with the assistance of various animals, he triumphed over adversities. Then he was called by Kalunga, God, who asked him who it was who boasted that he gave birth to himself. Kalunga said that he himself created all men. Nambalisita and Kalunga then vied with each other to show who was the greater: Nambalisita led his animals before Kalunga, and Kalunga revealed his great kraal of livestock. Nambalisita's rhinoceros gored Kalunga's bull. God showed off his great fields of millet and sorghum, preparing a meal for Nambalisita with two kinds of porridge. A fly warned Nambalisita to eat the dark porridge, not the light. When Kalunga shut him in a doorless room, Nambalisita called his animals, and they made a passage for his escape, at the same time filling the room with pumpkins. In the meantime, Kalunga set the room on fire. The pumpkins, when heated, burst, and Kalunga was satisfied that these were the sounds of Nambalisita dying. But Nambalisita then appeared. He left Kalunga's home, and had other experiences.

Nana-Buluku Creates the Universe (Fon/Benin, Togo) Nana-Buluku is the supreme god. The divine couple, Mawu and Lisa, owes its existence to this archaic androgyne. It was she who prefabricated the universe, leaving to her two successors the task of its completion. 🄴 To Mawu, the woman, was given command of the night; to Lisa, the man, command of the day. Mawu, therefore, is the moon and inhabits the west, while Lisa, who is the sun, inhabits the east. At the time their respective domains were assigned to them, no children had as yet been born to this pair, though at night the man was in the habit of having a rendezvous with the woman, and eventually she bore him offspring. This is why, when there is an eclipse of the moon, it is said the celestial couple are engaged in lovemaking; when there is an eclipse of the sun, Mawu is believed to be having intercourse with Lisa. *See also:* Lisa, Mawu, Mawu-Lisa.

Nangaban and the Marvelous Crocodiles (Habbe/Mali) Nangaban was a mythic hunter. The Habbe were originally a forest people, defeated and driven out of their country in the ancient wars by the invading conqueror Samori. 🄴 With their women and children, they wandered until they came to the banks of the Niger River, where a band of crocodiles came out of the water miraculously and transported them to the other side on their backs. Resuming their wanderings, guided and forced to go on by their priests, saved from their pursuers, but soon in a barren land where they underwent terrible hardships of hunger and thirst, they arrived at last at the foot of these cliffs and mountains. They camped on the slope, while Nangaban, the great hunter, with his two dogs, went ahead. He and his dogs wandered among the rocks, were lost for days and were on the point of dying from thirst when they reached a great pool from which a spring gushed, the pool swarming with crocodiles. Despite the fact that the crocodiles of the Niger had saved the Habbe, Nangaban was on the point of doing battle with these in order that he and his dogs might drink and afterward have meat for the community. But the dogs rushed into the water and began lapping it, and Nangaban withheld his spear when he saw that the crocodiles did not harm the dogs, but let them drink peacefully. He also drank, and presently bustards and baboons came to drink. These he killed, returned to the people, recounting the miracle, and led them up into the mountain, for the Habbe had reached the end of their wanderings and had come to their promised land. ▣ Establishing themselves there and beginning to explore the neighboring cliffs, they had found them inhabited by friendly cave-dwellers, a people of superhuman origin whose ancestors had had wings, and whose religion was a phallic cult with great priapic altars. The Habbe settled and remarried among them, adopted the new religion while retaining their own beliefs, built houses on the cliff tops and ledges, joined the cave-dwellers in their struggle against invading Peul, and became one people.

Nanna Tala and the Wonderful Spring of Water (Berber/Tunisia) Nanna Tala was a mythic woman from Uqatres. ▣ She quarreled with her family. Departing, she took with her a jar of water and a few dates, her distaff, and her two children. She set out and came to a place in the throat of a ravine, where she is now buried. She came to a mound and stopped there with her children. Every day, she gave them dates to eat and water from the jar to drink, and they went to sleep. In the morning, they found the dates, and the jar full of water, as before. Then she began to spin with her distaff. She dropped the distaff from the mound, down into the ravine, and a spring of water burst forth where it fell. Her relatives searched for her, and found her on this mound. They told her to come back with them. She said, "This is my country, and I will abide here. But I shall die. When I am dead, bury me here on this mound, together with my children, one on each side of me." Then she died suddenly, and her children died also. They buried her on that mound and built above her a great mosque at the very spot where her distaff fell, and they dug a large pit that became full of water and that is never dry at any time of year. People make pilgrimages to her, because she is a holy woman. They bring her offerings, slaughter goats and bullocks, and all those who come there eat of this meat, dividing the meat into equal shares for every person. If the person who assigns the portions to each person makes any mistake, the pit of water becomes red as blood, and when the color of the water changes the pilgrims know that there has been some mistake and they investigate the matter. When they have discovered the mistake, the pit returns to its former condition, and when the mistake has been set right, the water again becomes clear white, as it was before.

!Nariba Creates the Sun (|Gwikwe/Botswana, Namibia) !Nariba is the creator of all things on earth and the stars. ▣ He took fire and burned the edges of a bird's wings, then tied the wings on a tree. One wing was tied to a piece of wood with a string. On the other end of the stick, he tied a coal, also with a string. He took the whole thing and tossed it up with a stick. As it fell, he caught it with a stick and tossed it again, hoping to throw it so far it would not fall again. A third time he tossed it and it remained in space: it is the sun,

cutting the night, making the day and the night. !Nariba had created light. In the light, he went hunting, crawling on his knees, stalking an eland. But the sun heated the earth so much that he burned his knees when crawling, and he was moaning in pain. Then a !kxare tree, the first tree, sprang from the ground. He went and stood in its shade. While he was resting in the shade, other trees sprang up—all the other trees. *See also:* Pishiboro.

Nawuge: The Rope to Earth (Topotha, Nyitopotha/Sudan) Nawuge, God, lives in the sky. He decides how long a man is to live, but takes little interest in the affairs of mankind. ⊡ Long ago, all the people lived up above with Nawuge. One day, a bird flew up from earth to heaven, carrying in its beak a long rope. The rope was seized by the people, who started sliding down it until they reached the earth, where they found grass and trees, cattle and sheep. They milked the cattle and liked the taste of the milk. A lot of people came down the rope, but some remained above. Presently, a woman who was near her time with twins tried to slide down, but the rope broke and some people were left above and some on earth. ⊡ Sacred fire-making plays an important part in Topotha ritual. Fire-makers have sacred fire sticks that are handed down from father to son. Fire-makers accompany fighting expeditions. When the party arrives near its objective, the warriors are halted and the fire-makers make a fire on the path leading to the attack. The column tramps through the fire until it is extinguished, and once he has passed through it on no account is a warrior allowed to look over his shoulder. The same ceremony is observed during hunting expeditions. In times of emergency, drought, sickness, cattle plague, rainmakers attend the council of the elders. They make the fire in which the sacrificed animal is burned.

Ndahura and the Bird that Blazed in the Dark (Nyoro/Uganda) Ndahura was a mythic hero. ⊡ When Isimbwa grew up, he married in the world of spirits and had a son called Kyomya. Unlike his father, Isimbwa could visit the world of living men, and on a hunting expedition he came to the capital, where a man named Bukuku reigned. He was unpopular, because he was a commoner and had no real right to rule, but there was no one else to do so. He had a daughter called Nyinamwiru, and when she was born diviners had told Bukuku that he would have reason to fear any child that she might bear. He therefore kept her in an enclosure that could only be entered through his own well-guarded palace. Isimbwa reached Bukuku's capital and was intrigued by this. He sent secret messages to Nyinamwiru through her maid, then climbed into her enclosure and, unknown to Bukuku, stayed there for three months. Then he left the kingdom and was not seen again for many years. In time, Nyinamwiru bore a son, to the consternation of Bukuku, who gave orders for the child to be drowned. The baby was thrown in a river, but by chance its umbilical cord caught in a bush, and the child was discovered by a potter, Rubumbi, who took it home and brought it up as a member of his family. He knew that it was Nyinamwiru's child, and he told

her that it was safe. Bukuku believed it to be dead. The boy, strong and spir-
ited, was constantly in trouble with Bukuku's herdsmen; when the king's
cattle were being watered he would drive them away, so that he could water
Rubumbi's cattle first. This angered Bukuku, who one day came to the
drinking trough himself to punish the unruly potter's son. But before
Bukuku's men could carry out his orders to seize and beat him, he rushed
around to the back of Bukuku's royal stool and stabbed him mortally with
his spear. He then sat down on the king's stool. The herdsmen were aghast,
and ran at once to tell Nyinamwiru what had happened. She was both glad
and sorry—glad because her son had taken the throne, sorry because of her
father's death. So Ndahura, which is what the young man was called, came to
his grandfather Isaza's throne: he is the first of the Chwezi kings. ▣ The
ancestors of the Bahweju originated from Karagwe in Tanzania, and they
entered Nkore through Mpororo. As they came into the country, a bird
descended from heaven and lighted on one of them. At that time, there was in
the land a clan of people called Abarara, who were seers and prophets. They
told the Bahweju to follow the bird wherever it would lead them, that it was a
sign that a kingdom awaited them. They followed the bird then, and it led
them. They followed it day and night, for it blazed in the dark. It led them from
Mpororo, through Buhweju and Toro, to Bunyoro, and there it disappeared. So
they went to King Ndahura of the Bachwezi. They had with them their sister, a
girl of great beauty. When King Ndahura saw her, he wanted to marry her. Her
brothers consented, and she was married to King Ndahura. In return, he gave
them this land. See also: Chwezi, Nyamiyonga, Ruhanga, Wamara.

Nehoreka Learns His Enemy's Secret (Shona/Zimbabwe) The Budya, a Shona-
speaking people, came from Mingare. ▣ The father of the Budya was
Nehoreka. He wanted to migrate, because there was no water in his land. He
and other men went in search of a better country. They passed through
many countries, and finally reached a country that was ruled by Makate. It
was fine, arable land, with much water. Nehoreka returned to Mingare, and
prepared his people to migrate. But because Makate's people outnumbered
his, he married a daughter of Dzivaguru, the leader of Choma, a man who
had power over the rain. Dzivaguru agreed to help him, but asked for a place
in the new land for his own family. Nehoreka took his army and moved to
Makate's land. The people were struck by the beauty of that land. Makate, no
fool, prepared for an invasion. When Nehoreka's people attacked, Makate's
armies rolled rocks on them and forced them to retreat. Nehoreka, defeated,
refused to return to Mingare. He knew that Makate had supernatural powers,
powers over lightning, wind, water. So he asked his beautiful sister to marry
Makate. Makate was pleased with her, and over time he came to love her so
deeply that he told her all his secrets, not realizing that a trap was being set.
Nehoreka's sister took the horns and magical paraphernalia of her husband
and returned to Nehoreka, who once again took his people to war on
Makate. When Makate saw that his magical horns were gone, he knew that

he could not win, so he departed with his people. When Nehoreka arrived, the houses were deserted, flies were buzzing everywhere. Makate came to a great rock floor. He took a tail-switch and hit the ground, and the rock floor opened and all his people went in, disappearing into the earth. The only clue as to the entrance in this rock floor was a hoe beaten into the rock. No one could remove the hoe. In the meantime, Makate and his people moved into a new and better country. The footprints of Makate's family and those of his livestock are still on the rock.

Neith Creates Light from Her Eyes (Egypt) Neith (Net) was the mother goddess, the national goddess of Lower Egypt, a great hunter whose symbol was a crossed bow and arrows. She always had a separate existence, was never paired with any male god. She was a creator goddess who formed all things. In the beginning, she found herself in the watery waste of Nun, and she formed herself when the world was still in shadow and when there was no earth on which to rest, when no plant grew. She first appeared as a divine cow, then as a Nile perch, more suitable to the watery environment, and went on her way. She created light from her eyes, then said this place where she was would become for her a platform of earth supported upon the primeval waters upon which she might rest. And it was so. ◧ The next to emerge was the land of Egypt. Neith, having created the thirty gods by pronouncing their names, then called in a loud voice to all that she had created and they came to her in a spirit of joy and happiness. But Ra, who could not see her, wept, and men sprang from the tears in his eyes. The gods rested in their shrines and guarded Ra in his place, his cabin on the solar boat. At the same time as Ra was born, Apopi was created, a serpent 120 cubits long: Apopi would become the core of the revolt against Ra, so that there would be then and forever a struggle between good and evil. *See also:* Horus, Isis, Osiris, Ra.

Ngai and the Message of Life (Kamba/Kenya) Ngai (Engai, Mulungu, Mumbi), the supreme being, dwells in the skies an indefinite distance away; he is well-disposed toward human beings, but beyond that has nothing to do with them. Ngai is in the sun. Prayers, especially for rain, are sometimes addressed to him. The original ancestor, Mulungu created the first men: the maker, he existed before death came into the world. He is thought to dwell in the sky among the clouds, while the Aimu, spirits, dwell in the earth or upon it. ◧ The first men are said to have been thrown from heaven onto a mountain in Kilungu district in southern Ulu. ◧ A frog, a chameleon, and a thrush were sent by Ngai to search for human beings: they would die one day and come to life again the next. The chameleon was in those days a very important person, and he led the way. They went on their mission, and presently the chameleon saw some people lying apparently dead. As they approached the corpses, he called out to them softly. The bird asked what he was making that noise for. The chameleon said he was calling the people who have gone forward to come back. The bird said that it was impossible to find people who come back to life. But the chameleon said it was possible, pointing out that he himself goes forward and comes back—referring to the movements of his body. The three reached the spot where the dead people were lying, and in response to the calling of the chameleon they opened their eyes and listened to him. But the bird told them that they were dead and must remain dead; they would not rise to life again. The bird then flew away, and the frog and the chameleon stayed behind. The chameleon told the dead that he was sent by Ngai to raise them, they should not believe the lies of the bird. But the spell was broken, his entreaties were of no avail. They returned to Ngai, and the chameleon told him what had happened. Ngai asked the bird if this was so, and the bird said that the chameleon was making such a mess of his errand that he felt obliged to interrupt him. Ngai believed the story of the bird, and, vexed with the way the chameleon had executed his commands, reduced him from his high estate, ordaining that ever after he would only be able to walk very, very slowly, and should never have any teeth. The bird came into high favor, Ngai delegating to him the work of waking up the inhabitants of the world. The thrush therefore to this day wakes up and calls out about 2 A.M., whereas the other birds awaken at only about 4 A.M. 🔲 A young man asked his father for livestock for a dowry. When his father refused, the youth ascended to the heavens, as his father watched. He remained there two days, and on the third he returned to earth. But the father agreed to provide livestock only at the end of the year. Not satisfied with this, the youth charged at a rock, hit it with his head, and disappeared into the rock. Then he again returned and asked his father for livestock. His father agreed, and the youth took all his father's cattle except for one cow. *See also:* Mulungu.

Ngai Saves an Old Man from Starvation (Kikuyu/Kenya) There is one God, Ngai (Mugai, Murungu, Mwenenyaga, Muikumbania, Maagu, Githuku), the creator and giver of all things. He has no father, mother, or companion of any kind. His work is done in solitude. He loves or hates people according to their behavior. The creator lives in the sky but has temporary homes on earth, situated on mountains, where he may rest during his visits. Ngai is a distant being and takes little interest in individuals in their daily walks of life. Yet at the crises of their lives he is invariably called upon. At the birth, initiation, marriage, and death of every Kikuyu, communication is established on his behalf with Ngai. Ngai, not visible to mortal eyes, manifests himself in various ways: the sun, the moon, the stars, rain, rainbow, lightning, and thunder are looked upon as manifestations of his powers. Through these signs, he expresses his love or hatred. 🔲 In prayers and sacrifices, Ngai is addressed by the Kikuyu as Mwene-Nyaga, possessor of brightness. This name is associated with Kere-Nyaga, Mount Kenya, a phrase that refers to that which possesses brightness. The mountain of brightness is believed to be Ngai's official resting place, and when people pray they turn toward Kere-Nyaga. The Kikuyu are descendants of an old man and his wife, who came to the present country from the other side of the great mountain of Kenya. While they were on the slopes of the mountain, they were on the point of starvation, and the old man went up the summit to see Ngai, who dwells there. Ngai on that occasion gave him sheep and goats, and from that gift all the flocks of today are descended. Ngai told the old man that his descendants should occupy the present Kikuyu country, and that they should live by tillage; that the Masai should hold the plains, and should have flocks and herds; that the portion of the Dorobo should be the wild game of the wilderness and nothing else. ▣ In the beginning, all the people of the earth were immortal. Long ago, the great god Ngai sent the chameleon to assure the people of the earth that they would never die. But when the chameleon left, Ngai changed his mind. He summoned a bird, and told him to go quickly and proclaim to all the people of the earth that they shall die, and never return. The bird flew swiftly and arrived on earth to hear the chameleon hesitantly stammering the message. Without hesitation, the bird proclaimed the divine message: "The great god has said that all men shall die and shall never return." The chameleon had stammered too long and had failed to announce its message. That is why all men must die.

Ngewo, Lonely, Creates a Man and a Woman (Mende/Sierra Leone) Ngewo is the supreme being, the creator of the universe. He created man, the animals and fishes, as well as the trees and plants. The more common of the two names of God is Ngewo; the other name, Leve, seems to be more ancient. In ancient times, the Mende may have conceived of Leve as the female deity consort of Ngewo, forming the feminine half of a cosmic creator couple. Ngewo or Leve, chief and father protector, is transcendent, living away from the everyday activities of this world. ▣ Ngewo was once a very big spirit who lived in a cave. He was so powerful that all he said would be done took place. But he lived alone with no one to talk to or to play with. So he went to the entrance of the cave and said, "I want all kinds of animals to live with me in this cave." So the animals came in pairs. Ngewo, having created a primal pair, a man and a woman, used to live among men, offering them free access to him whenever they had a request to make. But the requests came so fast that he felt constrained to remove himself to a safe distance to avoid being worn out. He therefore retreated to the sky, where he now lives. Ngewo did return to bid mankind farewell, advising men to be charitable to one another and not to wish each other evil. He gave them two chickens, which he had created before making the descent, telling them that when one does another wrong, he must call God back to adjudicate, and when God returns the people must return his chicken to him. ▣ Ngewo sent two messengers to a certain town to carry news of death and life. The dog was sent to say that the people would not die, and the toad was sent to say that death was coming. They set out together. On the way, the dog met a woman cooking food for her child. He lay down and waited, and in due course received some food from the woman. The dog then ran on. But the toad had not stopped along the way. He reached the town first and entered, crying, "Death has come!" Then the dog came running, crying, "Life has come!" But he was too late. The toad had brought death first. That is why people die. *See also:* Leve.

Ngoma-lungundu, A Drum That Is the Voice of God (Venda/South Africa, Zimbabwe) The Drum of the Dead was brought to its present location by the Senzi people, who are today called the Venda. ▣ The sacred drum of the Senzi belonged to their departed ancestors at the time when they were living in the north. Among all their musical instruments, the greatest, and that which was feared and revered most by all the people, was this instrument of the royal ancestor spirits, the Drum of Mwali, the ancestor god of the Senzi and the Kalanga. This drum was called the Voice of the great God, Mambo wa Denga (King of Heaven), the lord of all the ancestor spirits. The king was feared because he could work miracles with this drum of the gods. His enormous city was built on a mountain. The drum was seen and beaten by no one except the high priest, Dzomo la Dzimu, the mouthpiece of God, and the king, Mwali. No one could look upon the king: he spoke through the high priest, whose voice reverberated in a terrifying way. The palace was guarded by lions, the dogs of the king, and by snakes who had heads on either end. When rain was needed, the king was petitioned, and when the drumming of Ngoma-lungundu was heard, they knew that the king had heard them. The drum could not be looked at. Once, when the people quarreled among themselves, Mwali, angry, spoke through the drum and many died. But the people continued to fight among themselves, and in the end Mwali left them, to go under the earth, to become the ancestor-god of the people. When they hear the earth shake, they know that he walks on the clouds or under the earth. When the king vanished, many people fled or died with him. Mwali bequeathed his powers to Tshilume, his eldest son, to whom he gave a small drum of the spirits, also called Ngoma-lungundu. This drum helped the prince when he was troubled by his enemies. It brought rain when it was needed. Some years later, Mwali's voice told the son to move his people to the land beyond the Limpopo. And so the people moved. The drum, enclosed, was carried by six men, with the injunction by Mwali that it must never touch the ground. During the migration, the people were protected by Mwali and the drum. They came to the Kalanga people, who were overwhelmed by their numbers and acquiesced to their presence. They continued to move south. They went to the country of the Nyai, and Mwali told them to move on. Then the drum of the spirits fell to the ground one day because it had not been placed carefully in a tree. A storm resulted, lions sent by Mwali ravaged the people, many died. The king went up a hill and did not return. Then all abated, and they continued under a new king to the valley of the Limpopo. When the king died, Hwami took over the leadership. Few people remained, but the drum made their enemies fear them. But the Pedi did not fear the drum, so Hwami and his people moved to another place. They migrated to the country of Tshivhula and settled. Dyambeu, Hwami's great-grandson, succeeded him, and they traveled to the east, using Ngoma-lungundu to subdue any who stood in their path. On the Plain of Tshisonga, they built a camp and prepared a shelter for Ngoma-lungundu. But at one point the drum, blown by the wind, fell to the ground, and the people were massacred and the drum taken by the enemy, the Tavhatsindi. With the help of Mwali, they recovered the drum and overcame the Tavhatsindi. The eldest son of Dyambeu, Bele, was selected king.

Nguleso Sends Beasts to Punish Men (Kakwa/Sudan) Nguleso, the supreme being, is god in the sky. Contrasted with him is a malevolent spirit, Ngulete, who causes illness and can be appeased by offerings. There are many Ngulete; they are children of beings called Jaguruba who live in the rivers. The spirits of the ancestors can, if neglected, send sickness or other misfortune. ▣ God threw a man down from the sky and taught him to cultivate. ▣ West of the Nile, the rainbow is believed to be the belched-forth breath of a gigantic python (Kakwa, Fajulu, Lululba, Moru), any approach to which is dangerous. ▣ Lightning lives in the sky, has almost personal attributes, but the body of a calf with the face and teeth of a lion. ▣ Long ago, some people were plagued by lions and wild beasts. They wondered, if Nguleso exists, why are they eaten by these beasts? Some said it was because they did not act properly, and because of this Nguleso sent the animals to devour the land. They thought about the deaths of these men, and concluded that Nguleso had treated them badly, that they had not taken another man's property, had not entered the house of another man, so he troubled them for no reason. They called together the spirits, Nguloki, and called upon Nguleso in the sky.

Ngulwe Causes a Child to Emerge from a Woman's Knee (Kuulwe/Tanzania) Ngulwe, the supreme being, is the creator of the world, but is too remote to interest himself in the affairs of men. ▣ There is an evil spirit called Mwawa, who sometimes appears in human form but usually takes the shape of a dog, running about in the villages stealing and biting. He also appears as a mouse. Mwawa is particularly associated with smallpox. ▣ The first human pair came down from heaven but did not produce offspring in the ordinary way. Ngulwe caused a child, known as Kanga Masala, to come out of the woman's knee.

Ngun Lo Ki and the Rope from Heaven (Bari, Fajulu/Sudan) God has a dual aspect: Ngun Lo Ki, God in the sky, associated with rain; and Ngun Lo Kak, God below the earth, concerned with earth and agriculture. The conception of Ngun is vague: he is armed with power, and like the moon, he comes and goes; as Ngun Lo Ki, he created men and keeps them alive, creating a hundred every month; as Ngun Lo Kak, he destroys them and they die, killing a hundred every month. ▣ Man originally lived with God in the sky, and came down to earth by means of a rope, which was subsequently broken, severing the connection. ▣ The rain chief, Fitia Lugor, has a holy stream called Kwe, to cross which is death. The rain chief operates by the manipulation and the washing of the sacred rain-stones after sacrifice. The stones are regarded as male and female, and in some cases seem to be old stone implements. He does not claim to make rain of himself; his ancestors were given their power and their rain-stones by God, and by the virtue of his ancestors he intercedes with God to send down the blessings of rain upon his people. Evil influences may bring the sun, scorching the crops; these it is his duty to combat. Sacred spears are also used for rainmaking. The power of the rain-maker descends in the male line, but not necessarily from father to son.

Nhialic and the Separation of Heaven and Earth (Dinka/Sudan) Nhialic (Nyalich, Acek, Jok), the supreme being, is associated with the firmament; the name means "in the above." Nhialic is higher than the spirits of the dead, jok; it was he who created the world and established the order of things, and it is he who sends the rain. Deng (literally, rain) is closely linked with Nhialic (in some regions, Deng is regarded as the supreme being and Nhialic is not mentioned, while in others Nhialic and Deng are believed to be the same spirit). ▣ Nhialic (and the sky) and men (and the earth) were originally contiguous; the sky then lay just above the earth. They were connected by a rope, stretched parallel to the earth and at the reach of a man's outstretched arm above it. By means of this rope, men could climb at will to Nhialic. At this time, there was no death. Nhialic granted one grain of millet a day to the first man and woman, and this satisfied their needs. They were forbidden to grow or pound more. Garang and Abuk, the first human beings living on earth, had to take care when they were doing their little planting or pounding, lest a hoe or a pestle should strike Nhialic, but one day the woman, because she was greedy, decided to plant more than the permitted grain of millet. In order to do so, she took a long-handled hoe. When she raised this pole to pound or cultivate, she struck Nhialic, who withdrew, offended, to his present great distance from the earth, and sent a small blue bird, the color of the sky, to sever the rope that had previously given men access to the sky and to him. Since that time, the country has been defiled, for men have to labor for the food they need, and are often hungry. They can no longer as before freely reach Nhialic, and they suffer sickness and death, which accompany their separation from Nhialic. ▣ Nhialic created Garang and Abuk in the east under a tamarind tree or on the bank of a great water. He made them so small—only half the length of a man's arm, of clay, and laid them in a pot, which he then covered. When he uncovered it, the two stood up and were complete and fully grown. In the morning, Garang was grown and carried the spear (the penis), and the breasts of Abuk were big, and they married. They bore children. The creator told them that their child would die but would return after fifteen days. Garang disagreed with this plan, saying that if people returned from the dead they would be too numerous, and where would people then build their homes? There would not be enough land. ▣ In the beginning, there was no light. In this darkness,

Nhialic created the first people, including a man named Aruu Pabek. Aruu, Dawn, twisted a rope, and Nhialic gave him eyes and he saw that he was in darkness. Aruu caught an animal with his rope and gave the foreleg to the wife of Nhialic, who suggested that Aruu should be rewarded. Aruu asked Nhialic to make an opening in the world so that people could see, but Nhialic refused. Instead, he offered him a spear, which he refused, then an ax, which he accepted. With the ax, Aruu struck the earth, and a part went up and a part below. Aruu said, "Why do you not light up?" and the earth lit up. So he divided the sky and the earth. Nhialic, angry, pushed Aruu down to earth and closed up the earth. He speared anyone who tried to emerge. Aruu took a stone and put it on his head, and when Nhialic speared him, the stone deflected the spear. Nhialic seized Aruu by the neck and said, "Why are you like a man?" *See also:* Abuk, Deng.

Njaajaan Njaay Lives in a River (Wolof/Senegal) Njaajaan Njaay was the mythic founder of the Waalo kingdom. 🔲 After the great flood, the children of Noah multiplied, and some settled in the area that would become the great empire of Ghana. Among them was Mbaarik Bo, who was converted to Islam by Bubakar Umar. He then followed Bubakar Umar, who moved to the west. Bubakar Umar was the father of Njaajaan Njaay, the first ruler of the Waalo empire. Bubakar, continuing his work of converting people to Islam, now lived among the Serer, and was wounded by Hamar, the leader of the Serer. As he prepared to go back east to die, he told his wife, Fatumata, not to marry a man whose body she might see while he was washing, a man whom she might see when he was relieving himself. And she must sleep with no man unless a mattress first falls on the floor. Mbaarik Bo overheard these instructions. Bubakar Umar died on his way to his eastern home. Mbaarik Bo made certain that he followed the instructions of Bubakar Umar, and Fatumata, who was until then able to marry no man because she had built a high pillar from which she watched the movements of men, married him. Njaajaan Njaay was taunted by other children because his mother was forced to marry her father's assistant. Furious, Njaajaan Njaay took weapons and tools, and threw himself into a river to commit suicide. But he was a good swimmer and could not drown himself. The river became his home, and he acquired a reputation for being a supernatural being. He hid in the reeds, moving from town to town, emerging from the waters, pale and hairy. He spent seven years in the river, then emerged when he saw children fighting over the fish they had caught. He taught them how to string the fish, and divided the fish for them. The children told their parents about this; they hid at the river, then caught Njaajaan Njaay as he came to the children. He refused to speak, until a man named Maramu Gaaya tricked him into speaking, pretending he did not know the correct way to balance a cauldron on three stones, pretending he did not know how to prepare and eat food. Njaajaan Njaay identified himself, and he went to Waalo, where he was made a chief of the army. In the meantime, his mother sent his younger brother to seek him, and the brothers were reunited. Njaajaan helped to develop a model government, and became one of the progenitors of the people.

Njambe: The Two Bundles (Boloki/CAR) Njambe is the supreme being. ▣ While a man was working one day in the forest, a little man with two bundles—one large and one small—went to him and asked, "Which of these two bundles will you have? This one," taking up the large bundle, "contains looking glasses, knives, beads, cloth, and this one," taking up the little bundle, "contains lasting life." The man answered, "I cannot choose by myself. I must go and ask the other people in the town." While he was gone to ask the other people, some women arrived, and the choice was put to them. The women tried the edges of the knives, bedecked themselves in the cloth, admired themselves in the looking-glasses, and without more ado they selected the big bundle and took it away. The little man, picking up the small bundle, vanished. On the return of the man from the town, both the little man and his bundles had disappeared. The women exhibited and shared the things, but death continued on the earth. ▣ Nkengo was the son of Libuta, and he noticed that the people were dying daily in great numbers. So one day he called out loudly, "You Cloud-people, throw me down a rope!" The Cloud-people heard, and they threw him a rope. Nkengo held on to it and was pulled up to the Cloud-land. When he arrived there, Nkengo had to wait one day, and in the morning the Cloud-people said to him, "You have come here to receive everlasting life and escape from death. You cannot

E.A. Wallis Budge, *From Fetish to God in Ancient Egypt* (London: Oxford University Press, 1934), p. 200.

Forms of Isis

make your request for seven days, and in the meantime you must not go to sleep." Nkengo was able to stay awake for six days, but on the seventh day he nodded and went to sleep. The Cloud-people woke him up, saying, "You came here to receive everlasting life and escape from death. You were able to keep awake six days. Why did you abandon your purpose on the seventh day?" They were so angry with him that they drove him out of Cloud-land and lowered him to the earth. The people on the earth asked him what had happened up above, and Nkengo replied, "When I reached Cloud-land, they told me that in order to gain everlasting life I must keep awake for seven days. I did not sleep for six days and six nights. But on the seventh day I nodded in sleep, whereupon they drove me out, saying, 'Get away with your dying. You shall not receive everlasting life, for every day there shall be death among you!'" His friends laughed at him because he went to receive everlasting life and lost it through sleeping. That is the reason why death continues in the world. *See also*: Libanza, Motu.

Njambi and the King of the Birds (Mpongwe/Gabon) Njambi is the supreme being. 🄴 All the birds lived together in the country of Njambi. One day they wondered who was the king of the birds. Each named himself, and to settle the issue they decided to go to Njambi. They told him that some birds could fly well, others speak well, others were strong. Which of these traits was the most important? Njambi asked the eagle to speak, then his wife; he asked the parrot to speak, then his wife; and all the birds in succession were asked to speak, along with their wives. Finally, he called the cock and told him to speak. But when Njambi asked the wife to speak, she observed that her husband said she could talk only if she bore children. So it is that when she lays an egg she speaks. So, asked Njambi, you do not speak like your husband? She said no. The cock said that he jeered at the other birds, husband and wife speaking alike. I do not allow this, he said. A husband should be at the head, it is not becoming that his wife talk as well as he does. Njambi then decreed that the cock would be the king of the birds. All the other birds, husband and wife, speak alike, he said. But the cock knows how to be the head of his family. But he also told the cock that he could not go back to the land of the birds—the other birds, jealous, might kill him. The cock must stay in Njambi's town. The other birds scattered then and lived in the forest with no king.

Nkongolo Insults Mbidi Kiluwe (Luba/DRCongo) Nkongolo is the rainbow king. 🄴 In the country of the east, Buhemba, on the right bank of the Lualaba River, there once were a man and a woman—Kiubaka-Ubaka, he who builds many houses, and Kibumba-Bumba, she who makes much pottery. Guided by the sound of chopping, the man discovered the woman, who was preparing firewood. They lived for a long time under the same roof, and brought forth twins of the opposite sex, who became inseparable companions. The twins found a place rich in fish, and spent the day catching fish, the night in each other's arms. In their turn, they brought forth twins, who lived in the same manner, far from their parents. This new generation took up trapping. So pairs of twins, moving in each generation a little farther westward, populated the country. ⬔ Nkongolo, the first divine king of the Luba, was the offspring of Kiubaka-Ubaka and Kibumba-Bumba. He brought all the lands of the west under his authority. He crossed the Lualaba with a large following, and he built a great village. About the same time, a hunter called Ilunga Mbidi Kiluwe left his village to conquer the peoples living between the Lualaba and Lubilash Rivers. On the way home, he met his brother-in-law, Nkongolo. Mbidi Kiluwe was shocked to see that Nkongolo ate and drank in the company of his people, and Nkongolo was astonished to see his guest disappear behind a screen at mealtimes. Mbidi Kiluwe angrily told him that he had conquered the country but had failed to observe the elementary prohibition that obliges a king to hide himself when he eats or drinks. He then departed from Nkongolo. When he arrived at the Lualaba River, he told the local chief that Nkongolo had insulted him. Mbidi Kiluwe had left behind Nkongolo's sisters, Mbidi's wives Mabela and Bulanda, who were pregnant. He entrusted them to the care of the diviner, Mijibu. The sons they would bring into the world were to rejoin Mbidi. He said that the chief would recognize them by their black skins, that if a red-skinned man asked permission to cross the river, he was to be refused. But if a black man asked, he should agree at once. At the village of Nkongolo, Mabela and Bulanda each gave birth to a boy, Kisula and Kalala Ilunga. Nkongolo invited his nephew, Kalala Ilunga, to a game, and, with Mijibu's help, Kalala Ilunga had no trouble beating his uncle. When Nkongolo invited his other nephew to a game, Mijibu magically made it possible for Kisula to win. Nkongolo's mother told her son not to contest with Kalala Ilunga. Angered by the growing renown of his nephew, Nkongolo caused a pit to be dug, lined with iron spikes, and hidden under a mat. He invited Kalala to dance in his honor. Mijibu gave Kalala two spears, and told him to brandish one while using the other to test the ground during his dance. Kalala Ilunga, dancing, hurled his spear at the mat. The weapon passed through it, revealing the trap. Kalala Ilunga fled, determined to join his father. Nkongolo pursued him, but the nephew had already crossed the Lualaba River when his uncle reached its bank. Faithful to Mbidi Kiluwe's orders, the local chief refused to allow the king to cross. Nkongolo tried in vain to build a stone causeway across the river: his iron implements were useless against rock. Nkongolo then decided to lure Kalala Ilunga to his side of the river. He compelled the diviner Mijibu and one Mungedi to climb to the top of a great tree and call the fugitive back. There was no response from Kalala to their calls. Mijibu and Mungedi spent two days without food at the top of the tree. Mijibu escaped, thanks to his magical powers. He crossed the Lualaba with a mighty leap. But Mungedi died of hunger. Mijibu succeeded in joining Mbidi Kiluwe, who raised a great army and entrusted its command to his son. Kalala Ilunga's army had seized the capital. Nkongolo took refuge. A woman discovered him, and

Kalala Ilunga's army encircled the hideout. Nkongolo was captured, beheaded, and castrated. The head and genitals of the dead king were sent in a basket to Kalala Ilunga's father. A miracle happened at the village of Lenga. When the man who was carrying the basket placed it on the ground, a termite hill formed over it with extraordinary speed, burying it under a mound of red earth. Mbidi Kiluwe reminded his son of the precise ritual observances required of divine kings. A king was obliged to take food and drink alone, and out of sight. A special house had to be devoted to the preparation of royal meals, because it was forbidden for the king to eat in a place where fire had been made. After securely establishing his rule over the country, Kalala Ilunga took the name of Ilunga Mwine Munza. *See also:* Kalumba

Nkulunkulu Emerges from the Reeds (Zulu/South Africa) Nkulunkulu, the supreme being, the ancient one, is the Zulu creator. ▣ Nobody knows where he is now; he came originally—that is, he broke off—from some reeds. Some say that he was the reeds, because the word for them, *uthlanga*, means source. It was he who broke off the people from the reeds and then the cattle and other peoples. He also broke off medicine men and dreams. He was really the first man and the progenitor of other men. A woman followed him out of the original reeds, then a cow and a bull, then the other pairs of animals. Nkulunkulu created everything that is—mountains, cattle, streams, snakes. He taught the Zulu how to hunt, how to make fire with sticks, and how to eat corn. He named the animals for them. Nkulunkulu is in everything; he is in the corn, the tree, the water. ▣ In another version of the myth, Nkulunkulu was the first man and there was nothing before him; he broke off from the source. He cut the little tree named *uluzi* and kindled fire by friction and told the people, "Be warm. Cook with it." Nkulunkulu cooked the first corn and ate it himself, to show the people how. He identified the wild animals for the people. Nkulunkulu broke off the stones and men, too, from the bed of reeds. The corn grew, and the first man said to the first woman, "Let's eat it." The woman said, "How?" "Cut it. Thrash it," said the man. "Find a stone. Go find another stone. Grind the corn between the stones." And this has been the way of mankind with corn ever since. ▣ Nkulunkulu sent a chameleon to tell men they would not die. The chameleon went slowly, loitering. Nkulunkulu sent a lizard after the chameleon, giving him the message that men would die. The lizard made great haste. The lizard arrived first with its message of death. When the chameleon finally arrived, the people would not hear its message of life.

Nomkhubulwana and the Girls (Zulu/South Africa) Nomkhubulwana is the daughter of Nkulunkulu, God. ▣ She came out on the same day that man came out of the earth. She orders the children to be weaned, tells the people when they will have a year of plenty. She presides over the growth of corn. ▣ This princess in heaven, Nomkhubulwana, heavenly princess, occasionally visits the cornfields and causes them to bear abundantly. For this princess, the people often set apart a small piece of cultivated land as an offering. One day is appointed especially for girls: they go out to the hills, fasting. They spend the entire day weeping, fasting, and praying, thinking that the more they fast and weep the more likely they are to be pitied by the princess. On that day, they wear men's clothing made of skins, and all men and boys are to keep out of their way, neither speaking to them nor looking at them. They start very early: at sunrise, they must be by the riverside, prepared to begin praying and weeping. They dig deep holes in the sand, and two or three girls sit in each of them. The holes are filled until nothing but the girls' heads show above the ground. There they remain, weeping and praying for some time. Girls about six years old are generally chosen for this purpose. Later, the older girls help them out and let them run home. The older girls then go to the mountains and weep. Then they go to their gardens, around which they walk, crying out to the princess to have pity on them and give them a good harvest. At sunset, they return to their homes and break their fast.

—— ✉ *Nongqawuse Seeks the Return of the Gods* ✉ ——

Humans Long for Their Heavenly Counterpart. In 1921, Simon Kimbangu (1889?-1951) healed the sick and raised the dead among the Kongo people in Central Africa. In 1700, in Sudan, a woman whose name was Quay mysteriously became pregnant and bore a son, Kejok, who grew to manhood in a few months and performed miracles. Years later, in 1921, it was said that he had risen from the dead and would bring his people an era of wealth and happiness. In Kenya in 1906, adherents to the Kiesu movement went into convulsions at the sight of a European. Maitatsine was a Cameroonian prophet killed in Nigeria in 1980. He attacked extravagance, demanded strict adherence to Islamic law, and precipitated violence that resulted in thousands of deaths. Peter Chileshe Mulenga, born in 1939, had a vision on November 26, 1958; he became a prophet in Zambia among the Bemba people. Chaminuka, whose historical identity is uncertain, fostered a cult that involved spirits with political implications among the Rozwi and Shona of Zimbabwe. Prophets and religious movements that sought a return to better conditions have occurred at various times and places in Africa. These "cargo cults" anticipated a new age during which the old order would give way to a new paradise, a return to God. ▣ (Xhosa/South Africa) In South Africa,

Nongqawuse was a Xhosa seer, from Centane District in the Transkei (1841-1898). She was a daughter of Mhlantla, raised by her uncle, Mhlakaza, a medical doctor of the Gcaleka people. Her home was on the banks of the Gxara, a small river in Centane District. In 1856, she declared that Xhosa ancestral spirits had spoken to her, telling her that the Xhosa people must kill all their cattle and destroy their grain. On a certain day, the sun would rise bloodred, then stand still in the sky, and the cattle pens and the grain pits would then be filled again, the old Xhosa leaders would rise from the dead with their warriors, and the whites would be driven into the sea. Her prophecy spread from the Gcaleka to the Ngqika (both Xhosa peoples). Great numbers of cattle, between 300,000 and 400,000, were killed, and grain was destroyed. On the appointed day, the Xhosa waited in suspense. Nothing happened. Famine then claimed thousands of human lives, perhaps 41,000 in the Ciskei alone, while the numbers in the Transkei remain unknown. Nongqawuse was taken prisoner, kept for some time on Robben Island, then spent the remainder of her life on a farm in Alexandria District. *See also:* Kejok.

Nun and the Rope to Earth (Mondari, Mandari/Sudan) Nun is a creator and protector spirit. The cosmos and the world are the work of the creator. The ancestral spirits, Nutu Ko Kak, visit the people from time to time and receive offerings of food. ▣ The earth and sky were originally joined by a perpendicular rope, allowing the creator and men to pass at will from the one to the other. In this primordial universe, the lower part, the earth, lacked natural and social diversity. The rope was eventually severed after the sin of fratricide was committed, and earth and the parts separated. The celestial realm was now largely inaccessible. When sky and earth were joined, there was direct communication; the ancestors came down the rope. Once it was apart, communication ceased, although kinship remained. This separation introduced death. At the time of this separation, the creator remained above together with a proportion of the people who were caught up there. Death allowed one to be reunited with the creator and the kin who had been separated when the rope was severed. ▣ Logobong is the archetypal man, the person who fathered the races. As creator and as another name for Nun, he symbolizes the spirituality of the procreative act, and is present when a man goes into his house with his wife. Logobong reunites the creator and man, who were early divided.

Nut Bears Ra, Who Returns to Her Body Each Day (Egypt) Nut is the sky god-dess. [] Nut spans the heavens, is the one who ascended from the primal waters, who gave birth to the earth. She gave birth to Ra, the sun, who returns each day to her body and is born each morning from between her thighs. She is the starry heavens, arching over her husband, Geb, the earth. *See also:* Ra.

Nyalutanga Instructs Girls as They Grow Up (Zaramo/Tanzania) Nyalutanga (Lutanga) was the first human being, and is related to the origin of all things. [] The earth is the great womb that gave birth to the first human being, Nyalutanga. The progenitor, Nyalutanga, appeared to a mother whose first daughter disappeared, because no one knew how to instruct her as to how to grow up, to become mature: she turned into an elephant. It was because of her that Nyalutanga appeared. She told the mother that she would instruct her daughters, and so it became possible for the girls to grow into full human beings.

Nyambe Moves Away from Aggressive Men (Lozi/Zambia) Nyambe (Mulimu) is God, the supreme being, the creator and origin of all things. He is superior to all spirits, is omniscient and omnipotent. He controls the universe, including the lives and fortunes of humankind. All members of the royal family have divine ancestry through their descent from Mbuyu, the daugh-ter of Nyambe. The three parts of Lozi religion consist of Nyambe, the spirits of the ancestors, and the shadows or spirits. [] The first man, Kamunu, was punished by Nyambe for killing and eating animals. When-ever Kamunu killed an animal, Nyambe deprived him of one of his own possessions, first his pot, then his dog. Finally, Kamunu brought death to humankind when Nyambe deprived him of his son. [] Nyambe lived on earth with his wife, Nasilele, but because of man's aggressive nature and intelligence in imitating him, he fled to heaven. After his ascension to heaven, the sun came to be regarded as the symbol of Nyambe and prayers to him were always made at sunrise.

Nyambe and the Origin of Death (Luyi/Zambia) Nyambe was the creator. [] He had a wife, Nasilele, who wanted humans to die forever. But Nyambe wanted them to live again once they had died. Nyambe had a favored dog that, when it died, he wanted to restore to life. But his wife objected because, she said, the dog was a thief. Later, Nasilele's mother died. When she asked her husband to restore her mother to life, he refused, reminding her that she had been opposed to giving new life to his dog. But after a time he relented. As he was bringing the mother to life, Nasilele, because of her curiosity, interfered, and the mother stayed dead. They then discussed the issue of whether eternal life should be given to mankind, and Nyambe sent the chameleon with that message. But the hare arrived on earth first, and told men that once dead they would remain dead.

Nyambi Flees from Assertive Men (Rotse/Zimbabwe) Nyambi (Nyambe) is the creator, the supreme being. ▣ He is symbolized by the sun, the moon symbolizing his wife. This woman became the mistress of the deity in the legendary night. She gave birth to the animals, then to men. There was a conflict between Nyambi and men. Nyambi manifested his power in resuscitating the animals man killed. But man was so cunning that Nyambi became afraid, and went up to heaven by means of a spider's web, and has been invisible ever since. ▣ In the beginning, Nyambi, having created all things, lived on the earth with his wife, Nasilele. One of Nyambi's creations was Kamonu, a man who imitated whatever Nyambi did. Nyambi was afraid of Kamonu, and was incensed when he killed animals. Animals are not meant to be killed, he told him. He drove Kamonu away, but Kamonu returned and Nyambi gave him a garden. Then, when animals came into his garden, Kamonu killed them. As he killed the animals, something began to happen to his own household—his dog died, his pot shattered, his child died. When Kamonu went to Nyambi and asked for help, Nyambi refused. And, to avoid Kamonu, to keep him from coming to him, God moved away, across a river. But Kamonu made a boat. When Nyambi created a mountain and went to the top, Kamonu climbed. Humans were plentiful now, and Nyambi could not find a place on the earth where he might be secure. So he went to a spider, who found a place for Nyambi in the sky. The spider spun a thread, and Nyambi climbed it, moving into the sky, putting the spider's eyes out so that he would not be able to find his way to heaven again. So it is that Nyambi moved deep into the sky. Now Kamonu and others constructed a tower to get to Nyambi's place in the heavens, but it collapsed, and Kamonu was never to find Nyambi.

Nyame and the Message of Death (Akan/Burkina Faso, Ghana) Nyame, the supreme being, is eternal, infinite, and the creator of the universe; he is remote from men and unconcerned with their daily life. He is one of the sources of fertility and father of the lesser spirits, or Abosom. A spark of fire enters the bloodstream of every individual from Nyame and so animates him. Man is the offspring of Nyame, the first member of the triune deity— Nyame, Odomankoma, and Nyankopon. Nyankopon is regarded as the great ancestor, source of all wisdom, bestowing on each man his unique talents. Odomankoma is the ultimate ancestor. Nana is the pattern and paradigm, mediator and exemplar, of the supreme ideal. Human life is one continuous stream flowing through all men. Man has to die to discover his completeness in the undying god. Daughters of Nyame include Asaase Afua, the goddess of fertility, and Asaase Yaa, the mother of the dead. ▣ In ancient times, men grew weary of dying and therefore decided to send a messenger to Nyame to complain. They selected a sheep to take the message. To assure that the messenger took the message correctly, they sent a second; for that purpose, they selected a dog. The dog, knowing that he was much swifter than the sheep, did not leave with the sheep but delayed for a time. As the sheep went along the road to Nyame's town, he came to where an old woman lived. She had found that some of her salt supply had been damaged by water, and it was not possible to dry it. She had therefore thrown the salt into the bushes outside the village. As the sheep moved along, he was eating the grass where the salt had been thrown, and, liking the taste, remained there a long time. In the meantime, the dog came along the same road but did not see the sheep in the countryside. He hurried on and reached Nyame's village first. He told Nyame that he and the sheep had been sent by men to deliver a message to him. When Nyame asked what the message was, the dog told him that men said that they wished to remain dead when they died and not to return here. Nyame said that it would be as they requested, and the dog returned. Along the way, he met the sheep and told him what he had done. The sheep explained that a mistake had been made, and they both returned to Nyame. But Nyame refused to alter his initial decision, which is why men die and do not come back again. *See also:* Aberewa, Odomankoma, Tano.

Nyame Sends a Python to Teach Humans to Mate (Asante/Ghana) Nyame (Nyankopon, Onyankopon, Odomankoma) is the supreme being, the creator, an ever-present force who is nevertheless somewhat remote from the affairs of humans. Lesser gods, Abosom, are the children of Nyame's sons (Apo, Bea, Bosomtwe, and Tano), and they deal with the day to day activities of humans on the earth. Nyame at one time sent his four sons to the earth to work with humans: they became identified with bodies of water. An Asante proverb suggests that if one wishes to say something to Nyame, one should speak it to the winds. Nyame's female side is represented by the moon; the male side by the sun. Humans were created with water by the female side of God; the life force came from the male side. There is a pantheon of gods, including Asase, the earth goddess. ⬛ The earth had been created by Nyame, and humans populated that earth. But in the beginning they did not conceive and bear children. Then Nyame caused a python to move to the earth, and that python taught humans to mate. ⬛ In another myth, Nyame journeyed around the earth creating the things of the earth at the same time that men and women worked out their own lives and activities. ⬛ In the beginning, Nyame lived on the earth, mingling with the humans he had created; they regularly visited with each other. But all of this came to an end one day: Nyame was watching some women as they pounded grain in mortars with pestles. The women, not happy with his presence there, told him to move on; when he did not move away quickly enough they rushed at him, striking him with their pestles. Nyame, angry at this treatment, left the earth and determined to remain away permanently. But he did not lose interest in those he had created; he retained concern for humans on the earth, and from the heavens he dispatched a goat to them with a hopeful message: he told the humans that Death would move among them, killing them. But he assured the humans that they would not remain dead, that they would in the end journey to the skies to be with God. So the goat set out; as he moved along with Nyame's message, he came to some fine looking grass, and he stopped to eat some of it. (The goat, not one of Nyame's favorite creatures, later became responsible for altering God's intentions regarding bodies of water on the earth.) In the heavens, Nyame saw what the goat was doing and, annoyed, he sent a sheep down to earth: the sheep was to carry the identical message to the humans. But the sheep garbled God's message; he told the people that God had decreed that when they died that would be the end. In the meantime, the goat continued his journey, and when he came to the humans he told them that Nyame had sent him with the message that, when humans died, they would go to him in the heavens. But it was too late: the humans told the goat that they had accepted the message of the sheep, and so death came among people.

Nyamiyonga Sends His Daughter to Subdue a King (Nyoro/Uganda) Nyamiyonga is the king of the underworld. There were three royal dynasties — first, the shadowy Tembuzi, of whom Kakama was the first and Isaza the last; second, the Chwezi, part-legendary hero-gods whose marvelous exploits are still spoken of; and third, the Bito, the line to which the present king belongs. Myths link these three dynasties together into a single line of descent, creating an unbroken chain between the present ruler and the very first king of Bunyoro. ☐ A story tells how Nyamiyonga, the king of the underworld, sent a message to King Isaza, asking him to enter a blood pact with him. Isaza's councillors advised against this, so Isaza had the pact made on Nyamiyonga's behalf with his chief minister, a commoner called Bukuku. When Nyamiyonga discovered that he had been united in the blood pact with a commoner, he was angry, and he determined to get Isaza into his power. So he sent his beautiful daughter, Nyamata, to Isaza's court, where she so attracted the king that, not knowing who she was, he married her. But he resisted all her efforts to persuade him to visit her home, for he could not bear to be parted from his cattle, which he loved more than anything else. Nyamiyonga thought of another plan. He caused two of his most handsome cattle to be discovered near Isaza's kraal, and these were taken to the king, who soon loved them most of all his herd. One day they disappeared, and the distracted Isaza went in search of them, leaving Bukuku to rule the kingdom in his absence. After much wandering, Isaza arrived in the country of spirits, where he found his two cattle and also his wife, Nyamata, who had gone home some time previously to bear him a child. Nyamiyonga welcomed the Nyoro king, but he had not forgiven him, and he never allowed him to return to the world of men. In due course, Nyamata's child was born and was named Isimbwa. *See also:* Ndahura, Ruhanga, Wamara.

Nyengebule Is Punished for Murder (Xhosa/South Africa) ☐ Nyengebule's two wives went to the forest to gather firewood. They found a bees' nest. The younger ate her share; the elder took some home to her husband. Nyengebule thanked the first wife for her thoughtfulness, and when his younger wife, Nqandamate, his favorite, told him that she had brought him no honey, he beat her, killing her. As he killed her, some feathers that she was wearing on her head fell down. He buried her, then went to her parents to demand that the dowry be returned. The feathers that had fallen from his wife's head now transformed into a bird, which flew after him. Along the way, he saw the bird. It identified him as his wife's killer. He killed the bird, but it came back to life and again pursued him. He killed it again, and it returned. Again, he killed it, and put it into a bag. When he arrived at his in-laws' place, they asked him for snuff, and he opened the bag. The bird flew out and again accused him of killing his wife. They seized him, and executed him.

Nyesowa Keeps Secrets from Men (Poro, Sande/Liberia) Nyesowa (Abi, Gala, Wala), God, created the world. When it is time for people to leave the earth, it is Nyesowa who calls them. ▣ God said to his wife that they should make people. He took earth from his home and put it with hers. He sent trees down from heaven, and when his wife asked him why he was sending these things from heaven, he said that his children must not be able to find out their secrets since they would not be staying with him in the sky. Then he brought water down to the earth so that the children he was about to send there would have something to drink.

Nyikang Throws an Adze at the Sun (Shilluk/Sudan) Shilluk kings are descended from Nyikang (Nyakang), the leader of the Shilluk during their heroic age, the mythic ancestor who led them into their present homeland, conquering it from its inhabitants. Nyikang, or the spirit of Nyikang, is believed to be in every king. He is a mythic personification of the timeless kingship that symbolizes the national structure, a changeless moral order. The kingship is the common symbol of the Shilluk people and, Nyikang being immortal, an abiding institution that binds the generations. It is not the individual at any time reigning who is the king, but Nyikang who is the medium between man and God (Juok) and is believed in some way to participate in God as he does in the king. The Shilluk believe in a supreme being who is greater than Nyikang or any other king. He is the creator of the world, but is far distant. The people feel the need to have someone to stand between them and God: Nyikang is that intermediary, a divine or semidivine being. He did not die but disappeared in a whirlwind during a festival. The spirit of Nyikang is present in certain places, men, and animals. ▣ In ancient times, the people came to the country of Kerau. Here Nyikang and his brother, Duwat, separated. Duwat asked him where he was going, and told him to look behind him. Nyikang looked back, and saw a stick for planting sorghum, which Duwat had thrown to him. Duwat told him that it was a thing with which to dig the ground of his village. Nyikang came to the country of Turo, the country of his son, Dak, who used to sit on the ashes of the village and play the *tom*, a stringed instrument. His uncles, the brothers of Nyikang, were jealous of Dak as the sole ruler of the country.

They sharpened their spears. But Dak was warned about the danger he was in. Nyikang got an ambach, hewed it, and made hands for it, so that it looked like a man. Dak sat in the same place and played his instrument. His uncles came and stabbed him—actually, they stabbed the ambach statue, and Dak went unhurt into his enclosure. Nyikang said, "My son has been killed by his uncles." His uncles, afraid, set a period of mourning for Dak. People came to mourn. Suddenly, Dak came out from his enclosure and danced. His uncles saw this and fled, and the mourning was finished. ▣ Nyikang went to a river, and the people settled on this river. The cow of Nyikang ran away because her calves were speared by him: whenever Nyikang came to a new place, he killed a calf. The cow came to the country of the sun. Ojul, the grey hawk, went to search for her. He found her among the cows of the sun. Garo, the son of the sun, asked Ojul what he was seeking. He said he sought the cow of Nyikang. Garo said there was no such cow there. But Ojul returned, and told Nyikang that the cow had been found among a herd of cows owned by a man who was very tall, just like Dak, wearing silver bracelets. Nyikang ordered an army to find the cow. Dak attacked Garo, threw him on the ground, cut off his hands, pulled the bracelets off them, and chased the enemy's army. He came to the sun. But there the army of Nyikang was chased, and it was destroyed. Nyikang himself came; he took an adze and aimed it at the sun. He hit the sun, and it returned to the sky. Nyikang took the bracelet. With it, he touched the dead of his army, and they returned to life. When the people came to the source of a river, they found it full of sudd. Nyikang wondered where it came from. Their way was barred. Obogo told Nyikang to put him under the sudd, then stab him, and he would part the sudd. So Obogo was stabbed under the sudd, and the sudd parted. They came to their place, and Nyikang settled with his people. Dak ruled, and, when he died, his son, Odak, ruled. He died while hunting game. Nyikang returned, and prepared a bier. Duwat ruled after him. *See also:* Gila, Juok, Ukwa.

Nzambi and the Land of the Dead (Kongo/Angola) Nzambi (Nzambi Mpungu), the sovereign master, is invisible. When people heard thunder, it was Nzambi and his people talking in the sky. Nzambi made the rain fall and planted seeds to grow into food to preserve mankind; he was responsible for their health and the birth of their children. Nzambi was very good, but there was also the matter of death: he killed people. Nzambi's body was like an immovable stone. ▣ Earth is a mountain over a body of water that is the land of the dead, called Mpemba, where the sun rises and sets just as it does in the land of the living. Between these two realms, the lands of the dead and the living, the water is both a means of access and an impenetrable barrier. The world is like two mountains opposed at their bases and separated by the ocean. At the rising and setting of the sun, the living and the dead exchange day and night. The setting of the sun signifies man's death and its rising his rebirth, or the continuity of his life. Man's life has no end, it constitutes a cycle. The sun, in its rising and setting, is a sign of this cycle, and death is merely a transition in the process of change.

Nzambi and the Great Flood (Kongo/DRCongo) Nzambi (Zambi, Nzambi-ampungu, Nyambi, Nzambe, Yambe), the supreme being, is the principal creator of the world and all living creatures. After his work of creation he withdrew himself, and, since then, he has taken little if any further interest in the world and its inhabitants. He is strong, rich, and good, so good that he will not hurt humans. ▣ The sky is like the ceiling of a house, and far away there are posts supporting this ceiling. Above the sky, or this ceiling, is a river that frequently wears away its bed and comes through in the form of rain. The thunder is the voice of a spirit called Nzaji, and the lightning is Nzaji himself. The sun sets every evening in the sea, but during the night, while people are sleeping, it steals back to the east ready to rise in the morning. ▣ The sun and moon once met, and the sun plastered some mud over a part of the moon, thereby covering up some of the light, which is why a portion of the moon is often in shadow. When this meeting took place, there was a flood, and the ancient people put their porridge sticks to their backs and turned into monkeys. The present race of people is a new creation. When the flood came, the men turned into monkeys and the women into lizards.

Nzambi Mpungu and the Race between Moon and Sun (Fiote, Fjort, Vili/Congo) Nzambi Mpungu is God, the father god who dwells in the heavens. Nzambici is God the essence, the god on earth, the great princess, the mother of all the animals, the one who promises her daughter to the animal who shall bring her the fire from heaven. Lightning is made by a blacksmith, Funzi, who lives in the center of Kongo country. Nzassi is thunder, and Lusiemo is lightning. The spirit that dwells in the sea is Chicamassi-chibuinji. The mystery of the earth, Nzambi, the mother of a beautiful daughter, gives mankind all laws, ordinances, arts, games, and musical instruments. Nzambi settles quarrels between animals, and in the stories giving her decision is embedded an immense amount of Fjort law. ▣ The creator is the great god, Nzambi Mpungu, the god who had fire and from whom Nzambi partially stole it; he did not give freely of his boxes of lightning. ▣ Nzambi Mpungu made the earth and sent Nzambi there. Then he came down and married his creation, thereby becoming the father of us all. Nzambi became the great princess who governed all on earth. ▣ Some women were busy planting in a country where water was scarce, so they brought their *sangas*, containing that precious fluid, with them. As they were working, an old woman, carrying a child on her back, passed by them, hesitated for a moment, then walked back to them and asked them to give her child a cup of water. The women said that they had carried the water from afar, and needed it for themselves, as there was no water just there. The poor old woman passed on, but told them that they would one day regret their want of charity. A man up in a palm tree placed a calabash at her feet. She told him to be there at the same time the next day. When he arrived, he found a great lake full of fish. The old woman told him that men could fish here, but women, because of the way they had treated her, would die if they ate the fish from the lake. "For I, Nzambi," she said, "have so ordered it." Nzambi then loaded the young man with many gifts, and told him to depart in peace. ▣ Ntangu, the sun, and Ngonde, the moon, are brothers. They lived in a village by the sea, and Ntangu wagered Ngonde that he could not beat him in a race. Ngonde caught up with Ntangu, and then Ntangu became annoyed and said that he would defeat Ngonde in a race, but he did not, so Ngonde won the wager. This is why the moon is seen during the day, with the sun, but the sun is never seen at night in company with the moon.

Nzame Re-creates the World (Fang/Cameroon, Equatorial Guinea, Gabon) In the beginning, there was nothing but Nzame, the supreme being. Nzame is really three: Nzame, Mebere, and Nkwa. ▣ Mebere made the first human out of clay, but in the form of a lizard. He put the lizard in the sea and left him there for eight days, after which he emerged as a man. It was the Nzame part of Nzame who created the universe and the earth and blew life into it. When he had done that, he called Mebere and Nkwa, the other parts of Nzame, to admire his work. They suggested that Nzame make a chief for the earth. Between them Nzame, Mebere, and Nkwa made a creature in their image. They named him Fam, Power. From Nzame the new creature gained strength; from Mebere he received leadership; and from Nkwa he had beauty. They instructed Fam to rule the world, then went back into the sky where they live. For a time, everything, even the first chiefs—the elephant, the leopard, and the monkey—obeyed Fam. But Fam grew arrogant, too proud of the qualities he had been given by Nzame. He began to mistreat the animals, even the first chiefs. He decided he did not need to worship Nzame, so Nzame brought down thunder and lightning, destroying everything. Only Fam was left, because he had been promised a deathless existence, and Nzame cannot take back his word. This is why, although Fam disappeared, we know he still exists and that he harms us when he can. ▣ Looking down at the parched earth, Nzame, Mebere, and Nkwa applied a new layer of earth to it, and when a tree grew it dropped its seeds and made new trees. Leaves that dropped into water became fish, and leaves that fell on the earth became animals. Soon, the earth was reborn. Nzame then created a new Fam, but one who could die. The new man was the ancestor, Sekume, who made the first woman, Mbongwe, from a tree. The first ancestors were made with both Gnoul (body) and Nsissim (soul). Nsissim gives life to Gnoul and is its shadow. When Gnoul dies, Nsissim does not die; he is the little shiny spot in the middle of the eye. This spot is like the star in the heavens or the fire in the hearth. Sekume and Mbongwe prospered and produced many children. Their only worry was the original Fam, who sometimes tunneled up from where Nzambe had left him under the earth and did evil things to them.

Nzazi and the Beautiful Dog (Luangu/DRCongo) Nzazi is lightning. 🔲 A man met a beautiful dog and was so pleased with its appearance that he took it home with him. It was raining heavily, so he took it with him inside his house. He lit a fire, and proceeded to dry and warm his new pet. Suddenly, there was an explosion, and neither man, dog, nor house was ever seen again. The dog, it is said, was Nzazi.

Nzeanzo Retreats from Earth Because His Potency Destroys Many (Bachama, Bata/Nigeria) Venin was the mother of all the Bachama gods. Her death is mourned annually; she is said to have come from the skies. Her brother was Wun, the god of death. Nzeanzo (Janzo, Njanjo), the most honored of the gods, was the youngest of Venin's five sons. His brothers were Gbeso, Hamagenin, Hamalbulki, and Ngbirrim, the founders of Bachama cults. Nzeanzo is the giver of rain; he is the corn god and the creator of man. He is not a remote god, but is immanent on earth, ever present with his people and engaged in a ceaseless contest with Wun. 🔲 While still in his mother's womb, Nzeanzo asked her to permit him to be born before his time. His mother said she had never heard of such a thing, but if he could devise a means of being born, then let him do so. Nzeanzo then came out of his mother's thigh. While he was still a small child, his mother left him behind while she went with her other children to visit her brother, Wun, to purchase cattle. Wun pretended to receive his sister joyfully, but resolved to devour her children. So he set things up so that her sons would sleep with his four daughters. Nzeanzo, fearing that some evil might befall his brothers, decided to follow them to the house of Wun, and arrived in the middle of the night. Divining the wicked intention of Wun, he transferred the clothes of Wun's daughters to his brothers, and the loin coverings of his brothers to the girls. Wun rose up in the darkness, and, feeling along the line of sleeping children, he seized each child who was wearing a boy's loincloth and cast it into a pot of boiling water. He then lay down again to sleep. Nzeanzo then roused his brothers, showed them the children of Wun boiling in the pot and the fate they had escaped. He set his mother and his brothers on the road back to earth and followed, riding on a hunting dog. When Wun woke up and found that he had been tricked, he hurled a river in front of Nzeanzo, but Nzeanzo caused the river to become a stream and leapt across. Wun then cast a marsh in his way, but Nzeanzo caused it to become merely a pool and, vaulting over it, reached home in safety. His brothers now knew that they were no match for Nzeanzo. 🔲 Nzeanzo once collected all the flies in the world and put them in a calabash. He warned his brothers not to open the calabash. But during his absence they opened it, and hence the plague of flies that men are now forced to endure. 🔲 One of Nzeanzo's brothers went to Kona, and when Nzeanzo visited his brother he was attracted by the women of Kona, and took one as a wife. The end of the god's life on earth is not clear. Some say that he died for the people, others that he withdrew from the earth because the potency of his person was causing the death of many.

Fantasy

The use of fantasy, mythic archetypes of antiquity and power, is complex. Fantasy has the effect of placing contemporary images into a fictional framework within which they are experienced and treated as empirical data, the common stuff of ordinary reality. A fantasy world is a secondary world whose metaphysical premises are different from those of the real world, but whose inhabitants are men and women like ourselves, who live in their reality just as we do ours. Fantasy treats mythic materials thus "realistically," not to debunk or to analyze them, but to give them new life, to reinvent them and by doing so give routine experience a new context. Images of fantasy implicitly or explicitly attempt to establish another universe as a mirror of or metaphor for our own. As Tolkien argues (1964, 43–50), the storyteller becomes a subcreator, fashioning a secondary world into which the mind can enter. Inside that world, the mythmaker reveals what is "true," in accordance with the laws of that world. One is now inside that world, and so believes it. But disbelief arises, Tolkien adds, the spell is broken, and the art has failed. The member of the audience is once again in the primary world, viewing the secondary world from outside. Fantasy establishes credentials for the supernatural. It is not enough for the audience to make the assumption that the characters in a myth could exist. The assumption must be made that their whole universe and the power that created it could exist. Fantasy contains essential ambiguity: it is unreal, is a spectral presence, suspended between being and nothingness. It takes the real, breaks it, reinvents it, recombines and inverts the real, but does not escape it.

Obassi Osaw and the First Fire (Ekoi/Niger, Nigeria) There are two deities, Obassi Osaw, the sky god, and the earth god, Obassi Nsi, and there are less powerful spirits. Between them, Obassi Osaw and Obassi Nsi made all things. ▣ They first dwelled together, but after a while agreed to have different lands. Obassi Osaw fixed his dwelling place in the sky, while Obassi Nsi came to earth and lived there. After this separation, Obassi Nsi grew in power, for when a child is born it falls to the earth, and when a man dies he returns to the earth, whence all things have sprung. Obassi Nsi is the governor of all crops that the earth ripens. The sky can be bad; it sometimes sends too much rain, sometimes not enough. Obassi Osaw's eyes are the heavens. The two biggest stars in the heavens are his son and his mother. ▣ In the beginning, Obassi Osaw made everything, but he did not give fire to the people who were on earth. Etim Ne sent a lame boy to ask Obassi Osaw for fire. Obassi Osaw, angry, sent the boy back quickly to earth to reprove Etim Ne for asking for fire. In those days the lame boy had not become lame, but could walk like other people. Etim Ne set out himself for Obassi Osaw's town and asked forgiveness, but Obassi would not pardon him. Etim went home, and the boy laughed at him—a chief, yet he could get no fire. The boy set out to steal fire. When he reached the house of Obassi, the people were preparing food. He helped them, and Obassi, seeing that the boy was useful, did not drive him out of the house. After several days, Obassi sent him to get a lamp from one of his wives. Knowing that it was in the house of the wives that fire was kept, the boy brought the lamp back quickly. On another day, Obassi sent him again, and this time one of the wives told him to light the lamp at the fire. The boy took a brand and lighted the lamp, then wrapped the brand in plantain leaves and tied it up in his cloth. He asked

Obassi for permission to leave for a time. The boy went outside the town where some dry wood was lying. He laid the brand among it, and blew until it caught alight. Then he covered it with plantain stems and leaves to hide the smoke, and went back to the house. That night, when all the people were sleeping, the thief tied his cloth together and crept to the end of the town where the fire was hidden. He found it burning, and took a glowing brand and some firewood and set out homeward. When earth was reached once more, the lad went to Etim and said, "Here is the fire which I promised to bring you." The first fire was made on earth. Obassi Osaw looked down from his house in the sky and saw the smoke rising. He told his eldest son, Akpan Obassi, to find out who had stolen the fire. The boy confessed. Akpan told him that from that day he would not be able to walk. It was the lame boy who brought fire to earth from Obassi's home in the sky.

Obatala Is Tempted with Palm Wine (Yoruba/Nigeria) Obatala was the creator. ◙ In the beginning, the earth was water. Olodumare, the supreme being and sky god, summoned Obatala (Orisa-nla), charging him with the first act of creation—the making of land. Obatala descended to earth with a hen with five toes, a pigeon, and a calabash containing a piece of dry soil. He dropped the soil on the surface of the water, then freed the hen and pigeon, who proceeded to scatter the soil. Obatala then returned to Olodumare to inform him that the earth had been created. Olodumare sent a chameleon to inspect what Obatala had done. The chameleon reported that the creation was a success, that there was much land. Olodumare then sent Obatala to earth once more, this time to create man. Obatala went to earth with the materials of creation. He descended upon Ife, the wide landmass, and began to create man out of clay. As he did this work, he became very tired. He came upon a receptacle filled with palm wine, and he drank and became drunk. As he continued his work, he created the victims of his drunkenness, various afflicted people. Finally, exhausted, he fell into a deep sleep. Some say that Esu, the divine trickster, Orunmila's messenger, unhappy with Obatala's success as a creator, tempted Obatala with the palm wine. Olodumare saw that Obatala was not doing his work properly, so he sent Oduduwa to complete the job. Oduduwa descended upon Ife and found Obatala asleep. He took the receptacle containing the means of creation away from him, peopled Ife with his own brand of humans, and settled them under his powerful leadership. Obatala later awakened, discovered that he had been replaced, and began a lengthy struggle with Oduduwa. (For another version of this story, *see*: Olodumare.) ◙ Some say that the earth and the heavens resemble each other, as a gourd and its cover which float on the water, the submerged part corresponding to the other world, or to the home of invisible forces. *See also*: Esu, Ifa, Oduduwa, Olodumare.

Odomankoma Creates the Universe (Akan/Ghana) Odomankoma is a creator and with Nyame and Nyankopon forms a triad. Nyame represents the revolving universe; Nyankopon, its Kra, or life-giving power; and Odomankoma, the visible world. Odomankoma is many and is everywhere visible. He alone created the world, working with his mind and his hands: a divine craftsman, he created the world by carving or hollowing it out from an inert substance devoid of Kra. He represents creative intelligence, and is venerated as the god of the earth with its mountains, plains, seas, rivers, and trees. 🔲 In his role as architect or craftsman (Borebore), he first created water, the primordial ocean. He then created heaven and earth by lifting up the one and setting down the other. Then other creatures followed, mankind and beasts, the thousands of powers, those things that are seen and those that are not, the numerous things in this world, and the seven-day week, each day of which is ruled by a planet. Odomankoma created Death and Death killed him; Odomankoma left his affairs in the hands of Nyame and Nyankopon. After his death, Odomankoma was resurrected. *See also:* Nyame.

Oduduwa and the Origin of Arable Land (Baoule/Côte d'Ivoire) There are two stages in creation, the first influenced by a primordial god, Oduduwa, the creator, and the second influenced by a couple, composed of Niamie, a heavenly being, and Assie, an underworld spirit. 🔲 Arable land originated from a particle in the sky, a particle that was torn away during a marital argument by Niamie with the intention of throwing it at his rebellious wife.

Oduduwa, Locked in the Darkness, in a Calabash (Yoruba/Nigeria) Oduduwa (Odudua, Oduwa) is the chief goddess of the Yoruba, the creator; she represents the earth. She is the wife of Obatala, but she is contemporary with Olorun—not made by him, as was her husband. She came from Ife, the holy city, in common with most of the other gods. Obatala and Oduduwa represent one androgynous divinity, an image of a human being with one arm and leg, and a tail terminating a sphere. But generally, Obatala and Oduduwa are regarded as two distinct persons. Oduduwa is both a primordial divinity and a deified ancestor. 🔲 Oduduwa was the creator of the earth and its inhabitants as a result of Obatala's failure through drunkenness to carry out Olodumare's injunction. (*See:* Obatala) 🔲 Obatala and Oduduwa, or heaven and earth, resemble two large cut-calabashes, which, when once shut, can never be opened. The shape of the universe is depicted by two whitened saucer-shaped calabashes, placed one covering the other, the upper one of which represents the concave firmament stretching over and meeting the earth, the lower one, at the horizon. According to a myth, Oduduwa is blind. At the beginning of the world, she and her husband, Obatala, were shut up in darkness in a large, closed calabash, Obatala being in the upper part and Oduduwa in the lower. They remained there for many days, cramped, hungry, and uncomfortable. Then Oduduwa began complaining, blaming her husband for the confinement, and a violent quarrel ensued, in the course of which, in a frenzy of rage, Obatala tore out her eyes, because she would not bridle her tongue. In return, she cursed him, saying, "You shall eat nothing but snails." ▣ Oduduwa is the patroness of love. She was once walking alone in the forest when she met a hunter, a man so handsome that the temperament of the goddess at once took fire. The advances that she made to him were favorably received, and they gratified their passion on the spot. After this, the goddess became still more enamored; unable to tear herself away from her lover, she lived with him for some weeks in a house that they constructed of branches at the foot of a large silk-cotton tree. At the end of this time, her passion had burned out, and, having become weary of the hunter, she left him, but before doing so she promised to protect him and all others who might come and dwell in the favored spot where she had passed so many pleasant hours. In consequence, many people came and settled there, and a town gradually grew up, a town named Ado, to commemorate the circumstances of its origin. *See also:* Ifa, Obatala, Ogun.

Ogboinba and the Creation Stone (Ijo/Nigeria) Ogboinba is a woman who oversteps her proper boundaries in an attempt to force the creator, Woyengi, to cure her barrenness by re-creating her. As a punishment for her arrogance, she is condemned to live forever in the eyes of pregnant women and other people, too. ▣ Into a field containing a huge iroko tree descended a table with dirt on it, a chair, and a creation stone. Amid thunder and lightning, Woyengi descended, sat on the chair, and, resting her feet on the sacred stone, took the earth from the table and created the first humans from it, breathing life into them. She told each to choose a gender, a way of life, and a way of death. All got what they asked for, including Ogboinba, who asked for sacred powers. Another woman asked for children who would be successful. Both of these women chose to be born in the same village, and, born of the same parents, they lived together as loving sisters. In time, they married, and one sister bore many wonderful children. Ogboinba produced only magic, and she yearned for children. Unhappy, she embarked on a long journey, going to Woyengi to request a change of fate. Everyone she met told her this would be impossible. She came to Woyengi as she had completed her work of creation and was about to ascend into heaven. She had already chosen her way of life, and this could not be altered. She challenged Woyengi, and God took Ogboinba's sacred and mystical powers away from her. Ogboinba fled into the eyes of a pregnant woman and remained in hiding, in the eyes not only of pregnant women but all eyes of all beings. So it is that when one looks into someone's eyes, Ogboinba looks back at one.

Oghene and the Origin of Death (Isoko, Urhobo/Nigeria) Oghene (Oghenukpabe) is the creator of the world and of life and death. Connected with the sky, he is at the junction of the earth and sky. Oghene is good and kind, though he punishes evil, even by death. An *emema* provided each child by Oghene is responsible for the child's welfare. At death, the personal spirit leaves the world and goes to the underworld where life continues much as it did on earth. ▣ Originally, Oghene created humans to live forever. When a man grew really old, he would be regenerated by sloughing off his old skin like a snake, and assume the skin and vigor of a young man. This process was to be repeated, and so man was to live forever. But as time went on, men increased and the earth became overpopulated. There arose an argument among the men and animals on earth as to what should be done to control the growing population. The dog argued that man should live forever, that Oghene should be implored to extend the frontiers of the earth to accommodate the increasing population. The dog's stand was prompted by his intimate association with man. The toad argued that anyone who dies should go home for good: space in the universe was limited and there was no room for further expansion of the earth. The dog and toad were told to take their views to Oghene in heaven. The views of the one who arrived there first would be accepted, after it had been ratified by Oghene, as the natural law about death. They started on their race to Oghene. The dog soon outran the toad. Convinced that it would get to Oghene before the toad, the dog relaxed, looking for food. It went off the road, overfed itself, and fell asleep. While the dog was sleeping, the toad continued its race. The toad got to heaven first, and said that man must not live forever but must die. The dog woke up later and hurried to cover lost ground, only to find to its dismay and that of man that the toad had already arrived and delivered its message, and that its opinion had been accepted as binding on all creatures. Death came into the world to stay.

Ogun Sinks into the Earth (Yoruba, Nigeria) Ogun is the god of war and iron, and he is the guardian divinity of barbers, blacksmiths, butchers, goldsmiths, hunters, all workers in iron and steel. Ogun stands for justice and is called on to witness covenants. ☐ When the divinities came to inhabit the earth, they encountered a thicket that they could not penetrate. Ogun was finally able to cut a path with his machete, and the gods were grateful. Ogun similarly assists humans as he did the gods at the beginning of time; he has the machete to clear the path and open the gate for wealth, health, and prosperity. But if he is neglected, he can cause ghastly accidents and bloody battles. ☐ Ogun, the son of Oduduwa, helped his father in wars against his enemies. Oduduwa therefore allowed him to reign over Ire, a town in Ekiti. Returning from a battle, Ogun came on a group of Ire people in Ajo Oriki, at a gathering where greetings were forbidden. Ogun, angry because no one greeted him, was further annoyed when he found that the palm-wine kegs were empty. He beheaded people in his fury and then, realizing what he had done, in anguish he thrust his sword into the ground, sat on it, and sank into the earth. Before he disappeared, he assured the people that whenever they needed him they should call on him. *See also:* Gu, Oduduwa.

Olodumare Moves Away from the Earth (Yoruba/Nigeria) The Yoruba have an elaborate hierarchy of deities, each with special duties and functions. They believe in a supreme but remote spirit, Olodumare, also known as Olorun, the lord of heaven and the creator. Some four hundred lesser gods and spirits, known individually and collectively as *orisa*, are recognized. An *orisa* is a person who lived on earth when it was first created and from whom present-day people are descended. Although the supreme being is transcendent, he is not removed from men; he is conceived a social being interested in the lives of people. He is accessible, and can be called on at any time. ▣ At one time, Olodumare and the sky that is his abode were nearer to earth than they are now, so near that one could reach up and touch the sky. Man then annoyed God by using the sky for food and wiping his hands on it. As a result, God and the sky separated themselves from the earth. Since that time, Olodumare has controlled the world from a distance. ▣ Earth was a marshy waste, Olodumare and other gods living in heaven above. But heaven and earth were so close that the denizens of heaven used to descend and ascend by means of a spider's web or a chain, going to earth to hunt. Olodumare, to create the solid earth, summoned Obatala (Orisa-nla), the archdivinity, to his presence, telling him to go and create it. (For another version of this story, see: Obatala.) He gave him loose earth in a snail shell, and, as tools, a hen and a pigeon. Obatala came to the marshy waste, threw the earth down, and released the hen and the pigeon, who immediately spread the earth. Land was created. Olodumare sent the chameleon to inspect the work. He reported that the earth was wide but was not yet solid. On the second inspection, the chameleon said that the work was ready. Olodumare then instructed Obatala to equip the earth. He took Orunmila, the oracle divinity, with him as his adviser and councillor. He was given the primeval palm tree that would provide food, drink, oil, and leaves for shelter. He was given three other trees full of juice to supply drinks for the inhabitants of earth, for as yet there was no rain. The original birds, the hen and the pigeon, were to increase on earth. Then Obatala was asked to lead to the earth sixteen persons already created by Olodumare. The head of these first human beings was Oreluere. Instructed by Olodumare, Obatala molded human forms, keeping the lifeless figures in one place until Olodumare came and breathed life into them. Obatala could create human forms, but that was all he could do; the principle of life was given only by the supreme being. *See also:* Obatala.

Ori and the Rope of Cows' Hide (Madi/Uganda) Ori, the supreme being, is an all-seeing, incorporeal creator who lives in the sky but takes little interest in human affairs. Another word for the supreme being is Rabanga, which stands for the supernatural force responsible for reproduction: Rabanga may be a spirit, Mother Earth, fertility, or the force from which the sun, moon, and stars sprang. ▣ At some time, Ori's wife or mother fell or was expelled from the sky in a shower of rain, and when on earth multiplied her kind. For some time, contact was maintained with the sky by means of a cowhide rope, but this was bitten by a hyena and human attempts to replace it with a bamboo tower failed. ▣ In another version of this myth, Ori is the creator, without body, all present, all knowing, but not interesting himself greatly in human affairs. He lives in the sky, where also man dwelled when he was created. At some time, a man and a woman were for some offense expelled from heaven in a shower of rain (some say that they fell down accidentally), and they increased and multiplied. The gods afterward made a rope of cowhide by which communication was kept up, each side going from time to time to dance with the others, until the hyena bit through the rope. The men thereafter tried to reach the sky by building a tower of bamboo, but after they had built it very high it collapsed.

Osa and the Breath of Life (Bini/Nigeria) Ogbora and a female deity, Odiong, gave birth to Osa (Osanobua), who became the ruler of the universe, the power of Ogbora only extending to the underworld. Osa, the supreme deity, took part in creation, and now prayers and sacrifices are made only to him: he rules the heavens and grants long life. To Ogbora was relegated the super-intendence of Ennimi-ne-Ehiamewin, the heaven of old shells, while his son, Osa, took his place as ruler of the universe. ◙ The next most power-ful of the deities is Ogiwu, the god of lightning, the son of Osalogbora and Adabinyan, who brings death. Ogiwu is always wise, solemn, and so power-ful that Osa cannot force him to obey his orders, especially as regards human beings, since he is the owner of the blood without which man cannot be made by Osa. Ogiwu is responsible for the blood of mankind, the sap in the trees, etc. His wife, Obiemi, the daughter of Osa and Agwa, is loved as kind and good. They had one son, called Okpanigiakon, who used to come down from heaven by a chain and demand the four front teeth from the eldest son of each leader, which he wore strung around his hat. He was at last killed by a slave named Ogiabo during the reign of the king, Ewuare. ◙ For this reason, Ogiwu began to vex the world. Once, in a quarrel, he plunged a sword into the body of Obiemi, so that one could see through her vertically and she could thereafter have no more children. It was because of this that the Omonusa spirits formed, from her excrement, the first man and woman, who, after being provided with blood by Ogiwu and the breath of life by Osa, came down to earth and founded the human race. Though it is Osa who ordains birth, the women pray to Obiemi for assistance in obtaining children and in delivery. ◙ The Ebbaw are believed to have been men who once lived on earth. One branch of them, called Ebami, supposed to number 221, were fol-lowers of Ewuare; they had a great reputation for knowledge and magic. Four-teen of the principal Ebbaw were called Ihe and lived in the earth. They seized the leader, Ewuare, on his travels and released him on condition that he sacri-fice one hundred animals every day, if he succeeded to the kingdom by their aid. After seven years, he grew tired of giving all these animals to them, and attempted, in vain, to burn them. His magic proved of no avail against the Ihe, and he was forced to retire for the three years before his death to Eshi.

Osanobua, Hurried, Creates an Incomplete Man (Edo, Igbo/Benin) Osanobua (Osa) is the creator of all beings both in the world in which humans live (called Agbo) and the other world, the world that cannot be seen, a world (called Erivi) of gods and spirits. Osanobua is like a divine king; his children are also divinities, the initial rulers of places on the earth, places like Benin and Ife. There are other gods: Ogu is the god of iron, Osu of medicine.

Ogiuwu is the king of death. And Oloku, the senior son of Osanobua, identified with water, the seas and the rivers, is also identified with fertility: he is the originator of children. The land of the earth has water on all sides, and if one is to move to Erivi, one must cross these waters. Humans typically make two journeys across these waters, once at birth and once at death. Oloku is therefore a significant figure in the religious beliefs of the people. When a person is about to make the journey to Agbo, the earth, he first stands before Osanobua (or Oloku), and informs him of his plans for his life. At the same time, he asks the creator for the wherewithal to achieve what it is he is setting out to do. Every person has a spiritual shadow, who lives in the other world, Erivi. That spiritual shadow at times mediates between the human and Osanobua. Yet another personal spirit has to do with a person's fortune.
▣ A myth tells of a young man who is being created by Osanobua, about to be born, about to make the journey to Agbo, and as he is being created he sees a beautiful woman and that makes him even more anxious to be born. But God is taking his time, and the young man impatiently hurries to his new world but with a body that is not wholly complete. God has not yet created his penis. And so he moves to Agbo, and his parents, when they discover that his body is not whole, are saddened. Then the parents die, and an old woman brings the boy up. As he moves to adulthood, it becomes evident that he is musically inclined. And when a princess hears his music, she informs her disinclined father that she wants to marry him. But a palmwine tapper sees from the upper reaches of the tree that he is tapping that the young man has no penis, and he tells the king, swearing on his life that what he reports is true. Now the king, who was not happy about the marriage from the start, makes a proclamation that all men must remove their clothing at a place designated in front of the palace. When the young man nervously tells the old woman of his situation, she casts a spell on him and he is transported back to Osanobua, his creator. He is angry as he moves back to the spiritual world because of his incompleteness, and he aggressively moves to fight even with Osanobua. God then provides him with a penis, and the youth returns to earth. And the day when all men must strip arrives. The youth reveals his body, and the king kills the palmwine tapper.   ▣   In another myth, Ovia, a king's wife, becomes a river as she mourns when her co-wives accuse her of making her husband sick.

— ▧ *Osiris, Killed by Set, Is Resurrected by Isis* ▨ —

God's Rebirth Prefigures Man's Rebirth. The two sides of God during the period of creation are frequently represented by antithetical characters—portrayed, for example, by the children of God (*see:* Kintu) or by the wife and brother of God, one representing order, the other chaos. In an ancient Egyptian myth, that dualism is linked to the seasons, and God's death and resurrection, caused by the two external characters, become emblematic of the annual death and rebirth of nature. ⊡ (Egypt) In the beginning, Osiris (Andjeti, Asari, Asartaiti, Aus, Heytau Osiris, Unneffer, Unno, Wenneffer), vegetation god and god of the dead, whose presence was manifested in the sprouting grain and the rising waters of the Nile, invented agriculture, writing, and the arts, and transformed humanity from barbarism to civilization. The goddess Nut, the wife of Ra, had an affair with Seb. When Ra discovered the intrigue, he cursed his wife and decreed that she not be delivered of her child in any month or in any year. The god Hermes, who also loved Nut, gambled with Selene and won from her the seventieth part of each day of the year; added together, these made five whole days. Hermes joined these to the three hundred and sixty days of which the year then consisted. On the first of these five days, Osiris was born; at the moment of his death, a voice was heard to proclaim that the lord of creation was born. In time, he became the king of Egypt; he devoted himself to civilizing his subjects and to teaching them the craft of agriculture, and he established a code of laws. When Egypt was flourishing because of his teachings, Osiris departed, going to instruct the other nations of the world. During his absence, his wife Isis ruled the state so effectively that Set, the evil brother of Osiris, could do no harm to the realm. When Osiris returned, Set plotted with seventy-two comrades and with Aso, the queen of Ethiopia, to kill him. Secretly, he took the measure of the body of Osiris, and built a handsome chest. This chest was brought into his banqueting hall when Osiris was present along with other guests. Osiris was induced to lie down in the chest, which was immediately closed by Set and his fellow conspirators, who conveyed it to the mouth of the Nile. The news was brought to Isis at Coptos; cutting off a lock of hair and putting on mourning apparel, she set out in deep grief to find her husband's body. With the help of children and of dogs, she learned that the chest had been carried by the sea to Byblos, where it had been deposited by the waves among the branches of a tamarisk tree; in a very short time, the tree grew to a magnificent size, enclosing the chest within its trunk. The king of the country, admiring the tree, had it cut down and made into a pillar for the roof of his house. When Isis heard of this, she went to Byblos, where she was made nurse to one of the king's sons. Instead of nursing the child in the ordinary way, Isis gave him her fingers to suck, and each night she put him into the fire to consume his mortal parts, at the same time changing herself into a swallow and bemoaning her fate. But the queen happened to see her son in flames, and cried out, and this deprived him of immortality. Isis then told the queen her story and begged for the pillar that supported the roof. This she cut open, then took out the chest and her husband's body. She wrapped the pillar in fine linen and, anointing it with oil, restored it to the queen. The lamentations of Isis were so terrible that one of the royal children died of fright. Isis then brought the chest by ship to Egypt, where she opened it and embraced the body of her husband, weeping bitterly. Then she sought her son, Horus, in Lower Egypt, first having hidden the chest in a secret place. But one night Set, hunting by the light of the moon, found the chest, and, recognizing the body, tore it into fourteen pieces, which he scattered up and down throughout the land. When Isis heard of this, she took a boat and gathered the fragments of Osiris's body. Wherever she found one, there she built a tomb. Osiris was then brought back to life, and his son, Horus, avenged his death. The story of Osiris, the dying and resurrected god, is also the story of the land: the Nile that settles within its banks during one season, only to overflow those banks and fertilize the land during another. This rhythmical movement of the seasons is linked to the annual ritual commemorating the death and rebirth of the god of agriculture. Osiris is a dualistic creator god, with Set representing his death-dealing side, Isis his life-giving side. *See also:* Horus, Isis, Ra.

Owuo:When His Eye Shuts, A Man Dies (Krachi/Togo) Owuo was Death. Long ago, there was a great famine in the world. A young man, searching for food and straying into a part of the countryside where he had never been before, saw a strange mass lying on the ground. It was the body of a giant, his silky hair stretching from Krachi to Salaga. Awed, the young man wished to withdraw, but the giant asked what he wanted. The young man requested food. The giant, telling him that his name was Owuo, or Death, agreed to give him food on condition that the youth would serve him for a while. He gave him wonderful meat that the boy had never tasted before. Pleased with his covenant, the boy served Owuo a long time, receiving much meat. Then he grew homesick. When he asked Owuo to give him a holiday, the giant agreed, but only if the youth would bring another boy in his place. He returned to his village, persuaded his brother to go with him, and gave him to Owuo. In time, the youth got hungry again and longed for the meat that

George Schweinfurth, The Heart of Africa: Three Years' Travel and Adventures in the Unexplored Regions of Central Africa from 1868 to 1871 (New York: Harper, 1874), p. 444.

A Zande Mythmaker

Owuo had given him, so he left the village and returned to the giant. He told the giant that he wanted more good meat. Owuo told him to enter the house and take as much as he liked, but he would have to work for him again. The youth agreed, entered the house, ate as much as he could, and again worked for the giant. The work continued for a long time, the boy eating his fill every day. But he saw nothing of his brother, and when he asked where his brother was, Owuo told him that he had sent him on an errand. When the youth asked the giant for permission to go home, he was told that he must return with him a girl who would become the giant's bride. At his home, he spoke to his sister, and she agreed to marry Owuo. With a slave as a maid, they journeyed to the home of the giant. The youth left the two girls and went back to the village. Not long after, he again grew hungry, so he made his way once more into the countryside and found the giant. Owuo was not pleased to see the boy, grumbling at being bothered a fourth time. He informed the youth that he could go into the house and get food. The young man entered and gnawed on a bone that he found there. But he soon saw that it was his sister's bone, and now he began to investigate, and he discovered that the meat in the house was that of his sister and her maid. Now he was afraid, and he fled from Owuo, hurrying to his home; when he arrived there, he told the people of his experiences. The people went to see the dread thing, but were afraid when they saw the monster. They returned to the village, then agreed to go to Salaga, where the giant's hair finished and set it on fire. When the hair was burning well, they returned to watch the giant. Beginning to feel the heat, he tossed and sweated. When the fire reached his head, the giant was dead. The young man saw that medicine had been concealed in the roots of the giant's hair. They sprinkled it on the bones and meat in the house, and the girls and the boy returned to life. The youth proposed to pour some of the medicine on the giant, but no one wanted the giant to return to life. The boy showered it into the eye of the dead giant; the eye opened and the people fled in terror. It is from that eye that death comes. Every time Owuo shuts that eye a man dies: he is forever blinking and winking.

Ozidi, Driven by His Grandmother, Fate (Ijo/Nigeria) Ozidi is a mythic hero.
🄷 Ozidi is confronted by impossible tasks. He completes the tasks because of his own extraordinary abilities and his courage, but also because the gods are with him, including the almighty god, Tamara. He is guided by his grandmother, Oreame, a supernatural being who is his fate. The epic tells of the posthumous birth of the general's son, the extraordinary manner of his growing up under the magic wings of his grandmother, Oreame, and of the numerous battles the hero engages in with all manner of men and monsters to regain for his family its lost glory. In this process, as J. P. Clark notes, he oversteps the natural bounds set to his quest, and it is not until he has received a divine visit from the Smallpox King that he emerges purged and is received back into the society of men. Ozidi is a supreme warrior who has

to perform a number of seemingly impossible feats to reach a destined end. Together, they spell out a mission arising out of a personal sense of wrong, the settlement of which determines the future course of public affairs in a powerful state. There is a period of tremendous preparation and initiation to pain, terror, and despair in their most naked forms. But it is not simple human power and courage that takes Ozidi triumphantly through his trials. Each of his opponents possesses these attributes, a good number of them to a greater degree. Ozidi overcomes them all because the gods are with him, including Tamara the almighty, and they are with him because of his filial piety, a devotion to duty. He is an instrument of justice, and wielding him all the time is his grandmother, Oreame, of the supernatural powers, who is fate as well as conscience driving him on. When Ozidi later forgets his true role and overreaches himself in a series of excesses, he is visited with divine punishment, and this time not even the supreme being his grandmother can save him. It is here that, by one quick turn of irony, humanity comes back into its own in the emergence of Ozidi's mother, Orea. She brings innocence and simplicity to the rescue of her heroic son so that, when he recovers purified, there is a general sense of relief and rejoicing that natural order has at last been restored.

Ngai ni mbui kwi wœnzi.
God is sharp, surpassing a razor.

—Kamba proverb

Pemba Moves to Earth on an Umbilical Cord (Bambara/Mali) In the heavens, God created two sets of twins, one a primordial pair, Musokoroni, a woman, and Pemba, her brother; the other, a contrasting pair, Faro and her brother. In the interaction of these pairs of twins the world was brought into being. Musokoroni revealed her rebelliousness from the outset; because of her confrontation with God, she and her brother journeyed to the earth by means of an umbilical cord that, when it was severed, broke their ties with the heavens. When they arrived on the earth, the twins indulged in reckless sexual activities. God, seeing this, angrily threw down the tree of the twins: from this action was born a society of giants who were then, in a sacrifice, destroyed by God. Only some dwarfs survived the cataclysm. But God's actions did not deter the twins, who continued their licentious ways, Musokoroni having sexual relations not only with her brother but with the earth itself, with the trees, the wind, the rays of the sun. The orgiastic activity became so devastating that brother and sister finally separated from each other, and continued their wild behavior. God, watching from the heavens, resolved to cleanse the cosmos. He created a ram, then destroyed it with lightning—it was a sacrifice. God created the second pair of twins, a boy and his sister, Faro. Now the sets of twins would be joined, as God sent this set from heaven in a golden canoe in which was contained the possibilities for the creation of the humans and the animals that would one day populate the earth. Musokoroni continued to defy, preparing the dwarfs to rebel, teaching them, instructing them. As she did this, her own body began to transform: she became uglier, her body bent. This made Musokoroni jealous, and she sought to turn men against Faro, in the meantime sending emissaries to the heavens to find an elixir of youth. But these emissaries were destroyed by God. Musokoroni

209

continued her struggle with Faro, luring men from her, having sexual relations with them, then destroying them. Again, God determined to purify the earth. He sent waters from the heavens, causing floods that drowned the people on the earth. Musokoroni was herself destroyed in the flood—another sacrifice. Faro took the golden canoe and rescued animals and humans, as the era of Musokoroni came to an end and that of Faro began. The ram that had been sacrificed in heaven was sent to the earth where it was, once more, sacrificed by Faro. *See also*: Faro, Mangala, Yo.

Pishiboro's Body Becomes Water, His Blood Becomes Rocks (|Gwikwe/Botswana, Namibia) Pishiboro is the supreme being. ▣ In the beginning, Pishiboro was bitten by a puff adder, and he died. The place where he died was an empty place, and when he died, the world was created: water flowed from his body and the rivers were created, blood coursed from his body and hills and rocks evolved, valleys were the result of his violent death throes, as his body resolved itself into rivers and his hair became the clouds that would create the rain. ▣ In the beginning, Pishiboro observed some of the beings he had created, the humans, and he concluded that they were not what he wanted them to be: they had no hair, they were unattractive. So it was that God determined to recreate them; when he did so he gave them hair, so that when he had completed his creation, the humans were now indistinguishable from the other animals. But the work of creation was not yet complete; now Pishiboro transformed some of these animals that he had made into people, into humans. Now the work of differentiation continued, as God identified some of the creatures he had created as gemsbok, some as wildebeest: these animals would multiply, and their flesh would be eaten by the people. He decreed that it was animals with horns that were to be eaten. People, on the other hand, were not to be eaten: they would walk upright, and when they died they would be buried. The people who had no horns, when they died, should be buried, not eaten. ▣ Today, Pishiboro lives under the ground. He emerges from time to time to destroy humans and to take them with him to his place beneath the earth. *See also*: ‡Gao!na, !Nariba

Polo, A Sphere in Two Parts (Lango/Uganda) Some Lango argue that there is a heaven, presided over by Jok; others insist that there is no heaven. But there is another world: *polo*, a realm that is an image, almost a mirror, of the world that we know. ▣ The universe is conceptualized by the Lango people as a sphere: the bottom part, that with which we are familiar, is the earth; the top part is another world, similar to ours. It also contains people and animals. That top part of the sphere, known as *polo*, is the sky. It is a shadowy world; it cannot be clearly seen from the earth. Between these two worlds is the heavens, and the planetary bodies, the sun, the moon, the stars, can be seen from both of the worlds. When it is day on earth, the moon and the stars can be seen in *polo*. As for the sun, it is said that when it moves to the west, it moves quickly again to the east, thence to begin its movement again in the morning. ⬛ The world of *polo*, that other world, is inhabited by people. Sometimes Jok—who is conceived of as being like the wind, never seen, always present—transports people of this world to the world of *polo*, and he also brings people of *polo* to earth. It is said that the inhabitants of the world of *polo* are much like the inhabitants of earth, except that there are no white people, and that the people have tails and eat fried flies. It is a world of plentiful livestock, enormous resources, unending plenty. The first inhabitants of this world of *polo* were a man, Olum, and his wife, and it is said that they also had tails. *See also:* Jok.

P

Mythmakers on the Emotions, I

Mdukiswa Tyabashe (1897–1970), a Xhosa mythmaker, spoke of the composition of a mythic work of art: "The way a poem is expressed," he said, "depends on the poet himself." The effectiveness of a mythmaker depends on the extent to which "their spirits push them." Emotions, he argued, are the essential ingredient: "If my feelings are indifferent to what's going on, then my poem will reflect this." The colors in the mythmaker's reservoir are brilliant—imperative, because they are meant to dynamically affect the emotions, first calling them forth, then working them into form. To understand myth, to comprehend story, one must have a rich sense of emotion and the way meaning becomes involved in emotion—more important, the way emotion provides the essence of meaning. "I feel it, I feel it!" exclaimed Ashton Ngcama, a Xesibe mythmaker also from South Africa, discussing the making of myth. He argued that the images of poetry, myth, came to him during the actual process of performance, as in a dream and without his conscious activity. He said that he stored these images in his mind; then, when he composed, he subconsciously brought them to the surface: "They simply come." When he evoked images of Mount Nolangeni, for example, to praise it as the mythic repository of Xesibe tradition, he was not consciously aware of what he was saying. When the performance came to an end, he did not know what he had been saying. It was as if he had been in a trance, he said. Nevertheless, mythmakers are fully cognizant of the central role played by feelings in their works.

Q

Qamatha Sends the Chameleon with a Message (Xhosa/South Africa) Qamatha is
the creator. The Xhosa name for God is Mdali, the supreme being. Other
names by which he is known are Thixo and Qamatha, a legacy from the
Khoi and possibly the San. Qamatha, the creator of all things, controls all
things. A Xhosa poet observed that in the absence of Qamatha, without the
rules laid down by Qamatha, there would be confusion on the earth, madness, uncertainty. Qamatha was usually addressed through the spirits of
the ancestors; these spirits provided necessary links between God and men.
▣ Man and beast emerged from a subterranean hole or cavern; in some
cases, the creator had a role in bringing them forth. Indentations on surrounding rocks are believed to be the footprints of the first men and their
animals. Generally, the place is reputed to be either in the north or in the
east, depending on the direction from which the people originally migrated,
and linked for some with the rising sun. There is a cavern in the east, which
is called *uhlanga*. This cosmological association with the east has a ritual
significance because traditionally the entrance to the main house in the
homestead faced east, and the chiefs were also buried facing east. The cattle
emerged first, followed by mankind, and then various beasts and birds, in
consecutive order. After many unsuccessful attempts, mankind eventually
domesticated the cattle. They were lured to the cavern entrance by the smell
of blood, and, as they stood around the spot bellowing, were surrounded and
taken. ▣ A certain man had three sons, whose names were Ibranana,
Xhosa, and Twa. Ibranana was a keeper of cattle, sheep, and goats, as was also
Xhosa, while Twa was satisfied with his honey bird and his game in the
desert. Ibranana, the ancestor of the Khoi, was not a tall man, and his complexion was sallow. Twa, the ancestor of the San, was shorter and more slen-

der, and also of a sallow complexion, but a shade lighter. And Xhosa was a tall, muscular man, and dark colored. ⊡ Qamatha sent the chameleon to earth to tell people that they would never die. The chameleon journeyed to the earth; on the way it got tired and rested. A lizard asked where the chameleon was going. Then the lizard ran and told the people that they would die. A big outcry erupted on the earth; people were crying because they were going to die. When the chameleon heard this outcry, it proceeded to the earth to tell the people that it would not be like that, they would never die. The people did not believe the chameleon, believing instead the word of the lizard. That is why people die. ⊡ Lightning was conceived as a bird, Impundulu or Intakezulu, the bird of heaven. Thunder was the beating of its wings. Impundulu was said to be dazzling in the brilliance of its different colors. It set its fat on fire and sent it down as lightning. Where this struck, it left its eggs. These resembled hen's eggs and were thought to bring bad luck to the neighborhood where they were laid. Another belief was that Impundulu was the servant of death of the supreme being, and was greatly feared as a messenger of death. *See also:* Mdali, Thixo.

Wakitega, Murungu eonza.
When you set the trap, God inspects it.

—Asu proverb

R

Ra, Enclosed in the Bud of a Lotus (Egypt) Ra (Re), the creator and supreme being, is the sun, sovereign lord of the sky. His principal sanctuary is at Heliopolis. Formerly, the sun god reposed, under the name of Atum, in the bosom of Nun, the primordial ocean. ▣ To assure that his luster not be extinguished, he kept his eyes shut. He enclosed himself in the bud of a lotus when, weary of his own impersonality, he rose by an effort of will from the abyss and appeared in splendor under the name of Ra. He then bore Snu and Tefnut, who, in their turn, gave birth to Geb and Nut, from whom issued Osiris and Isis, Set and Nephthys. These are the eight gods who with their chief Ra (Ra Atum) form the divine company or Ennead of Heliopolis. ▣ Ra drew from himself and without recourse to woman the first divine couple. Men and all other living creatures came from Ra's tears. At the same time, Ra created a first universe, different from the present world, which he governed from Heliopolis. But Ra grew old, and Isis took advantage of the god's senility and made him reveal his secret name so that she might acquire sovereign power. The ingratitude of men inspired in Ra a distaste for the world and a desire to withdraw himself beyond reach. So on the orders of Nun, the goddess Nut changed herself into a cow and took Ra on her back. She raised him high into the vault of heaven, and at the same time the present world was created. ▣ From the moment the sun god left the earth for heaven, his life was immutably regulated. During the twelve daylight hours, he rode in his boat from east to west across his kingdom. He had to take care to avoid the attack of his eternal enemy, Apep, the great serpent who lived in the depths of the celestial Nile and sometimes succeeded in swallowing the solar barque (total eclipses were the result). Apep was always at last vanquished by Ra's defenders and cast back into the abyss. During the twelve hours of darkness, the perils that Ra faced were even greater. But they, too, were overcome. Ra was born each morning in the guise of a child who grew until midday and afterwards fell into decline, to die that night an old man. *See also*: Horus, Isis, Neith, Nut, Osiris.

Raluvhimba, Flame on a Platform of Rock (Venda/South Africa) Raluvhimba (Raluvhimbi, Mwari), the supreme being, the creator, is a monotheistic deity. He is the maker and shaper of everything, providing for the community of humans, rewarder of good, punisher of evil. Ancestral gods, Badzimu (singular, Mudzimu), are mediators between humans and Raluvhimba. When a human dies, he becomes a Mudzimu. If he dies far from home, he returns to the mountain of his people to join his ancestors. After a period of some years, he is worshiped. 🔲 At a place called Luvhimbi is a cave which is visited at times by Raluvhimba. It is here that he presents himself to the people. 🔲 It is said that Raluvhimba is in all natural phenomena, in thunder and the stars. And when there is a rain storm, he reveals himself in the thunder, making his demands known. When he is angry with the people, he expresses his anger with drought or flood. It is with the chief that Raluvhimba is most closely tied; so it is that when rain is desired, it is the chief who performs a ritual which brings him into contact with God. When rains come, Raluvhimba is seen in a fire near the chief's home. *See also*: Mwari.

Rasoalavavolo Transforms Stones into People (Malagasy/Madagascar) The home of Rasoalavavolo is under the water. She is beautiful, has very long hair, which is why she is called Rasoalavavolo, long-haired. Some say that she is a Vazimba, one of the original inhabitants of Madagascar, and others argue that she belongs to one of the conquered royal families. 🔲 A woman named Rasoavolovoloina went to visit her and asked for a child. She offered Rasoalavavolo two silver rings and gave her two round smooth stones, which thereupon became two male children. When the two brothers grew up, they went to visit Rasoalavavolo under the water to offer her a gift, a string of coral beads, but she was asleep when they came and so did not speak with them. The brothers were the ancestors of the people who have since inhabited Madagascar.

Rdah Umm Zayed, Doomed from Birth (Arabic/Tunisia) Rdah Umm Zayed is a woman cursed from the outset of her life. 🔲 A childless king prays for a child. An angel appears, telling him to choose between a daughter with a misfortune but who survives, and a son with a misfortune who dies. A daughter is born, and the king builds a glass palace for her so that she might avoid misfortunes. She grows up in the glass palace. One day, she taps on the floor, it breaks open, and for the first time she sees people other than her parents and the maid. She hears a woman singing and invites her to the palace. The woman is amazed at the daughter's beauty, and tells her that she needs musk oil to perfume her hair. The princess falls ill, and tells her father that she wants musk oil. The father is angry and suspicious, fearing that this is the beginning of her misfortune. The queen tells him to get the oil. Hmid al-Hilali learns of this beautiful woman and seeks her. He is told that hell is at the end of the path he has chosen, but he persists. He gets nearer Tunis, and the perfume is now stronger. A woman shows him the way to the glass palace. The maid tells Rdah of the handsome knight, and Rdah asks him how he can aspire to a tree he can never climb. But they spend three nights together; she gives him her necklace and sends him to her father. But he first goes to his own land and asks his cousin to see the king on his behalf. He goes to his wife, who is bitter and says they must go their separate ways. The king receives the cousin, learns of what has happened, and orders his daughter thrown out in rags. Rdah is abused by the two men sent by the cousin of Hmid al-Hilali; she becomes sick because of the heat of the sun, is dying, and the men say to let her die. She dies, and the cousin finds a new bride and veils her. But Hmid al-Hilali will not accept her; he sighs and dies.

Rhampsinitus and the Headless Man (Egypt) Rhampsinitus was a king of Egypt.
He was rich and greedy, and had so much gold and silver he had no place to put it. He had a mason build a strong room with no windows in a corner of the palace; the gems and gold filled that place, and the king was happy and secure. The mason who had built the room, however, had been badly paid by the king. Now he was dying and had nothing to leave to his two sons. He told them of a mark he had made on a stone in the king's room. When it was removed, they would have access to the valuables. One night, they went there and took as much gold and silver as they could carry. This went on and on, until the king began to notice that his treasure was diminishing. Finally, he set a trap big enough to hold a man's leg. When the two brothers entered, one was caught in the trap. He told his brother to cut off his head so that the king would not know who had penetrated his room; otherwise, the brother would be killed as well. Reluctantly, he did that, and the king was amazed the next day when he went into the room and found the headless man. The king, to catch the thief's accomplice, had the body hung on a wall to see if anyone came to mourn. The other son told his mother what had happened, and she said he must get the body and bury it, that she would tell the king what had happened if he did not do this. The son then placed leather sacks of wine on the backs of six asses, wine he had purchased with the king's money. He drove the asses to the wall where his brother's body was hanging, and allowed the wine to trickle onto the ground. He tore his hair, crying out, trying to keep the wine from dripping, and the guards hurried and got cups to catch the wine to drink it. They became drunk, fell asleep, and the youth, having shaved the beards of the soldiers, took his brother's body from the wall and buried it. In the morning, people laughed at the soldiers, the king was furious, and he sent a herald around the country to say that rather than punish the inventive man who had stolen the money he would give him his daughter in marriage. But he must first tell the

king how he gained access to the treasure room. When the young man came forward and confessed, the king concluded that Egyptians were cleverer than other men, and that this youth was cleverer than all the Egyptians.

Rugaba Calls Niavingi to Him (Ziba/Tanzania) Rugaba is the supreme being. ◙ Long ago, the people of Mpororo decided that they wanted a queen, not a king. They asked a woman of brilliance to be their queen. Giving her spear and shield, they submitted to her. She was called Niavingi, and she was queen for many years; the people loved her. One day, the chief minister sought her and found her lying dead on her bed. He decided not to tell the people that she had died. Instead, he told them that she had gone to Rugaba, God, that God said that she had done her duty and now wanted her to live near him in his city and he would reward her. He told the people, and no one wept. They rejoiced that their queen was living near God.

Ruhanga and the Three Seeds of Life (Nyankole, Nyankore/Uganda) Ruhanga (Katonzi, Kazooba, Rugaba), who lived in the sky, was known as the creator, the powerful one. ◙ Ruhanga created a man, Rugabe, and his wife, Nyamate, and sent them to people the earth. They had a son, Isimbwa, the first of a dynasty of kings who ruled the country and did not die but became gods of the people. The first deified kings included Isimbwa, son of Rugabe, Ndahura, and Wamara. The mother of Kyomya, another deified king, was a princess and the sister of Wamara, who married her; Kyomya was their son. Later, Wamara sent the woman away but kept the son, who became a trader and wandered to Bukoba with salt, coffee berries, cats, and other goods. When he returned to Ankole, he herded livestock for a cowman named Kyana, who also made him gather firewood. Soon, the wife of Kyana began to suspect that Kyomya was not an ordinary mortal, and she and her husband laid traps for him, but he evaded them all. One day, while he was gathering firewood, Kyomya discovered the sacred drums that his father, Wamara, had received from the moon and that Kyana had stolen. He flicked his fingers, and the drums came to him. A few days later, he left Kyana to take the drums back to his father at Ruwanda in Ankole near Kabula. After that, he left the world and became a god. ◙ When Ruhanga created the first man and woman, he also created a peasant man and woman to be their servants, and these were the ancestors of the serfs. ◙ In the beginning, Ruhanga put three seeds into the ground, and in one day three calabashes had grown, all on one stem. He took a man and a woman out of the first calabash, and a man and a woman out of the second, while out of the third he took a man only. The men he called, respectively, Kakama, Kahima, and Kairu. He then put them through a test to show their worth. To each he gave a milk pot full of milk, and he led them to a water hole, where they were told to remain for the night, and they were warned against going to sleep, lest they spill their milk. Ruhanga left them, saying that he would return in the morning. At midnight, Kairu went to sleep, and though the other two woke him up from time to time, he spilled his milk. It is for this reason that, by Ruhanga's command, Kairu, even now, gets his food from the ground. Later in the night, Kakama also began to doze, and Kahima woke him up; but he got so sleepy after a while that Kahima was unable to awaken him, so he spilled half his milk. In the morning, Ruhanga came and found Kahima had only half of his milk in the pot, and he inquired why. Kahima told him that Kakama had spilled half his milk and asked Kahima to fill up his pot for him. Kahima had agreed to do that and had filled Kakama's pot, so that Kahima's pot was left only half full. Ruhanga told Kakama that he would be supplied with milk forever by Kahima, who had given away his luck to the other; he would obtain food grown by Kairu, as Kakama's milk had mixed with that of Kairu when it trickled into the water hole. Kakama was the ancestor of the Kama, or rulers of Ankole; Kahima was the ancestor of the Hima, or cattle-men; while Kairu was the ancestor of the Iru, or agriculturists. ▣ The sun is held up by an old woman named Nyakakaikuru, lest it should fall on the earth. The sun is created each morning in the east by Ruhanga. It then travels to the west, where it is killed and eaten by Nyakakaikuru. She then throws a small piece of the meat onto the sky and it travels to the east, where it is used by Ruhanga to make a new sun. *See also*: Chwezi, Kana, Ndahura, Wamara.

Ruhanga Fails to Prevent the Coming of Evil (Nyoro/Uganda) Ruhanga (Katonzi, Kazoba, Mukameiguru, Nyamuhanga, Rugaba) was the creator of all things. People did not call upon him for assistance, because he had done his work and there was no need to ask further favors of him. Other gods could assist in multiplying humans, cattle, and crops; they could also heal sickness and prevent plagues. The creator was therefore not troubled about these matters, nor was he thought of except when they desired to give him the honor that was due him as the maker of all things. The spiritual beings with whom Nyoro have most organized interaction are Chwezi spirits and ancestral spirits. The Chwezi spirits, Mbandwa, derive from the legendary Chwezi, who founded a dynasty in Bunyoro centuries ago, then, after ruling for a generation or two, vanished mysteriously. They possessed remarkable wisdom and skills, and left behind them a technique of spirit possession, of which they themselves were the subjects. By this means, their successors could gain access to the power and knowledge that they embodied and enjoy through them protection, well-being, and, especially, fertility. The Chwezi spirits traditionally numbered nineteen—some were associated with plenty, smallpox, harvest, royalty, healing, weather, and cattle. ▣ Bunyoro traditions distinguish three dynasties. The source of the first, very obscure dynasty is the supreme god called Ruhanga. He separated the sky and the earth, retired forever into the sky, created the conditions of life on earth, but failed to prevent the advent of evil and death, and finally established the unequal roles of the three social components: the king and his clan, the herdsmen, and the farmers. ▣ The last king of this mythical dynasty, Isaza, was approached by the king of the netherworld, who proposed a blood pact and sought to take over entirely the earthly world by the other two. A shrewd little servant maid invited Isaza to thwart the plan by sending not his own blood but that of his servant, Moon. But the king of the underworld, informed about this trick, decided to lure Isaza into the netherworld against his better judgment by first sending him his daughter, Nyamata. This trick failed. He then sent him two beautiful cows, who made him fall into a fatal abyss and finally made him a captive of the netherworld. But Nyamata bore him a son, Isimbwa, who later went hunting on earth with his own son, Kyomya. On earth, a usurper reigned, Bukuku, Isaza's former porter, and the diviners foretold that the son who would be born of his daughter would kill him and succeed him. To forestall his daughter's seduction, Bukuku shut her up in an enclosure without doors and left her only one eye and one ear. The wandering Isimbwa found her nevertheless and gave her a son, Ndahura, who was taken in by a potter; later Ndahura killed Bukuku, and after a few more adventures became the first king of the supernatural dynasty of the Chwezi, who originally came from the sky and from Ruhinda, but reemerged from the netherworld to reign on earth for the great happiness of mankind. Ndahura expanded his dominion over a vast empire, the Kitara, which encompassed the whole western zone and beyond. He did not die, but disappeared, and left his succession to his son Wamara, who brought the dynasty to a close. *See also:* Chwezi, Ndahura, Nyamiyonga, Wamara.

Ryangombe, Killed by an Unwed Mother (Nyarwanda/Rwanda) Imana is the creator god. The visible world is set against a world populated by spirits and evil influences. Among these is Ryangombe (known as Kiranga in Burundi), a spirit, a god-king. He is an invisible spirit, generally malevolent, greatly feared, but a sort of minister of Imana, carrying out his orders. He gives good things to those who pray to him, and preserves them from evil. ▣ The god-king Ryangombe is a prominent hunter, is close to nature, and provides benefits to his faithful followers. But his hunting activities are a threat to cultural order. He is closely linked with nature, and neglects his obligations to the society, including his relations with women. Because of his preoccupation with gaming, hunting, and sex, he overlooks these broader obligations. He is king of the Imandwa, an army of ruffians who become helpful spirits; after his tragic end, they follow him to the afterworld. Ryangombe is killed by an unwed mother without breasts who transforms into a buffalo. Dying, Ryangombe establishes his cult, promising the Hutu, Tutsi, and Twa that, if they pay him homage, they will thereby have the prosperity denied them by ancestral spirits and ineffectual rites. *See also:* Imana.

Mythmakers on the Emotions, II

"When I am praising," says the Xhosa mythmaker, "I cannot repeat the poem once I have completed it, because it is not I who says it. It comes on its own. When I visualize something, be it a king or someone who is, let us say, reading a book, or a preacher, or someone who is praying—when I look at this person, the brain wave gets to me. When it has come, then I have to say something about him. And when I have said it, I won't know it again, I won't be able to repeat it. Now I don't know where this thing comes from. It's as if I were dreaming, because when I'm praising, I don't think. My mind stops functioning; I cannot think. If, perhaps, someone behind me is thinking something, I may well express it before that person actually articulates it. He says, 'My! You're saying what I was thinking, and yet I haven't uttered it to anyone!' But I did not know what I was saying, it is only when this other person tells me what I was saying that I realize the subject of my words." One does not undergo an apprenticeship to learn how to do it. "It's a feeling! It's a feeling!" he exclaims. "If a preacher approaches, you have a feeling—it's the same thing. It comes to the same thing. When we say our prayers, we don't know what we have said. We cannot repeat them. It comes in that way—that's how it comes to me, you see. I have been asked by many chiefs to create poetry, but I can't, because I don't remember. Even what I am saying now, I cannot repeat it. It belongs to *ithongo*, dreams." He concludes, "I don't know why *umoya*, the spirit, comes to one. But it is *umoya* that causes me to do it."

Sabenas and the Drum of Iron (Tuareg/Western Sahara) Sabenas was a mythic ancestor. The important noble clans of the Kel Ferouan drum-group (a drum is the insignia of the chief in all Tuareg groups)—namely, the true Kel Ferouan and the Kel Azel—are said to be matrilineally related, as the ancestor of the Kel Azel was a woman of the Kel Ferouan clan. ◨ She married, tradition says, an Arab who was killed at her request. Sabenas was the ancestor of the noble clan and the first ruler of the Kel Ferouan drum-group. Her drum was made of iron. ◨ The chief of the noble Kel Ferouan clan had the only drum of the group of which he was supreme chief. The drum followed him on journeys, and there were various signals used to summon his subjects. These signals should be obeyed not only by members of all vassal clans but also by the noble Kel Azel. The drum is made of wood and covered with skin. It has a mystic power. Therefore, when the skin was worn and had to be replaced, the man charged with this task would do it looking away from the drum, lest he be struck blind. The drum must never come into contact with soil or water, and it must never be touched by women. Drum-chiefs are installed by a vassal Tuareg of the group, who, appointing the chief, wraps a new veil or turban around his head. The drum-chief sanctions the election of all chiefs of clans belonging to his group. He installs them ceremoniously, providing them with veils. The drum-chief had the supreme jurisdiction over his group.

Sagbata and the Bird That Reconciled (Fon/Benin) In the earth pantheon, Sagbata (Azo) is the god of smallpox. Sagbata comes from Mawu and Lisa. Mawu is one person with two faces, that of a woman, Mawu, the eyes of whom are the moon, and that of a man, Lisa, the eyes of whom are the sun.

Mawu directs the night; Lisa, the day. Mawu-Lisa gave birth first to twins called Dada Zodji (male) and Nyohwe Ananu (female). These twins mated and produced several children, who are the Sagbata gods. Mawu-Lisa divided the realms of the universe among their offspring. ⊡ A quarrel between two of the children, Sagbata and Hevioso, arose over the division of the universe. As a result, Sagbata, being the eldest child, went to live on the earth, taking his parents' riches with him. However, he either forgot or was unable to carry with him the rain, which was one of the creator's most important riches. Consequently, Hevioso was able to withhold the rain from the earth to avenge himself on his brother. There was a great drought, and the earth was in danger of conflagration. Through the intervention of a bird called Otutu (Wututu) which rises high into the air, the two brothers were eventually reconciled, and since then there has been no danger of a perpetual drought. *See also:* Hevioso, Legba, Lisa, Mawu, Mawu-Lisa.

Sa Na Duniya Supports the Earth on Its Horn (Hausa/Niger, Nigeria) Sa Na Duniya is the Bull of the World. ⊡ The earth is said to be a female, supported on one of the horns of the Sa Na Duniya, Bull of the World, and when he gets tired holding it on one, he tosses it to the other, and it is this that makes the earth quake. It is flat like a plate, divided in two by a wall, and it meets the sky. ⊡ The stars were once human beings. Long ago, some Maguzawa boys began to throw stones at an old woman, the world, who was sweeping the ground in front of her house, and she was annoyed by this. So she gave them her calabash of rubbish to empty, and immediately after they began to rise in the air, and at last they reached the sky. When they arrived there, God told them to remain, and so they have been there ever since. ⊡ In another version of this myth, the stars were always stars, but were once quite near the earth, being moved up above by the old woman because the boys were throwing stones at them. ⊡ When stars fall, it shows that they are fighting among themselves; some are running away and are being killed. They foretell battles upon earth, because they thus induce warfare among human beings. Shooting stars are thrown by angels at demons that have been prying into the secrets of paradise to tempt the inhabitants.

Sango and the Lightning Charm (Yoruba/Nigeria) Sango is the solar and thunder divinity, the lightning god. His wives were the rivers Awya (the Niger), Oshun, and Obba, who perhaps represented the tornado, the darkness, and the storm clouds. Among his servants were the wind, Afefe, and the rainbow, Oshumare, whose duty it was to carry up water from the earth to his palace. He is also the god of the chase. ⊡ Sango, the storm god, was the fourth king of Oyo. He was a tyrannical and powerful man, and so flamboyant that he is said to have sent out clouds of fire and smoke from his mouth. One version of the myth says that Sango discovered a charm by means of which he could call down lightning from heaven, and he went up a hill near the city to try its effect. The charm worked too well: a storm blew up at once, but the lightning descended on Sango's own palace and destroyed it. Most of his wives and children perished in the fire, and Sango was so broken in spirit that he hanged himself on an *ayan* tree of which wood the axes are made. ▣ Another version says that Sango ascended to heaven during a storm, or that he disappeared into the earth on a long chain. ▣ Sango's consort is Oya, the Niger River. In one story, he is said to have chased her across the sky, rising like the sun and following her all day until he reached the place where heaven and earth meet, and she hid in the sea. Oya has some storm characteristics; she is fierce and bearded, her face so terrible that no one can look at it, and her anger is greatly feared. She is said to strike down houses, and is often identified with the wind that blows when no rain follows.

Segbo and the Children with Wands (Fon/Benin) Segbo (Dada Segbo, Da Segbo) was king of the gods, early ruler of the world of men, the supreme soul. ▣ In ancient times, a man and a woman came down from the sky in the rain, the first family on the earth. They wore long skirts, and carried a wand and a calabash. The rain continued for seventeen days. They did not speak during this time, except to repeat, "Segbo," the name of the one who sent them to the earth. Seven days later, another man and woman descended from the sky, wearing Lisa's beads. They came to teach the worship of Mawu and Lisa, and when they had sacrificed to those creator gods, it rained again, and other people came down from the sky with the rain. When the ceremony was over, they returned to the sky. After other such rituals, and after establishing shrines to the gods, the couple wearing Lisa's beads returned to the sky, leaving behind them the beads and a daughter. She gave birth to a son and a daughter, each with a small wand in hand that grew as they grew. Seven years passed, and their parents returned to the sky. The children, always with the wands and therefore never lost, grew up and continued to teach the worship of the sky gods. ▣ The first pair who came from the sky had a chameleon with them, sent by Lisa to protect them. To shield the people against the enemies who might refuse to accept their teaching about the gods, the smooth skin of the chameleon reflected what occurred behind their backs: when the enemy came from behind, that was reflected in the skin of the chameleon, who was sacred to the god, Lisa. *See also*: Lisa, Mawu, Mawu-Lisa.

Sheuta and the Man-killing Woman (Bondei, Shambaa, Zigula/Tanzania) Sheuta was the primeval ancestor. ▣ A hunter who lived in a cave in the wilderness was befriended by a lion that shared its meat with him. Sheuta went hunting with his dogs and met an elephant that grabbed hold of Sheuta's penis and stretched it until it was long enough for Sheuta to sleep with the elephant. It then gave Sheuta a magical charm for making his penis longer or shorter at will. At this time, there was a woman named Bangwe who killed men once they had slept with her. Men from all over Shambaai were dying until Sheuta came and murdered Bangwe by lengthening his penis as he was having intercourse with her. The Shambaa were so happy at having rid the land of its scourge that they made Sheuta chief. He came through the wilderness from the south to an island in the middle of the river, in the land of women in which a woman was chief. Sheuta, naked, hid himself. He had with him his bow and arrows, roasted meat, and honey. When the women discovered him, Sheuta gave each one a taste of honey from his finger, which he dipped and then offered. At night, Sheuta slept in one part of the great house with the chief of the women, while those who served her slept in another part. The chieftainess became familiar with the masculine body, and with the functions of the various organs. The next morning, when she explained to the women what she had seen, heard, and felt, the women demanded that they be given men of their own. When their leader refused, the women decided to make Sheuta their chief, and their former leader became his wife. *See also*: Mbegha.

Shibeika, the Sword of Munshattih (Nuba/Sudan) Shibeika was a mythic sword. ▣ After journeying from Shendi, where they parted from Mek Nimr, Mek Musa'ad and his son, Munshattih, went to Ethiopia and raided the Ethiopians until the rainy season ceased their warfare. Because they had no salt, the climate there did not suit them, and as a result Mek Musa'ad and most of his followers died there. Munshattih led the remainder of his people to the country of Beshir el Ghul (who had founded a semi-independent kingdom on the Ethiopian border), and dwelled near him. He fell into want and sold his sword, the famous Shibeika, to Beshir el Ghul for a hundred ounces of gold, promising him that it would cut through two iron fetters. After two days, Beshir, wanting to test the sword, brought it out in his council, and after producing two rings of iron, struck at them, but the sword did not cut even one. They sent to Munshattih, and told him that he had sold them a poor piece of iron. It would cut through nothing, they said, and they demanded that he return their money. Munshattih came to Beshir el Ghul and his brother, and told them to bring more iron. They laughed, but brought two more rings and laid them on the first. Munshattih took the sword from them and, kneeling on one knee, struck with it, and it cut through all the iron and buried itself in the ground. He stood up and put the sword on his shoulder, saying, "I sold you the sword. Can I sell you my arm as well?" Mounting his horse, he went to his people, taking both gold and sword, saying, "He who wishes to overtake me, let him do so." But the Hamada, marveling at his strength, concluded that they could not fight this man, that he would destroy them. So they let him go. Munshattih gathered the rest of his people and went to Runga, where he dwelled near the Fung king. Later, the people of Beshir el Ghul overcame him by means of a beautiful slave girl, a sorcerer, who insinuated herself into his presence at a drinking party and put a charm on his vitals. Munshattih, in great pain, called his slave and told him to bring Shibeika and his two other swords and his horse, saddled. When the slave had done that, Munshattih told him to take the three swords and ride and give them to his uncle, Mek Nimr, that if he did that he would be free, he and his wife and his children, all of them. Then he died, sitting there in his chair with his eyes open, and angry, so that all who came and saw him sitting there were afraid and went back. So he stayed three days, until they smelled the smell of him and knew that he was indeed dead. Then they took him and washed him, shrouded him, and buried him.

Shida Matunda and the Blood of a Dead Woman (Nyamwezi/Tanzania) Shida Matunda was the creator. 🔲 He made the earth and everything in it, then created two women and took them as his wives. When his favorite wife died, Shida Matunda buried her in her house, watering her grave each day. After a time, a plant grew from the grave, and Shida Matunda knew that the dead woman would rise again. The other wife was not allowed to come near the grave, but one day, curious, she went to the grave, saw the plant, and jealously cut it. The blood of the dead woman gushed out, filling the house. Shida Matunda saw the blood and was afraid. Because she had killed her co-wife, all men, animals, and plants would die. From that co-wife, all other humans descended.

Shikwembu, Who Dwells Under the Earth (Tsonga/South Africa) Shikwembu is the creator. 🔲 A person, when he dies, becomes a Shikwembu, an ancestral spirit. The ancestor gods, Psikwembu, dwell in a place under the earth, in a village where everything is white.

Sidi Adjille Mahomet and the Mule's Feed Bag (Arabic/Morocco) Sidi Adjille was a saint. 🔲 Mouley Mahomet summoned Sidi Adjille to come to Morocco or he would be put into prison. The saint refused to go until the prince had sent him pledges of safety. He began his journey to Morocco, and did not eat or sleep during the three days of the trip. The prince told him that he could have anything that he wanted at the palace. So Sidi Adjille asked that his mule's feed bag be filled with wheat. The prince ordered that the feed bag be filled. The door of the first granary was opened, and wheat was put into the feed bag until the granary was empty. Another granary was opened and the wheat in it was exhausted, then a third and a fourth and a fifth—until all the granaries of the king were emptied. The prince was told that the granaries were all empty, yet they had not been able to fill the feed bag of the saint's mule. Then the people saw donkey drivers from many countries, taking wheat on mules and camels. The drivers said it was the wheat of Sidi Mahomet Adjille. The king asked the saint why he acted this way, considering that the granaries were empty. He and his council decreed that Sidi Adjille's head should be cut off. The saint finished his ablutions, then he lifted his eyes to heaven, got into the tub where he was washing, and he vanished.

Silamaka and the Sacred Serpent of the Woods (Fulani/Mali) Silamaka, a historical figure, is also a mythic hero. As a leader, Ardo, of the Fulani, he lived under Da Monzon, King of Segu, and rebelled against him. 🔲 Silamaka, shortly after birth, reveals great ability. When Da Monzon's messengers see a horsefly sucking blood from his forehead, they conclude that he is to be feared, and Da Monzon concludes that he must be killed. But nothing can kill Silamaka and his companion, Puluru, the son of a slave. When Silamaka grows up, a young woman challenges him to confront Da Monzon. Silamaka discovers that, to become invulnerable, he has to capture a sacred snake alive and wear it as a belt. He does what no other warrior has been able to do. A hero, Hambodedio insults Puluru, and, during their struggle, Silamaka spares him. The next year, Silamaka insults Da Monzon, and defeats Da Monzon's armies. But in the end, he has to flee to his home, and is assisted by Puluru and his sister. Now Da Monzon's armies set out against Silamaka, and Silamaka's small group is able to fend them off. A diviner prophesies the death of Silamaka. Before his final battle, he sends Puluru with a message to Hambodedio, telling him he is about to die and that Hambodedio will assume leadership. Silamaka is then killed by an uncircumcised albino, and his horse carries him home to a grieving Puluru. Puluru and Silamaka's sons then flee from the armies of Da Monzon, and, with the mystical spear of Silamaka, Puluru is able to disperse those armies. When night comes, everyone disappears, some say to heaven. Hambodedio becomes ruler of the area claimed by Silamaka. *See also:* Da Monzon.

Sno-Nysoa's Sons Refuse to Return from Earth (Kru/Liberia) Sno-Nysoa is God the creator (without the prefix, Nysoa or Nyensoa refers to God). ⊡ Sno-Nysoa has four sons to whom he is greatly attached. He has given them each a necklace of leopard teeth. He sends them to visit his big friend, Earth. They fail to return, and Sno-Nysoa asks Earth to send them home. "I have told them many times to return," answers Earth, "but they say that their new home is so interesting and beautiful, they have no desire to return." Sno-Nysoa finds his sons and admonishes them. "Do you not know that your father's life is sad without you, and that his heart cannot lie down while you're away?" They answer, "Yes, we know, but this is such a pleasant place to live, food is so plentiful, Earth so kind and good, we have decided to remain here always." Sno-Nysoa warns Earth that he intends to do something that very night to get his sons back. "I beg you, Sno-Nysoa," cries Earth, "do not rob me of your sons!" That night, all the sons go to sleep as usual, but in the morning the eldest does not awake. Earth ascends the broad way to the home of Sno-Nysoa, and begs him to give over using his secret power. Sno-Nysoa tells Earth not to trouble himself about his sons: whenever one does not awake, he should merely bury him. "I have simply called him home. I leave the body with you." Then Sno-Nysoa calls and shows Earth the eldest son. Suddenly one morning, it is found that the second son cannot be awakened. Earth again visits Sno-Nysoa, where he sees the second son alive and happy. A long time passes, then the third child fails to awake. Earth goes along the same wide way to Sno-Nysoa, only to find the third son well satisfied. "Perhaps you will remember, friend Earth, I told you long ago that when I really decided to have my sons again, I should get them. The time has now come to fulfill my words entirely. Tomorrow morning, you will find that my fourth son cannot be awakened. He will come to join his brothers here with me." Earth tries to keep the fourth son with him, but fails. The next day, the fourth son, like his brothers before him, cannot be awakened. In his misery, Earth starts out to go to Sno-Nysoa, but Sno-Nysoa has removed the open way to his home, and Earth can never find it again. To this day, Sno-Nysoa uses his secret power to remove people from the world, and the way to see them afterward is barred, because of Earth's action long ago.

Sogbo, with Lightning from His Mouth (Ewe, Fon/Benin) So, the offspring of Mawu-Lisa, was like them, androgynous. So gave birth to the gods of the thunder pantheon. The thunder god is So (Sogbo, Hevioso), sometimes represented as a ram painted red: lightning is coming from his mouth and two axes ending in curves like lightning stand by his side. ⬛ Sogbo, living in the sky, produced a number of children. She is the greatest of all gods, but her son, who is called Agbe, exercises control over what occurs in the universe. He is charged with the care of the earth, but all who worship him know that Sogbo, his mother, actually created the world. Agbe came to earth the better to fulfill the mission Sogbo gave him, and for him the sea was created as a place in which to reside. The great parent on high no longer looks after the earth, because the world of men and beasts is too small to occupy her. The dominions of the sky, which are infinitely more populous, engage her attention. Thus, when Sogbo confided the rule of the earth to Agbe, she really assigned him a relatively small task. *See also:* Hevioso, Mawu-Lisa, Sagbata.

Soko and the Origin of Death (Nupe/Nigeria) Soko is the sky god, who created the world and then withdrew himself from communion with man. God, having created the world, gave men access to certain mystical forces, making them at the same time subject to these and leaving them to make use of these powers and of the material world. ⬛ In the beginning, there was a man called Ancestor Ada and a woman called Ancestor Adama. They had two children, one male, one female, who in turn begot two children, male and female. The male child died immediately after birth, while the girl remained alive. When she grew up, she spoke a strange language that her parents could not understand. But a bull who one day rose from the river when the girl was standing on the bank understood the language. Later, the bull became the girl's lover, and she bore him a male child. This child again spoke and understood the strange language. When the boy grew up, he would go to the bank of the river to talk to the bull, until one day the bull climbed out of the river and followed the boy on dry land wherever he went. This boy was the ancestor of the Cow Fulani, and the bull the first of the Fulani cattle. Ancestor Adama had a third child, a girl called Mureamu, who had three children, two sons and a daughter. When they grew up, the two young men both desired their sister. They quarreled and one was killed.

So it was that death and murder first appeared in the world. The couple that remained did not know what to do with the dead body. They carried the corpse on their shoulders for three days, lamenting and crying, but could not get rid of it. At last, Soko caused the earth to open, and they placed the body inside, and the practice of burial and three days' mourning for the dead began. The couple now stayed together and begot a male child, who became the ancestor of the Nupe people. *See also:* Tsoede.

Somal: A Saint Passes through a Mountain (Somali/Somalia) Somal was the mythic founder. Barbarah (Berberah), according to the Kamus (an Arabic dictionary), is a well-known town in El Maghrib, and a people located between El Zanj—Zanzibar and the coast—and El Habash. They are descended from the Himyar chiefs, Sanhaj and Sumamah, and they arrived at the time of the conquest of Africa by the king Afrikus. These, the progenitors of the Somal, are a part of the Galla nation Islamized and semiticized by repeated immigration from Arabia. ▣ Somal is the name of the father of a people, so called because he thrust out his brother's eye. ▣ In A.H. 666 (A.D. 1266-1267), the Sayyid Yusuf al Baghdadi visited the port of Siyaro near Berberah, then occupied by a traditionalist magician, who passed through mountains by the power of his gramarye. The saint summoned to his aid Mohammed bin Yunis el Siddiki of Bayt el Fakih in Arabia, and by their united prayers a hill closed upon the unbeliever.

——— ⧫   Sudika-Mbambi Descends to Earth   ⧫ ———

God's Continued Presence on Earth Is Revealed in Human Rituals. When the mythic hero, godlike and heroic, undertakes to move through the stages of a ritual, he establishes a model for all humankind. In this story, his mortal brother becomes the stand-in for humanity, following in the hero's footsteps, repeating the stages of the ritual as laid down by this godly forebear. In the end, when God returns to heaven, becoming a part of the firmament, his brother and the rest of humans continue to echo the experience of that ideal person. ▣ (Kimbundu/Angola) Before Sudika-mbambi is born, his home is destroyed by many-headed ogres. He and his brother, Kabundungulu, are born miraculously: they speak in the womb, when they are born they wondrously erect homes. Sudika-mbambi goes to avenge his people, and along the way meets Kipalende, supernatural helpers, who turn against him, envious of his great powers. In a contest with the Kipalende, Sudika-mbambi wins a bride from an old destructive woman. The Kipalende throw him into a hole, and he moves to the bowels of the earth to the home of Kalunga-ngombe, god of the underworld. To marry Kalunga-ngombe's daughter, Sudika-mbambi undertakes tasks set by the reluctant father-in-law. He overcomes the many-headed Kinioka kia Tumba, then moves to Kimbiji, a crocodile, which swallows him. Sudika-mbambi's brother, Kabundungulu, sets out to rescue his brother from the belly of the swallower, and then the brothers fight over Sudika-mbambi's brides. They tire of fighting, and Sudika-mbambi moves to the heavens, where he becomes the thunder, with Kabundungulu, also in the sky, echoing that thunder.

Museum voor Volkenkunde, Leiden

Bronze Figure of Olokun, Sea God of Benin

Contending Forces Move Man to Godliness. During the transformation period, Sunjata goes through various stages: miraculous birth, coming to manhood, magical acts, accomplishing impossible tasks that reveal him as a great man destined for towering achievement, the epic struggle with Sumanguru, discovering the villain's fateful secret, the destruction of Sumanguru, the story of Sunjata's companions, especially Tira Makhang. Several ideas are being juggled here: tale, myth, and heroic poetry traditions, conventions of the trickster—the epic tradition is a broad gathering of all of these. While the tale and myth traditions link the epic hero to the gods and to the traditions of the society, both of which linkages are critical, this figure goes beyond these; he is often a revolutionary, in the sense that he espouses change. Sunjata becomes the embodiment of the culture and its great historical shift. The tale and myth contain bits of history, just as the heroic poem contains bits of fantasy. The epic hero, partaking of both fantasy and reality or history, is in the process of changing matters even as he changes, and that is where the traditions of the trickster come in. Tales, myths, and heroic epics all deal with uncertain periods in the lives of individual humans, of the universe, of the culture. People are in the process of transformation, people who will assure that these uncertain periods (the period of the trickster) will be successfully navigated. This is especially clear in the case of the individual in the tale: a person stands on the threshold of a new event in his life. But it is earthshaking only for him; the culture remains constant, and his rite of passage is a part of that constancy. This continuity is not the case in the myths and epics. Here the society is being altered drastically. In the myths, we stand on the threshold of human civilization; in the epics, we stand on the border of wholly new societies. Sunjata is a least likely hero, but he is heroically born. He must experience a pattern of struggles to prove himself, while the impostor-hero is on the throne. Sumanguru holds all the power, retaining it because of his father's magic. All around Sunjata are the bards, singing his praises, tying him to his historical and cultural lineage, giving him legitimacy. And he begins to do wonderful things. In the end, he has proven himself. Then, with the aid of his sister, he gets the secret of his nemesis's greatness, and, overcoming Sumanguru, takes the throne. He will now create the Mandinka empire. ▣ (Mandinka/Gambia, Mali) Sunjata's mother was pregnant with him for seven years, and once during that time she had a fright. Sunjata was born first, and was to be the heir to the kingdom of his father, but the birth of another son was announced earlier because of a delay by a messenger. Sunjata crawled for seven years, and when he was ready to be circumcised, iron rods were made for him, but they buckled under his weight. His mother helped him to stand. A test followed: the one who could wear a pair of enormous trousers would become king. Only Sunjata could put them on. When his father died, Sunjata said he wanted no inheritance except his father's bards. His brothers enlisted sorcerers to work against Sunjata. He left his home, and in an alien land was again tested: he removed a ring from boiling wax, another indication that he would be king of Manding. Sunjata initially failed in another test, shooting a silk-cotton tree, but when his mother told him the truth about his birth, that she had a fright, he was successful. In the meantime, his brothers were killed by Sumanguru, the blacksmith king of Susu, who was attempting to take over Manding as well. Sunjata's mother died, and when the ruler of the land where she died demanded payment for the burial plot, Sunjata vowed to destroy him one day. Sunjata went home and prepared to do battle with Sumanguru. The first battles went in favor of the enemy, but Sunjata's sister went to him and wrested the secret of his supernatural power from him: his father was a seven-headed jinn who lived in a hill, and could be killed only with an arrow tipped with a cock's spur; if his father were killed, Sumanguru's power would end. He would then change into various objects, which he enumerated, but he stopped before revealing the final object. Sunjata then overwhelmed Sumanguru, but the villain escaped because of the final transformation. Now Sunjata assumed the kingship of both Manding and Susu. The story unfolds within a context of praises and historical events, making plain Sunjata's cultural universality and historical presence. The epic is Sunjata's transformation period, from his miraculous birth to his coming to manhood, the impossible tasks that reveal him as a man destined to towering achievement, the epic struggle with Sumanguru, and the movement to kingship. The epic tradition is the essence of the society, built on tales the images of which are quickened and energized by myth.

S

Kwa Nyinalesa pepi, kwa Nyinamuntu kutali.
To the village of God's mother is near,
   to the village of man's mother is distant.

              —Lamba proverb

Tamuno Creates the World from Mud (Kalabari/Nigeria)   ⊡   Tamuno, the supreme deity, the creator, created the world from mud. She has no husband. The lesser spirits are sometimes referred to as her children; she created them as she created everything else in the world. Tamuno is everywhere, and is associated with the sky, so "heaven" is another term commonly used to refer to the supreme being.   ⊡   Everyone has his own personal Tamuno, whom he addresses as "My Tamuno, my mother." A person's Tamuno creates him by joining his spirit to his body, keeps him alive by maintaining the bond between the two, and brings death by separating them. Before a person's spirit is joined to his body, it tells Tamuno what fortunes it wishes on earth. This is accepted by Tamuno, and the wishes in it become the individual's personal So. Henceforward, as his So, these wishes guide the entire course of his life. Though a man's career is in the hands of his So, he does not necessarily know what this holds in store for him, and he may not always take the trouble to find out.

Tanit Creates the Universe (Berber, Carthaginian/Tunisia)   The goddess Tanit (Tini, Tinith, Tinnit) of Carthage was a moon and firmament goddess. She was worshiped as an armed divinity, symbolized by a broad arrowhead and a spear with a triangular blade. She was considered a giver of life and death, as a fertility deity, and was venerated as a great mother. The name is apparently Libyan, and the growth of her cult is associated with the acquisition of territory in Africa, with pronounced fertility aspects. Other deities in Carthage included Astarte, Eshmoun, identified with Aesculapius, the healer; and Melkart, the protector of the mother city, Tyre.   ⊡   Tanit had given birth to the universe without having first conceived. The title, Tanit-Pene-Baal, Tanit, the face of Baal, expresses Tanit's bisexual aspect. Tanit represented the visible moon and firmament, which is matter, whereas Baal represented the power that vitalized the matter. Tanit gave birth to the universe without the help of a male partner. *See also:* Baal Hammon.

Tano Struggles with Death (Akan, Asante/Ghana; Agni/Côte d'Ivoire) The river god of Ghana and the lower Ivory Coast is Tano or Ta Kora. Kora means "the immense"; Ta may be derived from a word meaning "father." Tano is a nature god, but he has heroic attributes. He was possibly once a thunder god as well. He was also invoked as a war god in time of military need. 🔯 Tano is the second son of Nyame, the supreme being. He cheated the elder son, Bia, of his inheritance, although Bia was Nyame's favorite. Bia, also a river god, therefore received only the more barren Ivory Coast lands, while Tano had the fertile land west of Ghana, for once Nyame had given these lands to the deceitful Tano he was unable to reverse the promise. In the Ivory Coast, the Agni people say that Bia cheated Tano of the blessing, then fled to the west. 🔯 Other myths say that Tano fought with Death, but they had to come to a compromise, so that while Tano was allowed to come to the town of man, Death came also. *See also:* Nyame.

Thingo Lwenkosikazi Lives With a Snake (Zulu/South Africa) The rainbow, Thingo Lwenkosikazi, is called the rod of the queen, the bow. 🔯 The rainbow is a fabulous animal that lives in a pool and is like a sheep. That is where the bow touches the earth: it drinks at a pool. Some fear to wash in a large pool, saying there is an incredible animal in it. If a man goes into the pool, the animal catches and eats him. If a person is properly prepared when he goes into the pool that has such a creature in it, the creature does not eat him but daubs him with ocher, and he emerges from the pool with snakes entwined about his body and goes home with them. 🔯 The rainbow is a rod of the great house. It appears in the heavens when the heavens rain. It lives with a snake. 🔯 Some say that the rainbow is a sheep that comes out of great pools and rests outside on the rocks. It comes out when the sky is clouded. A man who goes out in the morning and encounters the rainbow will be poisoned by it.

Thixo Creates Three Nations (Khoi, Xhosa/South Africa) Thixo, the supreme being, is the creator. 🔯 Thixo is derived from Tsui‖Goab (Tsuni-‖Goam), the great hero of the Khoi from whom they are said to have taken their origin. The meaning of the name is usually given as "sore or wounded knee." Tsui‖Goab was a great chief and warrior who went to war with another chief, ‖Gaunab, because the latter was always killing great numbers of his people. They had numerous battles until Tsui‖Goab became strong enough to kill ‖Gaunab. However, his enemy managed to give him a blow on the knee before expiring, and henceforth he was lame. As the conqueror, he became deified by later generations. 🔯 He was reputed to have had considerable powers during his lifetime; besides being a renowned warrior of great strength, he was said to be a powerful magician and a seer. Legend credits him with coming to life several times after dying. He came to be regarded as the personification of the natural forces producing rain. ▣ Three nations were created: the whites, the Xhosa, and the Khoi. A day was appointed for them to appear before Thixo to receive whatever he might apportion to each group. While they were assembling, a honey bird came flying by, and the Khoi ran after it, whistling. Thixo remonstrated with them about their behavior, but they ignored him. He thereupon denounced them as a people who would have to exist on wild roots and honey beer, and possess no stock whatever. When the fine herds of cattle were brought, the Xhosa became very excited, one of them exclaiming, "That black and white cow is mine!" and another, "That red cow and black bull are mine!" and so on, until at last Thixo, whose patience had been severely taxed by their shouts and unruly behavior, denounced them as a restless people who would only possess cattle. The whites patiently waited until they received cattle, horses, sheep, and all sorts of property. The whites have therefore got everything. The Xhosa have only cattle, while the Khoi have nothing. *See also:* Mdali, Qamatha, Tsui‖Goab.

Tianza Ngombe and the Division of the World (Lunda/DRCongo) Tianza Ngombe was the primordial serpent. ▣ The mother of all things, Tianza Ngombe (Chinaweshi, Chinawezi), divided up the world with the lightning, Nzashi, her husband. Nzashi set himself up in the sky with the sun, the moon, Venus, and the stars; his urine became the beneficial rain. Tianza Ngombe had the earth and the rivers. When the thunder rumbles in the sky, Tianza Ngombe responds in the waters and the rivers become swollen. ▣ Tianza Ngombe bore a son, Konde, and a daughter, Naweshi. These two had incestuous relations, and they had three children, among them Lueshi (Lueji). At the confluence of two rivers, Lueshi met Chibinda Ilunga, the master hunter and chief. *See also:* Chibinda Ilunga, Chinawezi, Lueji.

Tilo: Emergence of Life from a Reed (Lenge/Mozambique) Tilo (heaven), the supreme being, does not seem to exercise much influence upon people's lives. Ancestral spirits in the direct male line are very important. Sacrifices are made to the spirits before sowing in June, and the digging in August and September is preceded by sacrifices offered to these spirits. At the end of November or the beginning of December, baskets of seeds are taken to the chief, and these are blessed. The feast of the first fruits is also a significant religious ritual. Ancestral spirits are invoked for rainmaking. ▣ The first man and the first woman came out of a reed.

Tilo and the Child Found in Heaven (Ronga/Mozambique) Tilo is the supreme being. ▣ A girl is sent to get water. On the way home, she breaks the vessel containing the water. She is afraid that she will be punished, so wishes for a rope. Suddenly, she sees a rope uncoiling itself from a cloud. She climbs the rope, and finds herself in the country above the sky: it is similar to her own country. She goes to a ruined village and sees an old woman. The old woman calls her, and the girl tells her the story. The woman tells the girl to proceed, that an ant will creep into her ear and tell her how to cope in this strange country. When she comes to another village, she hears a whisper: she should not go in, just sit by the gate. Some old men in white come to her; she tells them she is seeking a baby. They take her to a house where women are working; they send her for corn. She brings it, following the instructions of the ant, and is praised for her efficiency. She is told to grind corn and make porridge, and she again has the advice of the ant, and is again praised by the Heaven-dwellers. Next day, the elders take her to a house where babies are laid out on the ground, some in white, some in red. The ant tells her to select a baby in white. The men give her cloth and beads, and send her home. Everyone is excited about the girl they had thought lost, but the younger sister is envious. She goes to the rope, climbs it, but refuses to heed the advice of the old woman, shakes the ant from her head, ravages the corn garden, does not grind the corn well or make satisfactory porridge. And she selects a baby wrapped in red. There is a sudden explosion, and she is struck dead. Tilo gathers her bones, and a man carries the bundle home. Along the way, the ant and the old woman tell her that she would not have died had she been less wicked. The bones are deposited at her home, and the conclusion is that Tilo, Heaven, was angry with her.

Tilo and the Cock of Heaven (Shangana, Tonga/Mozambique, South Africa, Zimbabwe) The word Tilo designates the blue sky, the heaven, from which come not only the terrific thunder and lightning but the life-giving rain and the health-giving sun. Tilo is a place and a power that manifests itself variously, regulating cosmic phenomena. Tilo gives and takes life. 🔲 Some think that thunder and lightning are caused by a bird, nkuku wa tilo, the cock of heaven, or psele tja tilo, the hen of heaven. 🔲 The first human beings came out from Lihlangu, a reed, or from Nhlanga, a marsh of reeds. One man and one woman suddenly emerged from one reed; it exploded, and there they were. Men of various groups emerged from a reed marsh, each group having its unique customs.

Tilo: The String to Heaven (Thonga, Tsonga/Mozambique, South Africa, Zimbabwe) Tilo, the blue sky, the heaven, is the supreme being. 🔲 A young girl who, having broken her jar and fearing a scolding from her mother, climbs her string and goes to Heaven, Tilo. There she finds a village. A child is given to her, because she is so gentle and obedient. Her sister tries to do the same thing. But she is ill-tempered and wicked. Heaven explodes, kills her by lightning, and her bones are blown right to her parents' house. 🔲 The first human beings came out of the reed, or the marsh of reeds. Some say that one man and one woman suddenly came out of one reed, which exploded. Others argue that people of different groups emerged from a marsh of reeds, each group with its own customs. When the first human beings emerged from the marsh of reeds, the chief of this marsh sent the chameleon, Lumpfana, to them, with this message: men will die, but they will rise again. The chameleon started walking slowly, according to his habit. Then the big lizard with the blue head, Galagala, was sent to tell men that they shall die and rot. Galagala started with his swift gait and soon passed Lumpfana. He delivered his message, and when Lumpfana arrived with his report, men said to him, "You are too late. We have already accepted another message." That is why men are subject to death.

Tindana, Murdered by a One-Eyed Giant (Dagomba, Mamprusi, Moshi/Ghana) Tindana was a mythic leader. ☐ Early in the Christian era, there lived in a cave among the hills around Mali, which tradition places far to the east, a man most loathsome to behold. He dwelled alone, but had acquired the reputation of being a fearless hunter. One day, when the people were hard-pressed by their enemies and disaster seemed in sight, they sent for this hunter to help them. He came, and his frightful appearance so terrified the foe that victory came to the people of Mali. The hunter returned to his cave, refusing all gifts and thanks. When his services were called for once more, he again triumphed. This time, the Mali people insisted on rewarding him, and he received as a wife their chief's daughter. By this marriage a son was born, a one-eyed giant even more revolting than his father. Inheriting his father's skill in warfare and the chase, the young man soon made himself a leader over his fellows, and shortly after reaching manhood he led a band of them westward to found a new country, as their own had been devastated by famine. This group eventually came to a town not far from the White Volta. The young man sat down at the watering place. Toward evening, women who lived there came to him and informed him that the city was the abode of the great Tindana (literally, "owner of the country"). He accompanied the women to the city, accepting the hospitality of the only daughter of the Tindana, a woman whose beauty attracted him. When he arrived at her house, he was hospitably received by the father and remained a time in the house as an honored guest. Then the day of the annual sacrifice arrived. For this event, people from all over the countryside gathered, as it was an event of national importance. The Tindana was to perform the sacrifice, and retired early to his bed. That night the young man murdered his host, and when morning came presented himself to the people dressed in the sacred robes of his victim. They were awed at the loathsome spectacle of the one-eyed giant and feared to touch the sacred emblems of the office he had usurped. At the same time, the youth's followers loudly acclaimed their chief and threatened to massacre any dissidents. His triumph was complete. He married the daughter of the unfortunate Tindana, and so founded the royal family of the Dagomba, and, with the aid of his own followers and the subdued townsfolk, he raided and conquered the neighboring country, and began an empire that is one of the greatest ever founded in Africa, the tri-dominion of Dagomba, Mamprusi, and Moshi.

Tlam and the Fifty Virgins (Kabyle/Algeria) Tlam is the underworld. 🈁 In the beginning, there were only one man and one woman, strangers to each other, who lived in Tlam beneath the earth. At a well, they had a quarrel, then they struggled, and ended by having sexual relations. In time, they had fifty sons and fifty daughters, but the two sexes remained strangers to each other. Their parents sent them, by separate ways, upward from Tlam. The fifty female virgins, curious, climbed out of a hole in Earth's crust and, addressing the plants, asked who made them. They replied that Earth had made them. When the virgins asked Earth who made him, he responded that he was always here. When the virgins asked the moon and stars who made them, they received no answer because the moon and stars were so distant. At the same time, the young men were also roaming on Earth's surface. They were bathing in a stream, when the boys and girls caught sight of one another. The virgins were shy, but a girl approached a handsome boy. Like their parents, they learned the joy of sexual intercourse, and the human race originated.

To Dino and the Great Flood (Fali/Cameroon) To Dino was the first man. 🈁 A male egg of a tortoise, a terrestrial animal, and a female egg of a toad, an aquatic animal, revolved in the atmosphere, beneath the arching sky. The tortoise was the first organizer of the world, moving in space from west to east, establishing east and west directions, creating the boundary between the known world and the unknown. 🈁 To bring an end to the flood that was about to submerge the earth, To Dino, the first man, was saved by the toad, who traced the route to be followed by the waters, dividing terrestrial space into four sectors. At the center point the beginnings of life would be concentrated, and from it they would spread to each of the parts of the earth. Through this point also, the earth entered communication with heaven and came to life. Later, when the heavenly ark came down to earth, carrying the emblems of all the species and of all knowledge, it would be divided in the same way. These four zones were linked in pairs, east and south on the one hand, west and north on the other hand, and between them were distributed the four elements that make up the universe, fire in the east, air in the west, water in the north, and earth in the south.

Tore and the Pot of Death (Efe/DRCongo) The soul goes to Tore (Arebati, Baatsi, Epilipili, Muri-Muri), the supreme being, in the sky, taken from the mouth of the dead man and wafted into the heavens by flies or by lightning. 🈁 Long ago, at the beginning, the earth was up where heaven is now, and heaven was down here. Because the Efe were hungry, they appealed to Tore. Then the earth with all its food supplies fell down below to the position it is now, and heaven went up in its place. The soul goes up there: all souls are gathered together there. ▣ Muri-Muri is the great spirit to whom the souls of all dead humans go. He frequently wanders in the depths of the forest, and he always kills anyone who encounters him. Muri-Muri's cry can be heard at night, a harbinger of woe or a hunt that will the following day be a successful one for hunters. ▣ In the beginning, all humans were evil and committed all sorts of crimes; as punishment, Muri-Muri threatened them with death. He laid down a code of instructions as to what they should and should not do. ▣ In the beginning, men did not die at all. In those early days, Muri-Muri gave a pot to a toad, ordering him to be careful not to break the pot, as death was shut up in it. If the pot got broken, he pointed out, all men were doomed to die. The toad went on his way, and he met a frog, who offered to carry the pot for him. The toad hesitated at first, but as the pot was very heavy, he eventually handed it over to the frog, warning him to be very careful with it. The frog hopped away with the pot, but let it fall. It broke into fragments, and death escaped from it. And that is how men first came to die. ▣ In the beginning, the earth was above and the heaven— that is, the throne of God—was below. Together with God were the moon and the lightning, two natural phenomena that play important roles in the mythology of the Efe. From above, dust and dirt drizzled down interminably and contaminated the food of God until he became weary of it and looked around for another dwelling place. He commanded the lightning to find a place above the earth, and with a great crash the lightning divided the earth and traveled upward. When a place in the heavens was prepared, God and the moon followed. The moon, however, is not greater or mightier than God. On the contrary, it comes under the godhead from whom it receives commands. When God looks toward the moon, it comes out of its dwelling place and shows itself to the world. *See also:* Arebati, Baatsi, Epilipili, Masupa, Tore (Mbuti).

Tore: The Arm of God (Mbuti/DRCongo) Tore (Arebati, Baatsi, Epilipili) is the creator, the supreme being. ▣ Tore, with the help of the moon, created Baatsi, the first man. The body was made by kneading, then clothed with a skin; blood was poured in, and the man lived. His creator then whispered to him that he would live in the forest and father children, that these children could eat of all of the trees of the forest save one, the tahu tree. Baatsi, warning his many children of the one forbidden thing, departed to join Tore, his creator, in the heavens. Then, one day, a pregnant woman craved the forbidden fruit. Her husband got it for her, hid the peel, but the moon, having seen it, told the creator what had happened, and he became so angry that he cursed the human race to die. ▣ Another myth about death tells how, in the beginning, there was only Masupa, who created for himself two sons and a daughter. He would speak unseen to them, and he gave them one commandment: never to try to see him. Masupa lived in a large house, apart, from which the sounds could be heard of hammering and forging. That was an altogether happy time, with no need to work. Or at least the two sons had no such need. To the daughter, the daily task had been given of fetching water and gathering firewood, to be placed at Masupa's door. She wanted to know what the one she was serving looked like, so one evening, as she set the water pot down, she decided to wait and see. She hid behind a post, and when Masupa's arm reached out for the pot, she saw it, richly adorned. Masupa was enraged. He informed his children that he now would leave them and that the days of their ease were ended. He gave them weapons and tools, taught them the use of the forge and of other things necessary for their maintenance; and, especially angry with his daughter, he told her that she would henceforth be a toiling wife and bring forth her children in pain. Then, secretly, he left them, passing downstream along the banks of the river, and no one has seen him since. Death came with the death of the woman's first child two days after its birth. She had named him, with a premonition, Death-is-coming. No one has escaped death since. For the Efe versions of these myths, *see:* Baatsi, Masupa.

Tororut and Animals That Did Not Fear Fire (Suk/Kenya; Pokot/Uganda)

Tororut (Ilat) is the supreme being, an omnipotent, omniscient being who is responsible not only for the creation of the world but for all the good and evil occurrences that have happened in it ever since. 🔲 A myth by Tiamolok, a Suk: Tororut is the supreme god. He made the earth and causes the birth of mankind and animals. No man living has seen him, though old men, long since dead, have. They say he is like a man in form, but has wings—huge wings—the flash of which causes the lightning, Kerual, and the whirring whereof is the thunder, Kotil. He lives above and has much land, stock, ivory, and every good thing. He knows all secrets; he is the universal father; all cattle diseases and calamities are sent by him as punishment to men for their sins. His wife is Seta, the Pleiades, and his firstborn son is Arawa, the moon. Ilat, the rain, is another son, as are Kokel, the stars, his other children. Topogh, the evening star, is his firstborn daughter. Asis, the sun, is his younger brother, who is angry in the dry season. All these are gods, and all are benevolently disposed toward mankind. 🔲 In the olden days, all cattle, sheep, and goats lived in the forests. Tororut called all the animals before him at a place in the forest, and he lit a large fire there. When the animals saw the fire, they were frightened and fled into the forests. There remained only the cattle, sheep, and goats who were not frightened. Tororut was pleased with these animals and blessed them, and decreed that henceforth they should always live with man, who would eat their flesh and drink their milk.

Tshawe and the Constricting Throat (Xhosa/South Africa)

Tshawe was the first man. 🔲 In the beginning, it is said, the first human came into being naturally. He achieved form as a human being; he quite clearly was a person. He came to be regarded as the archetype, the first human being. That was the beginning of what came to be known as a human being among the Xhosa.

That first person, the archetypal human being as far as the Xhosa are concerned, was Tshawe. Now the Xhosa divided themselves, and increased. It is said that in those days death was unlike the death that we know today. It used to be that a person's throat would become more and more difficult for him. Finally, he would be able only to drink milk, to swallow but a spoonful. But that would be sufficient for him. So it went, until such a person could breathe no more. He would then be taken and put into a secret place. No hole was dug in those days; no one said that a "burial" had taken place. The people would see that he was no longer breathing. He had grown old and was no longer able to get up. But his death was not caused by aches and pains; he just died gently. He became old; then, because of his age, he was unable to walk. And when his breath was no more, he was taken away and put in a hidden place, far from home. That is the way things were.

Tsibiri: The Sarki and the Red Snake (Hausa/Nigeria) 🔲 In 1343, Tsamiya was killed by Usman Zamnagawa, who in turn was succeeded by Yaji, "the hot-tempered one." At about this time, Islam was brought to the Hausa from Mali. There was opposition to Islam from traditionalist forces in the city: they defiled the mosque until they were suddenly all struck blind and turned away. Under Bugaya, the twelfth king, the Maguzawa traditionalists of Kano were ordered to leave their rocky fastness of Fongui and disperse themselves throughout the land. His successor, Kanajeji (1390-1410), son of Yaji, was the first Hausa king to introduce quilted-cotton armor, iron helmets, and coats of mail. 🔲 One of Kanajeji's wars was with Zukzuk (Zaria). At first, he was repulsed and his army was taunted by the men of Zukzuk, who wondered sarcastically where Kano was. Furious at his defeat, Kanajeji renounced Islam, and turned to the Tsibiri spirit. He was told by the Sarkin Tsibiri that he should reestablish the god of his ancestors. Kanajeji asked how this was to be done, and the Sarkin Tsibiri told him to cut a branch from a certain tree. When the Sarki had done so, he found a red snake in the branch. He killed the snake, and from its skin made two slippers. Then, from the branch, he made four long narrow drums and eight small round drums. He took these to Dankwoi and threw them into the water and went home. After waiting forty days, he came back to the water and took the objects to the house of Sarkin Tsibiri, who sewed the rest of the snake's skin around the drums and told Kanajeji that whatever he wished for in this world, he should do as his forefathers did. Kanajeji asked him to show him how, and the Sarkin Tsibiri took off his robe, put on the snakeskin slippers, and walked around the tree forty times, singing the song of Barbushe. Kanajeji did the same. The next year, he again warred with Zukzuk, and the men of Kano killed the Sarkin Zukzuk and overwhelmed his army. The Sarkin Kano entered Zukzuk and the people paid him tribute.

Tsoede and the Fruit That Cured (Nupe/Nigeria) The earliest history of Nupe centers around the figure of Tsoede or Edegi, the culture hero and mythical founder of Nupe kingdom. ▣ At that time, there was no kingdom of Nupe, only small chieftainships. The Nupe people were tributary to the Atta (king) of the Gara, at Eda (Idah), far down the Niger. Tribute was paid in slaves, and every family head had annually to contribute one male member of his house. These slaves were always sisters' sons. The son of the Atta Gara came hunting to Nku in Nupe country. He met the daughter of the chief of Nku, and fell in love with her. When he had to return to his country to take the throne of the Gara because of the death of his father, this woman was pregnant. He left her a charm and a ring to give to their child when it was born. This child was Tsoede. Then the old chief of Nku died, his son became chief, and when Tsoede was thirty years old the new chief sent him, as his sister's son, as slave to Eda. The Atta Gara recognized that his new slave was his son; he could tell because of the charm and ring that he was wearing. He kept him near, treating him almost like his legitimate sons. Tsoede stayed for thirty years at his father's court. Then the king fell victim to a mysterious illness that nobody could cure. A diviner said that only a fruit from a high oil-palm outside the town, plucked by one man, would cure the king. His legitimate sons vainly tried to reach the precious fruit. Finally, Tsoede made the attempt and succeeded. But he cut his lip so badly that he looked almost like a man born with a split lip. His achievement, which made him all the more beloved by his father and honored by the court, evoked the jealousy of his half brothers. When the Atta felt his death coming, he advised his son to flee, to return to his own country the rule of which he bestowed on him as a parting gift. He assisted him in his flight, giving him riches, bestowing on him the insignia of kingship. Tsoede had an adventurous flight from Eda, traveling up the river, hotly pursued by his half brothers and their men. On the way, he was helped by two men, whom he later rewarded by making them chief and second-in-command of the Kyedye people. When he reached the Kaduna River, he went into a creek called Ega, and remained in hiding until his pursuers, tired of their fruitless search, returned to Eda. Tsoede and his men left the canoe and sank it in the river. He then went to Nupeko, a village nearby, killed the chief, and made himself chief of the place. He conquered Nku, the town of his maternal uncle, made himself ruler of all Beni (or Nupe), and assumed the title Etsu, king. He made the twelve men who had accompanied him from Eda the chiefs of the twelve towns of Beni and bestowed on them the sacred insignia of chieftainship. *See also:* Soko.

Tsui∥Goab Is Given a Blow to the Knee by a Dying Foe (Nama/Namibia; Khoi/South Africa) Tsui∥Goab (∥Kaang, ∣Kaggen, Khub, Nanub) was the supreme being, the celestial god of the Khoi. He was omnipresent, wise, a notable warrior of great physical strength, a powerful magician. Although he died several times, he was reborn. He sent rain and caused the crops to grow and flourish. Tsui∥Goab was the first Khoi, from whom all the Khoi peoples originated. He was a creator, having made the rocks and stones from which the first Khoi came. ▣ Tsui∥Goab had a rival, another male figure, ∥Gaunab, the personified spirit of evil. Evil spirits, people said to have lived wickedly when alive, were known as ‖Gaunab and Sares; the whirlwind believed to bring sickness and death was also occasionally known as ‖Gaunab. Tsui‖Goab went to war with ‖Gaunab, because he killed great numbers of Tsui‖Goab's people. In this fight, Tsui‖Goab was repeatedly overpowered by ‖Gaunab, but in every battle he grew stronger. He was finally so strong and big that he easily destroyed ‖Gaunab by giving him one blow behind the ear. While ‖Gaunab was expiring, he gave his enemy a blow on the knee. Since that day, the conqueror of ‖Gaunab received the name Tsui‖Goab, "wounded knee." Henceforth, he could not walk properly because he was lame. ▣ A hare was sent to the world by the moon with the message, "As I die and dying am born again, so you shall die and dying live again." The hare got confused over the message and put a "not" in. It thus reversed the message, saying, "As I die and dying am born again, so you shall die and dying *not* be born again." When it returned to the moon and explained how it had delivered the message, the moon was angry with it for being so stupid. So the moon took a stick and hit the hare on its nose, splitting its lip. Ever since, the hare has had a split lip. *See also:* ⧻Gama-⧻Gorib, Heitsi-Eibib, Thixo.

Tsumburbura: His Sacred Place (Hausa/Nigeria) Tsumburbura is God. ▣ The earliest inhabitants of Kano were descendants of a Gaya smith named Kano who had come to the Dala hill in search of ironstone. ▣ Dala was of unknown origin, but came to this land, and built a house on Dala hill. He and his wives lived there, and had seven children—four boys and three girls. Garageje, his oldest child, was the grandfather of Nuzame, the father of Barbushe, chief of the Kano people, a giant who killed elephants with a stick and carried them for miles on his head. By his wonders and sorcery, and the power he gained over his brothers, he became chief and lord over them. He was high priest to the god, Tsumburbura (Tsunburburai), whose shrine was a tree called Shamus, surrounded by a wall. No one could enter the shrine but Barbushe: whoever else entered died. Barbushe descended from Dala two days a year, when mystic rites were performed in a grove. People came from all over to participate in the ceremonies, meeting at the foot of Dala hill at evening. When darkness came, Barbushe emerged with his drummers. He prayed to Tsumburbura, and the people responded. Then Barbushe descended, and the people went with him to the god. And when they drew near, they sacrificed what they had brought with them—a black dog, a black fowl, a black goat. Barbushe entered the sacred palace—he alone—saying that he was the heir of Dala and, like it or not, the people had to follow him. The people agreed to follow him. They marched around the sacred place until dawn, then rose, naked, and ate. Then Barbushe came and told them what would happen during the coming year.

Ture Brings Fire (Zande/DRCongo, Sudan) Ture is a divine trickster, the hero of a cycle of stories known as the Sangbwa Ture. ▣ Ture arose to go to his maternal uncles, who were the Abare peoples, and he met them under their forge, beating out their iron. They greeted him. Ture began to work their bellows for them. With deceit, he came and took fire for everybody, for once upon a time people did not have fire. Ture went on blowing the fire, then he left, telling them, "I will return tomorrow to dance for you." When the next day came, Ture gathered worn-out barkcloth around him at his home, a big stretch of it, and came and blew fire for a long time, then he arose and put his foot over the fire on one side, and his barkcloth glowed, catching fire. The people put it out. Then he jumped over the fire and dropped on the other side, and the fire caught his old barkcloth, and they put it out again. But it was not extinguished; they tried in vain to put it out. It glowed on Ture's barkcloth. The Abare gathered together to put out the fire on Ture; they tried in vain to put it out. Ture ran away with this fire and went with it into the dry grass, and the fire spread everywhere in the dry grass in Ture's tracks. He went on running. Because of Ture, people have fire.

T

Shadows

A myth is never performed outside a rich and varied context of other experiences, other myths. Hovering about it are the many versions and variants of that story, along with images that are common to stories that seem on the surface to be very different. Taken together, a single myth weaves into all of the other myths in the system, so that the performance of a single story actually animates the entire tradition, and every image is given a deep resonance not apparent on the story's surface. One myth, then, exists within and can only be comprehended within the entirety of the tradition. This complex of interacting experiences during performance is made even more labyrinthine considering that the stories of every member of the audience are also playing a role here—their own biographies are being shaped by the performance at the same time that their life's experience shape their experiences of those stories. But this biographical diversity, so important to the performer, and all of the varied emotions that it evokes, are slowly moved into union, so that, as the myth comes to an end, members of the audience are for the moment of performance welded in a single formal unity. That unity is now so robustly teeming with meaning and contained emotion that it calls upon all of the artistic skills of the performer to keep it focused. And with the completion of the myth, all comes apart, and the members of the audience go their separate ways. Emotions of the present, emotions engendered by images of the past, memories richly recalled, events only dimly recollected, the feelings enveloped in history and biography—these are the shadows that inform the story being performed.

Ukwa and the Women from the River (Shilluk/Sudan) Ukwa was a mythic ancestor. ⬚ In the beginning was Juok, the great creator; he created a great white cow, called Deung Adok, that came up out of the Nile. The cow gave birth to a man-child, whom she nursed and named Kola. Kola begat Umak Ra, or Omaro, who begat Makwa, or Wad Maul, who begat Ukwa. These people lived in a far-off country, nobody knows where. ⬚ Ukwa was one day sitting near the river when he saw two beautiful women with long hair rise out of the river and play about in the shallows. He saw them many times after that, but they would have nothing to do with him, merely laughing at him. Their lower extremities were like those of a crocodile. One day when Ukwa found them sitting on the banks, he came up behind and seized them. Their screams brought their father, Ud Diljil, out of the river to see what was the matter. Ud Diljil, whose right side was green in color and in form like a crocodile, while his left side was that of a man, protested mildly, but he allowed Ukwa to take away his daughters and wed them, at the same time uttering a series of prophecies. Nik-Kieya, the elder sister, gave birth to two sons and three daughters, and Ung-Wad, the younger, to one son only, named Ju, or Bworo. The eldest son of Nik-Kieya was called Nyikang; he inherited the crocodile attributes of his mother and grandfather. Meanwhile, Ukwa married a third wife, whose eldest child, a son, was named Duwat. On Ukwa's death, there was a quarrel between Nyikang and Duwat as to who should succeed Ukwa. It ended by Nyikang, with his sisters, Ad Dui, Ari Umker, and Bun Yung, his brother, Umoi, and his half brother, Ju, acquiring wings and flying away to the south of the Sobat (Bahr El Asraf). They found the Shilluk country inhabited, so they drove the people out and founded a successful kingdom. *See also:* Juok, Nyikang.

249

Unumbotte and the Origin of Languages (Bassari/Togo) Unumbotte was the creator. ◘ Unumbotte made a human being, naming him man. He made an antelope and a snake, giving them their names. At this time, there was one tree, a palm. The ground of the earth was still rough. Unumbotte ordered that the earth be made smooth. He gave the three seeds of all kinds, and told them to plant them. He returned and saw that the man, antelope, and snake had not yet smoothed the earth. They had planted the seeds, one of which had sprouted and grown: it was a tree, and it was tall and bore red fruit. Unumbotte returned every seven days, each time plucking one of the red fruits. Then the snake said that they should eat those fruits as well, rather than go hungry. The antelope responded that they knew nothing about the fruit. But man and his wife ate the fruit. When Unumbotte came down from the sky, he asked who ate the fruit, and the humans said that they ate it. Unumbotte asked them who told them that they could eat the fruit, and they said that the snake told them that, and they heeded the snake because they were hungry. Unumbotte asked the antelope if he was hungry too, and the antelope said that when he got hungry he ate grass. Since that time, the antelope has lived in the wild, eating grass. Unumbotte gave sorghum to man, along with yams and millet. The people gathered in groups that ate from the same bowl, never the bowls of the other groups. This is the way differences in language arose. Since then, the people have ruled the land. But Unumbotte gave the snake a medicine with which to bite people.

Urezhwa's Wife Is Buried (Yeye/Botswana) Urezhwa was the great being. ◘ He created men, then took for himself a wife. The wife fell sick, and so Urezhwa shut her in a cave and went on a long journey to fetch medicines. He told the people who watched her on no account to bury his wife if she died in his absence. However, she died soon after he left, and the people were so disgusted with the dead body that they buried it. When the creator came back, he found what they had done, and in anger said that if they had only obeyed him he would have raised her up to life, and would have given them power to become alive again after death. Now they must suffer for their disobedience. He then went above into the heavens, where he is often seen to pass with a bright light, and his voice is heard during thunder. ◘ There were at first only two men in the world, a Korana and a San. Then a woman came out of the ground, and the Korana married her. From this connection, the country was peopled. The Korana employed the San to kill game. They quarreled over some game that the San killed unfairly. They divided their mutual property. The San lost his cattle and was severely scratched by thorns. The Korana had smeared his body with butter that he accidentally obtained from the milk, and when the San came upon the Korana he was ashamed of himself and left without the cattle.

Usunu kudi lubeta kwizeulu.
Today there is a court above.

—Ila proverb

Vere Learns to Make Fire (Pokomo, Sanye/Kenya, Somalia) Vere was an ancestor who appeared in an uninhabited country. The Buu people of the Pokomo trace their descent from Vere. He was sometimes spoken of as a preternatural being without father or mother. ▣ Vere wandered about alone in the forests of the Tana Valley, feeding on wild fruits and raw fish, for he had no knowledge of fire and no means of making it. After two years, he met with one Mitsotsozini, a Wasanye, who showed him how to make fire by means of two sticks and cook his food. Some of the Buu clans trace their descent from Mitsotsozini, as well as from Vere.

Performance

It is not simply the word that expresses the myth, but the combination of the word, including images of present and past, nonverbal elements, the relationship between performer and audience, and all the memories and experiences that haunt and give definition to the myth under construction. That myth being constructed, at the center of performance, has no life without history, biography, and the tradition that remembers and accompanies it. No single myth travels alone, nor is the unique performance meant to be the subject of analysis. Story is at the heart of performance—not simply the linear organization of images in a move from conflict to resolution: that linear movement is certainly an organizing part of the story, but it is far from being the essential meaning. Narrative linearity is one form of organization; patterning of images is another. And each of those two organizing devices does more than simply organize words—in linear fashion, in cyclical fashion. There is a larger reason for these two activities: they exist more significantly to gather and then to shape the emotions generated by the images that are given linearity and cyclical strength. The performance of a myth then is itself a form of worship, a means of transporting members of audiences to the bosom of their beliefs, of their gods, and the transporting mechanism is emotion. Performance gathers the diverse aspects of the storytelling event and gives form to the emotions of the individual members of the audience, and, equally important, brings the varied experiences of the separate members of the audience into harmony. This performance experience is the means to God; perhaps it contains God within it.

Wac and the Rope to the Sky (Jo Luo/Sudan) Wac, Spider, is the divine trickster. ▣ Wac is often outrageous in his actions. But sometimes he is positive: he saves the people, for example, by advising Juok not to create a second sun that would have burned mankind. ▣ Wac is the savior who releases the people and animals from the stomach of a water spirit, and he tries to climb into the sky. The spider says that he wants to find Juok, wherever he is. He fastens a small drum under his armpit and asks the people to pull him up by a rope into the sky. The spider also has a small stick with him, and he tells the people to cut the rope if they hear him beating his drum. But before he reaches the sky he knocks the drum accidentally with his elbow. So the people think that he has already arrived in the sky, and they cut the rope. The spider falls down and breaks into small pieces. Since then, there have been a lot of spiders. *See also:* Juok.

Waga (Waqa) and the First Man (Konso/Ethiopia) Waga is God; he is a deity of justice, the bringer of life-sustaining rain, the originator of morality, the initiator of social order. He withdrew from the world, but his presence is detected in certain natural phenomena, in the rainbow, for example. And, though he is now remote, he remains the source of morality and continues to intervene to punish sinners and to judge between those who have called on him by oath in a dispute. Waga is the creator, responsible for the life of humans. There are different explanations as to how man was born—some say that the first humans were born of snakes; others argue that they emerged from a gourd. But however humans were born, it was Waga who gave them breath. When man was born, he had all the familiar physical aspects of the human body, except for one thing: he did not move, he did not eat, he did not speak. Waga's wife, when she saw this, asked if Waga had a cure for this, if he had some speech medicine, and it is then that Waga provided humans with breath, and when he had done so man began to move, to speak, to eat. Then, when man died, the breath was returned to Waga.

Wainaba, the Serpent Ruler (Kush/Ethiopia) A mythic dragon or serpent called Wainaba ruled the country for four hundred years. ⬛ The monster was slain by a man called Angabo, the predecessor and father of the Queen of Sheba on the throne of Abyssinia. This serpent lived in Tamben, a district to the south of Aksum, and when it became known that it was coming to Aksum, Angabo promised the Aksumites that he would kill the monster if they would agree to make him king. To this they assented, and Angabo made plans to kill the serpent. He worked magic on the road by which it would come, and he hid a magical object in the form of an iron instrument, or weapon, under the surface of the road, presumably with the view of wounding the serpent. Wainaba set out on the road for Aksum, and as he proceeded on his way he shot out fire from his body on the right hand and on the left, and passing on between the flames he came to Aksum and died. He was buried in May Wayno where his grave is to be seen to this day.

Waka and the Message of Life (Galla/Ethiopia) Waka (Waqa, Qak) is the supreme being, the creator and lord of the earth. Some believe that he once came to earth and talked with men. ⬛ Waka called men and all the animals together and explained to them that he was about to make a time for sleeping, and commanded them all to cover their faces with their hands while he did so. All obeyed, but the lion, leopard, and hyena peeped between their fingers and saw night being created. It is not stated what they saw, but the result is that they can see in the dark, while men and other creatures are unable to do so and put the night to its legitimate use. ⬛ Two stories about the origin of death: The Galla attribute the mortality of man and the immortality of serpents to the mistake or malice of a certain bird that falsified the message of eternal life entrusted him by God. The creature that did this great wrong is a black or dark blue bird with a white patch on each wing and a crest on its head. It perches on the tops of trees and utters a wailing note like the bleating of sheep. The Galla call it the sheep of God. ⬛ Once, God sent that bird to tell men that they should not die, that when they grew old and weak they should slip off their skins and so renew their youth. In order to authenticate the message, God gave the bird a crest to serve as a badge of his high office. The bird went off to deliver the glad tidings of immortality to man, but he had not gone far when he met a snake that was devouring carrion in the path. The bird looked longingly at the carrion and said to the snake, "Give me some of the meat and blood, and I will tell you God's message." The snake responded that he did not want to hear the message, and he continued his meal. But the bird pressed him to listen to his message, and the snake finally consented to hear it. "The message," said the bird, "is this. When men grow old they will die, but when you grow old you will cast your skin and renew your youth." That is why people grow old and die, but snakes crawl out of their old skins and renew their youth. For this perversion of the message, God punished the wicked bird with a painful internal malady from which he suffers to this day. That is why he sits wailing on the tops of trees.

Wala Sends the First People Down (Mano/Liberia) Wala is the creator. 🔲 When he sent the first people down, Wala dispatched them with dirt to form the place in which they were to stay. That was the beginning of things. These first people brought along with them the animals and all other things, including plants, rocks, and water. Zomia, the first man sent by Wala, gave water to Boya, his son. The water was kept in a big hole. Boya walked about everywhere, distributing it. The water began to run, forming streams that carried it off and so preventing the earth's surface from becoming covered with it. He also put some under the ground so that wherever one might dig, one would find water.

Walumbe's Fatal Admonition (Ganda/Uganda) Walumbe was the god of death, the brother-in-law of Kintu, the first king; he lived with his father, Gulu (Mugulu), in the sky. The king alone made offerings to this god, and he only did so at the bidding of the other gods in order to prevent Death from killing the people wholesale. Each king, when crowned, sent an offering to Walumbe to appease him. The souls of the dead had to go to Ntanda, where Walumbe's temple was located, to give an account of their deeds; when they had done this, they were free to return to their own families, to be near the graves in which their bodies were laid. 🔲 Mpobe was a hunter. He hunted rats with his dogs one day, and, after a long chase, pursued the rats into a large hole. Deep in the hole, he saw people, a garden, houses. He kept going and finally came to Walumbe, Death, who allowed him to return to his home—with the admonition that he must not speak about the place. But at his mother's urging, he told her of his experience in the land of the dead. That evening, he heard Death calling him. He kept putting Death off, finally hiding in the forest. Death allowed him to remain alive until he had settled his affairs and consumed his property, and then Death took him. *See also:* Kintu.

Wamara and the End of the Chwezi (Nyoro/Uganda) Wamara was a mythic king. There were only three—some say two—Chwezi kings: Ndahura, his half brother Mulindwa, and his son Wamara. 🔲 During Wamara's reign things began to go badly. They called their diviners, and an ox was cut open so that its entrails could be examined. The diviners were astonished to find no trace of the intestines, and they did not know what to say. At that moment, a stranger from north of the Nile appeared. He said that he was a diviner and would solve the riddle for them. But first he insisted on making a blood pact with one of the Chwezi, so that he could be safe from their anger if his findings were unfavorable. Then he took an ax and cut open the head and hooves of the ox. At once, the missing intestines fell out of these members, and as they did so a black smut from the fire settled on them and could not be removed. The Nilotic diviner then said that the absence of the intestines from their proper place meant that the rule of the Chwezi in Bunyoro was over. Their presence in the hoofs meant that they would wander far away; in the head, that they would, nonetheless, continue to rule over men. And the black smut meant that the kingdom would be taken over by dark-skinned strangers from the north. So the Chwezi departed from Bunyoro, no one knows where. Meantime, the diviner went back to his own country in the north, and there he met the sons of Kyomya, who was Isimbwa's son by his first wife. Kyomya had married in the country to the north of the Nile, and had settled down there. The diviner told Kyomya's sons that they should go south and take over the abandoned Nyoro kingdom of their Tembuzi grandfathers. There were four brothers altogether: Nyarwa, the eldest; the twins Rukidi Alpuga and Kato Kimera; and Kiiza, the youngest. They were the first Bito. When the Bito first arrived in Bunyoro, they seemed strange and uncouth to the inhabitants. It is said that half of Rukidi's body was black and half white, a reference to his mixed descent. So began the reign of the powerful Bito dynasty, which has lasted up to the present. *See also:* Chwezi, Ndahura, Nyamiyonga, Ruhanga.

Wan Dyor and the Stone That Became Human (Dinka/Sudan) The Wan Dyor were blessed men. 🄴 At Bor dwelled a very old woman who lived on fish that she fetched from the river. One day, she was splashed by a merman and became pregnant; after eight years, she gave birth to a son, whom she called Aiwel. But her daughter, also very old, would not accept Aiwel as a real brother, saying that her mother had long since passed the age of childbearing. So Aiwel lived as a poor man among the people and was badly treated by them. The headman of the village, Fadol, kept him as a herdboy and gave him a cow to share with his own son. When this cow was milked, the milk used to stream abundantly toward Aiwel's side, which was noticed by Fadol; he eventually gave the cow to Aiwel. The cow yielded milk continuously until it gave birth to a calf of yellow color, which grew until it became a spotted bull, and the people were amazed; Aiwel henceforward was known as Aiwel Longar in remembrance of this miracle. 🄴 During a period of barren grazing because of a lack of rain, Fadol's cattle were in charge of Aiwel Longar, and they never lacked grazing or water, for Aiwel would beat the ground and grass and water sprang up, while other people's cattle could find none. One day, Fadol followed Aiwel as he drove off the cattle as usual, but soon Aiwel caught sight of him, and Fadol at once fell dead. Thereupon, Aiwel went to Fadol's son and asked him to avenge his father's death, but Fadol's son said, "No, you are keeping Fadol's cattle alive, so have been giving life to Fadol." Aiwel then went and touched Fadol, restoring him to life. Then they returned to the village and Fadol collected all the herds, and gave to Aiwel a present of two beautiful women and cattle, and relinquished the leadership of the people to him. 🔲 Once, when out grazing their goats, Aiwel's sons found another herdsman pasturing his cattle in the mountains. They took the news to their father and were told to bring him in. They returned to do so, but the strange herdsman turned himself into a flame of fire. Aiwel's sons retaliated by becoming a sheet of water, which overcame the fire and resolved it into a stone, and then they regained their natural shape. They brought in this stone to their father, who put it in a house by itself, allowing only girls to enter, telling them to lie down by the stone, and should the stone again become human, the girls were to do whatever it wished. Eventually, a beautiful woman entered the house and the desired metamorphosis occurred. She became the herdsman's wife; the pair withdrew to the mountain and the herdsman was given the name of Koor, stone. Aiwel Longar and Koor were both known to all Dinka as Wan Dyor, blessed men, and their descendants as Man Dyor, sons of blessed men. *See also:* Aiwel, Deng, Longar.

Wanjiru Sinks into the Earth, and Rain Falls (Kikuyu/Kenya) Wanjiru was a mythic woman. 🔲 For three years, there was no rain; crops died, and hunger was rampant. A wise man told the people that a young woman named Wanjiru must be bought if rain is to fall. Each man would have to contribute a goat for the payment. Wanjiru, learning of her fate, was distraught, and her parents wept. Her feet began to sink into the ground; she sank to her waist, to her breast. But the rain did not come. When she sank to her neck, the rain came heavily. But no one came forward to save her, and she concluded that she had been undone by her people. She sank to her eyes. Whenever a member of her family moved to save her, someone would give him a goat, and that person would fall back. And Wanjiru vanished. There was a deluge. A warrior who loved Wanjiru took his weapons and went to the place where she had disappeared. Then he, too, sank into the ground. Under the earth, he traveled a long road until he saw her. She was miserable. He took her on his back and they rose to the open air. At night, he went to his mother, told her of what had happened, and she killed goats and fed the fat to Wanjiru and she again grew strong. With the skins, beautiful clothing was made for her. The next day, at a dance, the warrior and Wanjiru attended, but he would not allow her family to get close to her. In the end, he repented, paid her family the dowry, and married her. *See also:* Asis.

Wantu Su's Nephew and the Drum (Sara/Chad, Sudan) Wantu Su is the supreme god. 🔲 He gave to his nephew, Wantu, a drum that contained a little of all that he had in the sky. He wanted Wantu to give this to mankind. The plan was this: Wantu would slide down a rope from heaven, then when he reached the earth he would beat a drum to announce his arrival. But a crow struck the drum as Wantu descended. The drum fell and broke, and men, fish, and plants were scattered throughout the world.

We Moves Higher into the Sky (Kasena/Burkina Faso, Ghana) We (Wea) is the supreme god. He is powerful, a power without limit. God is invisible here below. Ancestral spirits are intermediaries between God and man. Tega, the earth goddess, is the wife of We. She receives her fertility through his superior power. The groves are points of contact of the earth with God. If from time to time God makes it rain, it is because his companion the earth has need of it. He watches over her because she has all that we need. He gives her night that she may have rest, and he gives her day that she may develop her various products. ☐ We (Wea), the supreme god, used to live on earth, but an old woman kept slicing bits off him to add to her soup. As a result, We, pained by this, decided to move higher, into heaven.

Wele and the House in the Air (Luyia/Kenya) The world was created by the supreme being, Wele Xakaba (Were, Isaywa, Khakaba, Nabongo, Nyasaye), giver of all things. He first created, by himself and like lightning, his own home, heaven, a place ever bright, supporting it with pillars. ☐ The first human couple lived at a place called Embayi, in a house that stood in the air, supported by poles. They descended by a ladder, and, when they went into the house, they pulled up the ladder so no one could enter their home. This was because there were monsters, Amanani, on earth, and they might attack the humans. ☐ The first humans did not know how to have intercourse, so lived many years without children. Later, Mwambu and Sela did have intercourse, and Sela bore a son, Lilambo. She bore another child later, a girl, Nasio. When Lilambo and Nasio grew up, they did not live in the air with their parents; they moved down to earth. They, too, had children, but they were in constant danger of being swallowed by the Amanani who stalked the earth. Sela bore two other daughters, Simbi and Nakitumba, and they were married to the sons born to Lilambo and Nasio. And so humans multiplied on the earth. ☐ The sun is a powerful, wealthy chief who lives in the sky. A young woman, having refused all the young men of her community, is carried to the sky by a rope. There she is received by the sun's mother, who tells her that her son wishes to marry her. The sun, returning from work in the gardens, courts her, offering her as gifts sorghum and eleusine and everything that grows on the earth. But the young woman refuses these gifts. Then the sun presents her with the rays of his brightness, and she agrees to be his wife. The rays of the sun are kept by her in a pot, which she keeps, covered, in her house. She gives birth to three sons, then asks her husband, the sun, for permission to return to earth to visit her parents. She takes her sons and her servants, and goes to earth by means of the same rope that had lifted her into the sky. Her parents are happy to see her; her father chooses a black cow as a purification sacrifice for her. But she refuses, and she continues to refuse cows of other colors, until her father selects a white cow. He sacrifices that cow; then, the next day, he gives her two white cows to take with her to heaven. She goes back to heaven with her sons and servants on the third day. When she arrives at the place of the sun, she opens the pot that contained the sun's rays so that they may shine down on the earth. There are cows in the rays, and they fall on her father's homestead. The whole earth is warmed by the rays of the sun, and things begin to grow luxuriantly, and the people live well. *See also*: Wele (Vugusu).

Wele Supports Heaven with Pillars (Vugusu/Kenya) The world was created by Wele Xakaba, the high god, the creator, giver of all things. ▣ Before he created the whole world with everything in it, he made his own abode, heaven. To prevent heaven from falling in, he supported it all around by pillars, just as the roof of a round house is propped up by pillars. Wele Xakaba created heaven alone, without the assistance of anyone else. In a miraculous way, he then created his two assistants, Wele Muxove and Wele Murumwa (or Wele Mu Oma). ▣ After God had created heaven, he made the moon, then the sun. In the beginning, the moon was larger and more luminous than the sun, who is his younger brother. But they fought with each other, and God had to separate them, saying that from that day the sun was to be brighter than the moon; this would be day. The moon was to shine only at night. ▣ God made clouds and put them into the sky. He created a big rooster from which lightning originates. This rooster lives among the clouds. Whenever it shakes its wings there is lightning, and whenever it crows there is thunder. ▣ God created stars to assist the sun and the moon. He created rain and put it into the clouds. To stop the rain from falling when it was not needed, he made two rainbows, a male one, which is narrow, and a female one, which is wider. The male rainbow alone cannot prevent the rain from falling, but the male and the female rainbows together can do so. To stop the rain, the male rainbow appears first and the female rainbow follows. ▣ It took God two days to create heaven and all the things in it. After he had created heaven and everything in it, he wondered where his two assistants and all the other things he had made could do their work. He therefore decided to create the earth. He did so in a mysterious way, providing the earth with mountains, valleys, and larger depressions. ▣ Having created the sun and given it the power of resplendence, he asked himself, "For whom will the sun shine?" This led to his decision to create the first man. The first man was called Mwambu. Because God had created him so that he could talk and see, he needed someone to whom he could talk. He therefore created the first woman, called Sela, to be Mwambu's partner. After God had provided the surface of the earth with water, he created all plants, animals, birds, and other creatures. The first human couple, Mwambu and Sela, lived at a place called Embayi. Their house did not stand on the earth but in the air, supported by poles. So whenever Mwambu and Sela wanted to walk on the earth, they had to descend from their house by means of a ladder. When back in their house, they pulled the ladder up so that no one could climb into their house. This was because there were monsters on earth who might have come to attack them. *See also*: Wele (Luyia).

Winnam Creates Four Brothers (Mossi/Burkina Faso) Winnam is the creator. 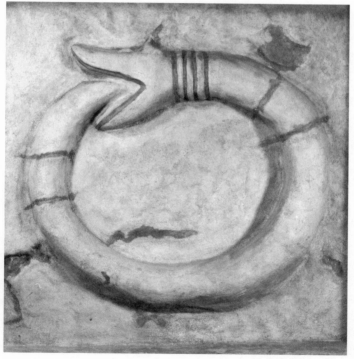 The Kurumba water spirit, Domfe, comes down to earth with rain and wind and the first food-bearing seeds. The culture hero of the Grusi is the first smith, sent by the spirit of the waters. ☒ In the beginning, Winnam (Naba Zidiwinde, Winde), the god of the sky, created four brothers and divided the earthly kingdom among them. The eldest went to a place that contained iron, and he became the first blacksmith; the second chose a place in which oxen were found, and he became the first Fulani; the third brother's place was full of bales and donkeys, and he was the first merchant; the youngest moved into a magnificent palace, and he was the first king, the leader of the earth. The elder brothers came to do the youngest homage, and from their collaboration rose the organization of the Mossi state.

Woot Takes Language from the Fly, the Tortoise, and the Dog (Kuba/DRCongo) Woot (Woto) was a mythic hero. The god, Mboom, had nine children, called Woot (Woto); each assisted in creating the world. Death came into the world when the eighth Woot killed the ninth Woot in a quarrel. ☒ Woot, drunk on palm wine, lay naked on the ground. His sons mocked him, but

Musée de l'Homme, Paris

The Snake of Eternity

261

his daughter covered his nakedness after approaching him modestly with her back turned. When Woot awoke, he rewarded his daughter by declaring that only her children would inherit from him. This is the origin of the matrilineal system. Woot punished his sons by making them undergo rituals of initiation. ◨ After committing incest with his sister, Mweel (Muele), Woot fled to the east and set himself up beside the Sankuru River. Mweel tried to make her brother return, for the village had been plunged into perpetual night since his departure. First, she sent human messengers to him. But these found the imprint of royal feet on a rock and turned back. Mweel then sent the tempest to her brother. But Woot refused to receive him. Next, Mweel sent the dog, Bondo, to whom Woot gave a bundle of meat wrapped in the mottled skin of the wild cat. He explained that day would come if the skin became white; but if it became completely black, night would continue to reign over the village. Woot forbade the messenger to eat the meat. But on the way back the dog could not resist temptation, and he therefore lost the power of speech. ◨ In a variant of the myth, the dog had two traveling companions, the fly and the tortoise. Woot offered his guests a house for the night, at the same time telling them not to touch anything. But the fly drank the palm wine, the tortoise smoked the pipe, and the dog ate the meat and cassava. To punish them, Woot deprived them of speech. He sent them back and blocked the road with a great stone. Then Mweel sent the woodworm, Bombo, which bored a way through the rock. The insect found Woot asleep. The cry of the leopard awoke him. The new messenger begged the fugitive to return to his sister so that daylight might reappear. Woot did not accede to this plea, but he called his daughter, Bibolo, and told her to collect presents for Mweel; these were a monkey, a cock, a sparrow, other birds, and a cricket. He gave these animals to Bombo, who returned with them to Mweel. The next day, the animals presented by Woot began to make their cries and the sun came up again. *See:* Mboom.

Wulbari and the Bird That Liked Human Flesh (Krachi/Togo) Wulbari is the creator god. ◨ Because of people's disrespect, Wulbari retreated from earth and rose to the sky. In the beginning, he and man lived close together and Wulbari lay on top of Mother Earth, Asase Ya. But as there was so little space to move about in, man annoyed the divinity, who in disgust went away, ascending to the present place, where one can admire him but not reach him. Various reasons are given for his retreat from the earth, out of the reach of men. An old woman, while making her fufu outside her house, kept knocking Wulbari with her pestle. This hurt him and, as she persisted, he was forced to go higher out of her reach. And there was this: the smoke of the cooking fires got into his eyes so that he had to go farther away. And this: Wulbari, being so close to men, made a convenient sort of towel, and the people used to wipe their dirty fingers on him. And this: he moved away because an old woman, anxious to make a good soup, used to cut off a bit of him at each mealtime, and he, being pained by this treatment, moved higher and higher, away from men. ▣ In the very olden time, Wulbari sent down some men by means of a chain, and they settled in the coppice between Nkomi and Krachi. At the same time, he sent down some women, also by a chain. They were on the other side of the Frao (Volta), and lived where Krachi itself now stands. Now, it happened that no men were born in Krachi and no women in the coppice. The young men did not seem to like this, and at last they arose one day and said to elders that they were dissatisfied with their enforced celibacy, adding, "Let us go to the women." Therefore they arose, and that is how Krachi came by its name and how the Krachi people originated. ▣ A certain bird, Animabri, the giant ground toucan, developed one day an evil liking for human flesh. He began to kill and devour all the men he encountered. And the men began to cry out. Their cries were heard by Wulbari, who asked what it was all about. When he was told, he called his court together and told them that in the future no one was to interfere with other people, but that each one of them was to mind his own business and not disturb his neighbor. He then asked each of his attendants to name his people and his place. The elephant told how he roamed in and controlled the far countryside—that was his people. Then all the other animals defined their respective realms. The goat said that his people were the grass; and finally the dog declared that men were his subjects. Wulbari gave the dog a medicine that would restore life to those dead whom the toucan had killed. Each then went to his kingdom. Now, the dog did not have far to go, but along the way he found a bone and, being hungry, put the medicine down by the roadside and began to chew on the bone. While he was doing this, the goat came along and saw the medicine lying there unguarded. So he took it and scattered it all over his people. The dog, when he finished his meal, could not find the magic drug. He returned to Wulbari, but God would do nothing. That is why to this day men die and do not return, but grass that dies every year comes back again.

Wuni Prohibits Intercourse (Dagomba/Ghana) Wuni is the supreme god.
▣ At the beginning of the world, Wuni, not wanting men and women to mix, arranged for the men to live in one town and the women in another. To assure that there would be no intercourse between them, he scattered masses of dry leaves all around the towns, so that if someone went out at night he would hear the rustling of the leaves and would be able to prevent his reaching the other town. Because the women did not approve of Wuni's idea, they collected pots of water and poured it on the leaves each night, making it possible for them to go to the men without Wuni's knowledge. This plan was satisfactory to the men. But one day all the women menstruated and they did not, therefore, arrange for the extra supply of water. Now, in the bachelors' town three young men grew impatient when their loved ones did not arrive, and they therefore went to see what was the matter. But as they left the town, the rustling of leaves awakened Wuni, who at once challenged them. When they explained what they were doing, Wuni became angry. To

punish the offenders, he said that, since they had broken his wishes, in the future they should suffer—women would no longer run to men, but men would ever have to chase and hunt down women. ▣ In the beginning of time, Wuni and Mother Earth lived close together, and Wuni lay on top of Mother Earth. But Wuni became annoyed when an old woman, while making her fufu (mashed yams) outside her house, kept knocking Wuni with her pestle. This hurt him, and as she persisted he was forced to go higher out of her reach. ▣ In the olden time, men did not die, and except for the chiefs they passed their whole time as slaves. They at last grew weary of this eternal bondage and decided to send a messenger to Wuni to beg him to put an end to their servitude. They chose for this duty their friend, the dog, and he departed on his errand. As he ran along the road that led to the dwelling place of Wuni, he came to a village where there was an old woman cooking a pot of something over a fire. The dog thought it a good chance to get some food and sat down nearby, gazing at the pot. The old woman tried to chase him away, but that made him more anxious to share what was in the pot. While he was waiting, a young goat who had overheard the message of the men came along, and seeing the dog tarrying decided he would do a good thing if he himself took the message and delivered it to Wuni. He therefore went on. Now, the dog had to wait a long time, and at last the pot was boiling. The old woman took it off and, taking a baby, opened the lid of the pot—the pot was only full of water, with which she began to wash the infant. The dog, annoyed, ran down the road to Wuni. On his way, he met the goat, who asked him where he was off to. The dog told him, and the goat replied that it was unnecessary to proceed, as he himself had given the message. The dog asked him what message, and when the goat told him that he had arrived at Wuni's compound and told God that men were tired of being slaves and now wanted to die, the dog was very upset and hurried to Wuni to correct the mistake. He came to God, who refused to listen to the new message, saying that he did not believe it and that he had already arranged for the death of men. So it is that death comes to all men and men remained slaves.

Wope aka asem akyere Onyankopon a, ka kyere mframa.
If you wish to tell anything to the supreme being, tell it to the winds.

Onyankopon nkum wo na odasani kum wo, wunwu.
If the supreme being does not kill you but a human kills you,
    you do not die.

Odomankoma bo owu ma owu kum no.
The creator created death only for death to kill him.

—Asante proverbs

Xu in a Two-Storied House in the Sky (Heikum/Namibia) Xu, who looks like a San and speaks !Kung, is the creator of all things, including mankind, and he sends the rain. ▣ He lives in the sky in a two-storied house, the lower story occupied by himself, his wife, and many children, while the upper is occupied by the souls of the dead. Honey, locusts, fat flies, and butterflies are found here in abundance, and the Great Captain dines on these. The souls of the dead eat nothing. Xu summons the musicians to play their music, and he gives them supernatural powers. He is the lord over rain and lightning, as well as over the spirits, ‖gaunab, and through their chief he sends good fortune in hunting or in the collection of foods. He is prayed to for rain, in sickness, before and after hunting, and before travel, and is often given the first offerings of the chase. He has neither wife nor children. He is benevolent and good. *See also:* Huwe.

An Aesthetic Space in a Familiar Cultural Place

A Zulu mythmaker directs the rhythmic movements of the myth with her hands, her fingers often outstretched, a supplementary movement when mimetic gestures are not in use. It is an abstract movement, frequently growing out of very particular, complementary movements. Her hands also act as directors; she moves characters, events, objects about in the space that she has claimed for herself and her performance, an aesthetic space existing in a very familiar cultural place. She ushers characters into the space, out of this space—characters from the real world, characters from the world of fantasy. She constructs images, brushes actions into being, burnishes characters, orchestrates complex movements and patterns, her hands also, usually in abstract fashion, indicating the passage of time. Complementary gestures become more important as she herself takes on the roles of the characters. She points to the various personae, gives directions, alludes to matters that are outside the range of her charted territory. She reveals the dimensions of people, objects, sketches in the contours of events. When the attention is on a character, she becomes that character, giving it flesh, breath. When she is not performing the roles of a character, she assumes the function of storyteller, mythmaker; it is in this mode that she escorts objects, images, people, events about within her space. These two roles define the mythmaker's functions in the performance. The body and the image build on the objects of physical reality and the unique feelings of an audience to take that audience beyond physical reality and into the realm of the gods.

Y

Yataa Puts Darkness in a Hamper (Kono/Sierra Leone) Two names are employed for the supreme being: Meketa and Yataa. Meketa, the old name, is used only occasionally now. Yataa is more commonly used: he is the great one, above and over all. He is above humans, far away in the sky. ☐ In the beginning, when Yataa made the world, the sun and the moon were in the sky, day and night were thereby defined, and the nights were pleasant, not dark and cold, and people were able to see clearly at night. Then, one day, God put the darkness into a basket and told the bat to take it to the moon. With the basket on his shoulder, the bat began his journey to the moon. But he became tired and put the basket down, and looked for food. In his absence, other animals found the basket, thought it might contain food, and they opened it. The bat returned as they did so, and he saw the darkness escape. Now, the bat sleeps during the daytime, and, when it gets dark, he flies about, attempting to catch the darkness, put it back into the basket so that he might carry it to the moon as God had instructed. But he is never able to do this, because the sun comes back and chases him away. Then the bat has to sleep until the darkness comes again, so that he may try once more to catch it. ☐ The first man and woman had one child, a boy, and Yataa told the three of them that they would never die, that when their bodies grew old he would give them new skins: the old ones would be shed, they would put on new ones, and they would become young again. God wrapped the new skins in a package and gave it to the dog to carry to the people. The dog carried the package until he met other animals who were eating, and the dog, anxious to share in the feast, put the package down and went to the food. One of the animals asked him what was in the package, and he told the story of the new skins. The snake heard the story and, when the dog was not looking, he stole the package, carried it home, and shared its contents with other snakes. When the dog reached home, the man asked him for the skins, and the dog told him how the snake had stolen them. They told Yataa about it, and God said that he could not take the skins from the snakes; from then onward the snake would not be allowed to live in the town with other animals, but would be driven out to live by himself. So now, when man grows old, he must die. Because the snake stole the skins, man always tries to kill him. *See also:* Dugbo, Meketa.

Yo, the Creative Spirit (Bambara/Mali) The creative spirit, Yo, begets three beings, named Faro, Pemba, and Teliko. Faro, the first of the three, is the master of the Word. He creates seven heavens, corresponding to the seven parts of the earth, which he fertilizes with life-giving rain. Teliko, the spirit of the air, gives life to creatures and conceives aquatic twins, ancestors of the fishermen, the first men. After whirling in space for seven years, Pemba creates the earth, with its mountains and valleys. Mixing dust with his saliva, Pemba creates a woman, Musokoroni, and after breathing into her a soul and a double, he makes her his wife. The animals and plants are the products of this marriage. ☐ Men are immortal, becoming seven-year-old children again each time they reach the age of fifty-nine. They live unclothed, have no physiological needs, and neither speak nor work. Insane with jealousy, Musokoroni attacks directly at the root of the evil. Roaming the land, she mutilates the sexual organs of both men and women, instituting the obligation of circumcision and excision. From then on, misfortunes, sickness, and death befall humanity—the golden age is over. Untamable, dirtying the earth with her impure touch, Musokoroni redeems herself, before dying, by teaching man to keep him from hunger the techniques of agriculture. *See also:* Amma, Faro, Pemba.

Y

Udwayi ufa leenziba zakhe.
The secretary bird dies with its feathers.

—Ndebele proverb

Z

Zambe Creates the Races (Bulu/Cameroon) Zambe was the creator. ⊡ Zambe, the son of Membe'e, the one who supports the world, was sent to create man, the chimpanzee, elephant, and gorilla, each of whom he named after himself. One of the men he created was black, another was white. Zambe gave his new creations water, tools, fire, the book. The new beings stirred the fire. When smoke got in the white man's eyes, he went away with the book. Chimpanzee left the fire and the other gifts, and went into the forest to eat the fruit there. Gorilla followed, and Elephant stood around. The black man stirred the fire, not bothering about the book. When the creator came for a visit, he called his creatures together and asked what they had done with the things he had given them. When Chimpanzee and Gorilla said what they had done, Zambe condemned them: they would have hairy bodies, big teeth, and live forever in the forest, eating fruit. Elephant received the same destiny. Then Zambe asked the black man where his book was. The black man replied that he had not had time to read it because he was tending the fire. Zambe told him that he would continue to do that, he would have to spend his life working hard for others because he lacked book knowledge. Zambe turned to the white man and asked him what he had done with the gifts. The white man said that he had read the book, and God said that the white man would continue to do that, that the white man would know many things but would need the black man to care for him because the white man knew nothing about keeping warm and growing food. So it is that the animals live in the forest, white men sit about reading a lot, and black men work hard and have control of fire.

Zambi and Zelo and the Knowledge of Fire (Gbaya/CAR) Humans were created by a man, Zambi, and a woman, Zelo, the first father and mother. ⊡ Zambi

271

and Zelo live in a village far in the west, neither eating nor drinking. They go naked without shame and devote themselves entirely to procreation. The first child born to this couple is ignorant of everything. His parents give him, as the first and most precious lesson, the knowledge of fire. They lead him into a forest where they find a tree named Bongo; in a bit of wood, they carve a hole, then apply a slender stick. The fire bursts out under this stick when it is vigorously rolled between the hands.

Zimu and the Message of Life (Transvaal Ndebele/South Africa) Zimu is the supreme being. 🔲 Zimu sent the chameleon with a message: "Go and tell the people that they will die and rise again." The chameleon set out but did not arrive quickly enough, so the lizard set out and ran hard and arrived before the chameleon, saying to the people, "You will die and you will not arise again." The chameleon arrived after the lizard and said, "You will die and arise again." But the people said to the chameleon, "We adhere to the word of the lizard."

Zobeyo Mebe'e and the Forbidden Basket (Bulu/Cameroon) Zobeyo Mebe'e is the creator. 🔲 Long ago, Zobeyo Mebe'e had four sons, Man, Dog, Sheep, and Rooster. All four of these sons stayed at home a long time without getting married. Rooster said, "I have lived as a bachelor long enough. I shall go and hunt for goods with which to get married." His father sent him to get kola nuts from Nkpwaevo. Nkpwaevo put kola nuts into a basket, along with a hen. He told Rooster not to open the basket. Rooster gave his father the kola nuts; then, in the house, his father untied the basket and put the hen on the ground and told Rooster, "There is your wife." Rooster took his wife, and they lived just behind the houses. Then Dog told his father that Rooster never worked, that Dog did all the work, yet his father did not help him to get a wife. So he set out to hunt for goods to get married. Zobeyo Mebe'e said the same to him as he had said to Rooster. Dog went and got a wife from Nkpwaevo in the same way as Rooster had done. Sheep did just as Rooster and Dog had done; he got a wife in the same way. At last Man came to Zobeyo Mebe'e and said that he was the oldest but still had no wife, although he did much work for his father. So he set out to hunt for goods to get married. Man, the son of Zobeyo Mebe'e, also arrived at the village of Nkpwaevo and gave him the message Zobeyo Mabe'e had sent him. Nkpwaevo loaded up and tied the basket, and besides the few kola nuts he put a woman into the basket. He warned the man not to untie the basket on his way home. After he had gone some distance, Man wondered what was in the basket. He untied the basket, and a young woman jumped out and ran back to Nkpwaevo. Man went home to his father, Zobeyo Mebe'e, and told him what he had done. His father said that he must start all over again. So Man again hunted for goods to take to Nkpwaevo as a dowry for his daughter. Not until after he had paid the full price of the dowry was he able to marry a woman. It is for this reason that men now always have to give goods as a dowry to marry a woman. It is because this first one acted foolishly and was unable to endure the heavy load. The dog and the rooster and the sheep do not give a dowry for marriage; they marry without giving any goods, because they did just as Nkpwaevo had told them.

Zong Midzi and the Quest for Immortality (Fang/Gabon) Zong Midzi is a mythic hero. ⬛ Zong Midzi of the land of Oku is engaged in a struggle with Angone Endong of the land of the immortals, Engong. Nkudang, an Engong woman with many suitors, is in love with Zong Midzi, though she has never seen him. But she knows that he is faithful to his wife, Esone Abeng. Nsure Afane is a youth who loves Nkudang, and as the two warring sides get closer he senses disaster. He takes Nkudang back to Engong, pursued by Zong Midzi, who seizes and beheads the woman. Nsure Afane beheads Zong Midzi's wife, then soars through the air on a magic ball and returns to Engong, carrying the two heads. Akoma Mba, the ruler of Engong, is watching these proceedings in a magic mirror. A decision is made that Nsure Afane should die, but he escapes on the mystic ball as Zong Midzi destroys his village. There is a pitched battle between the two, and when other Engong enter the fray Zong Midzi must escape under the ground to the safety of ancestral spirits. Four days later, with magic weapons, he returns, and the battles continue until Zong Midzi is blinded by some feathers. He is captured and taken to Engong, and the land of Oku is attacked. He escapes and returns to his ancestors, who begin to make him immortal. But their work is interrupted by Scorpion, sent by Engong, while Akoma Mba watches all in his mirror. Zong Midzi's move to immortality arrested, he is normal again, and his ancestors give him a magic gun. But a warrior from Engong overcomes him and brings him back to Engong, where he is divested of his magical ability, Akoma Mba makes him explode, and he dies. *See also:* Akoma Mba.

Zra Creates Death (Dan/Côte d'Ivoire) Zra, the creator, made death, but formerly Death was in the countryside and did not come to the villages. Men did not die. ⬛ One day, at the time when Death was in the countryside and killed only game, a hunter journeyed. He was a very good hunter. In the countryside, he found some fire on which Death was cooking meat. Nobody had seen Death until then, but the hunter met him. Death told him, "You have seen my game, so you have seen me. You are a hunter, I am a hunter. We are fellow hunters." The man stayed with Death for several days. Death gave him some meat. He thanked Death, and brought some meat back to his village. But he did not know that he was now in debt. One day, Death came to the village to ask for payment. He demanded that the hunter repay his debt. But the hunter said that he thought the meat was a gift. Death said that the hunter had come to him in the countryside, that he had taken all of Death's meat, and he therefore demanded repayment. The hunter then told Death to take one of his children. Death caught the child, saying, "I have come to you. You are in the village, you did not know that I was in the countryside. I killed game in the countryside, you came and took away my meat, and when I asked for payment you would not pay."

The Storyteller as Mythmaker

If the mythmaker is necessarily a storyteller, it is also true that the storyteller is a mythmaker: all storytellers, whether working with myth, tale, or epic—or, for that matter, history—have at the center of their craft emotion-evocative images—mythic images. The tale is never without mythic content, and it is that mythos that animates the tale, that welds it to the tradition. The tale is composed of everyday human activities and aspirations; myth links those activities and hopes to the ages. Storyteller, mythmaker—theirs is the same activity, dependent on like materials. The ancient images are decisively present in all stories in this collection; what remains is to bring them into effective communion with images from the present. So it is that the stories created by the mythmakers, stories of gods and origins and death, become the prototypes for the stories created by laic storytellers. They dip their brushes into the same palettes. The epic heroes who are a part of this dictionary are necessarily present here, because their stories make no sense without myth. And, as the tale characters' everyman and everywoman undergo the changes in their lives, those changes unfold within the embrace of myth. Inevitably and fundamentally, the storyteller is always a mythmaker—or there is no story.

> Un pays qui n'a plus de légendes, dit le poète, est condamné à mourir de froid. C'est bien possible. Mais un peuple qui n'aurait pas de mythes serait déjà mort
>
> —Dumézil, 15

So the early efforts to climb a tree to God were not so surreal. Mdi Msumu, the story tree, reaches from earth to heaven, our sole means of establishing linkages with our gods.

All storytellers depend on myth.

The Python's Shining Stone

by Okun Asere

Sheep lived in a certain town. He became a close friend of Antelope, whose home was in the bushes. When the two animals had grown up, they went out and cleared farmland. Sheep planted plantains in his, while Antelope set his with coco-yams.

When the time came for the fruits to ripen, Sheep went to his farm and cut a bunch of plantains, while Antelope dug up some of his coco-yams.

Each cleaned his food and put it in the pot to cook. When all was ready, they sat down and ate.

Next morning, Antelope said, "Let's trade. I saw a bunch of plantains on your farm that I would like to have. Will you go to mine and take some coco-yams?"

That was arranged, and Antelope said to Sheep, "Try to beat up some fufu."

Sheep tried, and found that it was very good. He gave some to Antelope, who ate all he wanted. Then he took the bunch of plantains and hung it up in his house.

Next morning, he found that the fruit had grown soft, so he did not care to eat it. He took the plantains and threw them away in the bushes.

During the day, Mbui Sheep came along and smelled the plantains. He looked around until he found them, then picked one up and began to eat. They were very sweet. He ate his fill, then went on, and later met a crowd of apes. To them he said, "Today I found a very sweet thing in the bushes."

In time, Antelope grew hungry again, and Sheep said to him, "If you're hungry, why don't you tell me?"

He went back to his farm and got four bunches of plantains. As he came back, he met the monkey people. They begged for some of his fruit, so he gave it to them.

After they had eaten all there was, they in their turn went on and met a herd of wild boars. To these they said, "There is very fine food to be got from Sheep and Antelope."

The wild boars therefore came and questioned Antelope: "Where is coco-yam to be had?"

Antelope answered, "The coco-yams belong to me."

The boars begged for some, so Antelope took a basket, filled it at his farm, and gave it to them.

After they were satisfied, they went on their way, and next morning they met Elephant. To him they said, "Greetings, Lord! Last night, we got very good food from the farms over there."

Elephant at once ran and asked the two friends, "Where do you get so much food?"

They said, "Wait a little."

Sheep took his long machete and went to his farm. He cut five great bunches of plantains and carried them back. Antelope got five baskets of coco-yams, which he brought to Elephant. After Elephant had eaten all this, he thanked them and went away.

All the beasts of the field came in their turn and begged for food, and to each the two friends gave willingly of all that they had.

Bush-cow was the last to come.

Now, not far from the two farms there was a great river called Akarram. In the midst of the river, deep down, dwelt Crocodile.

One day, Bush-cow went down into the water to drink, and from him Crocodile learned that much food was to be had nearby.

Crocodile came out of the water and began walking towards the farm. He went to Sheep and Antelope, and said, "I am dying of hunger. Please give me food."

Antelope said, "To the beasts who are my friends, I shall give all that I have. But to you I shall give nothing, for you are no friend of mine."

But Sheep said, "I do not like you very much, but I shall give you one bunch of plantains."

Crocodile took them and said, "Do not close your door tonight when you lie down to sleep. I'll come back and buy more food from you at a great price."

Crocodile then went back to the water and sought out a python that dwelled there.

To him he said, "I have found two men on land who have much food."

Python said, "I too am hungry. Will you give me something to eat?"

So Crocodile gave Python some of the plantains that he had brought. When Python had tasted one of them, he said, "How sweet it is! Will you go back and bring more?"

Crocodile said, "Will you give me something with which to buy?"

Python answered, "Yes, I'll give you something with which you can buy the whole farm!"

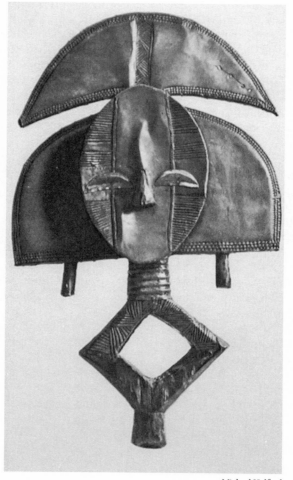

Michael Holford

Ancestral Spirit

Then he took from within his head a shining stone and gave it to the crocodile, who began his journey back to the farm. As he went, night fell, and all the road grew dark. But he held in his jaws the shining stone, and it made a light on his path so that all the way was bright. When he neared the dwelling of the two friends, he hid the stone, and called out, "Come out and I will show you something that I have brought."

It was very dark when they came to speak with him. Slowly the crocodile opened his claws in which he held up the stone, and it began to glimmer between them. When he held it right out, the entire place became so bright that one could see to pick up a needle or any small thing.

He said, "The price of this object that I bring to you is one whole farm."

Antelope said, "I cannot buy. If I give up my farm, nothing remains to me. What is the use of this great shining stone if I starve to death?"

But Sheep said, "I shall buy—oh, I shall buy, I shall give my farm full of plantains, for what you bring fills the whole earth with light. Come, let us go. I shall show you my farm. From here to the waterside, all around is my farm. Take it all, do what you choose with it. Only, give me the great shining stone so that when darkness falls the entire earth may still be light."

Crocodile said, "I agree."

Then Sheep went to his house with the stone, and Antelope went to his. Sheep placed the stone above the lintel so that it might shine for all the world, but Antelope closed his door and lay down to sleep.

In the morning, Sheep was very hungry, but he had nothing to eat because he had sold all his farm for the great white stone.

Next night and the night after, he slept filled with hunger. But on the third morning, he went to Antelope and asked, "Will you give me a single coco-yam?"

Antelope answered, "I can give you nothing, for now you have nothing to give in exchange. It was not I who told you to buy the shining thing. To give something when plenty remains is good, but no one but a fool would give his all so that a light may shine in the dark!"

Sheep was very sad. He said, "I have done nothing bad. Formerly, no one could see in the night. Now the python's stone shines so that everyone can see to go wherever he chooses."

All that day, Sheep still endured, though nearly dying of hunger, and at night he crept down to the water, very weak and faint.

By the side of the river he saw a palm tree, and on it a man trying to cut down clusters of ripe kernels, but this was hard to do because it had grown very dark.

Sheep said, "Who is there?"

The man answered, "I am Effion Obassi."

Sheep called, "What are you doing?"

Effion Obassi replied, "I am trying to gather palm kernels, but I cannot do so because it is so dark among these great leaves."

Sheep said to him, "It is useless to try to do such a thing in the dark. Are you blind?"

Effion Obassi answered, "I am not blind. Why do you ask?"

Then Sheep said, "Good. If you are not blind, I beg you to throw me down only one or two palm kernels, and in return I shall show you a thing brighter and more glorious than anything you have seen before."

Effion Obassi replied, "Wait a minute, and I will try to throw a few kernels down to you. Afterward, you can show me the shining thing, as you said."

He threw down three palm kernels, which Sheep took. They stayed his hunger a little.

Then he called, "Please try to climb down. We'll go together to my house."

Effion Obassi tried very hard, and after some time he stood safely at the foot of the tree by the side of Sheep.

When they got to his house, Sheep said, "Will you wait here a little while I go to question the townspeople?"

First, he went to Antelope, and asked, "Will you not give me a single coco-yam to eat? See, the thing that I bought at the price of all that I had turns darkness to light for you. But as for me, I shall die of hunger."

Antelope said, "I shall give you nothing. Take back the thing for which you sold everything, and we'll stay in our darkness as before."

Then Sheep begged all the townsfolk to give him a little food in return for the light that he had bought for them. But they all refused.

So Sheep went back to his house, and he took the shining stone and gave it to Effion Obassi, saying, "I love the earth folk, but they do not love me. Now take the shining thing for which I gave all my possessions. Go back to the place from which you came, because I know that you belong to the sky people. And when you reach your home in the heavens, hang my stone in a place where all the earth folk may see its shining and be glad."

Effion Obassi took the stone and went back by the road on which he had come. He climbed up the palm tree, and the great leaves raised themselves upward, pointing to the sky, and they lifted him up until, from their points, he could climb into heaven.

When he reached his home, he called all the lords of the sky and said, "I have brought back a thing today that can shine so that all the earth will be light. From now on, everyone on earth or in heaven will be able to see at the darkest hour of the night."

The lords looked at the stone and wondered. Then they consulted together and made a box.

Effion Obassi said, "Make it so that the stone can shine out only from one side."

When the box was finished, he set the globe of fire within it and said, "This stone is mine. From this time, all the people must bring me food. I shall no longer go to seek any for myself."

For some time, they brought him plenty of food, but after a while they grew tired. Then Effion Obassi covered the side of the box, so that the stone would not shine until they brought him more food.

That is the reason the moon is sometimes dark and people on earth say, "It is the end of the month. The people have grown weary of bringing food to him, and he will not let his stone shine out until they bring him a fresh supply."

Song of the Mythmaker

All creatures must die, be buried and rot.
Kings and heroes die, are buried and rot.
I, too, shall die, shall be buried and rot.
But the Dausi,
The song of my battles,
Shall not die.
It shall be sung again and again
And shall outlive all kings and heroes.
Hoooh, that I might do such deeds!
Hoooh, that I may sing the Dausi!
Wagadu will be lost,
But the Dausi shall endure and shall live!

(Frobenius and Fox, 1937, p. 101)

Sources

Primary sources are in bold print.

Abasi, Abbassi (Anang/Nigeria)—Messenger, 1982, 65–68; **Talbot, 1926, 73–74.**

Abasi, Abassi (Efik/Nigeria)—**Beier, 1966, 60–61**; Hackett, 1989, 32–34, 39–40; Noah, 1974, 85–88; **Simmons, 1956, 3, 19–20**; Talbot, 1926, 73–74.

Abasi, Abasi Ibom, Abasi Enyong, Chuku (Ibibio/Nigeria)—Abasiattai, 1991, 85–91; Forde and Jones, 1950, 78; Hackett, 1989, 33–34; Oduyoye, "Names," 1983, 352; Talbot, 1924–1925, 184; **Talbot, 1926, 61–63, 73–74, 117–19**; Ukpong, 1982, 162–63.

Aberewa (Akan, Asante/Ghana)—**King, 1986, 26**; **Parrinder, 1949, 47–48.**

Abradi (Nyimang, Ama/Sudan)—Ikenga–Metuh, 1987, 91; Kronenberg, 1959, 198–99, 208; Stevenson, 1940, 95–97; **Stevenson, 1950, 209–13, 216–20.**

Abua (Abua/Nigeria)—**Talbot, 1932, 28–30.**

Abuk (Dinka/Sudan)—**Bently, 1995, 9**; King, 1986, 52.

Abu Zayd, Zaydan, and Dhiyab (Bani Hilal, Banu Hilal/Tunisia)—**Norris, 1980, 25–28.**

Adoudoua (Agni, Baoule/Côte d'Ivoire)—American University, 1962, 150–51.

Adro, Adroa, Adronga (Lugbara/DRCongo, Sudan, Uganda)—Baxter and Butt, 1953, 123–24; **Middleton, 1960, 230–38, 252–56**; Middleton, 1963, 261, 271; Middleton, 1965, 18–19, 47–51; Middleton, 1973, 493–94.

Agipie (Turkana/Kenya)—**Dundas, 1910, 69.**

Aido–Hwedo (Fon/Benin)—**Argyle, 1966, 177–78**; Herskovits and Herskovits, 1958, 107–8

Aiwel (Bor, Dinka/Sudan)—**Seligman and Seligman, 1932, 148–49**; Willis, 1928, 195–97.

Ajok, Naijok (Lotuko/Sudan)—**Huntingford, Northern, 1953, 90–91**; **Seligman and Seligman, 1932, 325–26.**

Akoma Mba (Fang/Cameroon, Gabon, Equatorial Guinea)— Awona, 1965, 180–213; Awona, 1966, 109–209; **Biebuyck, "Heroic," 1978, 347–49**; Pepper, 1972.

Akongo (Ngombe/DRCongo)—**Davidson, 1950, 163–70, 175–76**; Ikenga-Metuh, 1987, 91.

Alatangana (Kono/Guinea)—Beier, 1966, 3–6; **Holas, 1964, 114–15.**

Ale, Ala (Igbo/Nigeria)—Beier, 1966, I, 364; Ezekwuga, 1987, 147; Ikenga-Metuh, 1987, 88–89; Iloanusi, 1984, 77–99; Leeming and Page, 1994, 38; Parrinder, 1949, 37–39; Talbot, 1927, 60, 134–35; **Talbot, 1932, 25–27.**

al-Khidr, Khadir, al-Khadir (Arabic Areas)— **Budge, 1933, 158–63**; **Norris, 1972,** 10, 14–24, 53–55; Qur'an, xviii: 60–82.

Ama (Jukun/Nigeria)—**Meek, Jukun, 1931**, 178–80, 189–90, 192–203; II, 520–23, 560.

Amma (Dogon/Burkina Faso, Mali)—Dieterlen, "Twins," 1991, 33–34; Griaule, 1965, 16–40; Griaule and Dieterlen, 1954, 83–110; **Griaule and Dieterlen, 1965**; de Heusch, 1985, 126–32; Holas, 1964, 110–13; Long, 1963, 26–27; Ottenberg, 1960, 367–68; Ray, 1976, 24–28; Sproul, 1979, 49–66.

Ananse, Anansi (Asante/Ghana)—**Rattray, 1930, 54–59.**

Andriambahomanana (Malagasy/Madagascar)—**Dahle, 1880, 44–45.**

Andriananahary (Betsileo, Malagasy, Merina/Madagascar)—**Carlyon, 1982, 17**; **Kottak, 1980, 69, 213–14**; Sibree, 1870, 375–77, 396–97.

Anna (Carthaginian/Tunisia)—**Grimal, 1985, 43.**

Antaeus (Libya, Morocco)—**Grimal, 1985, 43, 424, 455.**

Antar, Sirat (North Africa)—**Norris, 1980, 5–6.**

Arebati (Efe/DRCongo)—**Schebesta, Revisiting, 1936, 168–86.**

Aruan (Kyama/Benin, Côte d'Ivoire)—**Baker, 1942, 145–51.**

Arum (Uduk/Ethiopia)—**Evans-Pritchard, 1940, 230; James, 1979, 67–78**; Buxton, 1963, 19–20.

Asis (Kipsigis/Kenya)—Huntingford, 1953, 38, 52; **Koech, 1977, 118–39.**

Asis, Asista, Chebonamuni, Chepkeliensokol, Chepopkoiyo, Cheptalil (Nandi/Kenya)—**Frazer, 1923, 21**; Hollis, 1909, 40–41, 97–98, 113–14; Huntingford, 1928, 189–90; Huntingford, Southern, 1953, 38.

Ataa Naa Nyongmo (Ga/Ghana)—**Kilson, 1971, 58–78.**

Baal Hammon (Berber, Carthaginian/Tunisia)—Britannica, 1998, I, 762; Meyerowitz, 1958, 130–31, 135–36; Norris, 1972, 8; Picard, 1956, 26–31; Warmington, 1969, 145–47, 151; Warmington, 1981, 453–54.

Baatsi (Efe/DRCongo)—**Beier, 1966, 63; Schebesta, Revisiting, 1936, 168–86.**

Bail (Dilling, Nuba/Sudan)—**Sagar, 1921, 143–44.**

Balewa Yola (Fulani, Fulfulde/Nigeria)—**Hogben and Kirk–Greene, 1966, 433–34.**

Bata (Egypt)—**Petrie, 1899, 36–65.**

Bateta and Hanna (Soko/DRCongo)—**Stanley, 1893, 5–25.**

Bayajida, Abuyazidu (Hausa/Niger, Nigeria)—Edgar, 1977, III, 125–28; Hassan and Shuaibu Na'ibi, 1962; Hogben and Kirk–Greene, 1966, 145–46, 148–49, 212; Palmer, 1967, 133; **Yahaya, 1988, 8–9.**

Bumba (Bushongo/DRCongo)—**Leach, 1956, 145–47**; Leeming and Leeming, 1994, 34–35; Leslau and Leslau, 1963, 11; **Torday and Joyce, 1910, 20–21.**

Bunzi (Woyo/DRCongo)—**Leeming and Page, 1994, 97–98.**

Chibinda Ilunga (Luba, Lunda/Angola, DRCongo)—De Carvalho, 1890, 58–76; **Duysters, 1958, 81–86**; Hall, 1965, 19; Labrecque, 1949; Pogge, 1880, 224–26; Struyf, 1948, 373–75; Torday and Joyce, 1911, 235–36; Turner, 1955, 1–26; Turner, 1967, 152–53; Turner, 1968, 58; Tweedie, 1966, 203–4; Van den Byvang, 1937, 429–35 (text, 1926).

Chido (Jukun/Nigeria)—**Meek, 1931, II, 456.**

Chinawezi (Lunda/Angola, DRCongo)—**Bently, 1995, 46–47.**

Chipimpi, Kipimpi (Lamba/Zambia)—Doke, 1931, 31; **Marchal, 1936, 7–28.**

Chiti Mukulu (Bemba/Zambia)—Brelsford, 1956, 38–39; **Labrecque, 1933,** 21–48; Maxwell, 1983, 36–38.

Chiuta (Tonga/Malawi)—MacAlpine, 1905, 187; MacAlpine, 1906, 377–79; Tew, 1950, 69.

Chuku (Igbo/Nigeria)—Beier, 1966, 56; Ezekwuga, 1987, 78; Forde and Jones, 1950; 25–26; Ikenga–Metuh, 1987, 88–89; Iloanusi, 1984, 77–99; **Meek, 1937,** 20–21, 23, 26, **52–62;** Oduyoye, "Names," 1983, 356; Ohadike, 1994, 98–99; **Parrinder, 1949,** 21–22; Talbot, 1926, 40–49, 52–60; Talbot, 1932, 19–20, 23–27.

Chwezi (Nyoro/Uganda)—**Beattie, 1961, 11–16; Ingrams, 1960, 183–84.**

Da Monzon (Bambara/Mali)—Bâ and Kesteloot, 1966, 165–205; **Biebuyck, "Heroic," 1978, 338–40;** Bâ, 1966, 99–127; Doucouré, 1966, 43–45.

Deng (Dinka/Sudan)—King, 1986, 52; **Seligman and Seligman, 1932, 148;** Willis, 1928, 195–97.

Dengbagine (Zande/Sudan)—**Evans–Pritchard, 1937, 199–200.**

Dente (Ewe/Ghana)—**Westermann, 1930, 228–32.**

Dido (Carthaginian/Tunisia)—**Grimal, 1985, 136–37;** Meyerowitz, 1958, 129.

Dikithi (Mbukushu/Angola, Botswana, Namibia)—**Larson, 1963, 179–82.**

Ditaolane (Sotho/Lesotho)—**Casalis, 1861, 347–49.**

Djakomba, Djakoba, Djabi (Bachwa/DRCongo)—**Schebesta, My Pygmy, 1936, 234–37.**

Dodo (Hausa/Niger, Nigeria)—Besmer, 1983, 62–120; Edgar, 1977, II, 63–188; Gunn, 1956, 114; Hunter, 1997, 4–7; Meek, 1925, II, 18–20; Meek, Tribal, 1931, II, 136; Tremearne, 1913, 123–28, 292–93.

Doni Dyu (Bambara, Bozo, Dogon, Malinke, Minyanka/Mali)—**Dieterlen, "Graphic," 1991, I, 30–32.**

Doondari (Fulani/Mali, Senegal)—**Beier, 1966, 1–2;** Dieterlen, "l'Initiation," 1965, 327.

Dugbo (Kono, Tembe/Sierra Leone)—**Parsons, 1950, 270.**

Dzemawon, Numbo (Ga/Ghana)—**Field, 1937, 4–5;** Manoukian, 1950, 94–98.

Dzivaguru (Shona/Zimbabwe)—**Wollacott, 1963, 116–17.**

Dzugudini (Lovedu/South Africa)—**Krige and Krige, 1943, 5–6.**

Ebele (Igbo/Nigeria)—**Leonard, 1906, 31–33.**

Effion Obassi (Ekoi/Nigeria)—**Talbot, 1912, 344–49.**

Ekineba (Kalabari/Nigeria)—**Horton, 1975, 33–36.**

Elijinen (Tuareg/Algeria, Libya, Mali, Niger, Nigeria)—**Rodd, 1966, 278–79.**

Enkai (Masai/Kenya)—Guirand, 1959, 476; **Hollis, 1905, 268–69, 272–73;** Huntingford, Southern, 1953, 125; Koenig, 1956, 87–88, 147; **Lindblom, 1920, 475–76;** Werner, 1933, 148.

Epaphus (Egypt, Libya)—**Grimal, 1985, 147.**

Epilipili (Efe/DRCongo)—**Schebesta, Revisiting, 1936, 168–86.**

Esu (Yoruba/Nigeria)—**Abímbólá, 1994, 106, 108;** Awolalu, 1979, 28–29; Booth, "God," 1977, 169; Courlander, 1973, 10–11; King, 1986, 11; **Parrinder, 1949, 56–57;** Wyndham, 1921, 11.

Fa (Fon/Benin)—**Argyle, 1966, 190, 193**; Herskovits and Herskovits, 1958, 173–79.

Faro (Bambara/Mali)—**Dieterlen, 1951, 88–82**; Heusch, 1985, 166–70.

Fi (Jen/Nigeria)—**Meek, Tribal, 1931, II, 520–23**.

‖Gamab (Berg Damara/Namibia)—**Vedder, "Berg," 1928, 61–62, 66**.

╪Gama–╪Gorib (Khoi/South Africa)—**Kidd, 1925, 410–15**.

╪Gao!na (!Kung/Namibia)—**Marshall, 1962, 228–38**.

Gassire (Djerma/Burkina Faso, Niger; Soninke/Burkina Faso, Gambia, Mali, Mauritania, Senegal)—**Frobenius and Fox, 1937, 97–133**.

‖Gauwa (!Kung/Angola, Namibia)—**Campbell, 1822, I, 306**; Estermann, 1976, 12–13; Hays, 1963, 273; **Marshall, 1962, 221–28, 234, 238–44**; Schapera, 1930, 184; Schoeman, 1957, 9–10; Stow, 1905, 130.

Gborogboro and Meme (Lugbara/DRCongo, Sudan, Uganda)—Middleton, 1960, 252–56; **Middleton, 1965, 18–19**.

Gihanga (Hutu, Nyarwanda, Tutsi/Rwanda)—**Guillebaud, 1950, 193–94**.

Gihanga (Nyarwanda/Rwanda)—**Heusch, 1985, 115–17**.

Gila (Anuak/Sudan)—**Seligman and Seligman, 1932, 109**.

Gion (Jukun, Kororofawa/Nigeria)—**Palmer, 1912, 409–11, 415**.

Goha (San/Botswana, Namibia, South Africa)—**Campbell, 1822, I, 305–7; II, 32**.

Goroba–Dike (Fulbe/Mali)—**Frobenius and Fox, 1937, 137–50**.

Gu (Fon/Benin)—Argyle, 1966, 178; **Herskovits, 1938, II, 105–7**; Mercier, 1954, 210–34.

Gueno (Fulani/Senegal)—**Kesteloot, in Bâ, 1988, 40–41, 103–4, 116, 152**.

Gurzil (Libya)—**Norris, 1972, 45**; Rodd, 1966, 295.

Hambageu, Khambageu (Sonjo, Sonyo/Tanzania)—**Gray, 1965, 56–58**; Ndula, 1953, 38–42; Simenauer, 1955, 23–30.

Hathor (Egypt)—**Budge, 1904, I, 428–29, 431**; Leeming and Page, 1994, 44.

Hathors (Egypt)—**Petrie, 1899, 13–27**.

Hebioso and Abui (Awuna/Burkina Faso)—**France, 1908, 79–81**.

Heitsi–Eibib (Khoi/South Africa; Nama/Namibia; San/Botswana, Namibia, South Africa)—**Bleek, 1864, 74–82**; Carstens, 1975, 82–84; **Dapper, et al., 1933, xiii**; Hahn, 1880, 65; **Kidd, 1925, 107, 410–15**; Smith, 1950, 92; Vedder, "Nama," 1928, 131–32.

Hevioso, Xevioso (Fon/Benin)—**Argyle, 1966, 180–83**.

Hishe, Hise (Aikwe, Auen, Naron/Namibia)—**D. Bleek, 1928, 44–45**; **Marshall, 1962, 221–28**; Smith, 1950, 90–91.

Holy Fire (Berg Damara/Namibia)—**Vedder, "Berg," 1928, 68**.

Horus (Egypt)—**Budge, 1904, I, 473–77**.

Huveane (Pedi, Venda/South Africa)—**Werner, 1933, 155–60**.

Huveane (Sotho/Lesotho)—**Werner, 1933, 41**.

Huwe, Xu (!Kung/Botswana)—**Marshall, 1962, 221–28, 234**; Schapera, *Khoisan*, 1930, 184.

Hyel (Bura, Pabir/Nigeria)—**Helser, 1930, 192–93**; Meek, *Tribal*, 1931, I, 258–61.

Iboniamasiboniamanoro (Malagasy/Madagascar)—**Becker, 1939, 7–136**.

Idris (Arab, Berber/Morocco)—**Legey, 1935, 23, 44–45.**

Ifa, Orunmila (Yoruba/Nigeria)—Bascom, 1969; Ellis, 1894, 56–64; **Forde, 1951,** 29–30; Talbot, 1926, 33.

Iju (Margi/Nigeria)—**Meek, *Tribal*, 1931, I, 221–27.**

Imana (Hutu, Nyarwanda, Tutsi/Rwanda)—Guillebaud, 1950, 181–94; Ikenga-Metuh, 1987, 92; **Johanssen, 1931, 351;** Loupais, 1908, 5–6; **Ray, 1976, 33–34.**

Imana (Hutu, Rundi, Tutsi/Burundi)—**Guillebaud, 1950, 193–94.**

Inusa (Bachama, Bwaare, Bwaatiye/Cameroon, Nigeria)—**Carnochan, 1967,** 629–33.

Ipupi (Kimbu/Tanzania)—**Shorter, 1969, 232.**

Irgam Yigfagna, al–Jabal al–Lamma (Berber/Algeria, Libya, Morocco, Tunisia)—**Norris, 1972, 4–13, 21–22.**

Isis (Egypt)—**Budge, 1928, I, 144.**

Jaki and Dribidu (Lugbara/DRCongo, Sudan, Uganda)—**Middleton, 1960,** 231–32, 252–56.

Jangare, Bori (Hausa/Niger, Nigeria)—**Besmer, 1983, 3–4,** 62–120; Nadel, 1954, 209–10; Tremearne, 1913, 146–50; Tremearne, 1914, 19–20, 255–56.

Jeki la Njambe (Batanga, Duala, Malimba, Pongo/Cameroon)—**Austen, 1995,** 8–9.

Jinn (Arabic/Sahara Regions)—**Norris, 1972, 9–10;** Smith, 1901, 119–20; Yahaya, 1988, 15–17.

Jok (Acholi/Uganda)—Boccassino, 1939, 195–201; Butt, 1952, 86–89; Grove, 1919, 169; King, 1986, 53–55; Nalder, 1937, 34; Seligman and Seligman, 1932, 122.

Jok (Lango/Uganda)—**Butt, 1952, 104–5; Driberg, 1923, 216–43.**

Juntel Jabali (Tukulor/Senegal)—**Dilley, 1987, 71–73.**

Juok (Anuak/Sudan)—Butt, 1952, 79; **Cummins, 1915, 34–35; Evans–Pritchard and Beaton, 1940, 56–58.**

Juok (Jo Luo/Sudan)—**Kronenberg, 1960, 237–51.**

Juok (Shilluk/Sudan)—Butt, 1952, 62–64; Freund, 1964, 5–6; Hays, 1963, 324; Seligman and Seligman, 1932, 74–77, 88–89, 96–97; **Westermann, 1912, xxxix, 155–57.**

Juon, Juong (Burun, Meban/Sudan)—Butt, 1952, 160; **Frazer, 1923, 10–11.**

Kabunda (Lamba/Zambia)—**Grévisse, 1946–1947, 68–69.**

|Kaggen (San/Botswana, Namibia, South Africa)—**Bleek and Lloyd, 1911, 44–55; Bleek and Lloyd, 1923, 5–9, 30–40;** Hodgson, 1952, 23; Leach, 1956, 152–55; Orpen, 1919, 143–52; Stow, 1905, 130.

Kahina (Lamtuna/Morocco)—**Norris, 1972, 108–9.**

Kaidara (Fulani/Senegal)—**Kesteloot, in Bâ, 1988, 42–43.**

|Kai |Kini (!Kung/Namibia)—**Marshall, 1962, 232–33.**

Kalala (Holoholo/DRCongo, Tanzania)—**Schmitz, 1912, 261–66; Heusch, 1982,** 64–65.

Kalitangi (Ovimbundu/Angola)—**Ennis, 1962, 244–51.**

Kalumba (Luba/DRCongo)—Denolf, 1933, 237–46; **Donohugh and Berry, 1932,** 180–81; Theuws, 1962, 222–23.

Kamangundu and Omumborombonga (Damara, Herero/Namibia)—**Beider-becke, 1880, 88–97**; Hahn, 1928, 1–2.

Kambili (Mandinka/Mali)—**Camara, 1974, xi–xiii**.

Kana (Ganda/Uganda)—**Beattie, 1960, 11–12**.

Kanu (Limba/Sierra Leone)—**Finnegan, 1967, 19–24, 231–35**; McCulloch, 1950.

Kapepe (Lenje/Zambia)—Biebuyck, "Heroic," 1978, 349; **Torrend, 1921, 98–144**.

Kar, Jakar (Nuer/Sudan)—**Evans–Pritchard, 1940, 230**; James, 1979, 73.

Karkur (Hausa/Niger, Nigeria)—**Tremearne, 1914, 213–15**.

Karunga (Herero/Namibia)—**Beiderbecke, 1880, 88–97**; Ikenga–Metuh, 1987, 95; Viehe, 1879, 67.

Kashindika (Lala/Zambia)—**Munday, 1942, 47–53**.

Kaumpuli (Ganda/Uganda)—**Roscoe, 1911, 308–9**.

Kaura Duna (Hausa/Nigeria)—**Muhammad, 1982, 397–415**.

Kejok (Dinka/Sudan)—**Fergusson, 1921, 163–65**.

Kemangurura (Kikuyu/Kenya)—**Cagnolo, 1952, 1–3**.

Kho (San/Botswana, Namibia, South Africa)—**Gray, 1985, 13**.

Khuzwane (Lovedu/South Africa)—**Krige and Krige, 1943, 231–32, 239**.

Kibo and Mawenzi (Chaga/Tanzania)—**Gutmann, 1909, 1914; quoted in *Tanganyika Notes and Records* 64 (1965): 50–53**.

Kibuka (Ganda/Uganda)—King, 1986, 35; **Roscoe, 1911, 301–3**.

Kintu (Ganda/Uganda; Masai/Kenya)—Beattie, 1960, 11–12; Guirand, 1959, 475; Ingrams, 1960, 215; **Roscoe, 1911, 136, 460–64** Werner, 1933, 152.

Kisra (Bargu/Benin)—**Hogben, 1930, 164–65**.

Kiumbi (Asu, Pare/Tanzania)—**Kimambo and Omari, 1972, 111–21**.

Ko (San/Botswana, Namibia, South Africa)—**Campbell, 1822, I, 29; II, 32–34**.

Korau (Hausa/Niger, Nigeria)—**Hogben and Kirk–Greene, 1966, 157–58**.

Koulotiolo, Koulo Tyolo (Senufo/Côte d'Ivoire, Mali)—**Holas, 1964, 116–19**.

Kudu (Benga/Equatorial Guinea, Gabon)—**Nassau, 1912, 129–33**.

Kudukese (Hamba/DRCongo)—**Biebuyck, "Heroic," 1978, 45–46; Jacobs, 1963, 33–36**.

Kwege (Zaramo/Tanzania)—**Werner, 1933, 87–91**.

Kwoth (Nuer/Sudan)—Crazzolara, 1953, 67–68; **Evans–Pritchard, 1956, 1–10, 28–29, 63**; Fergusson, 1923, 148–49.

Legba, Elegba (Fon/Benin)—Argyle, 1966, 188–90; Ellis, 1890, 41–46; Herskovits, 1938, II, 109; **Herskovits and Herskovits, 1958, 142–48**; Leeming, 1990, 171–72; Parrinder, 1967, 91.

Lesa (Lala/Zambia)—Hall, 1965, 13; **Munday, 1942, 46–53**.

Lesa (Lamba/Zambia)—Doke, 1927, 15–23; **Doke, 1931, 30–32, 222–29**; Whiteley, 1950, 63–64.

Leve (Mende/Sierra Leone)—**Sawyerr, 1970, 85–91**.

Leza (Fipa/Tanzania)—**Frazer, 1923, 26**.

Leza (Ila, Kaonde/Zambia)—Idowu, 1973, 157; Jaspan, 1953, 41; Smith, 1907, 300; **Smith and Dale, 1920, II, 101–2, 197–200**.

Lianja (Mongo, Nkundo/DRCongo)—**Heusch, 1994, 229–32**.

Libaka (Ngombe/DRCongo)—**Davidson, 1950, 163–70, 175–77**.

Libanza (Boloki/CAR)—**Weeks, 1913, 200–4.**

Libanza (Upoto/DRCongo)—**Lindeman, 1906, 23.**

Libya (Libya)—Graves, 1955, I, 205–6; Grimal, 1985, 259–60.

Likuube (Nyamwezi, Sukuma, Sumbwa/Tanzania)—Abrahams, 1967, 77–78; **Cory, 1960, 15–16.**

Liongo (Pokomo, Swahili/Kenya)—**Steere, 1869, 440–53;** Werner, 1933, 146.

Lisa (Fon/Benin)—Akinjogbin, 1976, I, 375; Ellis, 1890, 65–66; **Herskovits, 1938, II, 106–7,** 289–92.

Lofokefoke (Mbole/DRCongo)—**Biebuyck, "Heroic," 1978, 345–47;** Jacobs, 1961, 81–92.

Loma, Hege (Bongo/Sudan)—Baxter and Butt, 1953, 135; Evans-Pritchard, 1929, 45; **A. and W. Kronenberg, 1962, 317–21.**

Loma Gubu (Bongo/Sudan)—**A. and W. Kronenberg, 1962, 317–21.**

Longar (Dinka/Sudan)—**Lienhardt, 1961, 169–92.**

Louliyya (Egypt)—**El–Shamy, 1980, 54–63.**

Luchyele (Lamba/Zambia)—**Doke, 1931, 30–32,** 222–29; **Hall, 1965, 11, 13.**

Lueji, Luweji, Lweshi (Lunda/DRCongo)—**Carvalho, 1890,** quoted in **Turner, 1955, 1–27.**

Lurubot (Lokoiya, Oxoriuk/Sudan)—**Nalder, 1937, 114–18.**

Lwanda Magere (Luo/Uganda)—**Imbo, private communication;** K'Okiri, 1970; K'Onyango, 1977; Omtatah, 1991.

Makeda (Amhara, Ge'ez, Tigre/Ethiopia)—Buxton, 1970, pp. 34, 37, 64; **Jones and Monroe, 1935, 10–16,** 18–19.

Malikophu (Xhosa/South Africa)—**Scheub, 1996, 163–86.**

Mangala (Mande/Mali)—**Dieterlen, 1957, 124–38;** Sproul, 1979, 66–75.

Maori (Makoni/Zimbabwe)—**Frobenius,** quoted in Beier, 1966, 15–17, and **Freund, 1964, 147–52.**

Masupa (Efe/DRCongo)—**Schebesta, Revisiting, 1936, 168–86.**

Matsieng (Hurutshe/South Africa)—**Breutz, 1953, 67–68.**

Mawu, Adanuwoto, Se (Anlo/Ghana)—**Gaba, 1969, 64–75.**

Mawu (Ewe/Benin, Ghana, Togo)—Booth, 1977, 161–62; **Cardinall, 1931, 15;** Ellis, 1890, 31–36; Frazer, 1923, 11; Manoukian, 1952, 45–53; Parrinder, 1949, 17–19; **Parrinder, 1950, 230–33;** Williams, 1936, I, 56.

Mawu (Fon/Benin)—**Booth, 1977, 161–62, 173; Herskovits, 1938, II, 101, 106–7, 289–92;** Herskovits and Herskovits, 1958, 159–62; Leach, 1956, 136–37; Sproul, 1979, 75–76.

Mawu–Lisa (Fon/Benin)—**Argyle, 1966, 176–80;** Herskovits, 1938, I, 159; II, 103–5, 129–31, 232 ; Mercier, 1954, 210–34.

Mbegha (Shambaa/Tanzania)—**Feierman, 1974, 43–45.**

Mbokomu (Ngombe/DRCongo)—**Davidson, 1950, 163–170, 175–77;** Feldmann, 1963, 38–39; Ikenga–Metuh, 1987, 91.

Mbomba Ianda (Mongo/DRCongo)—**Ross and Walker, 1979, 80–87.**

Mboom (Kuba/DRCongo)—Denolf, 1954, 134, 280; Torday, 1925, 124–25; Torday and Joyce, 1911, 20, 235–37; **Vansina, 1955, 145, 726–27; 1958, 732; 1963,** 111–12; 1966, 30; **1978, 30–31.**

Mbori (Zande/Sudan)—**Baxter and Butt,** 1953, 94–95; Evans–Pritchard, 1936, 33–39; 1937, 11.

Mbumba (Yombe/DRCongo)—**Bittremieux,** 1936, 244–65; **Heusch,** 1982, 42–43.

Mbungi (Boloki/CAR)—**Weeks,** 1913, 207–9.

Mdali (Xhosa, Zulu/South Africa)—**Gqoba,** 1885, 93; **Holden,** 1866, 299; Ikenga–Metuh, 1987, 95; Soga, 1931, 149–51.

Mdi Msumu (Chaga/Tanzania)—Gutmann, 1914, 152–53; **Werner, 1933, 70.**

Mebege (Fang, Pahouin/CAR, Congo, Gabon)—de Veciana, 1958; **Fernandez,** 1982, 53–57, 315–18, 325–37; Gollenhoffer and Sillans, 1972, 221; Largeau, 1901, 210–13, 261, 394–406; Tessman, 1913, II, 62.

Meketa, Yataa (Kono/Sierra Leone)—Ikenga–Metuh, 1987, 96; Parsons, 1950, 260–61; **Willans, 1908–1909, 131–32, 136–37, 292–93.**

Mekidech (Kabyle/Algeria)—Lacoste, 1965, 136–53; **Paulme, 1967, 56–57.**

Melqart (Carthaginian/Tunisia)—Meyerowitz, 1958, 129; Warmington, 1981, 453.

Miseke (Nyarwanda/Rwanda)—Hurel, 1922, 21–27; **Werner, 1933, 57–61.**

Mkhulumnchanti, Mvelingqangi (Swati/Swaziland)—Idowu, 1973, 158; Kidd, 1925, 101; **Kuper, 1947, 191–93; 1952, 42–44;** Pettersson, 1953, 102–3; Read, 1956, 158–60.

Modimo, Ralabepa (Sotho/Lesotho, South Africa)—Kropf, 1879, 32–33; Nürnberger, 1975, 179–80, 183–90; Pettersson, 1953, 103–4; **Setiloane, 1976,** 77–86; **Sheddick, 1953, 65–66.**

Modimo (Tswana/Botswana, South Africa)—**Brown, 1926, 91–125, 162–71;** Kidd, 1925, 102; Pauw, 1960, 12–13; Schapera, 1953, 59–60.

Monje Ngumyu (Tangale/Nigeria)—**Hall, 1994, 35–43.**

Mosuor (Talensi/Ghana)—**Fortes, 1945, 21–23.**

Motu (Boloki/CAR)—**Weeks, 1913, 205–7.**

Mpaca (Nyanga/DRCongo)—**Biebuyck and Mateene, 1970, 186–89.**

Mregho (Chaga/Tanzania)—**Marealle, 1965, 59–61.**

Mrile (Chaga/Tanzania)—Gutmann, 1914, 153–56; **Raum, 1909, 307–18.**

Mubila (Lega/DRCongo)—Biebuyck, 1953, 68–74; 1972, 257–73; **Biebuyck, "Heroic," 1978, 344–45.**

Mujaji, Modjadji (Lovedu/South Africa)—Branford, 1980, 179, 229–30; Dicke, 1936, 9–14; **Krige and Krige, 1943, 1–2, 271–75, 283; van S. Bruwer, 1972, VII,** 636–37.

Mukasa (Ganda/Uganda)—King, 1986, 36; **Roscoe, 1911, 290–92.**

Mukunga M'bura (Kikuyu/Kenya)—**Routledge and Routledge, 1910, 307–14.**

Muluku (Makua/Malawi, Mozambique)—**Guirand, 1959, 475.**

Mulungu (Gogo/Tanzania)—**Cole, 1902, 312–13, 332;** Idowu, 1973, 151.

Mulungu (Kamba/Kenya)—**Lindblom, 1920, 125, 209–11, 229, 243–44, 253,** 353–54, 476, **507;** Mbiti, 1966; Muthiani, 1973, 98.

Mulungu (Yao/Malawi, Mozambique)—Feldmann, 1963, 35; Leach, 1956, 143–44; **Macdonald, 1882, 295–98;** Smith, 1950, 59; Tew, 1950, 18; Werner, 1906, 73–74; 1933, 21.

Mumbi Mukasa (Bemba/Zambia)—**Mushindo, 1977,** 1–33.

Mungu (Nandi/Kenya)—**Huntingford, 1927, 447–48.**

Mungu (Swahili/Kenya, Tanzania)—Prins, 1961, 113–14.

Murungu, Ngai, Mwene inya (Meru/Kenya)—**Bernardi, 1959, 52–53, 123, 125.**

Mvelinqangi (Zulu/South Africa)—**Leslie, 1875, 207–9.**

Mwari (Shona/Zimbabwe)—**Aschwanden, 1989,** 11–12, 31–32; Bullock, 1927, 525–27; Daneel, 1970, 16–17, 43–45, 80–84; Kuper, 1954, 32–34; Nelson, 1983, 121–22; Posselt, 1929, 57; Stayt, 1931, 230; Zvarevashe, 1970, 44–47.

Mwindo (Nyanga/DRCongo)—Biebuyck, Biebuyck, *Hero and Chief,* 1978; "Heroic," 1978; **Biebuyck and Mateene, 1970.**

Naka (Sonjo, Sonyo/Tanzania)—**Gray, 1963,** 98.

Nambalisita (Ambo/Angola)—**Estermann, 1976, I,** 181–82, 185–88.

Nana Buluku (Fon/Benin, Togo)—Booth, 1977, 162, 174; **Herskovits, 1938, II,** 101–2; Holas, 1964, 119; Parrinder, 1949, 29, 53–54; 1950, 226–27.

Nangaban (Habbe/Mali)—**Seabrook, 1931, 253–54.**

Nanna Tala (Berber/Tunisia)—**Buselli, 1923–1924, 290–92.**

!Nariba (|Gwikwe/Botswana, Namibia)—**Stephens, 1971, 40–41.**

Nawuge (Topotha, Nyitopotha/Sudan)—Gulliver and Gulliver, 1953, 92; **Nalder, 1937,** 65–66, **69, 81.**

Ndahura (Nyoro/Uganda)—**Beattie, 1960,** 12–15; Ingrams, 1960, 199–200.

Nehoreka (Shona/Zimbabwe)—**Whiteley, 1964, 38–50.**

Neith (Egypt)—**Sauneron, 1962, 253–65;** Seton-Williams, 1992, 28–31.

Ngai (Kamba/Kenya)—**Hobley, 1910,** 85, 89, 91–92, 107–8; **Lindblom, 1920,** 13–14, **244–47;** Lindblom, 1935, 96–99.

Ngai (Kikuyu/Kenya)—**Beecher, 1938, 81–82;** Cagnolo, 1933, 18–19, 26–27; Freund, 1964, 160; **Kenyatta, 1938,** 3–8, 22–24, 70–72, **225–27, 233–43,** 252–61; Lonsdale, 1992, 343–45; Middleton and Kershaw, 1965, 60–61; Njururi, 1966, 71–79; Routledge, 1910, 225–27, 283–84; Wanjohi, 1978, 139–41, 145–46.

Ngewo (Mende/Sierra Leone)—Boone, 1986, 8–9; Harris, 1950, 278–79, 291, 293; **Harris and Sawyerr, 1968, 2–9;** Idowu, 1973, 155; Ikenga-Metuh, 1987, 89–90; Little, 1967, 217–18; McCulloch, 1950, 39–42; Sawyerr, 1970, 62–67, 71, 82–86, 92.

Ngoma–lungundu (Venda/South Africa, Zimbabwe)—Mudau, in **van Warmelo, 1940,** 8–32.

Nguleso (Kakwa/Sudan)—Huntingford, *Northern,* 1953, 55; **Nalder, 1937,** 32–34, 213–16.

Ngulwe (Kuulwe/Tanzania)—**Werner, "African Mythology," 1925,** 156–57.

Ngun Lo Ki (Bari, Fajulu/Sudan)—**Nalder, 1937, 32,** 124, **130–31.**

Nhialic, Nyalich, Acek, Jok (Dinka/Sudan)—Butt, 1952, 130–31; Deng, 1973, 50–53; Idowu, 1973, 157; King, 1986, 50–51; **Lienhardt, 1961, 29–30, 33–36;** Seligman and Seligman, 1932, 179, 184–86, 198–99.

Njaajaan Njaay (Wolof/Senegal)—**Diop, 1993, 56–93.**

Njambe (Boloki/CAR)—**Weeks, 1913, 217–18.**

Njambi (Mpongwe/Gabon)—**Nassau, 1912, 54–57.**

Nkongolo (Luba/DRCongo)—Burton, 1961, 3–15; Colle, 1913; d'Orjo de Marchovelette, 1950, 354–68; **Heusch, 1982, 11–14**; Verhulpen, 1936.

Nkulunkulu (Zulu/South Africa)—Bleek, 1952, 1–3; **Callaway, 1870, 1–104**; Döhne, 1857, 178; Holden, 1866, 299; **Kidd, 1906, 76–79, 96–107, 281–85**; Leach, 1956, 148–51; Pettersson, 1953, 102; Smith, 1950, 105–9; Theal, 1910, I, 43.

Nomkhubulwana (Zulu/South Africa)—**Lancaster, 1880, 12**; **Samuelson, 1911, 192–93**.

Nongqawuse (Xhosa/South Africa)—Abraham, 1966, 29–37; Dillon–Malone, 1985, 123–25; Fergusson, 1921, 163–65; Hassan, 1992, 234–35; Isichei, 1987, 194–96, 201; Lindlom, 1920, 239–40; Peires, 1989; **Scheub, 1996, 304–13**; Selous, 1881, 331; 1893, 113–17.

Nun (Mondari, Mandari/Sudan)—Buxton, 1963, 101–2; **Buxton, 1973, 17–25**; Huntingford, *Northern*, 1953, 66.

Nut (Egypt)—Leeming and Page, 1994, 13–14.

Nyalutanga, Lutanga (Zaramo/Tanzania)—**Swantz, 1986, 258–61**.

Nyambe, Mulimu (Lozi/Zambia)—Hall, 1965, 13; **Mainga, 1972, 95–96**, 99–100; Smith, 1950, 159–61; Turner, 1952, 48–51.

Nyambe (Luyi/Zambia)—Jacottet, 1896, 116–17; **Werner, 1933, 32–33**.

Nyambi, Nyambe (Rotse/Zimbabwe)—Beier, 1966, 7–14; Bertrand, 1899, 277; Feldmann, 1963, 36–37; **Smith, 1950, 156–61**.

Nyame, Nyankopon, Odomankoma (Akan/Burkina Faso, Ghana)—Danquah, 1944, 27, 30–77; Evans, 1950, 243–57; Field, 1948, 158; King, 1986, 21–25; Manoukian, 1950, 55–58; Meyerowitz, 1951, 23–25, 69–74; Quarcoopome, 1987, 62–66; Rattray, 1923, 216; Sawyerr, 1970, 14–31.

Nyame, Nyankopon, Odomankoma (Asante/Ghana)—**Clarke, 1930, 436–53**; **Frazer, 1923, 23–24**; Ikenga–Metuh, 1987, 87–88; Parrinder, 1949, 15–16, 26–27, 53; Rattray, 1923, 141–42, 145–46.

Nyamiyonga (Nyoro/Uganda)—**Beattie, 1960, 12–15**.

Nyengebule (Xhosa/South Africa)—**Callaway, 1879, 74–79**; Werner, 1933, 104–6.

Nyesowa (Poro, Sande/Liberia)—**Francis, 1985, 65–66**.

Nyikang (Shilluk/Sudan)—Butt, 1952, 62–64; **Evans-Pritchard, 1948, 9–19**; 1962, 74–75; Oyler, 1918, "Nikawng" and "Nikawng's Place"; Seligman and Seligman, 1932, 74–77, 80, 102; Westermann, 1912, xxxix–xliv, 155–64.

Nzambi, Nzambi Mpungu (Kongo/Angola)—Fukiau kia Bunseki, in **Janzen, 1974, 34**; Kunzi Yelemia, in **Janzen, 1974, 71–72**; Van Wing, 1921, 170ff.

Nzambi (Kongo/DRCongo)—**Weeks, 1914, 276–87, 293**.

Nzambi Mpungu (Fiote, Fjort, Vili/Congo)—**Dennett, 1898, 2–10, 18, 74–76**, 120–22; 1906, 166; Ikenga–Metuh, 1987, 95; **Kingsley, 1899, 404–5**.

Nzame (Fang/Cameroon, Equatorial Guinea, Gabon)—**Beier, 1966, 18–22**; Ikenga–Metuh, 1987, 95; Leach, 1956, 135.

Nzazi (Luangu/DRCongo)—**Dennett, 1906, 138**.

Nzeanzo, Janzo, Njanjo (Bachama, Bata/Nigeria)—**Meek, 1930, 323–31, 341–43**; **Meek, *Tribal*, 1931, I, 25–28**.

Obassi Osaw (Ekoi/Niger, Nigeria)—Leach, 1956, 138–39; Talbot, 1912, 13, 70–71, 357, 340–74.

Obatala, Orisa–nla (Yoruba/Nigeria)—Adedeji, 1972, 322–24, 332; Awolalu, 1979, 21–22; Beier, 1966, 47–50; Courlander, 1973, 10; Ellis, 1894, 38–39; Holas, 1964, 120; King, 1986, 10.

Odomankoma (Akan/Ghana)—Meyerowitz, 1951, 81–82; Meyerowitz, 1958, 46.

Oduduwa, Assie, Niamie (Baoule/Côte d'Ivoire)—Holas, 1964, 119.

Oduduwa (Yoruba/Nigeria)—Awolalu, 1979, 25–27; Ellis, 1894, 41–43; Idowu, 1962, 22–24, 27.

Ogboinba (Ijo/Nigeria)—Beier, 1966, 23–41; Okpewho, 1979, 305–6.

Oghene (Isoko, Urhobo/Nigeria)—Bradbury and Lloyd, 1957, 159–62; Erivwo, 1983, 362; Ikenga–Metuh, 1987, 96; Nabofa, 1983, 297–316.

Ogun (Yoruba/Nigeria)—Awolalu, 1979, 31–33; Booth, 1977, 170; Ellis, 1894, 67; King, 1986, 13; Wyndham, 1921, 62.

Olodumare, Olorun (Yoruba/Nigeria)—Awolalu, 1979, 11–16; Beier, 1966, 57; Booth, 1977, 160–61; Courlander, 1973, 15–23; Ellis, 1894, 35–38; Forde, 1951, 29–30; Idowu, 1962, 18–22, 39–47, 50–55; Ikenga–Metuh, 1987, 89; King, 1986, 8–9; Meek, 1925, II, 28–29, 31; Oduyoye, "Names," 1983, 357; Parrinder, 1949, 19–21; Parrinder, 1950, 227–30; Quarcoopome, 1987, 59–62; Sawyerr, 1970, 45–56; Talbot, 1926, 29; Williams, 1936, II, 156–57.

Ori, Rabanga (Madi/Uganda)—Baxter and Butt, 1953, 118; Nalder, 1937, 186–87.

Osa, Osanobua (Bini/Nigeria)—Parrinder, 1950, 236; Talbot, 1926, 35–38, 93–97.

Osanobua (Edo, Igbo/Benin)—Bradbury and Lloyd, 1957, 52–59; Okpewho, 1998, 6–7.

Osiris (Egypt)—Plutarch, 1880–1882.

Owuo (Krachi/Togo)—Cardinall, 1931, 30–33; Paulme, 1967, 51–53.

Ozidi (Ijo/Nigeria)—Biebuyck, "Heroic," 1978, 342–43; Clark, 1977, xx–xxi.

Pemba (Bambara/Mali)—Heusch, 1985, 166–70.

Pishiboro, Pisiboro (|Gwikwe, San/Botswana, Namibia)—Stephens, 1971, 27a–27c, 38a–38b.

Polo (Lango/Uganda)—Driberg, 1923, 216–43.

Qamatha (Xhosa/South Africa)—Alberti, 1810, 259; Alberti, 1968, 13; Ayliff, 1846, v–vi; Bleek, 1952, 2–3; Bokwe, 1914, 3, 37; Bryant, 1905, 758; Callaway, 1870, 1–125; Callaway, 1880, 56–60; Campbell, 1815, 365, 368; Chalmers, 1877, 354–56; Gqoba, 1885, 93; Grevenbroek, in Dapper, et al. 1933, 255; Hodgson, 1982, 18–25, 33–35, 41–48, 53–55, 62–63, 70; Holden, 1866, 299; Jenkinson, 1882, 15–16; Junod, 1927, II, 100–1; Kaye, n.d., 157–64; Kidd, 1906, 100–1, 119–20; Lichtenstein, 1812, I, 314; Nkonki, 1968, 28, 50–53, 143–47; Pettersson, 1953, 101–2; Schapera, 1933, 255; Shooter, 1857, 159; Soga, 1931, 59–60, 149–50; Steedman, 1835, 247–48.

Ra (Egypt)—Budge, 1904, 294–300, 359–71; Freund, 1964, 79–80; Guirand, 1959, 11–13; Leach, 1956, 217–20; Long, 1963, 99–101, 183–84.

Raluvhimba (Venda/South Africa)—Junod, 1921, 209–11; Stayt, 1931, 230–32.

Rasoalavavolo (Malagasy/Madagascar)—Sibree, 1896, 259–60.

Rdah Umm Zayed (Arabic/Tunisia)—Hejaiej, 1996, 140–48.

Rhampsinitus (Egypt)—Cox, 1868, 307–12.

Rugaba (Ziba/Tanzania)—Johanssen, 1931, 536–37; Rehse, 1912–1913, 103–6.

Ruhanga (Nyankole/Uganda)—Fisher, 1911, 69–83; Morris, 1964, 2–3; Roscoe, 1915, 91; Roscoe, Banyankole, 1923, 23–25; Taylor, 1962, 110–11; Williams, 1951, 39–40.

Ruhanga (Nyoro/Uganda)—Dunbar, 1965, 10–14; Roscoe, Bakitara, 1923, 23; Smith, 1991, 78; Taylor, 1962, 17, 38–39; Thomas, 1950, 204.

Ryangombe (Nyarwanda/Rwanda)—Guillebaud, 1950, 181–82; Heusch, 1985, 117–18.

Sabenas (Tuareg/Western Sahara)—Nicolaisen, 1959, 91–95.

Sagbata (Fon/Benin)—Argyle, 1966, 183–84, 186–87; Herskovits, 1938, II, 129, 131–34, 136; Herskovits and Herskovits, 1958, 125–32, 136–37.

Sa Na Duniya (Hausa/Niger, Nigeria)—Tremearne, 1914, 213, 215–16.

Sango (Yoruba/Nigeria)—Awolalu, 1979, 33–36; Booth, 1977, 171–72; Ellis, 1894, 46–56; King, 1986, 12; Parrinder, 1949, 32–33, 45; Quarcoopome, 1987, 62; Talbot, 1926, 32.

Segbo (Fon/Benin)—Herskovits and Herskovits, 1958, 136–37.

Sheuta (Bondei, Shambaa, Zigula/Tanzania)—Feierman, 1974, 67–68; Karasek, 1911, 221.

Shibeika (Nuba/Sudan)—Nalder, 1931, 81–82.

Shida Matunda (Nyamwezi/Tanzania)—Beier, 1966, 62.

Shikwembu (Tsonga/South Africa)—Pettersson, 1953, 103.

Sidi Adjille (Arabic/Morocco)—Basset, 1901, 226–27.

Silamaka (Fulani/Mali)—Bâ and Kesteloot, 1968, 5–36; Biebuyck, "Heroic," 1978, 240–41.

Sno–Nysoa (Kru/Liberia)—Bundy, 1919, 407–8.

Sogbo, So (Ewe, Fon/Benin)—Argyle, 1966, 181–82; Booth, 1977, 172–73; Herskovits, 1938, II, 151–53, 156–58; Parrinder, 1949, 31.

Soko (Nupe/Nigeria)—Forde, et al., 1955, 45; Idowu, 1973, 161; Nadel, 1954, 9–10, 11, 13, 17–18.

Somal (Somali/Somalia)—Burton, 1856, 86–87.

Sudika–mbambi (Kimbundu/Angola)—Chatelain, 1894, 84–97.

Sunjata (Mandinka/Gambia, Mali)—Biebuyck, "Heroic," 1978, 341–42; Innis, 1974; Niane, 1960.

Tamuno (Kalabari/Nigeria)—Horton, 1970, 193–97; Talbot, 1926, 60; 1932, 19.

Tanit (Berber, Carthaginian/Tunisia)—Meyerowitz, 1958, 130–32, 136–37; Warmington, 1969, 145–51; Warmington, 1981, 453.

Tano (Agni/Côte d'Ivoire; Akan, Asante/Ghana)—Meyerowitz, 1951, 76–77; Parrinder, 1949, 46–47, 59.

Thingo Lwenkosikazi (Zulu/South Africa)—Callaway, 1868, 290–95.

Thixo (Khoi, Xhosa/South Africa)—Bain, 1880, 21–23; Hodgson, 1982, 91–92; Kidd, 1925, 104–5; Lichtenstein, 1812, I, 311–12; Schapera, 1930, 376–89.

Tianza Ngombe (Lunda/DRCongo)—Roelandts, 1966, xvi, in **de Heusch, 1985,** 182–83.

Tilo (Lenge/Mozambique)—**Earthy, 1933,** 182–96.

Tilo (Ronga/Mozambique)—**Werner, 1933,** 62–65.

Tilo (Shangana, Tonga/Mozambique, South Africa, Zimbabwe)—**Smith, 1950,** 113–14.

Tilo (Thonga, Tsonga/Mozambique, South Africa, Zimbabwe)—**Junod, 1927, II,** **348, 350, 429–32.**

Tindana (Dagomba, Mamprusi, Moshi/Ghana)—**Cardinall, 1920,** 3–5.

Tlam (Kabyle/Algeria)—**Freund, 1965,** 130–31.

To Dino (Fali/Cameroon)—**Lebeuf, 1965, 338–40.**

Tore (Efe/DRCongo)—Baxter and Butt, 1953, 114; **Schebesta, 1933,** 234–42; **Schebesta, Revisiting, 1936, 168,** 182–84.

Tore (Mbuti/DRCongo)—Campbell, 1983, 107–8; Schebesta, 1933, 182–84, 238; **Schebesta, Revisiting, 1936, 177–80.**

Tororut (Suk/Kenya; Pokot/Uganda)—**Beech, 1911, 19–20, 39;** Huntingford, *Southern,* 1953, 89.

Tshawe (Xhosa/South Africa)—**Zenani, 1992,** 9–10.

Tsibiri (Hausa/Nigeria)—**Hogben and Kirk–Greene, 1966,** 185–89.

Tsoede (Nupe/Nigeria)—**Nadel, 1942,** 72–76, 406; 1954, 31–32.

Tsui‖Goab (Nama/Namibia; Khoi/South Africa)—Alexander, 1838, I, 169; Carstens, 1975, 80–82; Casalis, 1861, vii; Chidester, 1992, 2–3; Dapper, et al., 1933, xii–xiv, 75; Frazer, 1923, 20; Grevenbroek, in Dapper, et al., 1933, 193, 255; Hahn, 1880, 61, 65, 124, 134–35, 145; Hodgson, 1982, 23–25, 91–92; **Kidd, 1925, 77–78,** 410–415; Kolb, 1741, 29; Mabona, 1973, 6; Marshall, 1962, 239; Schapera, 1930, 188–89, 389; Schapera, 1933, 193; Smith, 1950, 92–94, 97; Stow, 1905, 130; Ten Rhyne, 1686, in Dapper, 1933, 140, 192–93; Theal, 1910, 110–11; Vedder, "Herero," 1928, 129–32; **Werner, 1925, 158–59;** Wikar, 1779, 95.

Tsumburbura (Hausa/Nigeria)—**Hogben and Kirk–Greene, 1966, 184–85.**

Ture (Zande/DRCongo, Sudan)—Baxter and Butt, 1953, 96; **Evans–Pritchard, 1964, 39–40,** 251–53, 258–60; 1967, 39–40.

Ukwa (Shilluk/Sudan)—**Westermann, 1912, 155–57.**

Unumbotte (Bassari/Togo)—**Campbell, 1983, 14;** Frobenius, 1924, I, 75–76.

Urezhwa (Yeye/Botswana)—Edwards, 1880, 34–37; Gibbs, 1965, 269; **Kidd, 1925, 78;** Stow, 1905, 314–15.

Vere (Pokomo, Sanye/Kenya, Somalia)—**Werner, 1925, 155.**

Wac (Jo Luo/Sudan)—**Kronenberg, 1960,** 237–51.

Waga (Konso/Ethiopia)—**Hallpike, 1972,** 222–28, 322–23.

Wainaba (Kush/Ethiopia)—**Budge, 1928, I,** 143–44.

Waka (Galla/Ethiopia)—Bonham–Carte, 1924, 7–8; **Frazer, 1919, I, 74–75;** Huntingford, 1955, 74–76; Lipsky, 1962, 100, 118–19; Werner, 1913, 90–91.

Wala (Mano/Liberia)—**Francis, 1985,** 66.

Walumbe (Ganda/Uganda)—**Roscoe, 1911, 465–67.**

Wamara (Nyoro/Uganda)—**Beattie, 1960,** 12–15.

Wan Dyor (Dinka/Sudan)—**Willis, 1928, 204–7**.

Wanjiru (Kikuyu/Kenya)—Radin, 1952, 272–73; **Routledge and Routledge, 1910, 287–89**.

Wantu Su (Sara/Chad, Sudan)—**Grimal, 1965, 530**.

We (Kasena/Burkina Faso, Ghana)—**Cardinall, 1931, 5**; Rattray, 1932, 42–45; **Williams, 1936, I, 48–49, 51–52**.

Wele (Luyia/Kenya)—**Wagner, 1954, 28–31**.

Wele (Vugusu/Kenya)—**Wagner, 1949, 169; 1954, 28–30**.

Winnam (Mossi/Burkina Faso)—**Grimal, 1965, 528**.

Woot (Kuba/DRCongo)—Achten, 1929, 192–93; Bently, 1995, 223; Denolf, 1933, 237–46; 1954, 134, 465–68; Torday, 1925, 106–7, 127–28; Torday and Joyce, 1911, 21–23, 240–41, 247–48, 250; **Vansina, 1955, 144; 1963, 93–95, 100–1; 1965, 257–300**.

Wulbari (Krachi/Togo)—**Cardinall, 1931, 15–23, 27–28, 230–31**; Radin, 1952, 28.

Wuni (Dagomba/Ghana)—**Cardinall, 1931, 15, 29–30, 231**.

Xu (Heikum/Namibia)—Marshall, 1962, 234; **Schapera, 1930, 184**.

Yataa, Meketa (Kono/Sierra Leone)—**Parsons, 1950, 261–65**, 269–71; Parsons, 1964, 22, 24, 39, 88, 109–11, 131, 155, 163–68.

Yo (Bambara/Mali)—**Holas, 1964, 107–10**.

Zambe (Bulu/Cameroon)—Krug, 1912–1913, 111–12; Leach, 1956, 140–42; **Leeming and Leeming, 1994, 37–38**; Sproul, 1979, 45–46.

Zambi and Zelo (Gbaya/CAR)—**Poupon, 1915, 143–44**.

Zimu (Transvaal Ndebele/South Africa)—**van Warmelo, 1930, 54–55**.

Zobeyo Mebe'e (Bulu/Cameroon)—**Krug, 1949, 350–51**.

Zong Midzi (Fang/Gabon)—**Biebuyck, "Heroic," 1978, 348–49**; Pepper, 1972.

Zra (Dan/Côte d'Ivoire)—**Paulme, 1967, 48**; Zemp, 1964, text 24.

Proverbs

R. Sutherland Rattray, *Ashanti Proverbs* (Oxford: Clarendon Press, 1914), 24, 27, 28.

A. F. Bull, "Asu (Pare) Proverbs and Songs," *Africa, Journal of the International Institute of African Languages and Cultures* (London) 6 (1933): 324.

George Charleton Merrick, *Hausa Proverbs* (London: Kegan Paul, Trench, Trübner, 1905), 14, 47.

Clement M. Doke, ed., *Lamba Folk-Lore* (New York: American Folk–Lore Society, 1927), 375.

Gerhard Lindblom, "Kamba Riddles, Proverbs and Songs," *Archives d'Études Orientales* 20 (1934): 34.

Marion S. Stevenson, "Specimens of Kikuyu Proverbs," *Festschrift Meinhof* (Hamburg: J. J. Augustin, 1927), 246.

Clement M. Doke, ed., *Lamba Folk-Lore* (New York: American Folk–Lore Society, 1927), 374.

M. Mary Senior, "Some Mende Proverbs," *Africa, Journal of the International African Institute* (London) 17 (1947): 204.

K. D. Leaver, "Proverbs collected from the Amandebele," *African Studies* 5 (1946): 139.

Albert Scheven, *Swahili Proverbs* (Washington, DC: University Press of America, 1981), 142, 246.

Henri Philippe Junod and Alexandre A. Jacques, *Vutlhari bya Vatonga* (Transvaal: Central Mission Press, 1936), 314–15.

James McLaren, "The Wit and Wisdom of the Bantu as Illustrated in Their Proverbial Sayings," *South African Journal of Science* 14 (1917): 344; John Henderson Soga, *The Ama-Xosa: Life and Customs* (Lovedale: Lovedale Press, 1931), 330.

C. L. Sibubiso Nyembezi, *Zulu Proverbs* (Johannesburg: Witwatersrand University Press, 1954), 148.

Other

page 2: Assia Djebar, *L'amour, la fantasia* (Paris: Éditions Jean–Claude Lattès, 1985), 200. Tran. *Fantasia: An Algerian Cavalcade*, trans. Dorothy S. Blair (Portsmouth, N.H.: Heinemann, 1993), 177.

page 275: Okun Asere, "The Python's Shining Stone," P. Amaury Talbot, *In the Shadow of the Bush* (London: William Heinemann, 1912), 344–349.

Bibliography

Abasiattai, Monday B. "Ibibio Traditional Religion and Cosmology." *The Ibibio: An Introduction to the Land, the People, and Their Culture.* Ed. Monday Abasiattai. Calabar: Alphonsus Akpan, 1991.

Abímbólá, Wándé. "Ifá: A West African Cosmological System." *Religion in Africa: Experience and Expression.* Ed. Thomas D. Blakely, Walter E. A. Van Beek, and Dennis L. Thomson. London: James Currey, 1994. 101–16.

Abímbólá, Wándé. *Sixteen Great Poems of Ifá.* Niamey: UNESCO, 1975.

Abraham, D. P. "The Roles of 'Chaminuka' and the Mhondoro—Cults in Shona Political History." *The Zambesia Past: Studies in Central African History.* Ed. Eric Stokes and Richard Brown. Manchester: Manchester University Press, 1966. 28–46.

Abrahams, R. G. *The Peoples of Greater Unyamwezi, Tanzania.* Ethnographic Survey of Africa. Ed., Daryll Forde. London: International African Institute, 1967.

Achten, L. "Over de geschiedenis der Bakuba." *Congo* 1, 2 (1929): 189–205.

Adedeji, Joel. "Folklore and Yoruba Drama: Obàtálá as a Case Study." *African Folklore.* Ed. Richard M. Dorson. Garden City, New York: Anchor, 1972. 321–339.

Akinjogbin, I. A. "The Expansion of Oyo and the Rise of Dahomey, 1600–1800." *History of West Africa.* Ed. J. F. A. Ajayi and Michael Crowder. New York: Columbia University Press, 1976. I, 373–412.

Alagoa, Ebiegberi Joe. "Idu: A Creator Festival at Okpoma (Brass) in the Niger Delta. *Africa, Journal of the International African Institute* (London) 34 (1964): 1–7.

Alagoa, Ebiegberi Joe. "The Niger Delta States and Their Neighbors, to 1800." *History of West Africa.* Ed. J. F. A. Ajayi and Michael Crowder. New York: Columbia University Press, 1976. I, 331–72.

Alberti, L. *De Kaffers aan de Zuidkust van Afrika, Natuur- en Geschiedkundig beschreven.* Amsterdam: E. Maaskamp, 1810. English trans.: *Alberti's Account of the Xhosa in 1807.* Cape Town: A. A. Balkema, 1968.

Alexander, James Edward. *An Expedition of Discovery into the Interior of Africa.* London: Henry Colburn, 1838. Two volumes.

American University. *Area Handbook for the Ivory Coast.* Washington, D.C.: Foreign Areas Studies Division, 1962.

Ardener, Edwin. *Coastal Bantu of the Cameroons.* Ethnographic Survey of Africa. Ed. Daryll Forde. *Western Africa*, Part II. London: International African Institute, 1956.

Argyle, William John. *The Fon of Dahomey: A History and Ethnography of the Old Kingdom.* Oxford: Clarendon Press, 1966.

Aristotle. *Aristotle qui ferebantur librorum fragmenta.* Ed. Valentin Rose. Stuttgart: Teubner, 1967 (1886).

Aschwanden, Herbert. *Karanga Mythology*. Gweru: Mambo Press, 1989.

Austen, Ralph A. *The Elusive Epic: Performance, Text and History in the Oral Narrative of Jeki la Njambè (Cameroon Coast)*. Atlanta: African Studies Association Press, 1995.

Awolalu, J. Omosade. *Yoruba Beliefs and Sacrificial Rites*. London: Longmans, 1979.

Awona, Stanilas. "La guerre d'Akoma Mba contre Abo Mama." *Abbia* 9–10 (1965): 180–213; 12–13 (1966): 109–209.

Ayliff, John. *A Vocabulary of the Kafir Language*. London: Wesleyan Mission House, 1846.

Bâ, Amadou Hampàté. *Kaïdara*. Trans. Daniel Whitman. Introduction, Lilyan Kesteloot. Washington, D. C.: Three Continents Press, 1988.

Bâ, Amadou Hampàté. "Monzon et le roi de Koré." *Présence Africaine* 58 (1966): 99–127.

Bâ, Amadou Hampàté, and Lilyan Kesteloot. "Les épopées de l'ouest africain." *Abbia* 14–15 (1966): 165–205.

Bâ, Amadou Hampàté, and Lilyan Kesteloot. "Une épopée peule: Silamaka." *L'Homme* 8 (1968): 5–36.

Bain, Thomas. "The Distribution of Animals, etc., after the Creation, as related by a Kafir." *Folk-Lore Journal* 2 (1880): 21–23.

Baker, Richard St. Barbe. *Africa Drums*. Oxford: George Ronald, 1942.

Bascom, William. *Ifa Divination: Communication between Gods and Men in West Africa*. Bloomington: Indiana University Press, 1969.

Basset, Rene. *Moorish Literature*. New York: Colonial Press, 1901.

Baxter, P. T. W., and Audrey Butt. *The Azande and Related Peoples of the Anglo-Egyptian Sudan and Belgian Congo*. Ethnographic Survey of Africa. Ed. Daryll Forde. East Central Africa, Part 9. London: International African Institute, 1953.

Beattie, John. *Bunyoro, An African Kingdom*. New York: Holt, Rinehart and Winston, 1960.

Beattie, John. "Group Aspects of the Nyoro Spirit Mediumship Cult." *Rhodes-Livingstone Journal* 30 (1961): 11–38.

Becker, R. "Conte d'Ibonia." *Memoires de l'académie malgache* 30 (1939): 7–136.

Beech, Mervyn W. H. *The Suk: Their Language and Folklore*. Oxford: Clarendon Press, 1911.

Beecher, Leonard J. "The Stories of the Kikuyu." *Africa, Journal of the International Istitute of African Languages and Cultures* (London) 11 (1938): 80–87.

Beidelman, T. O. *The Matrilineal Peoples of Eastern Tanzania*. Ethnographic Survey of Africa. Ed. Daryll Forde. East Central Africa, Part 16. London: International African Institute, 1967.

Beiderbecke, H. "Some Religious Ideas and Customs of the Ovaherero." *Folk-Lore Journal* 2 (1880): 88–97.

Beier, Ulli, ed. *The Origin of Life and Death: African Creation Myths*. London: Heinemann, 1966. Reprinted by permission of Heinemann Educational Publishers, a division of Reed Educational and Professional Publishing Ltd.

Belcher, Stephen. "Heroes at the Borderline: Bamana and Fulbe Traditions in West Africa." *Research in African Literatures* 29 (1998): 43–65.

Bently, Peter, ed. *The Dictionary of World Myth*. New York: Facts on File, 1995.

Bernardi, Bernardo. *The Mugwe, A Failing Prophet*. London: Oxford University Press, 1959.

Bertrand, Alfred. *The Kingdom of the Barotsi, Upper Zambezia; A Voyage of Exploration in Africa, Returning by the Victoria Falls, Matabeleland, the Transvaal, Natal, and the Cape.* Trans. A. B. Miall. London: T. F. Unwin, 1899.

Besmer, Fremont E. *Horses, Musicians, and Gods: The Hausa Cult of Possession-Trance.* South Hadley, Mass.: Bergin and Garvey, 1983.

Biebuyck, Daniel P. "The African Heroic Epic." *Heroic Epic and Saga: An Introduction to the World's Great Folk Epics.* Ed. Felix J. Oinas. Bloomington: Indiana University Press, 1978. 336–67.

Biebuyck, Daniel P. "The Epic as a Genre in Congo Oral Literature." *African Folklore.* Ed. Richard M. Dorson. Garden City: Doubleday, 1972. 257–73.

Biebuyck, Daniel P. *Hero and Chief: Epic Literature from the Banyanga (Zaire Republic).* Berkeley: University of California Press, 1978.

Biebuyck, Daniel P. "Mubila: Een epos der Balega." *Band* 12 (1953): 68–74.

Biebuyck, Daniel P., and Kahombo C. Mateene, ed. and trans. *Anthologie de la littérature orale nyanga.* Brussels: Académie Royale des Sciences d'Outre–Mer, 1970.

Biebuyck, Daniel P., and Kahombo C. Mateene, ed. and trans. *The Mwindo Epic from the Banyanga (Congo Republic).* Berkeley: University of California Press, 1971.

p'Bitek, Okot. *African Religions in Western Scholarship.* Nairobi: East African Publishing House, 1970.

Bittremieux, Léo. *La société secrète des Bakhimba au Mayombe.* Brussels: Falk fils, 1936.

Bleek, Dorothea F. *The Naron: A Bushman Tribe of the Central Kalahari.* Cambridge: Cambridge University Press, 1928. Reprinted with permission of Cambridge University Press.

Bleek, Wilhelm Heinrich Immanuel. *Reynard the Fox in South Africa; or, Hottentot Fables and Tales.* London: Trübner, 1864.

Bleek, Wilhelm Heinrich Immanuel. *Zulu Legends.* Ed. J. A. Engelbrecht. Pretoria: J. L. Van Schaik, 1952.

Bleek, Wilhelm Heinrich Immanuel, and Lucy C. Lloyd. *The Mantis and His Friends.* Ed. Dorothea F. Bleek. Cape Town: T. Maskew Miller, 1923.

Bleek, Wilhelm Heinrich Immanuel, and Lucy C. Lloyd. *Specimens of Bushman Folklore.* London: G. Allen, 1911.

Boccassino, Renato. "The Nature and Characteristics of the Supreme Being Worshipped among the Acholi of Uganda." *Uganda Journal* 6 (1939): 195–201.

Boelaert, Edmond. *Nsong'a Lianja: L' épopée nationale des Nkundo.* Anvers: De Sikkel, 1949.

Boelaert, Edmond. "La Procession de Lianja." *Aequatoria* 25 (1962): 1–9.

Bohannan, Laura and Paul. *The Tiv of Central Nigeria. Ethnographic Survey of Africa.* Ed., Daryll Forde. *Western Africa,* Part 8. London: International African Institute, 1953.

Bokwe, J. K. *Ntsikana: The Story of an African Convert.* Lovedale: Lovedale Press, 1914.

Bonham-Carter, Edgar. "Notes on Frazer's Folk Lore in the Old Testament." *Sudan Notes and Records* 5 (1924): 5–17.

Bonnefoy, Yves, ed. *Mythologies.* Trans. Wendy Doniger, et al. Chicago: University of Chicago Press, 1991. A translation of *Dictionnaire des mythologies et des religions des sociétés traditionnelles et du monde antique.* Paris: Flammarion, 1981.

Boone, Sylvia Ardyn. *Radiance from the Waters: Ideals of Feminine Beauty in Mende Art*. New Haven, Conn.: Yale University Press, 1986.

Booth, Newell S., Jr., ed. *African Religions: A Symposium*. Lagos: Nok, 1977.

Booth, Newell S., Jr. "God and the Gods in West Africa." *African Religions: A Symposium*. Ed. Newell S. Booth, Jr. Lagos: Nok, 1977. 159–81.

Booth, Newell S., Jr. "Islam in Africa." *African Religions: A Symposium*. Ed. Newell S. Booth, Jr. Lagos: Nok, 1977. 297–343.

Bradbury, R. E., and P. C. Lloyd. *The Benin Kingdom and the Edo-Speaking Peoples of South-Western Nigeria and The Itsekiri. Ethnographic Survey of Africa*. Ed. Daryll Forde. *Western Africa*, Part 13. London: International African Institute, 1957.

Branford, Jean. *A Dictionary of South African English*. Cape Town: Oxford University Press, 1980.

Brelsford, William Vernon. *The Tribes of Northern Rhodesia*. Lusaka: The Government Printer, 1956. 2nd edition: *The Tribes of Zambia*. Lusaka: Government Printer, 1965.

Breutz, P. L. *The Tribes of Marico District*. Pretoria: Government Printer, 1953.

Brisley, Thomas. "Some Notes on the Baoulé Tribe." *Journal of the African Society* 8 (1908–1909): 296–302.

Brown, J. Tom. *Among the Bantu Nomads*. Philadelphia: J. B. Lippincott, 1926.

Bryant, Alfred T. *A Zulu-English Dictionary*. Pinetown, Natal: Mariannhill Mission Press, 1905.

Budge, Ernest A. Wallis. *The Alexander Book in Ethiopia*. London: Oxford University Press, 1933.

Budge, Ernest A. Wallis. *From Fetish to God in Ancient Egypt*. London: Oxford University Press, 1934.

Budge, Ernest A. Wallis. *The Gods of the Egyptians*. London: Methuen, 1904. Two volumes.

Budge, Ernest A. Wallis. *A History of Ethiopia, Nubia and Abyssinia*. London: Methuen, 1928. Two volumes.

Bull, A. F. "Asu (Pare) Proverbs and Songs." *Africa, Journal of the International Institute of African Languages and Cultures* (London) 6 (1933): 323–28.

Bullock, C. "The Religion of the Mashona." *South African Journal of Science* 24 (1927): 525–29.

Bundy, Richard C. "Folk–Tales from Liberia (in Abstract)." *Journal of American Folk-Lore* 32 (1919): 406–27.

Burton, Richard Francis. *First Footsteps in East Africa; or, An Exploration of Harar*. London: Longman, Brown, Green, and Longmans, 1856.

Burton, William Frederick Padwick. *Luba Religion and Magic in Custom and Belief*. Tervuren: Annales du Musée royal de l'Afrique centrale, 1961.

Buselli, Gennaro. "Berber Texts from Jebel Nefûsi (Žemmàri Dialect)." *Journal of the African Society* 23 (1923–1924): 285–93.

Butt, Audrey. *The Nilotes of the Sudan and Uganda. Ethnographic Survey of Africa*. Ed. Daryll Forde. *East Central Africa*, Part 4. London: International African Institute, 1952.

Buxton, David. *The Abyssinians*. London: Thames and Hudson, 1970.

Buxton, Jean. "Mandari Witchcraft." *Witchcraft and Sorcery in East Africa*. Ed. John Middleton and E. H. Winter. New York: Frederick A. Praeger, 1963. 99–121.

Buxton, Jean. *Religion and Healing in Mandari.* Oxford: Clarendon Press, 1973.

Cagnolo, C. *The Akikuyu, Their Customs, Traditions and Folklore.* Nyeri, Kenya: Mission Printing School, 1933.

Cagnolo, C. "Kikuyu Tales." *African Studies* 11 (1952): 1–21, 62–71, 122–31.

Callaway, Henry. "A Fragment Illustrative of Religious Ideas among the Kafirs." *Folk-Lore* 2 (1880): 56–60.

Callaway, Henry. "Intsomi ka 'Nyengebule." *Folk-Lore Journal* 1 (1879): 74–79.

Callaway, Henry. *Nursery Tales, Traditions, and Histories of the Zulus.* Springvale, Natal: John A. Blair, 1868.

Callaway, Henry. *The Religious System of the Amazulu.* London: Trübner, 1870.

Camara, Seydou. *The Songs of Seydou Camara.* Volume one, Kambili. Tran. Charles Bird. Bloomington: African Studies Center, 1974.

Campbell, John. *Travels in South Africa, Undertaken at the Request of the Missionary Society.* London: Black, Parry, 1815. 2d ed.

Campbell, John. *Travels in South Africa, Undertaken at the Request of the Missionary Society, Being a Narrative of a Second Journey in the Interior of that Country.* London: Francis Westley, 1822. Two volumes.

Campbell, Joseph. *Historical Atlas of World Mythology.* Vol. 1, *The Way of the Animal Powers.* San Francisco: Harper and Row, 1983.

Cardinall, Allan Wolsey. *The Natives of the Northern Territories of the Gold Coast; Their Customs, Religion and Folklore.* London: G. Routledge and Sons, 1920.

Cardinall, Allan Wolsey. *Tales Told in Togoland.* London: Oxford University Press, 1931.

Carlyon, Richard. *A Guide to the Gods.* New York: Morrow, 1982.

Carnochan, J. "The Coming of the Fulani: A Bachama Oral Tradition." *Bulletin of the School of Oriental and African Studies* 30 (1967): 622–33.

Carstens, Peter. "Some Implications of Change in Khoikhoi Supernatural Beliefs." *Religion and Social Change in Southern Africa.* Ed. Michael G. Whisson and Martin West. Cape Town: David Philip, 1975. 78–95.

Carvalho, Henrique Augusto Dias de. *Etnografia e historia tradicionale dos povos da Lunda.* Lisbon: Imprensa Nacional, 1890.

Casalis, E. *The Basutos; or, Twenty-three Years in South Africa.* London: James Nisbet, 1861.

Cerulli, Ernesta. *North-eastern Africa, Part 3. Peoples of South-west Ethiopia and Its Borderland. Ethnographic Survey of Africa.* Ed. Daryll Forde. London: International African Institute, 1956.

Chalmers, John Aitken. *Tiyo Soga: A Page of South African Mission Work.* Edinburgh: Elliot, 1877.

Chatelain, Heli. *Folk-Tales of Angola.* New York: American Folk–Lore Society, 1894.

Chidester, David. *Religions of South Africa.* London: Routledge, 1992.

Clark, John Pepper. *The Ozidi Saga.* Ibadan: Ibadan University Press, 1977.

Clarke, Edith. "The Sociological Significance of Ancestor–Worship in Ashanti." *Africa* 3 (1930): 431–71.

Clifford, Miles. "Notes on the Bassa–Komo Tribe in the Igala Division." *Man* 44 (1944): 107–16.

Cole, H. "Notes on the Wagogo of German East Africa." *Journal of the Royal Anthropological Institute* 32 (1902): 305–38.

Colle, Pierre. *Les Baluba (Congo Belge)*. Brussels: Dewit, 1913. Two volumes.

Conrad, David C., ed. *A State of Intrigue: The Epic of Bamana Segu According to Tayiru Banbera*. Oxford: Oxford University Press, 1990.

Cooke, C. K. *Rock art of Southern Africa*. Cape Town: Books of Africa, 1969.

Cory, Hans. "Religious Beliefs and Practices of the Sukuma/Nyamwezi Tribal Group." *Tanganyika Notes and Records* 54 (March 1960): 14–26.

Cory, Hans, and M. M. Hartnoll. *Customary Law of the Haya Tribe, Tanganyika Territory*. London: Percy Lund, Humphries, 1945.

Courlander, Harold. *Tales of Yoruba Gods and Heroes*. New York: Crown, 1973.

Cox, George W. *Tales of Ancient Greece*. Chicago: Jansen McClurg, 1879.

Crazzolara, Joseph Pasquale. *Zur Gesellschaft und Religion der Nueer*. Vienna: Missionsdruckerei St.Gabriel, 1953.

Cummins, A.G. "Annuak Fable." *Man*, Royal Anthropological Institue of Great Britain and Ireland 15 (1915): 34–35.

Dahle, L. "The Lost Sons (or Children) of God." *Folk-Lore Journal* 2 (1880): 44–45.

Daneel, M. L. *The God of the Matopo Hills: An Essay on the Mwari Cult in Rhodesia*. The Hague: Mouton, 1970.

Daneel, M. L. *Old and New in Southern Shona Independent Churches; Volume I: Background and Rise of the Major Movements*. The Hague: Mouton, 1971.

Danquah, Joseph Boakye. *The Akan Doctrine of God: A Fragment of Gold Coast Ethics and Religion*. London: Lutterworth, 1944.

Dapper, Olfert, Willen Ten Rhyne, and Johannes Gulielmus de Grevenbroek. *The Early Cape Hottentots*. Trans. I. Schapera and E. Farrington. Cape Town: Van Riebeeck Society, 1933.

Davidson, J. "The Doctrine of God in the Life of the Ngɔmbe, Congo." *African Ideas of God: A Symposium*. London: Edinburgh House, 1950. 162–79.

Davis, Kortright, and Elias Farajaje–Jones, eds. *African Creative Expressions of the Divine*. Washington, D.C.: Howard University School of Divinity, 1991.

Dayrell, Elphinstone. *Folk Stories from Southern Nigeria West Africa*. London: Longmans, Green, 1910.

De Contenson, H. "Pre-Aksumite Culture." *General History of Africa*. Volume II, *Ancient Civilizations of Africa*. Ed. G. Mokhtar. Paris: United Nations Educational, Scientific and Cultural Organization, 1981. 341–59.

Deng, Francis Mading. *The Dinka and Their Songs*. Oxford: Clarendon Press, 1973.

Dennett, Richard Edward. *At the Back of the Black Man's Mind*. London: Macmillan, 1906.

Dennett, Richard Edward. *Notes on the Folklore of the Fjort (French Congo)*. Introduction by Mary H. Kingsley. London: David Nutt, 1898.

Denolf, Prosper. *Aan de rand van de Dibese*. Bruxelles, Institut royal colonial belge, 1954.

Denolf, Prosper. "De Oto-legenden." *Congo* 1, 2 (1933): 237–46.

De Rop, A. *Lianja, L'épopée des Móngo*. Brussels: Académie royale des sciences d'outre mer, 1964.

Detienne, Marcel. *L'invention de la mythologie*. Paris: Éditions Gallimard, 1981. Translation: *The Creation of Mythology*. Trans. Margaret Cook. Chicago: University of Chicago Press, 1986.

de Veciana, Vilaldach A. *La Secta del Bwiti en la Guinea Española*. Madrid: Instituto de Estudios Africans, 1958.

Dicke, Bernard Heinrich. *The Bush Speaks: Border Life in Old Transvaal*. Pietermaritzburg: Shuter and Shooter. 1936.

Dieterlen, Germaine. *Essai sur la religion bambara*. Paris: Presses Universitaires de France, 1951.

Dieterlen, Germaine. "Graphic Signs and the Seed of Knowledge: The 266 Basic Signs in West Africa." Yves Bonnefoy, ed. *Mythologies*. Trans. Wendy Doniger, et al. Chicago: University of Chicago Press, 1991. I, 30–32.

Dieterlen, Germaine. "L'Initiation chez les pasteurs peul (Afrique Occidentale)." *African Systems of Thought*. Ed. Meyer Fortes and Germaine Dieterlen. London: Oxford University Press, 1965. 314–27.

Dieterlen, Germaine. "The Mande Creation Myth." *Africa* 17 , 2 (1957): 124–38.

Dieterlen, Germaine. *Textes sacrés d'Afrique Noire*. Paris: Gallimard, 1965.

Dieterlen, Germaine. "Twins, A Dominant Theme in West African Mythologies." Yves Bonnefoy, ed. *Mythologies*. Trans. Wendy Doniger et al. Chicago: University of Chicago Press, 1991. I, 33–35.

Dillon–Malone, Clive. "The Mutumwa Church of Peter Mulenga." *Journal of Religion in Africa* 15 (1985): 122–41.

Dilley, R. M. "Tukulor Weaving Origin Myths: Islam and Reinterpretation." *The Diversity of the Muslim Community: Anthropological Essays in Memory of Peter Lienhardt*. Ed. Ahmed Al–Shahi. London: Ithaca Press, 1987. 70–79.

Diop, Samba. "The Oral History and Literature of the Wolof People of Waalo, Northern Senegal: The Master of the Word (Griot) in the Wolof Tradition; Performance of *The Epic Tale of the Waalo Kingdom* and the Transmission of Knowledge*. Diss., U. Cal. Berkeley, 1993.

Djebar, Assia. *L'amour, la fantasia*. Paris: Éditions Jean–Claude Lattès, 1985. Tran: *Fantasia, An Algerian Cavalcade*. Tran. Dorothy S. Blair. Portsmouth, NH: Heinemann, 1993.

Döhne, Jacob Ludwig. *A Zulu-Kafir Dictionary*. Cape Town: G. J. Pike, 1857.

Doke, Clement M. *Lamba Folk-Lore*. New York: American Folk-Lore Society, 1927.

Doke, Clement M. *The Lamba of Northern Rhodesia: A Study of Their Customs and Beliefs*. London: G. G. Harrap, 1931.

Donohugh, Agnes C. L., and Priscilla Berry. "A Luba Tribe in Katanga: Customs and Folklore." *Africa, Journal of the International Institute of African Languages and Culture* (London) 5 (1932): 176–83.

d'Orjo de Marchovelette, E. "Historique de la chefferie Kabongo." *Bulletin des juridictions indigènes et du droit coutumier congolais* 12 (1950): 354–68.

Doucouré, Amadou. "Défi, de Déissé-Koro, roi du Kaaarta à Da Monzon, roi de Ségou." *France-Eurafrique* 171 (1966): 43–45.

Douglas, Mary. "The Lele of Kasai." *African Worlds: Studies in the Cosmological Ideas and Social Values of African Peoples*. Oxford: Oxford University Press, 1954. 1–26.

Douglas Mary. *The Lele of the Kasai*. Oxford: Oxford University Press, 1963.

Driberg, Jack Herbert. *The Lango, A Nilotic Tribe of Uganda*. London: T. Fisher Unwin, 1923.

Dumézil, Georges. *Heur et Malheur du Guerrier*. Paris: Flammarion, 1985.

Dunbar, Archibald Ranulph. *A History of Bunyoro-Kitara.* Nairobi: Oxford University Press, 1965.

Dundas, K. R. "Notes on the Tribes Inhabiting the Baringo District, East Africa Protectorate." *Journal of the Royal Anthropological Institute* 40 (1910): 49–69.

Durkheim, Émile. *L'année sociologique.* Paris: Félix Alcan, 1899.

Duysters, L. "Histoire des Aluunda." *Problèmes d'Afrique centrale* 40 (1958): 79–98.

Dymond, G. W. "The Idea of God in Ovamboland, South–West Africa." *African Ideas of God: A Symposium.* Ed. Edwin W. Smith. London: Edinburgh House, 1950. 135–55.

Earthy, Emily Dora. *Valenge Women: The Social and Economic Life of the Valenge Women of Portuguese East Africa.* London: Oxford University Press, 1933.

Edgar, Frank. *Hausa Tales and Traditions: An English Translation of* Tatsuniyoyi Na Hausa. Trans., Neil Skinner. Madison: University of Wisconsin Press, 1977. Three volumes.

Edwards, S. H. "Tradition of the Bayeye." *Folk-Lore Journal* 2 (1880): 34–37.

Ellis, Alfred Burdon. *The Ewe-speaking Peoples of the Slave Coast of West Africa, Their Religion, Manners, Customs, Laws, Languages, etc.* London: Chapman and Hall, 1890.

Ellis, Alfred Burdon. *The Yoruba-speaking Peoples of the Slave Coast of West Africa, Their Religion, Manners, Customs, Laws, Language, etc.* London: Chapman and Hall, 1894.

El–Shamy, Hasan M. *Folktales of Egypt.* Chicago: University of Chicago Press, 1980.

Ennis, Merlin. *Umbundu; Folk Tales from Angola.* Boston: Beacon Press, 1962.

Erivwo, Samuel. "The Worship of Oghene." *Traditional Religion in West Africa.* Ed. E. A. Ade Adegbola. Accra: Asempa, 1983. 358–65.

Estermann, Carlos. *The Ethnography of Southwestern Angola.* Ed. and Trans. Gordon D. Gibson. Vol. 1, *The Non-Bantu Peoples, The Ambo Ethnic Group.* New York: Africana, 1976. Vol. 2, *The Nyaneka-Nkumbi Ethnic Group.* New York: Africana, 1979. Vol. 3, *The Herero People.* New York: Africana, 1981.

Evans, St. John R. "The Akan Doctrine of God." *African Ideas of God: A Symposium.* Ed. Edwin W. Smith. London: Edinburgh House Press, 1950. 241–59.

Evans-Pritchard, Evan Edward. "The Bongo." *Sudan Notes and Records* 12 (1929): 1–61.

Evans-Pritchard, Evan Edward. *The Divine Kingship of the Shilluk of the Nilotic Sudan.* Cambridge: Cambridge University Press, 1948.

Evans-Pritchard, Evan Edward. *Essays in Social Anthropology.* London: Faber and Faber, 1962.

Evans-Pritchard, Evan Edward. *The Nuer: A Description of the Modes of Livelihood and Political Institutions of a Nilotic People.* Oxford: Clarendon Press, 1940.

Evans-Pritchard, Evan Edward. *Nuer Religion.* Oxford: Clarendon Press, 1956.

Evans-Pritchard, Evan Edward. "A Preliminary Account of the Ingassana Tribe in Fung Province." *Sudan Notes and Records* 10 (1927): 69–83.

Evans-Pritchard, Evan Edward. "Some Zande Texts—Part 3." *Kush* 12 (1964): 251–81.

Evans-Pritchard, Evan Edward. *Witchcraft, Oracles and Magic among the Azande.* Oxford: Clarendon Press, 1937.

Evans-Pritchard, Evan Edward. "Zande Theology." *Sudan Notes and Records* 19 (1936): 5–46.

Evans-Pritchard, Evan Edward. *The Zande Trickster.* Oxford: Clarendon Press, 1967.

Evans-Pritchard, Evan Edward, and A. C. Beaton. "Folk Stories of the Sudan." *Sudan Notes and Records* 23 (1940): 55–74.

Ezekwuga, Christopher U. M. *Chi:The True God in Igbo Religion.* Alwaye, India: Pontifical Institute of Philosophy and Theology, 1987.

Fallers, Margaret Chave. *The Eastern Lacustrine Bantu (Ganda and Soga). Ethnographic Survey of Africa.* Ed. Daryll Forde. *East Central Africa,* Part 11. London: International African Institute, 1968.

Feierman, Steven. *The Shambaa Kingdom: A History.* Madison: University of Wisconsin Press, 1974.

Feldmann, Susan, ed. *African Myths and Tales.* New York: Dell, 1963.

Fergusson, V. H. "The Holy Lake of the Dinka." *Sudan Notes and Records* 5 (1921): 163–66.

Fergusson, V. H. "The Nuong Nuer." *Sudan Notes and Records* 4 (1923): 146–55.

Fernandez, James W. *Bwiti, An Ethnography of the Religious Imagination in Africa.* Princeton: Princeton University Press, 1982; reprinted by permission of the publisher.

Field, Margaret Joyce. *Akim-Kotoku: An Oman of the Gold Coast.* Accra: Crown Agents for the Colonies, 1948.

Field, Margaret Joyce. *Religion and Medicine of the Gã People.* London: Oxford University Press, 1937.

Finnegan, Ruth. *Limba Stories and Story-telling.* Oxford: Clarendon Press, 1967.

Fisher, Ruth B. *Twilight Tales of the Black Baganda.* London: Marshall Brothers, 1911.

Forde, Daryll, ed. *African Worlds: Studies in the Cosmological Ideas and Social Values of African Peoples.* London: Oxford University Press, 1954.

Forde, Daryll, ed. *Efik Traders of Old Calabar.* London: Oxford University Press, 1956.

Forde, Daryll. *The Yoruba-Speaking Peoples of South-Western Nigeria. Ethnographic Survey of Africa.* Ed. Daryll Forde. *Western Africa,* Part 4. London: International African Institute, 1951.

Forde, Daryll, Paula Brown, and Robert G. Armstrong. *Peoples of the Niger-Benue Confluence. Ethnographic Survey of Africa.* Ed. Daryll Forde. *Western Africa,* Part 10. London: International African Institute, 1955.

Forde, Daryll, and G. I. Jones. *The Ibo and Ibibio-Speaking Peoples of South-Eastern Nigeria. Ethnographic Survey of Africa. Western Africa,* Part 3. Ed. Daryll Forde. London: International African Institute, 1950.

Fortes, Meyer. *The Dynamics of Clanship among the Tallensi.* London: Oxford University Press, 1945.

Fortes, Meyer. *The Web of Kinship among the Tallensi; The Second Part of an Analysis of the Social Structure of a Trans-Volta Tribe.* London: Oxford University Press, 1949.

Fortes, Meyer, and G. Dieterlen, eds. *African Systems of Thought.* London: Oxford University Press, 1965.

Fortier, Joseph. *Le mythe et les contes de Sou en pays Mbaï-Moïssala.* Paris: Julliard, 1967.

France, Harry. "Worship of the Thunder–god among the Awuna." *Journal of the African Society* 8 (1908): 79–81.

Francis, Michael K. "Traditional African Religions and Christianity." *A Compendium of Lecture and Round-Table Discussion Papers Presented during the Liberia Segment of the 1985*

Seminar. Ed. James T. Tarpeh. Monrovia: United States Department of Education and United States Educational and Cultural Foundation in Liberia, 1985. 59–67.

Frazer, James George. *Folk-lore in the Old Testament, Studies in Comparative Religion, Legend and Law.* London: Macmillan, 1919. (Three volumes.) Abridged edition, 1923.

Frazer, James George, ed. *Anthologia Anthropologia; The Native Races of Africa andMadagascar.* London: Percy Lund, Humphries, 1938.

Freund, Philip. *Myths of Creation.* New York: Washington Square Press, 1964.

Frobenius, Leo. *Dämonen des Sudan: Allerhand Religiöse Verdichtungen.* Jena: Eugen Diederichs, 1924.

Frobenius, Leo. *Volksdichtungen aus Oberguinea.* Vol. I, *Fabuleien Drier Volker.* Jena: Eugen Diederichs, 1924.

Frobenius, Leo, and Douglas C. Fox. *African Genesis.* New York: Stackpole, 1937.

Gaba, C. G. "The Idea of a Supreme Being among the Anlo People of Ghana." *Journal of Religion in Africa* (Brill) 2 (1969): 64–79.

Gamble, David P. *The Wolof of Senegambia. Ethnographic Survey of Africa.* Ed. Daryll Forde. *Western Africa,* Part 14. London: International African Institute, 1957.

Gardiner, Allen F. *Narrative of a Journey to the Zoolu Country in South Africa.* London: William Crofts, 1836.

Gibbs, James L., ed. *Peoples of Africa.* New York: Holt, Rinehart and Winston, 1965.

Gollenhoffer, J. O., and R. Sillans. "Textes religieux du Bwiti-fan et de ses confréries prophétiques dans leurs cadres rituels." *Cahiers d'études africaines* 46 (1972): 197–253.

Goody, Jack. *The Myth of the Bagre.* Oxford: Clarendon Press, 1972.

Gqoba, William. "The Native Tribes, Their Laws, Customs and Beliefs." *Christian Express,* 15, 179 (June 1, 1885): 93.

Graves, Robert. *The Greek Myths.* Harmondsworth: Penguin, 1955. Two volumes.

Gray, Robert F. "Some Parallels in Sonjo and Christian Mythology." *African Systems of Thought.* Ed. M. Fortes and G. Dieterlen. London: Oxford University Press, 1965.49–63.

Gray, Robert F. *The Sonjo of Tanganyika.* Oxford: Oxford University Press, 1963.

Gray, Stephen, ed. *The Penguin Book of Contemporary South African Short Stories.* Harmondsworth: Penguin, 1985.

Greenberg, Joseph H. *The Influence of Islam on a Sudanese Religion.* New York: J. J. Augustin, 1946.

Grévisse, F. "Les traditions historiques des Basanga et de leurs voisins." *Bulletin du CEPSI* 2 (1946–1947): 50–84.

Griaule, Marcel. *Dieu d'Eau, entretiens avec Ogotemmêli.* Paris: Fayard, 1966. Trans., *Conversations with Ogotemmeli: An Introduction to Dogon Religious Ideas.* London: Oxford University Press, 1965.

Griaule, Marcel, and Germaine Dieterlen. "The Dogon." *African Worlds: Studies in the Cosmological Ideas and Social Values of African Peoples.* Ed. Daryll Forde. London: Oxford University Press, 1954. 83–110.

Griaule, Marcel, and Germaine Dieterlen. *Le renard pâle.* Paris: Institut d'ethnologie, 1965.

Grimal, Pierre. *The Dictionary of Classical Mythology.* Trans. A. R. Maxwell–Hyslop.
New York: Blackwell, 1985.

Grimal, Pierre, ed. *Larousse World Mythology.* Trans. Patricia Beardsworth. New York:
Putnam, 1965. Trans. from *Mythologies de la Méditerranée au Gange* and *Mythologies des
Steppes, des Iles et des Forêts.* Paris: Augé, Gillon, Hollier–Larousse, Moreau, 1963.

Grove, E. T. N. "Customs of the Acholi." *Sudan Notes and Records* 2 (1919): 157–82.

Guillebaud, Rosemary. "The Idea of God in Ruanda–Urundi." *African Ideas of God: A
Symposium.* London: Edinburgh House Press, 1950. Ed. Edwin W. Smith.
180–200.

Guirand, Felix, ed. *Larousse Mythologie Générale.* Paris: Augé, Gillon, Hollier–Larouse,
Moreau, 1959. *New Larousse Encyclopedia of Mythology.* Trans. Richard Aldington
and Delano Ames. London: Paul Hamlyn (Prometheus Press), 1959. New ed.,
1968, Octopus Publishing Group.

Gulliver, Pamela, and P. H. Gulliver. *The Central Nilo-Hamites.* Ethnographic Survey of
Africa. Ed. Daryll Forde. *East Central Africa,* Part 7. London: International African
Institute, 1953.

Gunn, Harold D. *Pagan Peoples of the Central Area of Northern Nigeria.* Ethnographic Survey of
Africa. Ed. Daryll Forde. *Western Africa,* Part 12. London: International African
Institute, 1956.

Gunn, Harold D. *Peoples of the Plateau Area of Northern Nigeria.* Ethnographic Survey of Africa.
Ed. Daryll Forde. *Western Africa,* Part 7. London: International African Institute,
1953.

Gunn, Harold D., and F. P. Conant. *Peoples of the Middle Niger Region, Northern Nigeria.*
Ethnographic Survey of Africa. Ed. Daryll Forde. *Western Africa,* Part 15. London:
International African Institute, 1960.

Gutmann, Bruno. "Chagga Folk–lore." (From *Dichten und Denken der Dschagganeger.*
Leipzig: Verlag der Evangelische-Lutherischen Mission, 1909; and *Volksbuch der
Wadschagga.* Leipzig: Verlag der Evangelische-Lutherischen Mission, 1914.) *Ta-
nganyika Notes and Records* 64 (1965): 50–55.

Gutmann, Bruno. *Volksbuch der Wadschagga.* Leipzig: Verlag der Evangelische-
Lutherischen Mission, 1914.

Hackett, Rosalind I. J. *Religion in Calabar: The Religious Life and History of a Nigerian Town.*
Berlin: Mouton de Gruyter, 1989.

Hahn, Carl Hugo Linsingen, et al. *The Native Tribes of South West Africa.* Cape Town:
Cape Times, 1928.

Hahn, Carl Hugo Linsingen. "The Ovambo." *The Native Tribes of South West Africa.* Ed.
Carl Hugo Linsengen Hahn, et al. Cape Town: Cape Times, 1928. 1–36.

Hahn, Theophilus. *Tsuni-‖Goam, The Supreme Being of the Khoikhoi.* London: Trübner,
1880.

Hakem, A. A., et al. "The Civilization of Napata and Meroe." *General History of
Africa.* Volume II, *Ancient Civilizations of Africa.* Ed. G. Mokhtar. Paris: United
Nations Educational, Scientific and Cultural Organization, 1981. 298–321.

Hall, John S. *Religion, Myth and Magic in Tangale.* Ed. H. Jungraithmayr and J. Adel-
berger. Köln: Rüdiger Köppe Verlag, 1994.

Hall, Richard. *Zambia.* London: Pall Mall Press, 1965.

Hallpike, C. R. *The Konso of Ethiopia: A Study of the Values of a Cushitic People.* Oxford: Clarendon Press, 1972. Revised edition in press.

Harris, William Thomas. "The Idea of God among the Mende." *African Ideas of God: A Symposium.* Ed., Edwin W. Smith. London: Edinburgh House Press, 1950. 277–97.

Harris, William Thomas, and Harry Sawyerr. *The Springs of Mende Belief and Conduct: A Discussion of the Influence of the Belief in the Supernatural among the Mende.* Freetown: Sierra Leone University Press, 1968.

Hart, George. *A Dictionary of Egyptian Gods and Goddesses.* London: Routledge and Kegan Paul, 1986.

Hassan, Alhaji, and Mallam Shuaibu Na'ibi. *A Chronicle of Abuja.* Trans. Frank Heath. Lagos: African Universities Press, 1962.

Hassan, Salah M. *Art and Islamic Literacy among the Hausa of Northern Nigeria.* Lewiston, NY: Edwin Mellen, 1992.

Hatfield, Colby Ray, Jr. "The Nfumu in Tradition and Change: A Study of the Position of Religious Practitioners among the Sukuma of Tanzania, East Africa." Diss. Washington, D.C.: The Catholic University of America, 1968.

Hays, Hoffman Reynolds. *In the Beginnings; Early Man and His Gods.* New York: Putnam, 1963.

Hejaiej, Monia. *Behind Closed Doors, Women's Oral Narratives in Tunis.* New Brunswick: Rutgers University Press, 1996.

Helser, Albert D. *African Stories.* New York: Fleming H. Revell, 1930.

Herodotus. *The History of Herodotus.* Trans., George Rawlinson. New York: Tudor, 1928.

Herskovits, Melville J. *Dahomey, An Ancient West African Kingdom.* New York: J. J. Augustin, 1938. Two volumes.

Herskovits, Melville J., and Frances S. *Dahomean Narrative: A Cross-cultural Analysis.* Evanston: Northwestern University Press, 1958.

Heusch, Luc de. *The Drunken King, or, The Origin of the State.* Tran. Roy Willis. Bloomington: Indiana University Press, 1982.

Heusch, Luc de. "Myth and Epic in Central Africa." Trans. Noal Mellott. *Religion in Africa: Experience and Expression.* Ed. Thomas D. Blakely, Walter E. A. Van Beek, and Dennis L. Thomson. London: James Currey, 1994. 229–38.

Heusch, Luc de. *Sacrifice in Africa: A Structuralist Approach.* Trans. Linda O'Brien and Alice Morton. Manchester: Manchester University Press, 1985.

Hobley, C. W. *Ethnology of A-Kamba and Other East African Tribes.* London: Frank Cass, 1910.

Hodgson, Janet. *The God of the Xhosa: A Study of the Origins and Development of the Traditional Concepts of the Supreme Being.* Cape Town: Oxford University Press, 1982.

Hogben, Sidney John. *The Muhammadan Emirates of Nigeria.* London: Oxford University Press, 1930.

Hogben, Sidney John, and A. H. M. Kirk-Greene. *The Emirates of Northern Nigeria: A Preliminary Survey of Their Historical Traditions.* London: Oxford University Press, 1966.

Holas, Bohumil. *Contes Kono: Traditions populaires de la forêt guinéenne.* Paris: Éditions G.–P. Maisonneuve et Larose, 1975.

Holas, Bohumil. "Mythologies of the World's Origins in Africa." Trans. Malcom Sylvers. Diogènes, 48 (1964): 105–24.

Holden, William C. The Past and Future of the Kaffir Races. London: Richards, Glanville, 1866.

Hollis, Alfred Claud. The Masai: Their Language and Folklore. Oxford: Clarendon Press, 1905.

Hollis, Alfred Claud. The Nandi, Their Language and Folklore. Oxford: Clarendon Press, 1909.

Horton, Robin. "Ekineba: A Forgotten Myth?" Òdùmá 2 (1975): 33–36.

Horton, Robin. "A Hundred Years of Change in Kalabari Religion." Black Africa: Its People and Their Cultures Today. Ed. John Middleton. London: Macmillan, 1970. 192–211.

Hountondji, Paulin J. Sur la philosophie africaine. Paris: F. Maspero, 1977.

Hunter, Linda. "The Communicative Power of Dodo in Saddik Balewa's K'asarmu Ce. (Unpublished paper, 1997.)

Huntingford, G. W. B. "Miscellaneous Records Relating to the Nandi and Kony Tribes." Journal of the Royal Anthropological Institute of Great Britain and Ireland. 57 (1927): 417–61.

Huntingford, G. W. B. North-eastern Africa, Part 2. The Gallo of Ethiopia. The Kingdoms of Kafa and Janjero. Ethnographic Survey of Africa. Ed. Daryll Forde. London: International African Institute, 1955.

Huntingford, G. W. B. The Northern Nilo-Hamites. Ethnographic Survey of Africa. Ed. Daryll Forde. East Central Africa, Part 6. London: International African Institute, 1953.

Huntingford, G. W. B. "Notes on Some Names for God." Man 28 (1928): 189–90.

Huntingford, G. W. B. The Southern Nilo-Hamites. Ethnographic Survey of Africa. Ed. Daryll Forde. East Central Africa, Part 8. London: International African Institute, 1953.

Hurel, Eugene. Le Poésie chez les primitifs. Bruxelles: Goemaere, 1922.

Idowu, E. Bolaji. African Traditional Religion: A Definition. Maryknoll, New York: Orbis Books, 1973.

Idowu, E. Bolaji. Olódùmarè: God in Yoruba Belief. London: Longmans, 1962.

Ikenga-Metuh, Emefie. Comparative Studies of African Traditional Religions. Onitsha: Imico, 1987.

Iloanusi, Obiakoizu A. Myths of the Creation of Man and the Origin of Death in Africa: A Study in Igbo Traditional Culture and Other African Cultures. Frankfurt am Main: P. Lang, 1984.

Imbo, Sam O. "Lwanda Magere." Private Communication, 1998.

Ingrams, William Harold. Uganda: A Crisis of Nationhood. London: Her Majesty's Stationery Office, 1960. Crown copyright is reproduced with the permission of the Controller of Her Majesty's Stationery Office.

Innes, Gordon. Sunjata: Three Mandinka Versions. London: School of Oriental and African Studies, University of London, 1974.

Isichei, Elizabeth. "The Maitatsine Risings in Nigeria 1980–85: A Revolt of the Disinherited." Journal of Religion in Africa 17 (1987): 194–208.

Jacobs, John. "Het epos van Kudukese, de 'Culture Hero' van de Hamba." *Africa-Tervuren* 9 (1963): 33–36.

Jacobs, John. "Le récit épique de Lofokefoke, le héros des Mbole (Bambuli)." *Aequatoria* 24 (1961): 81–92.

Jacottet, Edouard. *Études sur les langues du Haut Zambèze.* Paris: Leroux, 1896.

James, Wendy. *'Kwanim Pa: The Making of the Uduk People.* Oxford: Clarendon Press, 1979.

Janzen, John M., and Wyatt MacGaffey. *An Anthology of Kongo Religion: Primary Texts from Lower Zaïre.* Lawrence, Kansas: University of Kansas Publications in Anthropology, 1974.

Jaspan, M. A. *The Ila-Tonga Peoples of North-Western Rhodesia. Ethnographic Survey of Africa.* Ed. Daryll Forde. *West Central Africa,* Part 4. London: International African Institute, 1953.

Jenkinson, T. B. *Amazulu.* London: W. H. Allen, 1882.

Johanssen, E. "The Idea of God in the Myths and Proverbs of Some East African Bantu Tribes." *International Review of Missions* 20 (1931): 345–55, 534–46.

Jones, Arnold Hugh Martin, and Elizabeth Monroe. *A History of Ethiopia.* Oxford: Clarendon Press, 1935.

Junod, Henri A. *Les chants et les contes des Ba-Ronga de la baie de Delagoa.* Lausanne: G. Bridel, 1897.

Junod, Henri A. *The Life of a South African Tribe.* London: Macmillan, 1927. Reprinted: New Hyde Park, New York: University Books, 1962. Two volumes.

Junod, Henri A. "Some Features of the Religion of the Ba–Venda." *South African Journal of Science* 17 (1921): 207–20.

Junod, Henri Philippe, and Alexandre A. Jacques. *Vutlhari bya Vatonga.* Transvaal: Central Mission Press, 1936.

Kagame, Alexis. *La divine pastorale.* Bruxelles: Éditions du Marais, 1952–1955.

Kagame, Alexis. *La naissance de l'univers.* Bruxelles: Éditions du Marais, 1955.

Karasek, A. "Beiträge zur Kenntnis der Waschambaa." Ed. A. Eichhorn. *Baessler-Archiv* 1 (1911): 155–222.

Kasenene, Peter. *Religion in Swaziland.* Braamfontein: Skotaville, 1993.

Kaye, William Kehale. "Kafir Legends, and History." Manuscript 172C, University of Cape Town Manuscripts Division, n.d.

Kenyatta, Jomo. *Facing Mount Kenya: The Tribal Life of the Gikuyu.* London: Secker and Warburg, 1938. Reprinted by permission of Random House Group.

Kesteloot, Lilyan. *L'épopée bambara de Ségou.* Paris: Harmattan, 1993. Two volumes.

Kesteloot, Lilyan, Amadou Traore, and Jean–Baptiste Traore. *Da Monzon de Ségou.* Paris: Fernand Nathan, 1972. Four volumes.

Kidd, Dudley. *The Essential Kaffir.* London: A. and C. Black, 1925.

Kidd, Dudley. *Savage Childhood: A Study of Kafir Children.* London: Adam and Charles Black, 1906.

Kilson, Marion. *Kpele Lala: Ga Religious Songs and Symbols.* Cambridge, Mass.: Harvard University Press, 1971.

Kimambo, I. N., and C. K. Omari. "The Development of Religious Thought and Centres among the Pare." *The Historical Study of African Religions.* Ed. T. O. Ranger and I. N. Kimambo. Berkeley: University of California Press, 1972. 111–21.

King, Noel Q. *African Cosmos: An Introduction to Religion in Africa*. Belmont, California: Wadsworth, 1986.

Kingsley, Mary Henrietta. *West African Studies*. New York: Barnes and Noble, 1899.

Klamroth, M. "Beiträge zum Verständnis der religiösen Vorstellungen der Saramo in Bezirk Daressalam (Deutsch–Ostafrika)." *Zeitschrift für Kolonialsprachen* I (1910–1911): 118–53.

Kobishanov, Y. M. "Aksum: Political System, Economics and Culture, First to Fourth Century." *General History of Africa*. Volume II, *Ancient Civilizations of Africa*. Paris: United Nations Educational, Scientific and Cultural Organization, 1981. 381–99.

Koech, Kipng'eno. "African Mythology: A Key to Understanding African Religion." *African Religions: A Symposium*. Ed. Newell S. Booth, Jr. Lagos: Nok, 1977. 117–39.

Koenig, Oskar. *The Masai Story*. London: Michael Joseph, 1956.

K'Okiri, Oguda. *The Death of Lwanda Magere*. Nairobi: Equatorial, 1970.

Kolb, Peter. *Description du cap de Bonne-Esperance*. Amsterdam: J. Catuffe, 1741.

Kollmann, Paul. *The Victoria Nyanza: The Land, the Races, and Their Customs*. London: Swan Sonnenschein, 1899.

K'Onyango, Ochieng. *The Debtors*. Ed. Chris Wanjala. Nairobi: East African Literature Bureau, 1977.

Kottak, Conrad Phillip. *The Past in the Present: History, Ecology, and Cultural Variation in Highland Madagascar*. Ann Arbor: University of Michigan Press, 1980.

Krige, Eileen Jensen. *The Social System of the Zulus*. Pietermaritzburg: Shuter and Shooter, 1936.

Krige, Eileen Jensen, and J. D. Krige. *The Realm of a Rain-Queen: A Study of the Pattern of Lovedu Society*. London: Oxford University Press, 1943.

Kronenberg, A. and W. "Loma: An Aspect of the Supernatural among the Bongo." *Kush* 10 (1962): 315–27.

Kronenberg, Andreas. "Jo Luo Tales." *Kush* 8 (1960): 237–51.

Kronenberg, Andreas. "Some Notes on the Religion of the Nyimang." *Kush* 7 (1959): 197–213.

Kropf, A. "The Gods of the Basuto." *Folk-Lore Journal* 1 (1879): 32–33.

Krug, Adolf N. "Bulu Tales." *Journal of American Folklore* 62 (1949): 348–74.

Krug, Adolf N. "Bulu Tales from Kamerun, West Africa." *Journal of American Folklore* 25 (1912–1913): 106–24.

Kuper, Hilda. *An African Aristocracy: Rank among the Swazi*. London: Oxford University Press, 1947.

Kuper, Hilda. *Southern Africa. Ethnographic Survey of Africa*. Ed. Daryll Forde. *Southern Africa*, Part 1. London: International African Institute, 1952.

Kuper, Hilda. *The Swazi. Ethnographic Survey of Africa*. Ed. Daryll Forde. *Southern Africa*, Part 1. London: International African Institute, 1952.

Kuper, Hilda, A. J. B. Hughes, and J. Van Velsen. *The Shona and Ndebele of Southern Rhodesia. Ethnographic Survey of Africa*. Ed. Daryll Forde. *Southern Africa*, Part 4. London: International African Institute, 1954.

Labrecque, Ed. "La tribu des Babemba. I: Les origines des Babemba." *Anthropos* 18, 5–6 (1933): 633–48.

Labrecque, Ed. "Histoire des Mwata–Kaembe." Lovania 16 (1949): 9–33; 17 (1949): 21–48.

Lacoste, E. Traduction des légendes et contes merveilleux de la Grande Kabylie recueillis par Auguste Moulieras. Paris: Geuthner, 1965.

La Fontaine, J. S. The Gisu of Uganda. Ethnographic Survey of Africa. Ed. Daryll Forde. East Central Africa, Part 10. London: International African Institute, 1959.

Lancaster Carbutt, Mrs. Hugh. "Some Minor Superstitions and Customs of the Zulus, Connected with Children." Folk-Lore Journal, II (1880), 10–15.

Lang, Andrew. Myth, Ritual, and Religion. London: Longmans, Green, 1887.

Lang, Andrew. "The Religion of the Fans." Man 5 (1905): 54–55.

Largeau, V. Encyclopédie Pahouine, Congo Français. Paris: Ernest Leroux, 1901.

Larson, Thomas J. "Epic Tales of the Mbukushu." African Studies 22 (1963): 176–89.

Lawrance, J. C. D. The Iteso; Fifty Years of Change in a Nilo-Hamitic Tribe of Uganda. London: Oxford University Press, 1957.

Leach, Maria. The Beginning: Creation Myths around the World. New York: Thomas Y. Crowell, 1956.

Leach, Marjorie. Guide to the Gods. Santa Barbara: ABC-CLIO, 1992.

Leaver, K. D. "Proverbs Collected from the Amandebele." African Studies 5 (1946): 136–39.

Lebeuf, Annie. "Le Système classificatoire des Fali (Nord–Cameroun)." African Systems of Thought. Ed. M. Fortes and G. Dieterlen. London: Oxford University Press, 1965. 328–40.

Leeming, David Adams. The World of Myth. New York: Oxford University Press, 1990.

Leeming, David, and Margaret Leeming. A Dictionary of Creation Myths. Oxford: Oxford University Press, 1994; ABC CLIO.

Leeming, David, and Jake Page. Goddess: Myths of the Female Divine. Oxford: Oxford University Press, 1994.

Legey, Françoise. The Folklore of Morocco. Trans. Lucy Hotz. London: George Allen and Unwin, 1935. (First published, in French, in 1926.)

Leonard, Arthur Glyn. The Lower Niger and Its Tribes. London: Macmillan, 1906.

Leslau, Charlotte and Wolf, eds. African Folk Tales. Mount Vernon, N.Y.: Peter Pauper Press, 1963.

Leslie, David. Among the Zulus and Amatongas. Ed. W. H. Drummond. Edinburgh: Edmonston and Douglas, 1875.

Lewis, I. M. Peoples of the Horn of Africa: Somali, Afar, and Saho. Ethnographic Survey of Africa. Ed. Daryll Forde. North Eastern Africa, Part 1. London: International African Institute, 1955.

Lichtenstein, Henry. Travels in Southern Africa in the Years 1803, 1804, 1805 and 1806. Trans. Anne Plumptre. London: Henry Colburn, 1812, 1815. Two volumes.

Lienhardt, Godfrey. Divinity and Experience: The Religion of the Dinka. Oxford: Clarendon Press, 1961.

Lindblom, Gerhard. The Akamba in British East Africa. New York: Negro Universities Press, 1920, 1969.

Lindblom, Gerhard. Kamba Folklore. II. Tales of Supernatural Beings and Adventures. Lund: Berlingska Boktryckeriet, 1935.

Lindblom, Gerhard. "Kamba Riddles, Proverbs and Sons." *Archives d'Études Orientales* 20 (1934): 1–58.

Lindeman, M. *Les Upotos*. Bruxelles: Vanderauwera, 1906.

Linton, Talph. *The Tanala, A Hill Tribe of Madagascar*. Chicago: Field Museum, 1933.

Lipsky, George Arthur, et al. *Ethiopia: Its People, Its Society, Its Culture*. New Haven, Conn.: Human Relations Area Files, 1962.

Little, Kenneth Lindsay. *The Mende of Sierra Leone: A West African People in Transition*. Rev. ed. London: Routledge and Kegan Paul, 1967.

Long, Charles H. *Alpha, The Myths of Creation*. New York: G. Braziller, 1963.

Lonsdale, John. "The Moral Economy of Mau Mau: Wealth, Poverty and Civil Virtue in Kikuyu Political Thought." *Unhappy Valley: Conflict in Kenya and Africa*. Book Two: *Violence and Ethnicity*. London: James Currey, 1992. 315–504.

Loupais, P. "Tradition et Légende des Batutsi sur la Création du Monde et leur Éstablissement au Ruanda." *Anthropos* 3 (1908): 1–13.

MacAlpine, Alexander G. "Tonga Religious Beliefs and Customs." *Journal of the African Society* 17 (1905): 187–90; 18 (1906): 257–68; 20 (1906): 377–80.

MacDonald, Duff. *Africana; or, The Heart of Heathen Africa*. London: Simpkin Marshall, 1882.

Mainga, Mutumba, "A History of Lozi Religion to the end of the Nineteenth Century." *The Historical Study of African Religions*. Ed. T. O. Ranger and I. N. Kimambo. Berkeley: University of California Press, 1972. 95–107.

Mair, Lucy Philip. *An African People in the Twentieth Century*. London: George Routledge and Sons, 1934.

Mamet, M. *La legende d'Iyanja*. Brussels: Dépositaire pour la Belgique et l'Étranger, 1962.

Manoukian, Madeline. *Akan and Ga-Adangme Peoples*. Ethnographic Survey of Africa. Ed. Daryll Forde. *Western Africa*, Part 1. London: International African Institute, 1950.

Manoukian, Madeline. *The Ewe-Speaking People of Togoland and the Gold Coast*. Ethnographic Survey of Africa. Ed. Daryll Forde. *Western Africa*, Part 6. London: International African Institute, 1952.

Manoukian, Madeline. *Tribes of the Northern Territories of the Gold Coast*. Ethnographic Survey of Africa. Ed. Daryll Forde. *Western Africa*, Part 5. London: International African Institute, 1951.

Marchal, R. "Histoire des Balamba." *Artes Africanae*, 3, 4 (1936): 7–28.

Marealle, Petro Itosi. "Chagga Customs, Beliefs and Traditions." Trans. R. D. Swai. *Tanganyika Notes and Records* 64 (1965): 56–61.

Marshall, Lorna. "!Kung Bushman Religious Beliefs." *Africa, Journal of the International African Institute* (London) 32 (1962): 221–52.

Maxwell, Kevin B. *Bemba Myth and Ritual: The Impact of Literacy on an Oral Culture*. Berne: Peter Lang, 1983.

Mbiti, John S. *African Religions and Philosophy*. New York: Praeger, 1969.

Mbiti, John S. *Akamba Stories*. Oxford: Clarendon Press, 1966.

Mbiti, John S. *Concepts of God in Africa*. London: S. P. C. K., 1970.

Mbiti, John S. *Introduction to African Religion*. New York: Praeger, 1975.

McCulloch, Merran. *The Ovimbundu of Angola*. Ethnographic Survey of Africa. Ed. Daryll Forde. *West Central Africa*, Part 2. London: International African Institute, 1952.

McCulloch, Merran. *Peoples of Sierra Leone*. Ethnographic Survey of Africa. Ed. Daryll Forde. *Western Africa*, Part 2. London: International African Institute, 1950.

McCulloch, Merran. *The Southern Lunda and Related Peoples*. Ethnographic Survey of Africa. Ed. Daryll Forde. *West Central Africa*, Part 1. London: International African Institute, 1951.

McCulloch, Merran, Margaret Littlewood, and I. Dugast. *Peoples of the Central Cameroons*. Ethnographic Survey of Africa. Ed. Daryll Forde. *Western Africa*, Part 9. London: International African Institute, 1954.

McLaren, James. "The Wit and Wisdom of the Bantu as Illustrated in Their Proverbial Sayings." *South African Journal of Science* 14 (1917): 330–44.

Meek, Charles Kingsley. *Law and Authority in a Nigerian Tribe: A Study in Indirect Rule*. London: Oxford University Press, 1937.

Meek, Charles Kingsley. "A Religious Festival in Northern Nigeria." *Africa, Journal of the International Institute of African Languages and Culture* (London) 3 (1930): 323–46.

Meek, Charles Kingsley. *The Northern Tribes of Nigeria*. London: Oxford University Press, 1925. Two volumes.

Meek, Charles Kingsley. *A Sudanese Kingdom: An Ethnographical Study of the Jukun-speaking Peoples of Nigeria*. London: Kegan Paul, Trench, Trübner, 1931.

Meek, Charles Kingsley. *Tribal Studies in Northern Nigeria*. London: Kegan Paul, Trench, Trübner, 1931. Two volumes.

Mercier, P. "The Fon of Dahomey." *African Worlds: Studies in the Cosmological Ideas and Social Values of African Peoples*. Ed. Daryll Forde. London: Oxford University Press, 1954. 210–34.

Merrick, George Charleton. *Hausa Proverbs*. London: Kegan Paul, Trench, Trübner, 1905.

Messenger, John C. "Ancestor Worship among the Anang: Belief System and Cult Institution." *African Religious Groups and Beliefs*. Ed. Simon Ottenberg. Meerut, India: Archana, 1982.

Meyerowitz, Eva Lewin–Richter. *The Akan of Ghana, Their Ancient Beliefs*. London: Faber and Faber, 1958.

Meyerowitz, Eva Lewin–Richter. *Akan Traditions of Origin*. London: Faber and Faber, 1952.

Meyerowitz, Eva Lewin–Richter. *The Divine Kingship in Ghana and Ancient Egypt*. London: Faber and Faber, 1960.

Meyerowitz, Eva Lewin–Richter. *The Sacred State of the Akan*. London: Faber and Faber, 1951.

Middleton, John. "The Concept of the Person among the Lugbara of Uganda." *La notion de personne en Afrique noire*. Paris: Éditions du centre de la recherche scientifique, 1973. 491–506.

Middleton, John. *The Lugbara of Uganda*. New York: Holt, Rinehart and Winston, 1965.

Middleton, John. *Lugbara Religion*. Oxford: Oxford University Press, 1960.

Middleton, John. "Witchcraft and Sorcery in Lugbara." *Witchcraft and Sorcery in East Africa*. Ed. John Middleton and E. H. Winter. New York: Frederick A. Praeger, 1963. 257–75.

Middleton, John, and Greet Kershaw. *The Central Tribes of the North-Eastern Bantu*. Ethnographic Survey of Africa. Ed. Daryll Forde. *East Central Africa*, Part 5. London: International African Institute, 1965.

Middleton, John, and E. H. Winter, eds. *Witchcraft and Sorcery in East Africa.* New York: Frederick A. Praeger, 1963.

Moore, Sally Falk, and Paul Puritt. *The Chagga and Meru of Tanzania. Ethnographic Survey of Africa.* Ed. John Middleton. London: International African Institute, 1977.

Morris, H. F. *The Heroic Recitations of the Bahima of Ankole.* Oxford: Clarendon Press, 1964.

Mudau, E. "Ngoma Lungundu." Nicolaas Jacobus van Warmelo. *The Copper Miners of Musina and the Early History of the Zoutpansberg.* Pretoria: Government Printer, 1940. 8–32, 109–32.

Mudimbe, V. Y. *The Invention of Africa: Gnosis, Philosophy, and the Order of Knowledge.* Bloomington: Indiana University Press, 1988.

Muhammad, Dalhatu. "The Tabuka Epic in Hausa: An Exercise in Narratology." *Studies in Hausa Language, Literature and Culture.* Ed. Ibrahim Yaro Yahaya et al. Kano: Bayero University, 1982. 397–415.

Munday, J. T. "The Creation Myth amongst the Lala of Northern Rhodesia." *African Studies,* 1, 1 (1942): 47–53.

Mushindo, P. B. *A Short History of the Bemba.* Lusaka: Neczam, 1977.

Muthiani, Joseph. *Akamba from Within: Egalitarianism in Social Relations.* Jericho, New York: Exposition Press, 1973.

Nabofa, M. Y. "Erhi and Eschatology." *Traditional Religion in West Africa.* Ed. E. A. Ade Adegbola. Accra: Asempa, 1983. 297–316.

Nadel, Siegfried Frederick. *A Black Byzantium: The Kingdom Nupe in Nigeria.* London: Oxford University Press, 1942.

Nadel, Siegfried Frederick. *Nupe Religion.* London: Routledge and Kegan Paul, 1954.

Nalder, Leonard Fielding. "Tales from the Fung Province." *Sudan Notes and Records* 14 (1931): 67–86.

Nalder, Leonard Fielding, ed. *A Tribal Survey of Mangalla Province by Members of the Province Staff and Church Missionary Society.* London: Oxford University Press, 1937.

Nassau, Robert H. Nassau. *Where Animals Talk, West African Folk Lore Tales.* Boston: Richard G. Badger, 1912.

Ndula, Simeon. "Hambegeu, The God of the Wasonjo." *Tanganyika Notes and Records* 35 (1953): 38–42.

Nelson, Harold D., ed. *Somalia, A Country Study.* Washington, D.C.: American University, 1982.

Nelson, Harold D., ed. *Zimbabwe, A Country Study.* Washington, D.C.: American University, 1983.

Niane, Djibril T. *Soundjata ou l'épopée manolingue.* Paris: Présence Africaine, 1960.

Nicolaisen, Johannes. "Essai sur la religion et la magie touarègues." *Folk, Dansk Etnografisk Tidsskrift* 3 (1961): 113–62.

Nicolaisen, Johannes. "Political Systems of Pastoral Tuareg in Air and Ahaggar." *Folk, Dansk Etnografisk Tidsskrift* 1 (1959): 67–131.

Njururi, Ngumbu, ed. *Agikuyu Folk Tales.* London: Oxford University Press, 1966.

Nkonki, Garvey. "The Traditional Prose Literature of the Ngqika." M.A. thesis, University of South Africa, 1968.

Noah, Monday Efiong. "Old Calabar (Circa 1800–1885): The City States and the Europeans." Diss., Howard U., 1974.

Norris, H. T. *The Adventures of Antar.* Warminster: Aris and Phillips, 1980.

Norris, H. T. *Saharan Myth and Saga.* Oxford: Clarendon Press, 1972.

Nürnberger, Klaus. "The Sotho Notion of the Supreme Being and the Impact of the Christian Proclamation." *Journal of Religion in Africa* 7 (1975): 174–200.

Nyembezi, C. L. Sibusiso. *Zulu Proverbs.* Johannesburg: Witwatersrand University Press, 1954.

Oduyoye, Modupe. "Àdàmú Órìsà." *Traditional Religion in West Africa.* Ed. E. A. Ade Adegbola. Accra: Asempa, 1983. 112–16.

Oduyoye, Modupe. "Names and Attributes of God." *Traditional Religion in West Africa.* Ed. E. A. Ade Adegbola. Accra: Asempa, 1983. 349–57.

Oduyoye, Modupe. "Patrilineal Spirits (The ntoro of the Akan, the tro-wo of the Ewe)." *Traditional Religion in West Africa.* Ed. E. A. Ade Adegbola. Accra: Asempal 1983. 289–96.

Ohadike, Don C. *Anioma: A Social History of the Western Igbo People.* Athens, Ohio: Ohio University Press, 1994.

Ojobolo, Okabou. *The Ozidi Saga.* Trans. J. P. Clark. Ibadan: Ibadan University Press and Oxford University Press, 1977.

Okpewho, Isidore. "African Mythology and Africa's Political Impasse." *Research in African Literatures* 29 (1998): 1–15.

Okpewho, Isidore. "Poetry and Pattern: Structural Analysis of an Ijo Creation Myth." *Journal of American Folklore* 92 (1979): 302–25.

Okpewho, Isidore. *Myth in Africa: A Study of Its Aesthetic and Cultural Relevance.* Cambridge: Cambridge University Press, 1983.

Omtatah, Andrew Okoiti. *Lwanda Magere.* London: Heinemann, 1991.

Orpen, J. M. "A Glimpse into the Mythology of the Maluti Bushmen." *The Cape Monthly Magazine* 9 (1874); reprinted in *Folklore* 30 (1919): 139–56.

Ottenberg, Simon and Phoebe, ed. *Cultures and Societies of Africa.* New York: Random House, 1960.

Oyler, D. S. "Nikawng and the Shilluk Migration." *Sudan Notes and Records* 1 (1918): 107–15.

Oyler, D. S. "Nikawng's Place in the Shilluk Religion." *Sudan Notes and Records* 1 (1918): 283–92.

Palmer, Herbert Richmond. *Sudanese Memoirs.* London: Cass, 1967 (1928.)

Palmer, Herbert Richmond. "Notes on the Korôrofawa and Jukoñ." *Journal of the African Society* 11 (1912): 407–15.

Parrinder, E. G. "Theistic Beliefs of the Yoruba and Ewe Peoples of West Africa." *African Ideas of God: A Symposium.* London: Edinburgh House Press, 1950. 224–40.

Parrinder, Geoffrey. *African Mythology.* London: Paul Hamlyn, 1967.

Parrinder, Geoffrey. *Religion in Africa.* Baltimore: Penguin, 1969.

Parrinder, Geoffrey. *West African Religion: A Study of the Beliefs and Practices of Akan, Ewe, Yoruba, Ibo, and Kindred Peoples.* London: Epworth, 1949.

Parsons, Robert Thomas. "The Idea of God among the Kono of Sierra Leone." *African Ideas of God: A Symposium.* Ed. Edwin W. Smith. London: Edinburgh House Press, 1950. 260–276.

Parsons, Robert Thomas. *Religion in an African Society; A Study of the Religion of the Kono People of Sierra Leone in Its Social Environment with Special Reference to the Function of Religion in that Society.* Leiden: E. J. Brill, 1964.

Paulme, Denise. "Two Themes on the Origin of Death in West Africa." *Man,* Royal Anthropological Institute of Great Britain and Ireland ns 2 (1967): 48–61.

Pauw, Berthold Adolf. *Religion in a Tswana Chiefdom.* London: Oxford University Press, 1960.

Peires, J. B. *The Dead Will Arise: Nongqawuse and the Great Xhosa Cattle-Killing Movement of 1856-7.* Johannesburg: Ravan Press, 1989.

Pepper, Herbert. *Un mvet de Zwè Nguéma: Chant épique Fang.* Paris: Armand Colin, 1972.

Petrie, William Matthew Flinders, ed. *Egyptian Tales.* London: Methuen, 1899.

Pettersson, Olof. *Chiefs and Gods: Religious and Social Elements in the South Eastern Bantu Kingship.* Lund: C. W. K. Gleerup, 1953.

Picard, Gilbert. *Carthage.* Trans. Miriam and Lionel Kochan. London: Elek, 1956. (*Le Monde de Carthage* [Paris: Éditions Corrêa, 1956].)

Plutarch. *Plutarch's Lives.* Trans. Aubrey Stewart and George Long. London: G. Bell, 1880–1882.

Pogge, Paul. *Im Reiche des Muata Jamwo: Beiträge zur Entdeckungsgeschichte Afrika's.* Berlin: D. Reimer, 1880.

Posselt, Friedrich Wilhelm Traugott. *Fables of the Veld.* London: Oxford University Press, 1929.

Poupon, A. "Étude ethnographique des Baya de la circonscription du M'bimou." *L'Anthropologie* 26 (1915): 87–144.

Prins, A. H. J. *The Coastal Tribes of the North-Eastern Bantu* (Pokomo, Nyika, Teita. Ethnographic Survey of Africa. Ed. Daryll Forde. *East Central Africa,* Part 3. London: International African Institute, 1952.

Prins, A. H. J. *The Swahili-speaking Peoples of Zanzibar and the East African Coast* (Arabs, Shirazi and Swahili). Ethnographic Survey of Africa. Ed. Daryll Forde. *East Central Africa,* Part 12. London: International African Institute, 1961.

Qu'ran. Trans. J. M. Podwell. London: J. M. Dent, 1909.

Quarcoopome, T. N. O. *West African Traditional Religion.* Ibadan: African Universities Press, 1987.

Radin, Paul. *African Folktales and Sculpture.* Princeton: Princeton University Press, 1952.

Rattray, Robert Sutherland. *Akan-Ashanti Folk-Tales.* Oxford: Clarendon Press, 1930.

Rattray, Robert Sutherland. *Ashanti.* Oxford: Clarendon Press, 1923.

Rattray, Robert Sutherland. *Ashanti Proverbs.* Oxford: Clarendon Press, 1914.

Rattray, Robert Sutherland. *Hausa Folklore, Customs, Proverbs, etc.* Oxford: Clarendon Press, 1913. Two volumes.

Rattray, Robert Sutherland. *Religion and Art in Ashanti.* Oxford: Clarendon Press, 1927.

Rattray, Robert Sutherland. *The Tribes of the Ashanti Hinterland.* Oxford: Clarendon Press, 1932.

Raum, Johannes William. *Versuch einer Grammatik der Dschaggasprache (Moschi-dialekt).* Berlin: Archiv für die Stud. Dtsch. Kolonialspr. 11 (1909): 307–18.

Ray, Benjamin C. *African Religions: Symbol, Ritual, and Community.* Englewood Cliffs, NJ: Prentice-Hall, 1976.

Read, Margaret. *The Ngoni of Nyasaland.* London: Oxford University Press, 1956.

Rehse, Hermann. "Die Sprache der Baziba in Deutsch-Ostafrika." *Zeitschrift für Kolonialsprachen* 3 (1912–1913): 81–123.

Rodd, Francis. *People of the Veil.* Osterhout: Anthropological Publications, 1966.

Roelandts, manuscript copied at Kikwit by de Sousberghe. Bastin has reproduced this text (1966, appendix, p. xvi). Quoted in de Heusch, 1985, pp. 182–93.

Roscoe, John. *The Baganda: An Account of Their Native Customs and Beliefs.* London: Macmillan, 1911.

Roscoe, John. *The Bagesu and Other Tribes of the Uganda Protectorate.* Cambridge: Cambridge University Press, 1924.

Roscoe, John. *The Bakitara or Banyoro.* Cambridge: Cambridge University Press, 1923. Reprinted with permision of Cambridge University Press.

Roscoe, John. *The Banyankole.* Cambridge: Cambridge University Press, 1923. Reprinted with permission of Cambridge University Press.

Roscoe, John. *The Northern Bantu.* London: Frank Cass, 1915.

Ross, Mabel H., and Barbara K. Walker. *"On Another Day ...": Tales Told among the Nkundo of Zaïre.* (March 1973, Narrator: Bongonda Michele, Location: Bolenge.) Hamden, Connecticut: Archon, 1979.

Routledge, W. Scoresby, and Katherine Routledge. *With a Prehistoric People: The Akikúyu of British East Africa.* London: Edward Arnold, 1910.

Sagar, J. W. "Notes on the History, Religion, and Customs of the Nuba." *Sudan Notes and Records* 5 (1921): 137–56.

Samuelson, L. H. "Some Zulu Customs." *Journal of the African Society* 10 (1911): 191–99.

Sauneron, Serge. *Les fêtes religeuses d'Esna aux derniers siècles du paganisme.* Cairo: Publications de l'institut française d'archéologie orientale d'Esna, 1962.

Sawyerr, Harry. *God, Ancestor or Creator? Aspects of Traditional Belief in Ghana, Nigeria and Sierra Leone.* Harlow: Longmans, 1970.

Schapera, Isaac, ed. *The Bantu-speaking Tribes of South Africa: An Ethnographical Survey.* London: Routledge and Kegan Paul, 1937.

Schapera, Isaac, ed. *The Early Cape Hottentots, Described in the Writings of Olfert Dapper (1668), Willen ten Rhyne (1686) and Johannes Gulielmus de Grevenbroek (1695).* Cape Town: Van Riebeeck Society, 1933.

Schapera, Isaac, ed. *The Khoisan Peoples of South Africa: Bushmen and Hottentots.* London: Routledge and Kegan Paul, 1930.

Schapera, Isaac. *The Tswana. Ethnographic Survey of Africa.* Ed. Daryll Forde. Southern Africa, Part 3. London: International African Institute, 1953.

Schebesta, Paul. *Among Congo Pygmies.* Trans. Gerald Griffin. London: Hutchinson, 1933.

Schebesta, Paul. *My Pgymy and Negro Hosts.* Trans. Gerald Griffin. London: Hutchinson, 1936.

Schebesta, Paul. *Revisiting My Pygmie Hosts.* Trans. Gerald Griffin. London: Hutchinson, 1936.

Scheub, Harold. *The Tongue Is Fire*. Madison: University of Wisconsin Press, 1996.

Scheven, Albert. *Swahili Proverbs, Nia zikiwa moja, kilicho mbali huja*. Washington, DC: University Press of America, 1981.

Schmitz, Robert. *Les Baholoholo*. Brussels: A. DeWit, 1912. 261–66.

Schoeman, Pieter Johannes. *Hunters of the Desert Land*. Cape Town: Howard Timmins, 1957.

Schweinfurth, George. *The Heart of Africa; Three Years' Travel and Adventures in theUnexplored Regions of Central Africa from 1868 to 1871*. New York: Harper, 1874.

Seabrook, William B. *Jungle Ways*. New York: Harcourt Brace, 1931. Copyright © 1931 by Harcourt, Inc., renewed 1958 by Mrs. Constance Seabrook, reprinted by permission of the publisher.

Seligman, Charles Gabriel, and Brenda Z. Seligman. *Pagan Tribes of the Nilotic Sudan*. London: Routledge and Kegan Paul, 1932.

Selous, Frederick Courteney. *A Hunter's Wanderings in Africa*. London: Richard Bentley, 1881.

Selous, Frederick Courteney. *Travel and Adventure in South-east Africa*. London: Rowland Ward, 1893.

Senior, M. Mary. "Some Mende Proverbs." *Africa, Journal of the International African Institute* (London) 17 (1947): 202–05.

Setiloane, Gabriel M. *The Image of God among the Sotho-Tswana*. Rotterdam: A. A. Balkema, 1976.

Seton-Williams, M. V. "Egypt: Myth and the Reality." *The Feminist Companion to Mythology*. Ed. Carolyne Larrington. London: Pandora Press, 1992. River Oram Press: 23–47.

Seydou, Christiane, ed. and trans. *La geste de Ham-Bodêdio ou Hama le rouge*. Paris: Armand Colin, 1976.

Seydou, Christiane, ed. and trans. *Silâmaka et Poullôri*. Paris: Armand Colin, 1972.

Shack, William A. *The Central Ethiopians: Amhara, Tigriña and Related Peoples*. Ethnographic Survey of Africa. Ed. Daryll Forde. North-Eastern Africa, Part 4. London: International African Institute, 1974.

Shack, William A., and Habte–Mariam Marcos. *Gods and Heroes: Oral Traditions of the Gurage of Ethiopia*. Oxford: Clarendon Press, 1974.

Sheddick, V. G. J. *The Southern Sotho*. Ethnographic Survey of Africa. Ed. Daryll Forde. Southern Africa, Part 2. London: International African Institute, 1953.

Shooter, Joseph. *The Kafirs of Natal and the Zulu Country*. London: E. Stanford, 1857.

Shorter, Aylward. "Religious Values in Kimbu Historical Charters." *Africa, Journal of the International African Institute* (London) 39 (1969): 227–37.

Sibree, James, Jr. *Madagascar and Its People*. London: The Religious Tract Society, 1870.

Sibree, James, Jr. *Madagascar before the Conquest*. London: T. Fisher Unwin, 1896.

Sibree, James, Jr. "Malagasy Folk–tales." *Folk-Lore Journal* 2 (1884): 49–55.

Simenauer, E. "The Miraculous Birth of Hambegeu, Hero–God of the Sonjo." *Tanganyika Notes and Records* 38 (1955): 23–30.

Simmons, D. "An Ethnographic Sketch of the Efik People." *Efik Traders of Old Calabar*. London: Oxford University Press, 1956, 1–26.

Skinner, Neil, ed. and trans. *Hausa Tales and Traditions*. Trans. of Frank Edgar. *Tatsuniyoyi Na Hausa*. Madison: University of Wisconsin Press, 1977.

Smith, Edwin William, ed. *African Ideas of God: A Symposium*. London: Edinburgh House, 1950.

Smith, Edwin William. *A Handbook of the Ila Language (Commonly Called the Seshuku-lumbwe) Spoken in North-western Rhodesia, South-central Africa*. London: Oxford University Press, 1907.

Smith, Edwin William. "The Idea of God among South African Tribes." *African Ideas of God: A Symposium*. London: Edinburgh House, 1950. 78–134.

Smith, Edwin William, and Andrew Murray Dale. *The Ila-Speaking Peoples of Northern Rhodesia*. London: Macmillan, 1920. Two volumes.

Smith, Pierre. "Sacred Kingship among the Bantu Speakers of the Great Lakes Region." Yves Bonnefoy. *Mythologies*. Transl. Wendy Doniger et al. Chicago: University of Chicago Press, 1991. I, 76–81.

Smith, W. Robertson. *Lectures on the Religion of the Semites*. London: Adam and Charles Black, 1901.

Soga, John Henderson. *The Ama-Xosa: Life and Customs*. Lovedale: Lovedale Press, 1931.

Sproul, Barbara C. *Primal Myths: Creation Myths around the World*. San Francisco: HarperCollins, 1979.

Stanley, Henry Morton. *Tales from Africa*. London: Sampson Low, Marston, 1893.

Stayt, Hugh Arthur. *The Bavenda*. London: H. Milford, 1931.

Steedman, Andrew. *Wanderings and Adventures in the Interior of Southern Africa*. London: Longmans, 1835.

Steere, Edward. *Swahili Tales*. London: Society for Promoting Christian Knowledge, 1869.

Stephens, Jean B. "Tales of the |Gwikwe Bushmen." M.A. thesis, Goddard College, 1971.

Stevenson, Maron S. "Specimens of Kikuyu Proverbs." *Festschrift Meinhof*. Hamburg: J. J. Augustin, 1927.

Stevenson, R. C. "The Doctrine of God in the Nuba Mountains." *African Ideas of God: A Symposium*. Ed. Edwin W. Smith. London: Edinburgh House Press, 1950. 208–23.

Stevenson, R. C. "The Nyamang of the Nuba Mountains of Kordofan." *Sudan Notes and Records* 23 (1940): 75–98.

Stow, George William. *The Native Races of South Africa; A History of the Intrusion of the Hottentots and Bantu into the Hunting Grounds of the Bushmen, the Aborigines of the Country*. Ed. George McCall Theal. London: S. Sonnenschein, 1905.

Struyf, Y. "Kahemba: Envahisseurs Badjok et conquérants Balunda." *Zaïre*, 2, 4 (1948): 351–390.

Stuart, J. uKulumetule. London: Longmans, Green, 1925.

Swantz, Marja–Liisa. *Ritual and Symbol in Transitional Zaramo Society, with Special Reference to Women*. Uppsala: Scandinavian Institute of African Studies, 1986.

Talbot, Percy Amaury. *In the Shadow of the Bush*. London: William Heinemann, 1912.

Talbot, Percy Amaury. *The Peoples of Southern Nigeria*. London: Frank Cass, 1926.

Talbot, Percy Amaury. "Some Foreign Influences on Nigeria." *Journal of the African Society* 24 (1924–1925): 178–201.

Talbot, Percy Amaury. *Some Nigerian Fertility Cults*. London: Oxford University Press, 1927.

Talbot, Percy Amaury. *Tribes of the Niger Delta, Their Religions and Customs*. London: Frank Cass, 1932.

Taylor, Brian K. *The Western Lacustrine Bantu*. Ethnographic Survey of Africa. Ed. Daryll Forde. East Central Africa, Part 13. London: International African Institute, 1962.

Tessmann, Günter. *Die Pangwe—Völkerskundliche Monographie eines Westafrikanischen Negerstammes*. Berlin: Ernst Wasmuth, 1913. Two volumes.

Tew, Mary. *Peoples of the Lake Nyasa Region*. Oxford: Oxford University Press, 1950.

Theal, George McCall. *Ethnography and Condition of South Africa before 1505*. Vol. 1 of *History of South Africa*. London: George Allen and Unwin, 1910.

Theuws, Th. *De Luba-mens*. Tervuren: Annales du Musée royal de l'Afrique centrale, 1962.

Thomas, H. B. "The Doctrine of God in Uganda." *African Ideas of God: A Symposium*. Ed. Edwin W. Smith. London: Edinburgh House Press, 1950. 201–07.

Tolkien, J. R. R. *Tree and Leaf*. London: George Allen and Unwin, 1964.

Torday, Emil. *On the Trail of the Bushongo*. London: Seeley, Service, 1925.

Torday, Emil, and T. A. Joyce. "Les Bushongo." *Annales du Musée de Congo Belge*, Ethnographie Anthropologie, Serie 4, t. 2 (1910): 20ff.

Torday, Emil, and T. A. Joyce. *Notes ethnographiques sur les peuples communément appelés Bakuba, ainsi que sur les peuplades apparentées—Les Bushongo*. Tervuren: Annales du Musée du Congo Belge, 1911.

Torrend, J. *Specimens of Bantu Folk-lore from Northern Rhodesia*. London: Kegan Paul, Trübner, 1921.

Tremearne, A. J. N. *The Ban of the Bori: Demons and Demon Dancing in West and North Africa*. London: Heath, Cranton, and Ouseley, 1914.

Tremearne, A. J. N. *Hausa Superstitions and Customs: An Introduction to the Folk-lore and the Folk*. London: John Bale, Sons, and Danielsson, 1913.

Triulzi, Alessandro. "Myths and Rituals of the Ethiopian Bertha." *Peoples and Cultures of the Ethio-Sudan Borderlands*. Ed. M. Lionel Bender. East Lansing, Mich.: African Studies Center, 1981. 179–214.

Turner, Victor W. *The Drums of Affliction: A Study of Religious Processes among the Ndembu of Zambia*. Oxford: Clarendon Press, 1968.

Turner, Victor W. *The Forest of Symbols: A Study of Religious Processes among the Ndembu of Zambia*. Oxford: Clarendon Press, 1967.

Turner, Victor W. *The Lozi Peoples of North-Western Rhodesia*. Ethnographic Survey of Africa. Ed. Daryll Forde. *West Central Africa*, Part 3. London: International African Institute, 1952.

Turner, Victor W., trans. and ed. "A Lunda Love Story and Its Consequences: Selected Texts from Traditions Collected by Henrique Dias de Carvalho at the Court of Mwatianvwa in 1887." *Rhodes-Livingstone Journal* 19 (1955): 1–27.

Tweedie, Ann. "Towards a History of the Bemba from Oral Tradition." *The Zambesian Past; Studies in Central African History*. Ed. Eric Stokies and Richard Brown. Manchester: Manchester University Press, 1966. 197–225.

Ukpong, Justin S. "Sacrificial Worship in Ibibio Traditional Religion." *Journal of Religion in Africa* 13 (1982): 161–88.

Ullendorff, Edward. *The Ethiopians: An Introduction to Country and People*. London: Oxford University Press, 1965.

Van S. Bruwer, J. P. "Mujaji." *Standard Encyclopedia of South Africa*. Cape Town: Nasou, 1972. VII: 636–37.

Van den Byvang. "Notice historique sur les Balunda." *Congo* 1, 4 (1937): 426–38; 1, 5 (1937): 548–62; 2, 2 (1938): 193–208.

Vansina, Jan. *The Children of Woot: A History of the Kuba Peoples*. Madison: University of Wisconsin Press, 1978.

Vansina, Jan. *Geshiedenis van de Kuba von ongeveer 1500 to 1904*. Tervuren: Annales Musée Royal de l'Afrique Centrale, Sci. Humaines, 44, 1963.

Vansina, Jan. "Initiation Rites of the Bushong." *Africa, Journal of the International African Institute* (London) 25 (1955): 138–53.

Vansina, Jan. *Kingdoms of the Savanna*. Madison: University of Wisconsin Press, 1966.

Vansina, Jan. *Les anciens royaumes de la savane*. Kinshasa: Université Lovanium, Institut de Recherches économiques et sociales, 1965.

Vansina, Jan. "Les croyances religieuses des Kuba." *Zaïre*, 12, 7 (1958): 725–58.

Van Warmelo, Nicolaas Jacobus. *The Copper Miners of Musina and the Early History of the Zoutpansberg*. Pretoria: Government Printer, 1940.

Van Warmelo, Nicolaas Jacobus. *Transvaal Ndebele Texts*. Pretoria: Government Printer, 1930.

Van Wing, R. P. *Études Bakongo: histoire et sociologie*. Bruxelles: Goemaere, 1921.

Vedder, Heinrich. "The Berg Damara." *The Native Tribes of South West Africa*. Ed. Carl Hugo Linsingen Hahn, et al. Cape Town: Cape Times, 1928. 37–78.

Vedder, Heinrich. "The Herero." *The Native Tribes of South West Africa*. Ed. Carl Hugo Linsingen Hahn, et al. Cape Town: Cape Times, 1928. 153–211.

Vedder, Heinrich. "The Nama." *The Native Tribes of South West Africa*. Ed. Carl Hugo Linsingen Hahn, et al. Cape Town: Cape Times, 1928. 106–52.

Vedder, Heinrich. *South West Africa in Early Times*. London: Frank Cass, 1938.

Verhulpen, Edmond. *Baluba et Balubaïsés du Katanga*. Anvers: L'Avenir Belge, 1936.

Viehe, G. "Some Customs of the Ovaherero." Ed. W. Coates Palgrave. *Folk-Lore Journal* I (1879): 37–67.

Wagner, Günter. "The Abaluyia of Kavirondo." *African Worlds: Studies in the Cosmological Ideas and Social Values of African Peoples*. Oxford: Oxford University Press, 1954: 27–54.

Wagner, Günter. *The Bantu of North Kavirondo*. London: Oxford University Press, 1949.

Wallmark, Patrik. "The Bega (Gumuz) of Wellegga: Agriculture and Subsistence." *Peoples and Cultures of the Ethio-Sudan Borderlands*. Ed. M. Lionel Bender. East Lansing, Michigan: African Studies Center, 1981. 79–116.

Wanger, W. "The Zulu Notion of God." *Anthropos* 19 (1924): 656–87; 20 (1925): 558–78; 21 (1926): 351–85.

Wanjohi, G. J. "An African Conception of God: The Case of the Gikuyu." *Journal of Religion in Africa* 9 (1978): 136–46.

Warmington, B. H. *Carthage*. New York: Praeger, 1969. Rev. ed.

Warmington, B. H. "The Carthaginian Period." *General History of Africa*. Volume II, *Ancient Civilizations of Africa*. Ed. G. Mokhtar. Paris: United Nations Educational, Scientific and Cultural Organization, 1981. 441–64.

Weeks, John H. *Among Congo Cannibals*. London: Seeley, Service, 1913.

Weeks, John H. *Among the Primitive Bakongo*. London: Seeley, Service, 1914.

Weeks, John H. *Congo Life and Jungle Stories*. London: Religious Tract Society, 1911.

Werner, Alice. *African Mythology*. London: Marshall Jones, 1925.

Werner, Alice. "African Mythology." *The Mythology of All Races*, Volume 7. Ed. John Arnott MacCulloch. New York: Cooper Square, 1964 (c. 1916–1932). London: Marshall Jones, 1925.

Werner, Alice. "The Bushongo." Journal of the African Society 11 (1912): 206–12.
Werner, Alice. Myths and Legends of the Bantu. London: George G. Harrap, 1933.
Werner, Alice. The Natives of British Central Africa. London: A. Constable, 1906.
Werner, Alice. "Two Galla Legends." Man 13 (1913): 90–91.
Westermann, Diedrich. The Shilluk People: Their Language and Folklore. Philadelphia: Board of Foreign Missions of the United Presbyterian Church of N. A., 1912.
Westermann, Diedrich. A Study of the Ewe Language. London: Oxford University Press, 1930.
Whiteley, W. H. Bemba and Related Peoples of Northern Rhodesia. Ethnographic Survey of Africa. Ed. Daryll Forde. East Central Africa, Part 2. London: International African Institute, 1950.
Whiteley, W. H., ed. A Selection of African Prose. Oxford: Clarendon Press, 1964.
Wikar, H. J. The Journal of Hendrik Jacob Wikar (1779). Ed. E. E. Mossop. Cape Town: Van Riebeeck Society, 1935.
Willans, R. H. K. "The Konnoh People." Journal of the African Society 8 (1908–1909): 130–44, 288–95.
Williams, F. Lukyn. "Ankole Folk Tales." Africa, Journal of the International African Institute (London) 21 (1951): 32–40.
Williams, Joseph J. Africa's God, II—Dahomey. Chestnut Hills, Mass.: Boston College Press, 1936.
Williams, Joseph J. Africa's God, I—Gold Coast and Its Hinterland. Chestnut Hills, Mass.: Boston College Press, 1936.
Williams, R. H. K. "The Konnah People." Journal of the African Society 8 (1909): 130–41.
Willis, C. A. "The Cult of Deng." Sudan Notes and Records 11 (1928): 195–208.
Willis, John Ralph. "The Western Sudan from the Moroccan Invasion (1591) to the Death of Al–Mukhtar Al–Kunti (1811)." History of West Africa. Ed. J. F. A. Ajayi and Michael Crowder. New York: Columbia University Press, 1976. I, 512–54.
Willis, Roy G. The Fipa and Related Peoples of South-West Tanzania and North-East Zambia. Ethnographic Survey of Africa. Ed. Daryll Forde. East Central Africa, Part 15. London: International African Institute, 1966.
Wiredu, Kwasi. Philosophy and African Culture. Cambridge: Cambridge University Press, 1980.
Wollacott, R. C. "Dziwaguru–God of Rain." NADA (Southern Rhodesia Native Affairs Department Annual) 40 (1963): 116–21.
Wyndham, John. Myths of Ifè. London: Erskine Macdonald, 1921.
Yahaya, Ibrahim Yaro. "Some Parallels in Unofficial Islamic Beliefs in Near Eastern and Hausa Folk Beliefs." Al-Mathura Al Sha'biyyah, No. 11 (July, 1988): 8–25.
Young, T. Cullen. "The Idea of God in Northern Nyasaland." African Ideas of God: A Symposium. Ed. Edwin W. Smith. London: Edinburgh House Press, 1950. 36–58.
Zemp, H. "La littérature des Dan (Côte d'Ivoire)." Diss., University of Paris, 1964.
Zenani, Nongenile Masithathu. The World and the Word, Tales and Observations from the Xhosa Oral Tradition. Madison: University of Wisconsin Press, 1992.
Zvarevashe, Ignatius M. "Shona Religion." Shona Customs. Ed. Clive and Peggy Kileff. Gwelo: Mambo Press, 1970. 44–47.

Appendix 1

Myths Listed by Country

Algeria
Arabic–al-Khadir
Berber–Irgam Yigfagna
Kabyle–Mekidech
Kabyle–Tlam
Tuareg–Elijinen
Tuareg–Sabenas

Angola
Ambo–Nambalisita
Kimbundu–Sudika-mbambi
Kongo–Nzambi,
    Nzambi Mpungu
Luba, Lunda–Chibinda Ilunga
Lunda–Chinawezi
Mbukushu–Dikithi
Ovimbundu–Kalitangi

Benin
Bargu–Kisra
Edo, Igbo–Osanobua
Ewe–Mawu
Fon–Aido-Hwedo
Fon–Fa
Fon–Gu
Fon–Hevioso
Fon–Legba
Fon–Lisa
Fon–Mawu
Fon–Mawu-Lisa
Fon–Nana Buluku
Fon–Sagbata, Azo
Fon–Segbo
Fon–Sogbo, So

Kyama–Aruan

Botswana
|Gwikwe–!Nariba
|Gwikwe–Pishiboro
!Kung–Huwe, Xu
Mbukushu–Dikithi
San–Goha
San–|Kaggen
San–Kho
San–Ko
Tswana–Modimo
Yeye–Urezhwa

Burkina Faso
Akan–Nyame, Onyame
Awuna–Hebioso and Abui
Djerma–Gassire
Dogon–Amma
Kasena–We, Wea
Mossi–Winnam, Ouennam,
    Winde, Naba Zidiwinde

Burundi
Rundi, Hutu, Tutsi–Imana

Cameroon
Bachama–Inusa
Batanga, Duala, Malimba,
    Pongo–Jeki la Njambe
Bulu–Zambe
Bulu–Zobeyo Mebe'e
Fali–To Dino
Fang–Akoma Mba
Fang–Nzame, Nyame

Central African Republic
  Boloki–Libanza
  Boloki–Mbungi
  Boloki–Motu
  Boloki–Njambe
  Pahouin, Fang–Mebege

Chad
  Sara–Wantu Su

Congo
  Fiote, Vili–Nzambi Mpungu
  Gbaya–Zambi and Zelo

Côte d'ivoire
  Agni, Baoule–Adoudoua
  Agni–Tano
  Anyi–Alouko Niamie
  Baoule–Oduduwa, Niamie, Assie
  Dan–Zra
  Kyama–Aruan
  Senufo–Koulotiolo

Democratic Republic of Congo
  Bachwa–Djakomba
  Bushongo–Bumba
  Efe–Arebati
  Efe–Baatsi
  Efe–Epilipili
  Efe–Masupa
  Efe, Mbuti–Tore
  Hamba–Kudukese
  Holoholo–Kalala
  Kongo–Nzambi, Zambi, Yambe
  Kuba–Mboom
  Kuba–Woot, Woto
  Lega–Mubila
  Luangu–Nzazi
  Luba–Kalumba, Sendwe Mwlaba
  Luba–Nkongolo
  Luba, Lunda–Chibinda Ilunga
  Lugbara–Adro, Adroa, Adronga
  Lugbara–Gborogboro and Meme
  Lugbara–Jaki and Dribidu
  Lunda–Chinawezi

Lunda–Lueji
Lunda–Tianza Ngombe,
    Chinaweshi, Chinawezi
Mbole–Lofokefoke
Mbuti–Mungu
Mongo–Lianja
Mongo–Mbomba Ianda
Ngombe–Akongo
Ngombe–Libaka
Ngombe–Mbokomu
Nyanga–Mpaca
Nyanga–Mwindo
Soko–Bateta and Hanna
Upoto–Libanza
Woyo–Bunzi
Yombe–Mbumba
Zande–Ture

Egypt
  Bata
  Epaphus
  Hathor
  Hathors
  Horus
  Isis
  Louliyya
  Neith, Net
  Nut
  Osiris
  Ra
  Rhampsinitus

Equatorial Guinea
  Benga–Kudu
  Fang–Akoma Mba
  Fang–Nzame, Nyame

Ethiopia
  Galla–Waka, Waqa,
    Wak
  Ge'ez, Amhara,
    Tigre–Makeda
  Konso–Waga
  Kush–Wainaba
  Uduk–Arum

Gabon
Benga–Kudu
Fang–Akoma Mba
Fang–Nzame, Nyame
Fang–Zong Midzi
Mpongwe–Njambi

Gambia
Mandinka–Sunjata

Ghana
Akan–Nyame, Onyame
Akan–Odomankoma, Damankama
Akan, Asante–Aberewa
Akan, Asante–Tano
Anlo–Mawu, Se
Asante–Ananse
Asante–Nyame, Onyame,
    Onyankopon
Dagomba, Mamprusi,
    Moshi–Tindana
Dagomba–Wuni
Ewe–Dente
Ewe-Mawu
Ga–Ataa Naa Nyongmo
Ga–Dzenawon
Kasena–We, Wea
Talensi–Mosuor

Guinea
Kono–Alatangana

Kenya
Kamba–Mulungu
Kamba–Ngai
Kikuyu–Kemangurura
Kikuyu–Mukunga M'bura
Kikuyu–Ngai, Mogai
Kikuyu–Wanjiru
Kipsigis, Lumbwa–Asis, Asista
Luyia–Wele, Were
Masai–Kintu
Masai–Ngai
Meru–Murungu, Ngai
Nandi–Asis, Asista

Nandi–Mungu
Pokomo, Sanye–Vere
Suk–Tororut, Ilat
Swahili–Mungu
Swahili, Pokomo–Liongo
Turkana–Agipie
Vugusu–Wele

Lesotho
Sotho–Ditaolane
Sotho–Modimo

Liberia
Kru–Sno-Nyosa, Nysoa, Nyensoa
Mano–Wala
Poro, Sande–Nyesowa, Gala, Wala,
    Abi

Libya
Antaeus
Arabic–al-Khadir
Berber–Irgam Yigfagna,
    al-Jabal al-Lamma
Epaphus
Gurzil
Libya
Tuareg–Elijinen

Madagascar
Betsileo–Andriananahary
Malagasy–Andriambahomanana
Malagasy–Andriananahary
Malagasy–Iboniamasiboniamanoro
Malagasy–Rasoalavavolo
Merina–Andriananahary

Malawi
Makua–Muluku
Tonga–Chiuta
Yao–Mulungu

Mali
Bambara–Da Monzon
Bambara–Doni Dyu
Bambara–Faro

Bambara–Pemba
Bambara–Yo
Bozo–Doni Dyu
Dogon–Amma
Dogon–Donu Dyu
Fulani–Doondari
Fulani–Silamaka
Fulbe–Goroba-Dike
Habbe–Nangaban
Malinke–Doni Dyu
Mande–Mangala
Mandinka–Kambili
Mandinka–Sunjata
Minyanka–Doni Dyu
Tuareg–Elijinen
Tuareg–Sabenas

Mauritania
Soninke–Gassire

Morocco
Antaeus
Arabic–al-Khadir
Arabic, Berber–Idris
Arabic–Sidi Adjille
Berber–Irgam Yigfagna, al-Jabal al-
    Lamma
Lamtuna–Kahina
North Africa–Antar

Mozambique
Lenge–Tilo
Makua–Muluku
Ronga–Tilo
Shangana, Tonga–Tilo
Thonga, Tsonga–Tilo
Yao–Mulungu

Namibia
Aikwe, Auen, Naron–Hishe
Berg Damara–‖Gamab
Berg Damara–Holy Fire
Damara, Herero–Kamangundu and
    Omumborombonga
|Gwikwe–!Nariba

Heikum–Xu
Herero–Karunga,
    Ndjambi Karunga, Mukuru
!Kung–≠Gao!na
!Kung–‖Gauwa
!Kung–|Kai |Kini
Mbukushu–Dikithi
Nama–Tsui‖Goab
Naron, Aikwe, Auen–Hishe
San–Goha
San–|Kaggen
San–Kho
San–Ko

Niger
Djerma–Gassire
Ekoi–Obassi Osaw
Hausa–Bayajida
Hausa–Karkur
Hausa–Korau
Hausa–Sa Na Duniya
Hausa–Tsumburbura
Tuareg–Elijinen
Tuareg–Sabenas

Nigeria
Abua–Abua
Anang–Abasi, Abbassi
Bachama, Bata–Nzeanzo
Bachama–Inusa
Bini, Edo–Osa, Osanobua
Bura, Pabir–Hyel
Efik–Abasi, Abassi
Ekoi–Effion Obassi
Ekoi–Obassi Osaw
Fulani, Fulfulde–Balewa Yola
Hausa–Bayajida
Hausa–Dodo
Hausa–Jangare, Bori
Hausa–Karkur
Hausa–Kaura Duna
Hausa–Korau
Hausa–Sa Na Duniya
Hausa–Tsibiri
Hausa–Tsumburbura

Ibibio—Abasi Ibom
Igbo—Ale, Ala
Igbo—Chuku
Igbo—Ebele
Ijo—Ogboinba
Ijo—Ozidi
Isoko, Urhobo—Oghene,
    Oghenukpabe
Jen—Fi
Jukun—Ama
Jukun—Chido
Jukun, Kororofawa—Gion
Kalabari—Ekineba
Kalabari—Tamuno
Margi—Iju
Nupe—Soko
Nupe—Tsoede
Tangale—Monje Ngumyu
Yoruba—Esu
Yoruba—Ifa
Yoruba—Obatala, Orisa-nla
Yoruba—Oduduwa, Oduwa,
    Odudua
Yoruba—Ogun
Yoruba—Olodumare
Yoruba—Sango

Rwanda
Nyarwanda—Gihanga
Nyarwanda, Hutu,
    Tutsi—Gihanga
Nyarwanda—Miseke
Nyarwanda—Ryangombe
Rundi, Hutu,
    Tutsi—Imana

Senegal
Fulani, Peul—Doondari
Fulani—Gueno
Fulani—Kaidara
Tukulor—Juntel Jabali
Wolof—Njaajaan Njaay

Sierra Leone
Kono, Tembe—Dugbo

Kono—Meketa, Yataa
Limba—Kanu, Masala, Masaranka
Mende—Leve
Mende—Ngewo

Somalia
Pokomo, Sanye—Vere
Somali—Somal

South Africa
Hurutshe—Matsieng
Khoi—‡Gama-‡Gorib
Khoi—Heitsi-Eibib
Khoi—Tsui‖Goab
Lovedu—Dzugudini
Lovedu—Khuzwane, Mwari
Lovedu—Mujaji, Modjadji
Ndebele—Zimu
Pedi, Venda—Huveane
San—|Kaggen
San—Kho
San—Ko
Thonga, Tsonga—Tilo
Tsonga—Shikwembu
Tswana—Modimo
Venda—Ngoma-lungundu
Venda—Raluvhimba, Raluvhimbi,
    Mwari
Xhosa—Malikophu
Xhosa, Zulu—Mdali
Xhosa—Nyengebule
Xhosa—Qamatha
Xhosa, Khoi—Thixo
Xhosa—Tshawe
Zulu—Mvelinqangi
Zulu—Nkulunkulu
Zulu—Nomkhubulwana
Zulu—Thingo Lwenkosikazi

Sudan
Ama, Nyimang—Abradi
Anuak—Gila
Anuak—Juok, Jwok
Bari, Fajulu—Ngun Lo Ki
Bongo—Loma, Hege

Bongo—Loma Gubu
Bor, Dinka—Aiwel
Burun, Meban—Juon
Dilling, Nuba—Bail
Dinka—Abuk
Dinka—Deng
Dinka—Kejok
Dinka—Longar
Dinka—Nhialic, Nyalich, Acek, Jok
Dinka—Wan Dyor
Ju Luo—Juok
Jo Luo—Wac
Kakwa—Nguleso
Lotuko—Ajok
Loyoiya, Oxoriuk—Lurubot
Lugbara—Adro, Adroa, Adronga
Lugbara—Gborogboro and Meme
Lugbara—Jaki and Dribidu
Mondari—Nun
Nuba—Bail
Nuba—Shibeika
Nuer—Kar
Nuer—Kwoth, Kwoth Nhial
Sara—Wantu Su
Shilluk—Juok, Jwok
Shilluk—Nyikang
Shilluk—Ukwa
Topotha, Nyitopotha—Nawuge
Zande—Dengbagine
Zande—Mbori, Bapaizegino
Zande—Ture

Swaziland
Swati—Mkhulumnchanti,
    Mvelingqangi.

Tanzania
Asu, Pare—Kiumbi
Bondei, Shambaa, Zigula—Sheuta
Chaga—Kibo and Mawenzi
Chaga—Mdi Msumu
Chaga—Mrile
Fipa—Leza
Gogo—Mulungu
Holoholo—Kalala

Kimbu—Ipupi
Kuulwe—Ngulwe
Nyamwezi—Shida Matunda
Nyamwezi, Sukuma,
    Sumbwa—Likube, Likuube
Shambaa—Mbegha
Sonjo, Sonyo—Hambegeu
Sonjo, Sonyo—Naka
Swahili—Mungu
Zaramo—Kwege
Zaramo—Nyalutanga, Lutanga
Ziba—Rugaba

Togo
Bassari—Unumbotte
Ewe—Mawu
Fon—Nana Buluku
Krachi—Owuo
Krachi—Wulbari

Tunisia
Arabic—al-Khadir
Arabic—Rdah Umm Zayed
Bani Hilal—Abu Zayd
Berber,
    Carthaginian—Baal Hammon
Berber—Irgam Yigfagna,
    al-Jabal al-Lamma
Berber—Nanna Tala
Carthaginian—Anna
Carthaginian—Dido
Carthaginian—Melqart
Carthaginian, Berber—Tanit, Tinith,
    Tini
Tuareg—Elijinen
Tuareg—Sabenas

Uganda
Acholi—Jok, Juok, Lubanga
Ganda—Kana
Ganda—Kaumpuli
Ganda—Kibuka, Kyobe
Ganda—Kintu
Ganda—Mukasa
Ganda—Walumbe, Warumbe

Lango—Jok
Lango—Polo
Lugbara—Adro, Adroa, Adronga
Lugbara—Gborogboro and Meme
Lugbara—Jaki and Dribidu
Luo—Lwanda Magere
Madi—Ori, Rabanga
Nyankole, Nyankore—Ruhanga,
     Katonzi, Yazooba
Nyoro—Chwezi
Nyoro—Ndahura
Nyoro—Nyamiyonga
Nyoro—Ruhanga
Nyoro—Wamara
Pokot—Tororut

Western Sahara
Arab (Sahara Regions)—Jinn

Zambia
Bemba—Chiti Mukulu
Bemba—Mumbi Mukasa
Ila, Kaonde—Leza

Lala—Kashindika
Lala—Lesa
Lamba—Chipimpi,
     Kipimpi
Lamba—Kabunda
Lamba—Lesa
Lamba—Luchyele
Lenje—Kapepe
Lozi—Nyambe,
     Mulimu
Luyi—Nyambe

Zimbabwe
Makoni—Maori
Rotse—Nyambi,
     Nyambe
Shangana,
     Tonga—Tilo
Shona—Dziwaguru
Shona—Mwari
Shona—Nehoreka
Thonga, Tsonga—Tilo
Venda—Ngoma-lungundu

Appendix 2

Myths Listed by Language and Culture

Abua (Nigeria), Abua
Acholi (Uganda), Jok
Agni (Côte d'Ivoire), Adoudoua, Assie
Agni (Côte d'Ivoire), Tano
Aikwe (Namibia), Hishe, Hise, Hisheya
Akan (Burkina Faso), Nyame, Nyanko-pon, Odomankoma
Akan (Ghana), Aberewa
Akan (Ghana), Nyame, Nyankopon, Odomankoma
Akan (Ghana), Odomankoma, Nyame, Nyankopon
Akan (Ghana), Tano
Ama (Sudan), Abradi
Ambo (Angola), Nambalisita
Amhara (Ethiopia), Makeda
Anang (Nigeria), Abasi
Anlo (Ghana), Mawu, Adanuwoto, Se
Anuak (Sudan), Gila
Anuak (Sudan), Juok, Jwok
Anyi (Ivory Coast), Alouko Niamie Kadio
Arab (Morocco), Idris
Arabic Areas, al-Khidr, Khadir, al-Khadir
Arabic (Morocco), Sidi Adjille
Arabic (Tunisia), Rdah Umm Zayed
Arabic (Western Sahara), Jinn
Asante (Ghana), Aberewa
Asante (Ghana), Ananse, Anansi
Asante (Ghana), Nyame, Nyankopon, Odomankoma, Onyankopon
Asante (Ghana), Tano
Asu (Tanzania), Kiumbi
Auen (Namibia), Hishe, Hise

Awuna (Burkina Faso), Abui and Hebieso
Awuna (Burkina Faso), Hebieso and Abui
Bachama (Cameroon, Nigeria), Inusa
Bachama (Nigeria), Nzeanzo, Janzo, Njanjo
Bachwa (DRCongo), Djakomba, Djakoba, Djabi
Bambara (Mali), Da Monzon
Bambara (Mali), Doni Dyu
Bambara (Mali), Faro
Bambara (Mali), Pemba
Bambara (Mali), Yo
Bani Hilal, Banu Hilal (Tunisia), Abu Zayd
Baoule (Côte d'Ivoire), Adoudoua, Assie
Baoule (Côte d'Ivoire), Oduduwa, Assie, Niamie
Bargu (Benin), Kisra
Bari (Sudan), Ngun Lo Ki
Bassari (Togo), Unumbotte
Bata (Nigeria), Nzeanzo, Janzo, Njanjo
Batanga (Cameroon), Jeki la Njambe
Bemba (Zambia), Chiti Mukulu
Bemba (Zambia), Mumbi Mukasa
Benga (Equatorial Guinea, Gabon), Kudu
Berber (Algeria), Irgam Yigfagna, al-Jabal al-Lamma
Berber (Libya), Irgam Yigfagna, al-Jabal al-Lamma
Berber (Morocco), Idris
Berber (Morocco, Tunisia), Irgam Yigfagna, al-Jabal al-Lamma

Berber (Tunisia), Baal Hammon, Baal Haman

Berber (Tunisia), Nanna Tala

Berber (Tunisia), Tanit, Tini, Tinith, Tinnit

Berg Damara (Namibia), ‖Gamab

Berg Damara (Namibia), Holy Fire

Bini (Nigeria), Osa, Osanobua

Boloki (CAR), Libanza

Boloki (CAR), Mbungi

Boloki (CAR), Motu

Boloki (CAR), Njambe

Bondei (Tanzania), Sheuta

Bongo (Sudan), Loma, Hege

Bongo (Sudan), Loma Gubu

Bor, Dinka (Sudan), Aiwel

Bozo (Mali), Doni Dyu

Bulu (Cameroon), Zambe

Bulu (Cameroon), Zobeyo Mebe'e

Bura (Nigeria), Hyel

Burun (Sudan), Juon, Juong

Bushongo (DRCongo), Bumba

Bwaare (Cameroon), Inusa

Bwaare (Nigeria), Inusa

Bwaatiye (Cameroon), Inusa

Bwaatiye (Nigeria), Inusa

Carthaginian (Tunisia), Anna

Carthaginian (Tunisia), Baal Hammon, Baal Haman

Carthaginian (Tunisia), Dido

Carthaginian (Tunisia), Melqart

Carthaginian (Tunisia), Tanit, Tini, Tinith, Tinnit

Chaga (Tanzania), Kibo and Mawenzi

Chaga (Tanzania), Mdi Msumu

Chaga (Tanzania), Mregho

Chaga (Tanzania), Mrile

Dagomba (Ghana), Tindana

Dagomba (Ghana), Wuni

Damara (Namibia), Kamandungu and Omumborombonga

Dan (Côte d'Ivoire), Zra

Dilling (Sudan), Bail

Dinka (Sudan), Abuk

Dinka (Sudan), Deng

Dinka (Sudan), Kejok

Dinka (Sudan), Longar

Dinka (Sudan), Nhialic, Nyalich, Acek, Jok

Dinka (Sudan), Wan Dyor

Djerma (Burkina Faso), Gassire

Djerma (Niger), Gassire

Dogon (Burkina Faso), Amma

Dogon (Mali), Amma

Dogon (Mali), Doni Dyu

Duala (Cameroon), Jeki la Njambe

Edo (Benin), Osanobua, Osa

Efe (DRCongo), Arebati, Baatsi, Epilipili

Efe (DRCongo), Baatsi

Efe (DRCongo), Epilipili

Efe (DRCongo), Masupa

Efe (DRCongo), Tore, Arebati, Baatsi, Epilipili, Muri-Muri

Efik (Nigeria), Abasi

Egypt, Bata

Egypt, Epaphus

Egypt, Hathor, Athyr, Hethert, Mentu, Qedeshet

Egypt, Hathors

Egypt, Horus

Egypt, Isis, Aset, Aust, Eset, Hest, Mert, Selkit, Unt

Egypt, Louliyya

Egypt, Neith

Egypt, Nut

Egypt, Osiris, Andjeti, Asari, Asartaiti, Heytau Osiris, Unneffer, Unno, Wenneffer

Egypt, Ra

Egypt, Rhampsinitus

Ekoi (Nigeria), Effion Obassi

Ekoi (Niger), Obassi Osaw

Ekoi (Nigeria), Obassi Osaw

Ewe (Benin), Mawu

Ewe (Benin), Sogbo, So, Hevioso

Ewe (Ghana), Dente

Ewe (Ghana), Mawu

Ewe (Togo), Mawu

Fajulu (Sudan), Ngun Lo Ki

Fali (Cameroon), To Dino

Fang (Cameroon), Akoma Mba

Fang (Equatorial Guinea), Akoma Mba

Fang (Gabon), Akoma Mba

Fang (CAR), Mebege

Fang (Congo), Mebege

Fang (Gabon), Mebege

Fang (Cameroon), Nzame, Mebere, Nkwa

Fang (Equatorial Guinea), Nzame, Mebere, Nkwa

Fang (Gabon), Nzame, Mebere, Nkwa

Fang (Gabon), Zong Midzi

Fiote, Fjort (Congo), Nzambi Mpungu

Fipa (Tanzania), Leza

Fon (Benin), Aido-Hwedo

Fon (Benin), Fa

Fon (Benin), Gu

Fon (Benin), Hevioso, Xevioso, So, Sogbo

Fon (Benin), Legba, Elegba

Fon (Benin), Lisa

Fon (Benin), Mawu

Fon (Benin), Mawu-Lisa

Fon (Benin), Nana Buluku

Fon (Benin), Sagbata, Azo

Fon (Benin), Segbo

Fon (Benin), Sogbo, So, Hevioso

Fon (Togo), Nana Buluku

Fulani (Mali), Silamaka

Fulani (Mali, Senegal), Doondari

Fulani, Fulfulde (Nigeria), Balewa Yola

Fulani (Senegal), Gueno

Fulani (Senegal), Kaidara

Fulbe (Mali), Goroba-Dike

Fulfulde (Senegal to Sudan), Khadir, al-Khadir, al-Khidr, Halilu, Hishiri

Ga (Ghana), Ataa Naa Nyongmo

Ga (Ghana), Dzemawon, Numbo

Galla (Ethiopia), Waka, Waqa, Wak

Ganda (Uganda), Kana

Ganda (Uganda), Kaumpuli

Ganda (Uganda), Kibuka, Kyobe

Ganda (Uganda), Kintu

Ganda (Uganda), Mukasa

Ganda (Uganda), Walumbe

Gbaya (CAR), Zambi and Zelo

Ge'ez (Ethiopia), Makeda

Gogo (Tanzania), Mulungu

|Gwikwe (Botswana), !Nariba

|Gwikwe (Namibia), !Nariba

|Gwikwe, San (Botswana), Pishiboro

|Gwikwe, San (Namibia), Pishiboro

Habbe (Mali), Nangaban

Hamba (DRCongo), Kudukese

Hausa (Niger), Bayajida, Abuyazidu

Hausa (Niger), Dodo

Hausa (Niger), Jangare

Hausa (Niger), Karkur

Hausa (Niger), Korau

Hausa (Niger), Sa Na Duniya

Hausa (Nigeria), Bayajida, Abuyazidu

Hausa (Nigeria), Dodo

Hausa (Nigeria), Jangare

Hausa (Nigeria), Karkur

Hausa (Nigeria), Kaura Duna

Hausa (Nigeria), Korau

Hausa (Nigeria), Sa Na Duniya

Hausa (Nigeria), Tsibiri

Hausa (Nigeria), Tsumburbura, Tchunburburai

Heikum (Namibia), Xu

Herero (Namibia), Kamangundu and Omumborombonga

Herero (Namibia), Karunga, Mukuru, Ndjambi Karunga

Holoholo (DRCongo), Kalala

Holoholo (Tanzania), Kalala

Hurutshe (South Africa), Matsieng

Hutu (Burundi), Imana

Hutu (Rwanda), Gihanga

Hutu (Rwanda), Imana

Ibibio (Nigeria), Abasi Ibom, Abasi Enyong, Chuku

Igbo (Benin), Osanobua, Osa

Igbo (Nigeria), Ale, Ala, Ane

Igbo (Nigeria), Chuku, Chukwu, Chi, Chi-uku, Chineke, Osebuluwa

Igbo (Nigeria), Ebele

Ijo (Nigeria), Ogboinba

Ijo (Nigeria), Ozidi
Ila (Zambia), Leza
Isoko (Nigeria), Oghene,
   Oghenukpabe
Jen (Nigeria), Fi
Jo Luo (Sudan), Juok (God)
Jo Luo (Sudan), Wac
Jukun (Nigeria), Ama
Jukun (Nigeria), Chido
Jukun (Nigeria), Gion
Kabyle (Algeria), Mekidech
Kabyle (Algeria), Tlam
Kakwa (Sudan), Nguleso
Kalabari (Nigeria), Ekineba
Kalabari (Nigeria), Tamuno
Kamba (Kenya), Ngai, Engai,
   Mulungu, Mumbi
Kamba (Kenya), Mulungu
Kaonde (Zambia), Leza
Kasena (Burkina Faso), We
Kasena (Ghana), We
Khoi (South Africa), ≠Gama-≠Gorib
Khoi (South Africa), Heitsi-Eibib
Khoi (South Africa), Thixo
Khoi (South Africa), Tsui‖Goab, Cagn,
   |kaang, Khub, Nanub
Kikuyu (Kenya), Kemangurura
Kikuyu (Kenya), Mukunga M'bura
Kikuyu (Kenya), Ngai, Githuku,
   Muikumbania, Murungu,
   Mwenenyaga
Kikuyu (Kenya), Wanjiru
Kimbu (Tanzania), Ipupi
Kimbundu (Angola), Sudika-mbambi
Kipsigis (Kenya), Asis, Chebtalel,
   Chebongolo
Kongo (Angola), Nzambi, Nzambi
   Mpungu
Kongo (DRCongo), Nzambi, Nzambi
   Mpungu, Yambe, Zambi
Kono (Guinea), Alatangana
Kono (Sierra Leone), Dugbo
Kono (Sierra Leone), Meketa
Kono (Sierra Leone), Yataa
Konso (Ethiopia), Waga

Kororofawa (Nigeria), Gion
Krachi (Togo), Owuo
Krachi (Togo), Wulbari
Kru (Liberia), Sno-Nysoa, Nysoa,
   Nyensoa
Kuba (DRCongo), Mboom,
   Mboomaash, Mboomyeec
Kuba (DRCongo), Woot, Woto
!Kung (Botswana), Huwe, Xu
!Kung (Namibia), ≠Gao!na
!Kung (Namibia), ‖Gauwa
!Kung (Namibia), |Kai |Kini
Kush (Ethiopia), Wainaba
Kuulwe (Tanzania), Ngulwe
Kyama (Benin), Aruan
Kyama (Côte d'Ivoire), Aruan
Lala (Zambia), Kashindika
Lala (Zambia), Lesa, Cuuta, Lucele,
   Mulenga
Lamba (Zambia), Chipimpi, Kipimpi
Lamba (Zambia), Kabunda
Lamba (Zambia), Lesa, Lyulu, Mulungu,
   Nyambi, Shyakapanga
Lamba (Zambia), Luchyele
Lamtuna (Morocco), Kahina
Lango (Uganda), Jok
Lango (Uganda), Polo
Lega (DRCongo), Mubila
Lenge (Mozambique), Tilo
Lenje (Zambia), Kapepe
Libya, Antaeus
Libya, Gurzil
Libya, Libya
Limba (Sierra Leone), Kanu, Masala,
   Masaranka
Lokoiya (Sudan), Lurubot
Lotuko (Sudan), Ajok, Adyok, Naijok
Lovedu (South Africa), Dzugudini
Lovedu (South Africa), Khuzwane,
   Mwari
Lovedu (South Africa), Mujaji, Mo-
   djadji
Lozi (Zambia), Nyambe, Mulimu
Luangu (DRCongo)–Nzazi
Luba (Angola), Chibinda Ilunga

Luba (DRCongo), Chibinda Ilunga
Luba (DRCongo), Kalumba, Sendwe
Mwlaba
Luba (DRCongo), Nkongolo
Lubanga (Acholi/Sudan, Uganda), Jok
Lugbara (DRCongo), Adro, Adroa,
Adronga
Lugbara (DRCongo), Gborogboro and
Meme
Lugbara (DRCongo), Jaki and Dribidu
Lugbara (Sudan), Adro, Adroa, Adronga
Lugbara (Sudan), Gborogboro and
Meme
Lugbara (Sudan), Jaki and Dribidu
Lugbara (Uganda), Adro, Adroa,
Adronga
Lugbara (Uganda), Gborogboro and
Meme
Lugbara (Uganda), Jaki, and Dribidu
Lunda (Angola), Chibinda Ilunga
Lunda (Angola), Chinawezi, Chinaweji
Lunda (DRCongo), Chibinda Ilunga
Lunda (DRCongo), Chinawezi, Chi-
naweji
Lunda (DRCongo), Lueji, Luweji,
Lweshi
Lunda (DRCongo), Tianza Ngombe,
Chinaweshi, Chinawezi
Luo (Uganda), Lwanda Magere
Luyi (Zambia), Nyambe
Luyia (Kenya), Wele, Wewle xakabo,
Were, Isaywa, Khakaba, Nabongo,
Nyasaye
Madi (Uganda), Ori, Rabanga
Makoni (Zimbabwe), Maori
Makua (Malawi), Muluku
Makua (Mozambique), Muluku
Malagasy (Madagascar), Andriamba-
homanana
Malagasy (Madagascar), Andrianana-
hary, Zanahary, Andriamanitra
Malagasy (Madagascar), Iboniamasi-
boniamanoro
Malagasy (Madagascar), Rasoalavavolo

Malimba (Cameroon), Jeki la Njambe
Malinke (Mali), Doni Dyu
Mamprusi (Ghana), Tindana
Mandari (Sudan), Nun
Mande (Mali), Mangala
Mandinka (Mali), Kambili
Mandinka (Gambia), Sunjata
Mandinka (Mali), Sunjata
Mano (Liberia), Wala
Margi (Nigeria), Iju, Ba-Chi, Hyel,
Tambi
Masai (Kenya), Enkai, Olparsai,
Emayian
Mbole (DRCongo), Lofokefoke
Mbukushu (Angola, Botswana,
Namibia), Dikithi
Mbuti (DRCongo), Tore, Arebati, Baatsi,
Epilipili, Muri-Muri
Meban (Sudan), Juon, Juong
Mende (Sierra Leone), Leve
Mende (Sierra Leone), Ngewo,
Ngewo-wa, Leve, Maanda
Meru (Kenya), Murungu, Ngai,
Mwene inya
Minyanka (Mali), Doni Dyu
Mondari (Sudan), Nun
Mongo, Nkundo (DRCongo), Lianja
Mongo (DRCongo), Mbomba Ianda,
Mbombianda
Morocco, Antaeus
Moshi (Ghana), Tindana
Mossi (Burkina Faso), Winnam, Naba
Zidiwinde, Winde
Mpongwe (Gabon), Njambi
Nama (Namibia), Tsui‖Goab, Cagn,
‖kaang, Khub, Nanub
Nandi (Kenya), Asis, Asista, Chebona-
muni, Chepkeliensokol, Chepo-
pkoiyo, Cheptalil
Nandi (Kenya), Mungu
Naron (Namibia), Hishe, Hise
Ndebele (Transvaal Ndebele) (South
Africa), Zimu
Ngombe (DRCongo), Akongo

Ngombe (DRCongo), Libaka
Ngombe (DRCongo), Mbokomu
North Africa, Antar, Antara, Sirat
Nuba (Sudan), Bail
Nuba (Sudan), Shibeika
Nuer (Sudan), Kar, Jakar
Nuer (Sudan), Kwoth, Kwoth Nhial
Nupe (Nigeria), Soko
Nupe (Nigeria), Tsoede
Nyamwezi (Tanzania), Likuube
Nyamwezi (Tanzania), Shida Matunda
Nyanga (DRCongo), Mpaca
Nyanga (DRCongo), Mwindo
Nyankole (Uganda), Ruhanga, Katonzi, Kazooba, Rugaba
Nyarwanda (Rwanda), Gihanga (first man)
Nyarwanda (Rwanda), Gihanga (king)
Nyarwanda (Rwanda), Imana
Nyarwanda (Rwanda), Miseke
Nyarwanda (Rwanda), Ryangombe
Nyimang (Sudan), Abradi
Nyitopotha (Sudan), Nawuge
Nyoro (Uganda), Chwezi, Cwezi
Nyoro (Uganda), Ndahura
Nyoro (Uganda), Nyamiyonga
Nyoro (Uganda), Ruhanga, Katonzi, Kazoba, Mukamiguru, Nyamuhanga, Rugaba
Ovimbundu (Angola), Kalitangi
Oxoriuk (Sudan), Lurubot
Pabir (Nigeria), Hyel
Pahouin (CAR), Mebege
Pahouin (Congo), Mebege
Pahouin (Gabon), Mebege
Pedi (South Africa), Huveane
Pokomo (Kenya), Liongo
Pokomo (Kenya), Vere
Pokomo (Somalia), Vere
Pokot (Uganda), Tororut, Ilat
Pongo (Cameroon), Jeki la Njambe
Poro (Liberia), Nyesowa, Abi, Gala, Wala
Ronga (Mozambique), Tilo

Rotse (Zimbabwe), Nyambi, Nyambe
Rundi (Burundi), Imana
San (Botswana), Goha
San (Namibia), Goha
San (Botswana), |Kaggen, Cagn, Dxui, Gao!na, ||Gauwa, Hishe, Huwe, |Kaang, Kho, Thora
San (Namibia), |Kaggen, Cagn, Dxui, Gao!na, ||Gauwa, Hishe, Huwe, |Kaang, Kho, Thora
San (South Africa), |Kaggen, Cagn, Dxui, Gao!na, ||Gauwa, Hishe, Huwe, |Kaang, Kho, Thora
San (Botswana), Kho, Cagn, Huwe, |Kaang, |Kaggen, Thora
San (Namibia), Kho, Cagn, Huwe, |Kaang, |Kaggen, Thora
San (South Africa), Kho, Cagn, Huwe, |Kaang, |Kaggen, Thora
San (Botswana), Ko
San (Namibia), Ko
San (South Africa), Ko
Sande (Liberia), Nyesowa, Abi, Gala, Wala
Sara (Chad), Wantu Su
Sara (Sudan), Wantu Su
Senufo (Côte d'Ivoire, Mali), Koulotiolo
Shambaa (Tanzania), Mbegha
Shambaa (Tanzania), Sheuta
Shangana (Mozambique), Tilo
Shangana (South Africa), Tilo
Shangana (Zimbabwe), Tilo
Shilluk (Sudan), Juok, Jwok
Shilluk (Sudan), Nyikang, Nyakang
Shilluk (Sudan), Ukwa
Shona (Zimbabwe), Dzivaguru
Shona (Zimbabwe), Mwari
Shona (Zimbabwe), Nehoreka
Soko (DRCongo), Bateta and Hanna
Soninke (Burkina Faso, Gambia), Gassire
Soninke (Mali), Gassire
Soninke (Mauritania), Gassire
Soninke (Senegal), Gassire

Sonjo (Tanzania), Hambageu, Kha-
  mbageu
Sonjo (Tanzania), Naka
Sotho (Lesotho), Ditaolane
Sotho (Lesotho), Huveane
Sotho (Lesotho), Modimo, Ralabepa
Sotho (South Africa), Modimo, Ra-
  labepa
Suk (Kenya), Tororut, Ilat
Sukuma (Tanzania), Likuube
Sumbwa (Tanzania), Likuube
Swahili (DRCongo), al-Khidr, Khadir,
  al-Khadir, Hidhiri, Hishiri
Swahili (Kenya), al-Khidr, Khadir, al-
  Khadir, Hidhiri, Hishiri
Swahili (Kenya), Liongo
Swahili (Kenya), Mungu
Swahili (Tanzania), al-Khidr, Khadir,
  al-Khadir, Hidhiri, Hishiri
Swahili (Tanzania), Mungu
Swati (Swaziland), Mkhulumnchanti,
  Mvelingqangi
Talensi (Ghana), Mosuor
Tangale (Nigeria), Monje Ngumyu
Tembe (Sierra Leone), Dugbo
Thonga, Tsonga (Mozambique), Tilo
Thonga, Tsonga (South Africa), Tilo
Thonga, Tsonga (Zimbabwe), Tilo
Tigre (Ethiopia), Makeda
Tonga (Malawi), Chiuta
Tonga (Mozambique), Tilo
Tonga (South Africa), Tilo
Tonga (Zimbabwe), Tilo
Topotha (Sudan), Nawuge
Tsonga (Mozambique), Tilo
Tsonga (South Africa), Shikwembu
Tsonga (South Africa), Tilo
Tsonga (Zimbabwe), Tilo
Tswana (Botswana), Modimo
Tswana (South Africa), Modimo
Tuareg (Algeria), Elijinen
Tuareg (Libya), Elijinen
Tuareg (Mali), Elijinen
Tuareg (Niger), Elijinen

Tuareg (Nigeria), Elijinen
Tuareg (Western Sahara), Sabenas
Tukulor (Senegal), Juntel Jabali
Turkana (Kenya), Agipie
Tutsi (Burundi), Imana
Tutsi (Rwanda), Gihanga
Tutsi (Rwanda), Imana
Uduk (Ethiopia), Arum
Upoto (DRCongo), Libanza
Urhobo (Nigeria), Oghene, Oghenu-
  kpabe
Venda (South Africa), Huveane
Venda (South Africa), Raluvhimba,
  Mwari
Venda (South Africa), Ngoma-lungundu
Venda (Zimbabwe), Ngoma-lungundu
Vili (Congo), Nzambi Mpungu
Vugusu (Kenya), Wele
Wolof (Senegal), Njaajaan Njaay
Woyo (DRCongo), Bunzi
Xhosa (South Africa), Malikophu
Xhosa (South Africa), Nyengebule
Xhosa (South Africa), Qamatha
Xhosa (South Africa), Thixo
Xhosa (South Africa), Tshawe
Xhosa, Zulu (South Africa), Mdali
Yao (Malawi), Mulungu
Yao (Mozambique), Mulungu
Yeye (Botswana), Urezhwa
Yombe (DRCongo), Mbumba
Yoruba (Nigeria), Esu, Elegba
Yoruba (Nigeria), Ifa, Orunmila
Yoruba (Nigeria), Obatala, Orisa-nla
Yoruba (Nigeria), Oduduwa, Odu-
  dwa, Odudua
Yoruba (Nigeria), Ogun
Yoruba (Nigeria), Olodumare, Olorun
Yoruba (Nigeria), Sango, Jakuta
Zande (DRCongo), Ture, Tule
Zande (Sudan), Dengbagine
Zande (Sudan), Mbori, Mboli,
  Bapaizegino
Zande (Sudan), Ture, Tule
Zaramo (Tanzania), Kwege

Zaramo (Tanzania), Nyalutanga, Lutanga

Ziba (Tanzania), Rugaba

Zigula (Tanzania), Sheuta

Zulu (South Africa), Mvelinqangi

Zulu (South Africa), Nkulunkulu

Zulu (South Africa), Nomkhubulwana

Zulu (South Africa), Thingo
   Lwenkosikazi

Appendix 3

The Grand Myth

The Argument of the Grand Myth

The mythmaker builds his repertory of stories around an initial sense of oneness that was surrendered, to be followed by an effort to regain the lost accord. Considering the many stories that comprise this collection of myths, a number of common threads can be discerned:

Beginnings   God created the universe, shaped it, and then created life. Two forces contended during the age of creation, forces of chaos and order.

First Connections   Initially, there were connections between heaven and earth, between God and the mortals he created.

Separation   But something occurred to provoke a separation—a disobedience, a struggle, an error, fate—and death came into the world. And in the end, the break was complete.

Struggle Between God and Man   On the earth, there was a continuation of the primal struggle between the forces of good and evil, as humans made efforts to regain and maintain their contacts with the heavens.

Second Connections   Heroes were emblematic of this struggle, containing within themselves both the positive godlike qualities and the negative qualities. In the tales, everyman and everywoman, obeying cultural injunctions and following social rituals, sought to restore the lost harmony: this was the second connection. Not just heroes are engaged in this gargantuan labor: everyman and everywoman are also contenders, which is why the tale is inevitably built around a mythic core.

Endings   But death in the end was victorious, although there are some suggestions of a reunion in death with the god of the beginnings.

⧗   Beginnings   ⧗

There are varied ideas about the initial shape of the universe and about the primal activities of creator gods —a cosmic egg, a mat hurled through the void, an earth perilously perched on a bull's horns, two worlds encased in a sphere. There was a flurried maelstrom of shaping, chiseling, organizing, hewing, sculpting industry in these formative periods, and out of the scramble of competing forces emerged man —from the heavens, from the earth, by means of serpents, spiders, chameleons, heavenly bodies, the rainbow, lightning, an egg, man himself. Animals also emerged, and trees and plants. People, sometimes suspended between heaven and earth, had connections in both realms.

---

fire, animals that do not flee are
    blessed–Tororut
fire, fox brings–Arum
fire, magical–Nawuge
fire-makers, sacred–Nawuge;
fire, origin of–‡Gao!na, Jaki and
    Dribidu, Juok (Anuak), Juok (Jo
    Luo), Kabunda, |Kai |Kini, Kalu-
    mba, Mawu (Ewe), Mboom, Motu,
    Mulungu (Yao), Nkulunkulu,
    Nzambi Mpungu, Obassi Osaw,
    Ture, Vere, Zambi
fire shoots out of hero's body–Wainaba
first being instructs girls–Nyalutanga
first beings children of God–Nzambi
    Mpungu
first beings non-human–Adro
first fruits–Mkhulumnchanti
first men thrown from heaven–Ngai
    (Kamba)
flame, God as a–Raluvhimba
food, origin of–Tore (Efe)
founding of a city–Dido
God clears paths for people–Ogun
God creates barriers of mountains and
    rivers–Longar
God vomits the world–Bumba
Gods fight, create
    thunderstorms–Agipie
Gods fight, result is drought or
    plenty–Baal Hammon,
    Jok (Lango)
God's world–Lesa (Lamba)
gourd, man born of–Waga
hairy house in the sky, God's–Huwe
hare gets split lip because of garbled
    message–Tsui‖Goab
head creates thunder–Chipimpi
heaven, humans fall to earth–
    Gihanga
heaven, origin of–Tore (Efe)
heavenly bodies–Gion
hole, as abode of the dead–Modimo
    (Sotho)
hole, God's abode–Modimo (Sotho)

hole of ancestors–‡Gama-‡Gorib,
    ‖Gauwa, Goha, |Kaggen, Matsieng,
    Modimo (Tswana), Qamatha, Tlam
hole, to contain god of
    plague–Kaumpuli
hole, woman emerges from–Urezhwa
horned animals to be meat for
    humans–Pishiboro
house of God in the sky–Xu
humans recreate the world–|Kaggen
humans superior to animals–Juok
    (Anuak)
husband as head of family–Njambi
imagination, creation from
    God's–|Kaggen
interaction of universes–Abasi Ikom
jealous gods create–Naka
jinn shows how to weave–Juntel Jabali
knee, child born from–Ngulwe
knee, God wounded on–Thixo, Tsui-
    ‖Goab
knowledge, God as the embodiment
    of–Kaidara
languages, origin of–Alatangana,
    Unumbotte
Libya, birth of–Epaphus
light, origin of–Alatangana, Nhialic
lightning and thunder caused by cock
    and hen of heaven–Tilo (Tonga)
lightning and thunder, gods
    in–Hebieso and Abui
lightning divides the sky and
    earth–Tore (Efe)
lighting is a rooster shaking its
    wings–Wele (Vugusu)
livestock from the finger of the rain-
    bow–Mukunga M'bura
lizards, humans will become lizards if
    sky tilts–Akongo
man gives birth to himself–
    Nambalisita
marriage, the origin of–Iboniamasibo-
    niamanoro
miraculous birth–Jeki la Njambe,
    Kejok, Lofokefoke, Wan Dyor

origin of wealth—Kahina
origin of weapons—Juok (Anuak)
original inhabitants of the
    earth—Mosuor
patrilineal filiation, end of—Kabunda
pillars prop up heaven—Wele (Vugusu)
potter, God compared to—Ama, Fi
primeval men—Osa
python teaches humans to
    mate—Nyame (Asante)
races, origin of activities—Zambe
rainbow the breath of a
    python—Nguleso
rainbows control the rain—Wele
    (Vugusu)
rain-stones from heaven—Lurubot
reed, God and people and animals
    from—Mdali, Mvelinqangi, Nku-
    lunkulu, Tilo (Lenge), Tilo
    (Tonga), Tilo (Tsonga)
rock, people emerge from—Tsui‖Goab
seed of creation—Doni Dyu
seeds, first—Mulungu (Kamba)
serpent encircles earth—Irgam
    Yigfagna, Mawu (Fon)
serpent, primordial—Tianza Ngombe
sexual relations result in creation of
    earth—Pemba
sky, first man falls from—Mwari, Ori
sky, first men come from—Djakomba,
    Ngulwe
sky, first men thrown from—Nguleso,
    Ori
sky, first people descend
    from—Nawuge, Segbo
sky, God travels through—Raluvhimba
sky, a spark from hell—Idris
sky supported by poles—Akongo
snake vomits the moon—Mungu
    (Swahili)
snakes, man born of—Waga
snakes slough off skin, live
    forever—Waga, Yataa
speech, fox brings to humans—Arum
speech, God gives to man—Waga

spiders, origin of their nocturnal char-
    acteristics—Juok (Jo Luo)
spirits live in a white village—Shi-
    kwembu
spring, miraculous—Nanna Tala
stars, creation of—Maori, Sa Na Duniya
stars fall, fighting among selves—Sa Na
    Duniya
stars, shooting—Sa Na Duniya
stone from heaven—Aiwel, Lurubot,
    Mwari
stone, people encased in—Akoma Mba
stones become first
    ancestors—Rasoalavavolo
struggle between gods—Mbumba
struggle between sun and moon—Juok
    (Jo Luo), Kalumba, Wele (Vugusu)
sun, as God's eye—Gueno, Horus
sun, creation by—Gueno
sun, creation of—|Kaggen, Kalumba,
    Kashindika, Lianja, !Nariba, Nut,
    Nzambi Mpungu, Ruhanga
    (Nyankole), Sango, Wele (Luyia),
    Woot
sun god—Gurzil
sun, movement of—Polo, Ruhanga
    (Nyankole)
sun, origin of—Alatangana, Kudukese
sun's rays released, cows fall to
    earth—Wele (Luyia)
tails, people with—Polo
teeth, child born with—Longar
teeth, men given by God—Gihanga
termite hill magically appears—
    Nkongolo
termite hole, humans emerge
    from—Enkai, Mulungu (Kamba)
thunder, God's voice in—Raluvhimba,
    Urezhwa
thunder is a rooster crowing—Wele
    (Vugusu)
toad creates life—Bateta and
    Hanna
transformation from animals
    to humans—Louliyya

transformation from undisciplined to protective leader–Mbegha
transformation into a bird–|Kai |Kini
transformation into a lion–Kambili
transformation into a water nymph–Anna
transformation into a woman–Akoma Mba
tree, creation of–!Nariba
tree of covenants–Libaka
tree of God–╪Gao!na
tree of life–Jok (Acholi), |Kaggen, Kudu
tree, origin of the primeval–Olodu-mare
universe created by virgin birth–Tanit
universe, shape of–Mawu-Lisa, Mboom, Nzambi (Kongo/DRCongo), Obatala, Oduduwa, Osanobua, Polo, Ra, Sa Na Duniya, To Dino, Tororut, Nzambi

urine of God becomes rain–Tianza Ngombe
wands from God–Segbo
water, miraculous appearance of–Wan Dyor
water, origin of–Wala
waters, control of–Hevioso
waters, movement of–Andriamba-homanana
weaving, a jinn shows how–Juntel Jabali
Well of Life–al-Khidr
woman created from rib of man–Mungu (Nandi)
woman from heaven–Mumbi Mukasa
woman tamed by hunter–Sheuta
women had spiritual husbands–Ngai (Kamba)
world on shoulders of a giant–Libya

⚌ First Connections ⚏

The first connections were present if not always firm. God moved on the face of the earth, leaving his footprints permanently inscribed on the earth's surface. A goddess arched over the earth, maintaining vigilance and concern. Chains, threads, ropes, strings, webs, trees connected heaven and earth, and God and man remained relatively close to each other.

---

cattle descend on strip of leather–Enkai
chain to heaven–Ifa, Sango, Wulbari
footprints on a rock–Chiti Mukulu, Goha, Khuzwane, Luchyele, Matsieng, Modimo (Sotho), Modimo (Tswana), Mulungu (Kamba), Nehoreka, Qamatha, Mboom, Woot
goddess arches over the earth–Nut

road to God–||Gamab
spider spins thread to heaven–Nyambi
spirits connect this world and the next–Bail
string to heaven–Tilo (Tsonga)
thread to heaven–Nyambi
tree to heaven–Arum, Kalala, Kalitangi, Kar, Libanza (Boloki), Mbumba
worship of gods, teaching–Segbo

——————————— ◪ *Separation* ◪ ———————————

But then the connections were severed, the ropes were cut, God became distant. Something went wrong, the harmony between heaven and earth was disrupted—by an errant pestle, perhaps, arrogant humans using the sky as a towel or as food. Or God was annoyed by humans who arrogantly proclaimed equality with him. There might have been a quarrel, the breaking of a prohibition. Whatever the impetus, the ordered ties with heaven are broken, the gods leave the earth, and man is left with a flawed environment. People try to reestablish contact with the heavens, building towers to the sky, but these crumble under their own weight and under the weight of their insolence. People scatter now, disperse, migrate—they are on their own.

---

bat lets the darkness escape—Yataa

child is born and paradise is lost—Mvelinqangi

crow beats drum, scatters people—Wantu Su

darkness because of a dog's greed—Woot

dispersion of peoples—Koulotiolo, Nangaban, Ndahura, Ngai (Kikuyu)

earth, humans lowered to because of a nuisance—Mbokomu

earthquake, reason for—Sa Na Duniya

evil, origin of—Mbokomu

expulsion because humans bore children—Mungu (Nandi)

forbidden basket—Motu

forbidden fruit—Kudu

forces of order and chaos on the earth—Amma

God becomes destructive—Hathor

God, drunk, creates afflicted beings—Obatala

God forbids procreation—Abasi (Efik)

God instructs men—Dente

God lives in seclusion, on a rock—Mukasa

God moves into the sky, his creation completed—Lianja, Luchyele

God moves to the earth to reign—Ruhanga (Nyoro)

God retreats because a woman cuts bits off him for soup—Wulbari

God retreats because a woman slices bits off him—We

God retreats because he is hit by a pestle—Wulbari, Wuni

God retreats because he is used as a towel—Wulbari

God retreats because his potency causes death—Nzeanzo

God retreats because humans bury his wife—Urezhwa

God retreats because man imitates him—Nyambi

God retreats because men use sky as food, wipe hands on it—Olodumare

God retreats because of a dirty calabash—Iju

God retreats because of an excess of requests—Ngewo

God retreats because of a quarrel—Kejok

God retreats because of a quarrel over a woman—Mboom

God retreats because of a trick—Esu

▶ Struggle between God and Man ◀

Now, separated one from the other, the gap between God and humans grows. Upheavals persist in heaven and earth—it is often an unhappy time, a time of evil unleashed, of omens, plagues, curses. But it is also a time of exhilaration, a time of new-found freedom. At times, man and God engage in contests, and other times humans take on limited roles of God and combat evil. The earthly struggle between order and chaos, between union and separation, is nowhere more graphically revealed than in the divine trickster, symbolic of this period.

animals assist human in struggle with God—Nambalisita

animals sent by God to punish men—Nguleso

bird, magical, accuses a murderer—Nyengebule

cheating results in land acquisition—Tano

childless parents given fearful option—Rdah Umm Zayed

darkness vs. light—Ra

deadly power on earth—Dodo

divine tricksters—Anansi, Dikithi, Esu, Huveane, |Kaggen, Kudu, Mekidech, Obatala, Ture, Wac

evil, a woman overcomes—Mpaca

evil spirit as a mouse, stealing and biting—Ngulwe

flame, man turns self into—Wan Dyor

giant, one-eyed, destroys spiritual leader, usurps position—Tindana

God and man have a contest—Nambalisita

God, transforming into a woman, delays an enemy—Dzemawon

love of woman leads man under the earth—Wanjiru

nature assists human in struggle with God—Nambalisita

ogre transforms into a woman—Mekidech

ox devoid of intestines, a bad omen—Wamara

plague, keeping under control—Kaumpuli

river, accused of making husband sick, a woman becomes—Osanobua

serpent as a friend to man—Jinn

serpent bites God—Isis

servants, origin of—Ruhanga (Nyankole)

sexual relations prohibited—Wuni

snails, God cursed to eat—Oduduwa

snake and sexual relations—Mwari

spirits struggle with each other—Elijinen

stone, man becomes—Wan Dyor

struggle between evil and good forces—Esu, ǂGama-ǂGorib, Mangala

sun burns mankind—Wac

woman persuades erring king to visit her home—Nyamiyonga

— 🖂   Second Connections—Restoring Links with God   🖂 —

Humans do not wish to cleave relations with the heavens. The towers have crashed, but they persist in their efforts, seeking new links, pursuing second connections, with God, striving to find that oneness, even if, as is evidenced in the tales, it is only within themselves. Mortals move to God, find aspects of God within, themselves become God, have relations with the gods, or experience the force of God in miraculous occurrences. Rainmaking, for example, becomes a way of making the connection, and God manifests himself in various ways to suggest that the connection remains a possibility, an option.

---

man moves to godliness—Bata

marriage to a mythic person—Kahina

merman makes woman pregnant—Wan Dyor

messenger of God—Mkhulumnchanti

mountain, saint passes through—Somal

mythical city of spirits—Jangare

nature responds to death and resurrection of a god—Osiris

parting the waters—Dengbagine, Heitsi-Eibib, Kisra, Lofokefoke

personal god—Tamuno

quest for that to which nothing can be compared—Akoma Mba

rain comes from sacrifice—Asis (Kipsigis), Wanjiru

rain, stealing the apparatus for making—Dzugudini

rainmaker comes to earth as water—Ajok

rainmaker disappears in a pool—Dzivaguru

rainmaking—Chido, Mujaji, Ngun Lo Ki

rock, youth moves into—Ngai (Kamba)

sacrifice: a beautiful girl sacrificed to God—Mregho, Wanjiru

sexual relations ritualized—Legba

sky people restored lost identity—Kwege

snake as rain-maker—Bunzi

snake skin and traditional beliefs—Tsibiri

spider, fantastic—Kudukese

stone, God deflects—Heitsi-Eibib

stones, adding to for assistance—Karkur

stories of the gods owned by Trickster—Anansi

sun falls to earth—Chido

sun's rays in a pot—Wele (Luyia)

thunderbolt as God coming to earth—Modimo (Sotho)

vanishing saint—Sidi Adjille

Water People take beautiful woman—Ekineba

water turns to blood—Nanna Tala

wings, people with—Nangaban

woman discovers God's vulnerability—Kibuka

⧅ Second Connections—Mythic Heroes ⧅

If tale characters find God in themselves, heroes bestride heaven and earth, assuring that the culture that they embody has heavenly sanction. Heroes, successful or not, sublime or not, provide the promise of union with the heavens. A stone falls from the sky, a hero emerges, and later, with a fearful noise, the stone splits—and rain falls. A hero comes out of an egg, and proceeds to struggle with God for ascendancy. Pale and hairy, a hero arises from the water and establishes a model government. A hero's strength is in his shadow, and as long as his secret remains safe, he plays the role of God. Waters part for the hero, miraculously born. The hero, mortal and flawed, has within him the capacity to reach godliness.

---

bird blazes in the dark—Ndahura

contending gods—Balewa Yola

gold and wisdom—Kaidara

hero, drunk, mocked by sons, protected by daughter—Woot

heroes into the abyss—Irgam Yigfagna

jinn battled by heroes—Abu Zayd, Jinn
lake contains the spirit of a mythic
   king—Aruan
man moves to a position of
   strength—Asis (Nandi)
mythic hero—Aiwel, Antaeus, Antar,
   Balewa Yola, Chibinda Ilunga, Da
   Monzon, Dido, Ditaolane, Ebele,
   Gassire, Hambageu, Iboniamasibo-
   niamanoro, Jeki la Njambe, Kahina,
   Kambili, Kapepe, Kaura Duna,
   Kejok, Kemangurura, Kisra, Korau,
   Kudukese, Lianja, Libanza (Boloki),
   Liongo, Lofokefoke, Longar, Lueji,
   Lwanda Magere, Makeda, Mbegha,
   Mbomba Ianda, Mubila, Namba-
   lisita, Ndahura, Nehoreka, Njaajaan

Njaay, Nkongolo, Nyalutanga,
   Nyikang, Ruhanga (Nyoro),
   Ryangombe, Shibeika, Silamaka,
   Tindana, Tsoede, Tsumburbura,
   Ukwa, Wainaba, Wan Dyor, Woot,
   Zong Midzi
rock, hero's body turns into—Lwanda
   Magere
serpent, hero kills and becomes
   king—Wainaba
snake, the destruction of means the
   kingship—Bayajida
spirits, struggle with by hero—Antar
waters, miraculous transportation
   over—Nangaban
woman divulges leader's vulnerability—
   Korau, Lwanda Magere, Nehoreka

⬕ Endings ◧

In the end, the death that was prefigured at the beginning is triumphant, and man must die, receiving in many ways the message that he is not eternal. Often this message seems unsubstantial, but that only reinforces the delicate balance of that which sustains and defines the human condition. A chameleon often brings the message of life, but is overtaken by a swifter rival or garbles the message. Sometimes the message of life is cruelly subverted, or it is lost because of a mortal craving for food or rest, or God changes his mind. Implied in many of the myths is the chance of everlasting life—tantalizing, tempting, teasing, but it remains only a vague promise, now lost. In some stories, humans out of greed, arrogance, curiosity, desperation, break a commandment, transgress a prohibition, overlook a possibility, misinterpret a message, and eternal life becomes a distant and haunting hope.

---

arm of God, and death—Tore (Mbuti)
bird falsifies message, result is
   death—Waka
bundle, forbidden, containing
   death—Lesa (Lamba), Njambe
burial facing the rising sun—Ko
burial of humans—Ale, Soko
burial with a spear—Ko

calabash containing plague of
   flies—Nzeanzo
calabash containing smallpox—
   Kalala
chameleon and the message of
   death—Chiuta, Iju, Lesa (Lamba),
   Luchyele, Mdali, Modimo
   (Tswana), Mulungu (Kamba),

Ngai (Kamba), Nyambe (Luyi),
Qamatha, Tilo (Tsonga), Zimu
dead, land of–Nzambi (Kongo)
death and confusion eliminated when
people turn to God–Leve
death and movement to new identity–
Malikophu
death and resurrection–Mubila
death and resurrection of
God–Melqart, Odomankoma
death and resurrection of God tied to
nature–Osiris
death and the holy fire–‖Gamab
death a pleasurable state–Adoudoua
death as a result of a backward
glance–Inusa
death as a result of a deal with
God–Alatangana
death as a result of a dog's
hunger–Ngewo
death as a result of a garbled message–Nyame (Akan), Nyame
(Asante), Tsui‖Goab
death as a result of a hyena's
greed–Murungu
death as a result of a message subverted by a hare–Kho
death as a result of a message subverted by a lizard–Lesa (Lamba),
Qamatha
death as a result of a message subverted by a serpent–Imana
death as a result of a race–Hyel,
Nyambe (Luyi), Oghene
death as the result of a
serpent–Mulungu (Yao)
death as a result of a stammered message–Mulungu (Kamba), Ngai
(Kikuyu)
death as a result of a wrong message
by dog–Mawu (Ewe)
death as a result of breaking God's
prohibition–Imana, Kintu
death as a result of burying a
corpse–Hyel, Iju, Lesa (Lala)

death as a result of curiosity about
God–Masupa
death as a result of discovery of fatal
flaw–Liongo
death as a result of eating forbidden
fruit–Murungu
death as a result of
disobedience–Nhialic
death as a result of indebtedness to
Death–Zra
death as a result of jealousy–Likuube,
Shida Matunda, Yo
death as a result of killing God's creatures–Nyambe (Lozi)
death as a result of man's
arrogance–Nzame
death as a result of man's
tardiness–Jok (Acholi), Libanza
(Upoto), Modimo (Tswana)
death as a result of pride–Doondari,
Mwari
death as a result of "the world-
destroyer"–Kashindika
death as a result of vanity–Njambe
death, as decreed by a hyena–Mulungu
death as in life–Oghene
death: attempt to move into heaven
before dying–Mawu (Anlo)
death attributed to an evil being–Modimo (Sotho)
death bathes in a field of fire–Iju
death because a frog broke the pot
containing death–Tore (Efe)
death because a mortal breaks a
promise–Walumbe
death because a toad loses a
contest–Mbori
death because a toad spills
medicine–Kanu
death because chameleon is so
slow–Luchyele, Mdali, Modimo
(Tswana), Mvelinqangi, Tilo
(Tsonga), Zimu
death, because forbidden fruit is
eaten–Tore (Mbuti)

God's sons are lost—Andriambahomanana, Andriananahary

hare wins race, death the consequence—Nyambe (Luyi)

hill closes on an unbeliever—Somal

hunting, a threat to culture, results in
death—Ryangombe

hyena intimates mole, brings
death—Murungu

instruction of God ignored, death
results—Abasi (Efik), Abuk

lizard and the message of death—Zimu

lizard cursed, death results—Arum

message of life is intercepted, garbled,
misinterpreted—Abradi, Asis
(Nandi), Chiuta, Imana

moon and the coming of death—Asis
(Nandi)

moon spits, death results—Arum

prohibition: forbidden city—
Janjare

prohibition: God's fruit—
Unumbotte

prohibition of God broken, man must
pay dowry—Zobeyo Mebe'e

prohibition of God ignored, death
results—Imana, Tore (Mbuti)

prohibition of God ignored, plague of
flies results—Nzeanzo

rabbit poisons man, brings
death—Abradi

resurrection from the dead—Ha-
mbageu, Isis, Kalala, Kudukese,
Mubila, Nzambi (Kongo), Wan
Dyor

resurrection of God—Melqart,
Odomankoma, Osiris

salamander gives the message of
death—Mdali

serpent brings death—Imana

sky, evildoer goes to—Dugbo

soul to kingdom of dead—Oduduwa

sun, moon, stars live forever, man
dies—Jok (Acholi)

toad brings a message of
death—Oghene

toad changes message, brings
death—Chuku, Ngewo

toad ignores God's instruction, brings
death—Arebati

underworld, journey from—Tlam

underworld, journey to—Jeki la
Njambe

woman sinks into the earth—Wanjiru

Index